INTERROGATING RACE AND RACISM

Edited by Vijay Agnew

It is a common misconception that, in the contemporary world, racism has been defeated or pushed to the boundaries of acceptable social behaviour. In fact, racism has taken on a subtler guise in the ways it is expressed, and this ambiguity has made it more insidious than ever. *Interrogating Race and Racism* examines the subject of racism with a view to uncovering the different ways in which it exists today.

Because of its many permutations, racism needs to be examined from a multidisciplinary perspective and this collection features contributors from a variety of backgrounds. Among the specific topics discussed are border politics and the search for asylum, exclusionary policies, and the struggle for substantive citizenship. This volume also includes an extended examination of racism in the workplace, an illuminating and important sequence of essays that expose the institutionalization of racist hiring procedures despite legislation to curb such practices. With the heightening of tensions in the post–9/11 period and a resurgence of racist attitudes, *Interrogating Race and Racism* is a timely analysis of cultural alienation and its impact on our lives.

VIJAY AGNEW is a professor in the Division of Social Science at York University.

Interrogating Race and Racism

EDITED BY VIJAY AGNEW

UNIVERSITY OF TORONTO PRESS
Toronto Buffalo London

© University of Toronto Press Incorporated 2007
 · Toronto Buffalo London
Printed in Canada

ISBN 978-0-8020-9356-1 (cloth)
ISBN 978-0-8020-9509-1 (paper)

Printed on acid-free paper

Library and Archives Canada Cataloguing in Publication

Interrogating race and racism / edited by Vijay Agnew.

ISBN 978-0-8020-9356-1 (bound)
ISBN 978-0-8020-9509-1 (pbk.)

1. Race.   2. Racism.   I. Agnew, Vijay, 1946–

HT1521.I59 2007   305.8   C2007-902098-4

This book has been published with the help of a grant from the Canadian
Federation for the Humanities and Social Sciences, through the Aid to
Scholarly Publications Programme, using funds provided by the Social
Sciences and Humanities Research Council of Canada.

The University of Toronto Press acknowledges the financial assistance to its
publishing program of the Canada Council for the Arts and the Ontario
Arts Council.

University of Toronto Press acknowledges the financial support for its
publishing activities of the Government of Canada through the Book
Publishing Industry Development Program (BPIDP).

For Nicole Agnew
Daughter of an immigrant mother

Contents

Acknowledgments

This past summer, as I was setting off on my daily walk, I met a neighbour that I like, a white woman whom I have known for some twenty years. During our chat she admonished me by saying, 'Vijay, you should stop thinking about race so much.' Since we are personal friends with different interests, she knows only that I am a professor and a feminist but nothing else about my professional life. Perhaps I had mentioned the word race once too often in our previous conversations for her liking. I laughed and continued with my walk.

A white woman is defined by race as much as a South Asian woman such as me. The difference, however, is that most white people are not conscious of their race and it does not impact their everyday interactions and therefore their sense of self. Racism renders non-white people unequal to others, and they come to believe that their identity circumscribes their ability to fully enjoy their rights as citizens. Consequently, understanding the phenomenon of race and racism has been an enduring passion of my academic career and advocacy work since I came to Canada thirty-five years ago. I do not appreciate racism and am not grateful to those who act in such a reprehensible way. I wish there were no racism and that people would embrace differences, so that all of us could feel we belong in Canada as equal participating citizens.

Over the course of my research and writing on race and racism, I have met a wide range of scholars with similar interests, some of whom have now become my dear friends. I owe a debt to them for helping me to understand race and racism. Together we have, over the years, created a body of literature that documents the life and settlement experiences of immigrants who come to Canada from Asia, Africa, and the Caribbean. I knew that much research on racism was being done among my colleagues and initiated the idea, as director of the Centre for Feminist Research at York University, for collecting and presenting this material in a book. I am indebted to my colleagues for entrusting me with the writings on which they have laboured for months and even years. Over the two years that it took to put this book together and have it reviewed by the Press, all the authors cooperated with my many demands for information and clarification. Now that the book is a reality, I hope we can collectively take pleasure in the contribution it will make to the burgeoning literature on race and racism in Canada.

I would like to thank Stephen Kotowych, senior editor at the University of Toronto Press, for shepherding this volume through the many steps that were necessary to have it published. Carol Pollock, Diane Young, and Janet Hutchinson did the copy-editing at the initial stages of preparing the manuscript for the Press, and I would like to thank them for their meticulous reading of the text. Maureen Epp copy-edited the final draft for the Press and I thank her as well. I am always amazed at the attention to detail that the copy editors bring to manuscripts that turns them from a rough stone into a polished gem.

A number of people were enthusiastic about the project and provided intellectual support at various stages of preparing this book – Professors Haideh Moghissi, Marlene Kadar, Suzie Young, Hira Singh, Merle Jacobs, and Peter Li. I would like to thank Professor Hira Singh for also reading 'Being White and Thinking Black' and suggesting ways to improve the presentation of the material. Annis Karpenko worked closely with me in communicating with the contributors to this volume, and I would like to thank her for generously supporting my work. Adinne Schwartz, Diane Emory, and Abhinava Kumar prepared the manuscript and got it ready for the Press. Their knowledge of computer functionality and the Internet smoothed out the many wrinkles that such preparation presents.

My husband, a white man and a scientist by profession, does not quite understand my passion for reading and writing about race and racism. My daughter, Nicole Agnew, believes her life and experiences to be different from my own (and I fervently hope that they prove to be so). Nevertheless, they both support me wholeheartedly in my work and for that I am grateful.

INTERROGATING RACE AND RACISM

Introduction

VIJAY AGNEW

When I was a young woman in the 1970s, I became a feminist, and the words 'oppression' and 'exploitation' became part of my everyday vocabulary. I was an Indian immigrant, recently arrived in Canada, where I had joined the graduate program at the University of Toronto. Before long, I became enamoured with discussions about gender that were then taking place at many North American universities. The prevailing wisdom at the time among feminists was that gender was the defining force in life, and that the inequities that women were just beginning to discover and name were not new; rather, they had a long history and were common to almost all cultures and societies. Adopting the language and the posture of the white, middle-class feminists whom I met at the university, I began to think of myself as an unwitting victim of capitalism and patriarchy.

I joined forces with these white, middle-class feminists and, for a time, accepted the notion of being oppressed by my gender and being their 'sister' in a common struggle. Like them, I was able to dredge up memories of the injustice of sex-differentiated socialization that had been imposed upon me as young girl by my family. The cultural and social sex roles (gender had yet to become part of the common parlance) that my family had inculcated in me had constructed my human potential in gender-specific ways. In retrospect, it seems ironical that a woman such as myself, who had enjoyed many privileges associated with birth, education, caste, and class, would seriously believe that she was a victim. But the feminist euphoria of the times swept me away, and enthused by the language of those around me, I clung, like many white, middle-class feminists, to the idea of being a victim and of victimization.

Living in Canada made me question both my past and present. My life in India had not encouraged any introspection or self-questioning. My experiences at the university, however, were imperceptibly but slowly and surely raising my consciousness of self, culture, and the society around me. Sometimes I would meet my friends at University College at the University of Toronto, where I was charmed by the old buildings whose architecture was inspired by British traditions and reminded me of Elphinstone College (named after a British governor), which I had attended in Mumbai. Inside the buildings, wood-panelled rooms and wide stairwells and halls were clean and uncluttered compared to my former college. I would walk through the buildings, sombrely thinking I was one in a parade of students that had passed through these halls for more than a hundred years. But if I hesitated in my walk or stopped to look around, a polite student or professor would offer to help me find my way. I did not know then that my clothes and the colour of my skin were, in themselves, unusual.

When I was with white feminists at these colleges or at the graduate student residence where I lived, we passionately discussed life and society around us, imagining that we were at the centre of it all. There were vigorous discussions about male and female roles and their consequent oppression of women's capabilities and opportunities. We unquestioningly assumed that these biases had existed from time immemorial and were common to all cultures and societies. The only important social difference between individuals, we confidently asserted, was that of sex.

Among the many issues that feminists debated earnestly were those relating to dress and to behavioural norms among men and women, which, they argued, encoded societal biases and assumptions. At the residence, we earnestly discussed the custom of men holding the door open for women; we wondered if it was an insult of some kind, however trivial in nature, signalling women's dependence on men or their lack of ability. But when I in my youthful enthusiasm rejected such courtesies from white males at the university, I'd note surprised or even shocked expressions on their faces. At the time, it was enjoyable. Now I wonder if these men, when they encountered me in buildings, said to themselves, 'There goes a militant bra-burning feminist.' Or did my appearance – my sari and the red *bindi* or dot painted on my forehead – make them think of me as a woman from a traditional culture who was unfamiliar with such courtesies? Or did the colour of my skin indicate my hopeless commitment to aggressive, uncivilized, and uncouth behaviour?

In India, I was perceived as a Hindu, the daughter of a successful businessman, and a mission-school-educated, English-speaking, westernized woman. When I lived there, I gave little thought to how my culture, caste, and class oppressed women. In Toronto, innumerable experiences from my day-to-day life made me conscious of my difference from the predominant white, middle-class norm. My experiences made me critical of the white feminist theorizing of the time and drew me to the writings of black feminists such as Angela Davis and bell hooks. By the time the 1980s rolled around, I had joined the 'women of colour' (the new terminology that came into use at that time to refer to non-white women).

Along with other women of colour, I chanted the mantra of race, class, and gender, and how these integrated and interconnected oppressions kept us down. Although like many women I accepted the theories of integrated oppressions, my passion was often reserved for locating, deconstructing, and challenging interpersonal and systemic racism and its harmful impact on our lives – and the lives of our families – in Canada. I did not give up the mantle of victimhood; rather, I developed an even more exaggerated notion of my own disadvantage and lack of privilege vis-à-vis some undefined other. Later, with more reading and increasing age and sobriety, I would think of myself less as a victim and more as a survivor of the many struggles of racism, sexism, and classism that I was engaging in as an activist. James Baldwin notes: 'That victim who is able to articulate the situation of the victim has ceased to be a victim; he or she has become a threat' (Baldwin 1976). Or at least a budding activist.

Identities arise in a 'structured field of relations' and are a consequence, not the cause, of conflicts. Cultural differences do not give rise to collective identities; rather, differences of identity are in many ways prior to those of culture. Identity, writes Appiah, is both who we are and what we are; that is, it incorporates ascriptive criteria such as race, gender, and sexuality but also a belief system that is associated with them (Appiah 2005, 64). Race, gender, religion, and sexuality make us, in the words of Ian Hacking, certain 'kinds of persons' that are brought into being 'hand in hand with our invention of categories labeling them' (Hacking 1986). 'Once labels are applied to people, ideas about people who fit the label come to have social and psychological effects. In particular these ideas shape the ways people conceive of themselves and their projects. So the labels operate to mold what we may call identification, the process through which individuals shape their projects – including their plans for their own lives and their conceptions of the good life – by reference to available labels, available identities' (Appiah 2005, 66).

Identification with a collective identity requires three factors. First, there needs to be an availability of terms in public discourse that can pick out bearers of the terms by their ascriptive criteria; for example, man, woman, white, or black. Usually a consensus exists around these terms that are organized around a set of stereotypes (which may be true or false); however, these terms are not accurate but rather are 'rough and ready' and change with time and place. Second, there needs to be an internalization of those identities or labels and a conception of one-self as a woman, man, white, or black in ways that 'make a difference' and shape one's feelings and actions. Third, identification with a collec-tive identity refers to a pattern of behaviour that is 'profoundly shaped (even in a sense produced) by histories of sexism, homophobia, racism, and ethnic hatred' (Appiah 2005, 69). Racial, sexual, and gender identi-ties are not a matter of convention but are derived from ascriptive crite-ria which are independent of the individuals' choices (70).

Experiences, theorists would argue, were making me conscious of my race, nationality, gender, class, and immigrant status, and their role in constructing my identity in Canada. Experience is not the 'endpoint but the beginning of an exploration of the relationship between the per-sonal and the social and therefore the political. And this connecting process, which is also a discovery, is the real, pedagogic process, the "science of social science"' (James 2000, 14). Language creates social meanings, has power relations embedded in it, and defines others; con-sequently, my university colleagues and I debated the assumptions underlying the words used to describe us. Some of these labels were seemingly innocuous and factual, such as 'foreign student,' 'Indian woman,' 'Third World woman,' 'immigrant,' and 'visible-minority woman.' Some of us who were familiar with Foucault's theories of dis-course, however, were perturbed by the hidden meanings embedded in labels that aimed 'not to discover truth (i.e., powerful knowledge) but to understand how truth is formed' (Henry and Tator 2002, 24).

Proctor explains that for Stuart Hall, discourse refers to 'a whole clus-ter of narrative statements and/or images on a particular subject that acquire authority and become dominant at a particular historical moment' (Procter 2004, 60). Discourse governs and empowers certain interpretations, while ruling out and delegitimizing others. Hall, unlike Saussure, gives importance in his analysis of discourse to the physical world outside language; for example, signifiers that refer us to skin colour, as in 'visible-minority women,' or signs that categorize certain individuals as outsiders, as in 'immigrants.'

Since language is used to convey a set of meanings and since it provides a bridge between the social world and us, we need to know in any given context who is saying what and why they are saying it. Language articulates by drawing upon the prevailing sociocultural and economic influences, as well as upon myths and fantasies prevalent in the culture. Thus, it is never neutral, objective, or detached. The social meanings of labels are often politicized and when they are challenged, reveal the embedded concepts of power that reflect the interests of the elites (Henry and Tator 2002, 25; Agnew 1996). In this volume, Li, Lee, McDonald, and Smith use discourse analysis to reveal the hidden biases in print media, including literature, and the negative assumptions and images associated with black people and those of Asian and Arab background. Similarly, Aiken and McDonald deconstruct legislation and show the hidden biases against immigrants and refugees.

The boundaries around labels such as 'Third World woman' included me willy-nilly and excluded me from the category of feminist. 'Third World woman' implies poverty, illiteracy, backwardness, traditionalism, and race, and its use circles all racialized immigrants in its embrace (Mohanty 1991). Bannerji responds to such labelling:

> Regardless of my official status as a Canadian citizen, I, like many others remained an 'immigrant.' The category 'Canadian' clearly applied to people who had two things in common: their white skin and their European North American (not Mexican) background. They did not all speak English. There were two colours in this political atlas – one a beige-brown shading off into black and the other white. These shades did not simply reflect skin colors – they reflected the ideological, political, and cultural assumptions and administrative practices of the Canadian state ... We are part of its [Canadian] economy, subject to its laws, and members of its civil society. Yet we are not part of its self-definition as 'Canada' because we are not 'Canadians.' We are pasted over with labels that give us identities that are extraneous to us. (1997, 24–5)

Whiteness was everywhere in the 1960s. Although at some levels it appeared to be nothing in particular, nevertheless it was the organizing principle in social and cultural relations. Whiteness remained unnamed in the late 1980s, yet it was still the unspoken norm against which others were measured.

Beginning in the mid-1980s and continuing throughout the 1990s, the characteristics used to define identity proliferated. Since these characteristics come together in individuals in many different combinations, the term *diversity* has become part of our language in talking about social justice for all Canadians. We all have multiple identities and no one lives only as a woman or as an Asian; at some moments, one or another aspect of our identities predominates. We play different roles in different situations, and our identities emerge 'through complex interaction with others as well as through constant dialogue and negotiations' (Lipsitz 1998, 57).

Stuart Hall prefers the use of the term *subject* to that of *identity*, noting that 'the sense of shared or common collective identity, of "cultural belongingness" becomes increasingly difficult to maintain within postmodern times. Globalization disrupts the relatively "settled" character of traditional cultures and collectivities structured around ideas of nationality, race, class, and gender.' For Hall, the self 'is internally fragmented, incomplete, multiple and is produced and positioned – that is subjected to and determined within – discourse' (Procter 2004, 110).

In putting together an anthology of poetry, Dunlop and Uppal, two second-generation South Asian professors, did not find an 'essentialized South Asian Canadian national or cultural identity.' The unifying experience among the South Asian poets lay in the imagination that is crucial to notions of self, family, and home rather than in categories of gender and nation (2004, 5). In a similar vein, Toni Morrison writes: 'My work requires me to think about how free I can be as an African-American woman writer in my genderized, sexualized, wholly racialized world ... for me, imagining is not merely looking or looking at; nor is it taking oneself intact into the other. It is, for the purposes of the work, *becoming*' (qtd in Hurtado 1999, 225).

Identity is central to a discussion of race and racism. The chapters included in this volume have been written by individuals with varied racial identities: whites, blacks, Chinese, South Asians, and Jews. These contributors examine changes and continuities in the content and form of racism and by tracing historical developments. Their scholarship questions some racist formulations and is in itself a form of resistance to expressions of racial domination and oppression.

This book is directed to readers with specialized interests in studying racism and to scholars – whether students or researchers – interested in the phenomenon or race and racism. The collection is interdisciplinary: the chapters have been written from the perspectives of sociology, political science, the humanities, law, geography, women's studies, and economics. The authors may or may not belong physically to the group they speak about, but they are sensitive to race dynamics, knowledge-able, and ideologically committed to anti-racism.

The Social Construction of Race, Racism, and Culturalism

Race reduces and fixes difference. Historically, race was presumed to be premised on biological characteristics and was thought to determine culture and personality. Academics argued that biology, whether phe-notypic or genetic, was merely the marker of race and could not and did not do the work of differentiation and distinction. Race as a fact of nature does not exist, yet 'it is an integral part of the classificatory sys-tem through which a racialized social order is produced and main-tained' (Torres, Miron, and Inda 1999, 5). All the papers in this collection use the word race as a socially constructed category; Li and Aiken put quotation marks around the word to further indicate its contested nature despite its continued usage. Aiken provides a very useful analy-sis of the meaning of race and racism and an introduction to critical race theory. Essentialism, a concept similar to that of race, is the belief that a fixed set of properties defines all members of a group, and proponents of essentialism make generalizations based on this assumption. Since generalized evaluations based on race and essentialism preclude the proper appreciation of difference, they have not provided a useful way of examining population groups and have thus been discredited.

The term *racialization* refers to the process that produces and con-structs the meaning of race and to the structures that accompany such a process (Small 1999, 49). Racialization occurs when meaning is attrib-uted to particular 'objects, features and processes in such a way that the latter are given special significance and carry or are embodied with a set of additional meanings' (Henry and Tator 2002, 11). Miles defines racialization as 'those instances where social relations between people have been structured by the signification of human biological charac-teristics in such a way as to define and construct differentiated social collectivities ... The concept therefore refers to a process of categoriza-tion, a representational process of defining an Other (usually, but not exclusively) somatically' (Miles 1989, 75).

Similarly, the report of the *Commission on Systemic Racism in the Ontario Criminal Justice System* (1995) defines racialization 'as the pro-cess by which societies construct races as real, different and unequal in ways that matter to economic, political and social life' (qtd in Ontario Human Rights Commission 2005, 9). Racialization extends to people and to their specific traits and attributes, such as accent, diet, name, beliefs and practices, and places of origin. Such traits are assumed to characterize some people and lead to their evaluation as 'abnormal and of less worth' (Ontario Human Rights Commission 2005, 9). The use of the term racialization, as opposed to race and racism, emphasizes that the definitions of white and black are inherently unstable, changing in different historical contexts and open to several meanings.

Race and racialization can be used to categorize and define white people as well as others. However, although race categorizes whites, racialization is a process that occurs in the context of power relations, whether this process takes place in discourses, is systemic to structures and institutions, or is merely a matter of everyday encounters. The Ontario Human Rights Commission therefore recommends the use of the term racialization to refer to only those groups that have experienced disadvantage and discrimination. The authors in this collection adopt this suggestion, using the word racialized to refer to subordinate and disadvantaged groups such as black people, those of Chinese and Arab origins, and so on.

The authors in this volume, particularly Li, Aiken, Hagey, Turrittin and Das Gupta, Smith, Creese, and I, analyse the processes that racialize individuals and groups in varied ways and in different contexts. Both Li and Aiken discuss ideological racialization by documenting how the discourse of immigrants and immigration becomes imbued with racial dimensions. Such discourses become racialized in a context where substantial numbers of immigrants are people of colour. As Li and Aiken argue, these discourses construct, differentiate, and exclude people. Similarly, Smith's chapter demonstrates how the reporting of stories in print media sometimes racializes crime by highlighting the race of the individuals alleged to be the perpetrators. The consequences of such racialization are the stigmatization and victimization of blacks in general and black men in particular.

'Racialized structures,' Small asserts, 'are the institutional pillars of society.' These he defines as 'routine, recurrent, and organized features of contemporary life' (Small 1999, 50). He notes that racialized structures have two key components: first, the distribution of valuable resources such as employment, education, and housing; and second, the routine, normal, and recurrent procedures of institutions that shape and constrain our daily lives, whether through politics, work, or social life (50). The behaviours and actions that racialized individuals and groups experience sustain the unequal distribution of resources.

Authors Pendakur and Pendakur, Wang and Lo, Hagey, Turrittin and Das Gupta, and Creese note that the practices of key institutions shape and determine who is rewarded or penalized, and who is included or excluded. Wang and Lo and Pendakur and Pendakur document racialized inequality, showing that despite equivalent qualifications, Chinese immigrants and other visible minorities earn less than white populations with similar characteristics. Hagey, Turrittin, and Das Gupta discuss the relationships between groups that are defined by their race in different ways, leading to racialized barriers and to the expression of hostility that creates impediments to the professional aspirations of black nurses. Creese argues that the racialization of black female identity fosters a characterization of black women as inferior and has the effect of excluding them at work and in interpersonal relations. Consequently, racialized females come to believe that they do not belong to Canada.

Racism

Racism is a loaded and ambiguous term that has a long history. Historians have used the word from ancient times to talk about xenophobia and tribalism, but in the 1930s it came into common usage with the persecution of the Jews (Fredrickson 2002, 5). In the preface to his *Anatomy of Racism*, Goldberg says, 'The prevailing critical presupposition of the social scientific attack on racism from its emergence in the 1930s is that racism is unvarying in its nature ... There is a growing recognition now ... that racist discourse is more chameleonic in nature' (Goldberg 1990, ix).

Now that belief in the biological dimensions of race has waned (with some exceptions, such as the theories of Philippe Rushton), it is thought that racism is a socially constructed phenomenon that 'is based on the false assumption that physical differences such as skin colour, facial features, and hair colour and texture are related to intellectual, moral, or cultural superiority' (Henry and Tator 2002, 11). Social construction, Code notes, is 'concerned with understanding how the language we use and the taken-for-granted categories we employ construct our experiences in ways which we then reify as "natural," "universal" and the "way things have to be"' (Code 2000, 451). The use of social construction in understanding race offers a possibility for uncovering fundamental processes of power that have shaped our sense of ourselves and structured the world around us. The authors in this volume argue that immigrants, asylum seekers, black people, women, and Muslims have been socially constructed in specific ways in Canada under discriminatory conditions. Their discussions show the contingency of historical construction and the influence of variables such as time and place.

Race is fluid, unfixed, and capable of multiple meanings. Race, like many other socially significant aspects of identity, such as gender, sexuality, and able-bodiedness, is socially constructed by oppressive relations in specific historical situations. The significance and meaning attached to skin colour, eyes, hair, or any other diacritical symbols are the products of histories of conquest, colonization, and imperialism in various parts of the world. Race articulates with other social phenomena, and thus there are historically specific 'racisms,' not a singular ahistorical racism. As Hall puts it, 'One cannot explain racism in abstraction from other social relations' (1980, 337). Several racisms are discussed in this book, including racism in post-apartheid South Africa, in the asylum policies of Britain, in Canadian immigration policies, and in the feminist movement in Canada.

Although the values and meaning attached to race change with time and place, sometimes they are weakened or merely replaced. For example, in the early part of the twentieth century in British Columbia, immigrants from China were publicly vilified as the 'yellow peril.' That racist image has now been replaced by a new stereotype – that of wealthy Chinese immigrants from Hong Kong who live in 'monster homes' in Vancouver and Toronto (Anderson 1991; Li 2004). In another example, discussed by Smith in this volume, public concern with safety and security in the post–September 11 period, partly fuelled by the media, has strengthened racism against black people and those of Arab descent. Since the meaning of race is fundamentally unstable, it allows for rearticulation. Frances Henry, interviewed in this volume, describes how she and other academics contested the meanings attached to race in Canada in the late 1960s. Their research constructed new knowledge and formed the basis of improved public and social policies. Research showed the falsity of the values attached to race and the discrimination experienced by the racialized population when it sought employment and housing. It also brought moral opprobrium on the expression of race-based biases. Thus, although race is historically contingent, it nevertheless requires 'mapping the relations of power, the patterns of contestation and struggle out of which such social constructions emerged' (Holt 2000, 18).

A racist ideology 'justifies and condones exclusion and exploitation as well as expulsion and extermination' (Fleras 2004, 434). Fredrickson notes that 'it is when differences that might otherwise be considered ethnocultural are regarded as innate, indelible, and unchangeable that a racist attitude or ideology can be said to exist. It finds its clearest expression when the kind of ethnic differences that are firmly rooted in language, customs, and kinship are overridden in the name of an imagined collectivity based on pigmentation, as in white supremacy, or on a linguistically based myth of remote descent from a superior race, as in Aryanism' (2002, 5). Racism as racialized language or discourse manifests itself in 'euphemisms, metaphors, and omissions that support given ideologies and policies. It is reflected in the collective belief systems of the dominant culture, and it is woven into the laws, languages, rules, and norms of Canadian society' (Henry and Tator 2002, 11). Racism is not, however, merely a set of attitudes, but finds expression in the practices, institutions, and structures that a sense of deep difference justifies and validates. Racism proposes to establish and sustain a racial order and a permanent group hierarchy.

Cultural Racism

Culture is another ambiguous and hard-to-define term. Since culture has, to a large extent, replaced the biological notions of race, it is a significant concept (Holt 2000, 14; Fleras 2004). 'If we think of culture as historically constructed, fluid, variable in time and space, and adaptable to changing circumstances, it is a concept antithetical to that of race. But culture can be reified and essentialized to the point where it becomes the functional equivalent of race' (Fredrickson 2002, 7). *Culturalism* or *cultural racism* is the inability or unwillingness to tolerate cultural difference. It is another way of talking about the very groups previously alleged to be biologically inferior and the use of rationalizations to exclude them or to maintain them in inferior positions. For example, it has been claimed that some groups have inferior cultures or are wedded to 'ways of life allegedly inconsistent with some vision of a particular national culture' (Blum 2004, 59).

In Canada, cultural racism was expressed before World War II by defining Asian immigrants as being culturally unsuited to Canadian norms (Anderson 1991). In the contemporary period, such racism is articulated by defining the 'mainstream' as 'culturally appropriate' and normal, and non-white groups as being 'culturally incompatible' and 'too different to comply or integrate.' Such racism uses 'coded language' that links 'social cohesion with national identity and preferred culture.' Similarly, subliminal cultural racism flourishes between the gap of 'inclusive principles and exclusionary practices.' This manifests itself in a disavowal of racism while appealing to high-minded principles; for example, concerns about fairness (criticism of refugees as economic migrants who are jumping the queue and taking advantage of liberal refugee policies) and national security that in essence support the status quo (Fleras 2004, 434–7).

Étienne Balibar defines culturalism as 'racism whose dominant theme is not biological heredity but the insurmountability of cultural differences, a racism which, at first sight, does not postulate the superiority of certain groups or peoples in relation to others but "only" the harmfulness of abolishing frontiers, the incompatibility of life-styles and traditions' (1991). Cultural racism assumes a situation in which the nation and the citizen are in a binary relation to the alien, foreigner, and immigrant, who are collectively defined as 'the other.' The other then poses a 'threat to the nation and must therefore be relegated to the margins of society, often blamed for all the social and economic ills that befall the nation ... [Although] cultural racism does not appear to exclude and marginalize populations on the basis of their biological heritage, one cannot really discount the element of biology since those who belong to the incommensurable cultures are most often non-white' (Torres, Miron, and Inda 1999, 9–10).

In this volume, Li demonstrates that the contemporary discourse on immigration is 'racially tinted' and that the term *diversity* is a 'coded word' and part of a 'syntax' that has been used widely to refer to non-white immigrants. Opinion polls on immigration ask what seem to be neutral and objective questions, but which have a strong undertone of concern with the presence of visible minorities or non-white immigrants in Canada. Although such polls may seem to be soliciting views about how many immigrants are thought to be desirable, the questions point subliminally to how many non-white immigrants are deemed acceptable. The respondents' opinions about race are not considered racist; rather, they are considered to be a 'genuine expression of "growing intolerance" and "cultural insecurity" based on legitimate concern that too many "nonwhites" would render Canadian values "slipping away."' Such opinions are 'noble concerns by citizens who only want to protect Canada's ideological tradition and the national unity' (Li 2004, 173–4).

Power and difference are two significant defining features of racism. Racism originates in a mindset that regards 'them' as different from 'us' in ways that are permanent and unbridgeable. This sense of difference justifies harming other ethnic groups by exploiting one's position of power. There are innumerable historical examples of this situation: in South Africa during apartheid; in pre–World War II Canada in the treatment of blacks, Chinese immigrants, and aboriginal populations; and in the subjugation of colonized populations in many countries in Africa and Asia. Racism, whether mild or severe, essentially asserts that it is impossible for the racializers and racialized to coexist, except in relations of domination and subordination.

Biology or Social Construction?

Although at the present time there is wide consensus about the wisdom of social construction, nevertheless a biological sediment remains in how we think of, experience, and respond to the physical markers of race. The physical encounter between the powerful and the powerless is important because it reveals who and what is seen and not seen (Razack 1998, 11). On the streets of Toronto in the 1970s, those of Asian descent and blacks were noticed, as demonstrated by seemingly innocent remarks such as, 'The mall was full of Chinese,' or 'The mall was full of blacks.' These comments reveal that the individual who made them – who was presumably not of Asian descent or black – noticed every Chinese or black person in the mall, and through such meticulous attention, those few individuals were transformed into an overwhelming majority. Those of Asian descent and blacks became visible, and the white majority in the mall became insignificant. Inversely, it could be said that a white woman in a bazaar in a city such as Chandigarh in India would be very visible to all those who were present on the scene.

The significance in these two scenarios is not merely the presence or visibility of someone of a different skin colour; rather, the significance lies in how a racist ideology constructs the individual and constructs the belief about whether it is appropriate for that person to be present in that location or not. In Canada in the 1970s, the presence of Asian immigrants and black people made some white people feel overwhelmed and intensified fears that 'Canadian' culture was under attack (Henry and Tator 2002; Li 2004). Although an individual may use common sense in evaluating people on the basis of skin colouring, eyes, and hair, significance lies in the racist ideology or racist stereotypes that she or he may, consciously or otherwise, use to label people in particular ways.

This ongoing problem, Holt argues, which lies in our own 'general failure to probe beyond the mantra of social constructedness, to ask what that really might mean in shaping lived experience, bears some responsibility for the shallowness both of the conception itself and of its repudiation in ordinary discourse' (Holt 2000, 10). Hartigan argues that the skepticism and questioning of race as a social construct arises from empirical research that has demonstrated that 'racial systems of inequality are inscribed in the very infrastructure of societies, in a realm that, while not attaining the permanence of genetic and biological orders, reflect a durability that exceeds simple individual intervention or tinkering' (Hartigan 1999, 185).

I could assert that the white men who sometimes held a door open for me many years ago attached stereotypical assumptions to the colour of my skin ('my race') and clothes ('my culture') and thus excluded me from the category of feminists while including me among 'traditional women.' Alternatively, it could be argued that these white men were crossing the cultural line by showing respect to a non-white woman. Such an argument captures one of the most difficult dilemmas of racism. The individual thinks, feels, and experiences racism, yet any action can lend itself to varying interpretations. It is incredibly hard to prove racism beyond any doubt, particularly in legal proceedings.

Perhaps I could be excused for coming to a conclusion that imputes racism to this act, because Canada has a history of race-based practices. In the pre–World War II period, race was used to exclude immigrants from Asia and include those from Europe. Race (that is, the beliefs associated with skin colour and eye colour) denied fair wages to Chinese male immigrants and exploited their labour in the early part of the twentieth century in British Columbia. Race categorized all Japanese-Canadians as 'enemy aliens,' which led to their internment and to the denial of their rights as citizens. Public antipathy to immigrants from India in British Columbia in the early 1900s led to the passing of the Continuous Journey legislation that barred their entry into Canada, and the subsequent challenge by potential immigrants to such exclusion led to the infamous *Komagata Maru* incident in 1914. Asian immigrants were excluded from citizenship rights by being denied the right to vote in British Columbia in 1871, resulting in their exclusion from certain occupations such as pharmacy, law, and political office (Anderson 1991, 47). The stigmatization of Asian immigrants was done not only to exploit their labour and to oppress them culturally, but also to preserve the value of whiteness. In all these cases, legislation defined what it means to be a low-wage Chinese immigrant, a gendered subject from India, or the white-skinned Canadian citizen.

In their respective chapters, Aiken, McDonald, and Smith discuss the significance of history and show how racism is not a thing of the past but continues in different forms at the present time. Racism in Canada, however, has taken different forms than elsewhere. Also included in this volume are studies that provide a basis for comparing situations in two different countries, such as increasing incidents of racism in Canada and the United States in the post–September 11 era.

Whiteness

Whiteness is hard to define because it seems to be everywhere and yet appears to be nothing much in particular (Razack 1998; Lipsitz 1998). Whiteness is the 'centre of the universe' and until recently was considered a 'natural' identity; a literary rendition of such a phenomenon is provided by Hurtado:

> If I am the center of the universe, you do not exist. If I am not the central actor in the drama I will not listen to you, I will not acknowledge your presence, and I will remove myself from the situation. My absence will highlight my centrality to all actions. I will not acknowledge your presence; my ability not to see you is my power. If I do not see you, you do not exist. If you only exist at my will, you are nothing without my attention. I am therefore the one that controls who is real and who is not. (1999, 228)

Until recently, whiteness remained unproblematized and not extensively studied. Whiteness is a race that is socially constructed. It is also an organizing principle of social relations that refers to its structural position of power and privilege historically, socially, politically, and culturally (Frankenberg 1993). Whiteness seems universal and natural because it has been dominant for centuries in many parts of the world. What at first glance may seem like neutral social and institutional arrangements are based on white dominance, and consequently whiteness and the behavioural and social norms associated with it have gained power and prestige.

Scholars such Frankenberg (1993), Lipsitz (1998), and Razack (1998) refer to whiteness as the colour of domination and argue that such dominance has become part of our social relations. A study of whiteness can thus reveal the racial interests inherent in some institutional arrangements and in the myriad behavioural and social relations that pervade our life and society. Although historically whiteness has dominated large parts of the globe, it is not homogenous; rather, it is heterogeneous and derives particular meanings from historical settings and from the time periods in which it was formed (Lipsitz 1998). Whiteness is lived through gender and class, like all other racial categorizations (Frankenberg 1993).

Whiteness is constructed in relation to those of different skin colour. Since whiteness is the unmarked category against which difference is structured, it has seldom been named or labelled and its role in racial inequality remained, until recently, untheorized. '"Racial" and "race" are typically used to characterize difference and deviance from social norms that have been seamlessly equated with what white people, generally speaking, do and think' (Hartigan 1999, 185). The present emphasis on naming whiteness allows us to reveal how it articulates with social formations, and when such relations of domination and subordination are made visible, they enable us to deconstruct and challenge them.

A discussion of whiteness raises much the same difficulties as any discussion of race. For example, does race really matter? What elements of biology creep into our definitions and discussions of whiteness? If the 'fact' of whiteness becomes established with certainty, then what is one to make of contingency and its significance for racial categories? Do the beliefs in a 'white culture' reify whiteness as a definable entity and undermine the social construction theory of race? How do changing political situations intersect with beliefs about white hegemony? I address some of these questions in this volume in an interview with Frances Henry, a white Jewish woman who was a victim of Nazi Germany and who has studied racism against black people in Canada throughout her academic career.

Whiteness is more than identifying white versus black; rather, it is the elevation of whiteness through the racialization of others that has resulted in tremendous economic gains and opportunities for white people throughout history, locally and globally. Lipsitz labels this as the 'possessive investment' in whiteness. He notes that 'race is a cultural construct, but one with sinister structural causes and consequences. Conscious and deliberate actions have institutionalized group identities in [Canada], and not just through the dissemination of cultural stories but also through systematic efforts from colonial times to the present to create economic advantage through a possessive investment in whiteness for European [Canadians]' (1998, 2).

Such investment is not merely a matter of history, but continues globally at the present time (for instance, through the exploitation of labour in China and India). In their chapter, Pendakur and Pendakur analyse statistical data from Canadian censuses to show that racialized individuals born in Canada earned less than their white Canadian counterparts. In this study, the authors eliminated the variable of social capital sometimes thought to be a negative factor affecting the earnings of first-generation immigrants, proving that regardless of social factors such as accent, dress, and behavioural norms, race matters. Wang and Lo show that although the characteristics of Chinese immigrants to Canada have changed recently and more of them have academic credentials and speak English proficiently, they still earn less than white Canadians.

Epistemology (or, Colonizer and Colonized)

Shards and fragments of history commingle with our present and define the colour and the cultural line that exclude and include. The political, economic, social, and intellectual legacy of white colonial rule has infiltrated almost every aspect of colonized societies. The knowledge produced by the colonizers about the colonized defined them as others from the standpoint of white European culture and society (Said 1978).

Knowledge produced by the colonizers about the colonized distorts and inflicts violence on them by denigrating their culture, history, and sense of themselves as a people and nation – a process referred to as *epistemic violence*. Frankenberg notes:

> Equally significant, while discursively generating and marking a range of cultural and racial Others as different from an apparently stable Western or white self, the Western self is itself produced as an *effect of* the Western discursive production of its Others. That means that the Western self and the non-Western other are constructed as discursive products, both of whose 'realness' stands in extremely complex relationships to the production of knowledge and to the material violence to which epistemic violence is intimately linked. (1993, 17)

India and other countries in South Asia have also helped shape the self-images of other cultures, although this is discussed more rarely. Western cultures have

> recurringly used India as a foil to define their own historical moments: to reassure or to doubt themselves. And Indians have also, on occasion, tried to work out their own 'indigenous' ways of knowing the West. It is impossible to sever these twisted bonds of mutual knowingness and ignorance: the plunder is constant, and neither side can retreat into a luxurious hermeticism. Any discussion of India is thus inescapably forced on to the treacherous fields of the politics of knowledge. These must be navigated, like any political activity, by one's wits. There is no privileged compass, no method, or idiom that can assist. (Khilnani 1998, 197)

The introduction by Western missionaries of English-language education for females was eagerly embraced by upper-middle-class Indians of all castes, particularly those in cities. I attended one such school, and my colonial education inculcated in me a set of beliefs and values about European societies, whiteness, and the culture associated with it, which moulded my intellect in particular ways. In Toronto and in the university classroom, I would discover that my education had oppressed me, devalued my culture, and such a discovery compelled me to engage in deconstructing the knowledge that was an integral part of who I was.

In Canada, whiteness seems almost invisible because of its predominantly normative nature. For example, in the 1970s immigrants from Third World countries were attracted to cities by the promise of economic and educational opportunities, changing the Anglo-Saxon whiteness that had characterized the Canadian city thus far. The 1967 immigration policy gave points for education, age, language, and skills, and in so doing was thought to make the criteria for entry into Canada objective and neutral and one that had universal applications. This immigration policy encouraged a rapid influx of immigrants from 1967–73 from Third World countries. A large proportion of them were settled in Ontario, particularly in Toronto (Simmons 1998). The presence of these new immigrants led to a public outcry in the media about the burden that they were imposing on 'our' social services and structures (Pitman 1977). Such concerns continue to be expressed at the present time in arguments that schools and social services are straining to meet the 'diverse' (read 'non-white') needs of immigrants (Li 2004, 130).

The social context of whiteness that predominated Canada in the period from 1967–73 defined 'us' and excluded 'them' – the new non-white immigrants. What distinguished 'us' from 'them' was not mere identity (that is, race) but a history that assigned power to some and made others less powerful (or even powerless). The meanings of race, Holt notes, articulate with a given social formation defined as 'all the interrelated structures of economic, political, and social power, as well as the system of signification (that is cultural systems) that give rise to and/or reflect those structures' (Holt 2000, 22). The power of white men in a predominantly white Canada is vastly different from that of a gendered, non-white immigrant.

The Canadian Nation

Whiteness has defined the Canadian nation. Such an identification is not unique to Canada; rather, it replicates the historical experience of the United States and some countries in Europe. The knowledge constructed by white men, historically, has been silent about the contributions of racialized immigrants and all women to nation building. (A detailed analysis of this literature is found in my book *Resisting Discrimination: Women from Asia, Africa, and the Caribbean and the Women's Movement in Canada*). Feminists have argued that the silences and absences pervasive in many different kinds of literature and emanating from a variety of disciplines have oppressed them. They have decoded the silence to reveal the values and norms guiding those who were constructing such knowledge – usually white, middle-class, university-educated men. Examples of such biases include the value placed on paid work over women's substantial unpaid labour in the family and the objectification and representation of black women's sexuality. The situation of racialized women in the United States was powerfully documented in the seminal work *Women, Race, and Class* by Angela Davis (1983). Another kind of silence is discussed by Ostow in this volume – in this case, the empty towers designed by the architect Daniel Libeskind for the Jewish museum in Berlin to represent the voids left in Berlin and throughout Jewish history.

Feminist epistemology has disputed the notion of the value-neutral and objective researcher and academic, arguing instead that all knowledge is constructed from a particular social, cultural, and political location and reflects that standpoint (Harding 1990). The absence of racialized immigrants in what was written about Canada, particularly prior to the 1970s, provides an insight into the identity of those typically thought of as 'Canadian.' Bannerji writes:

'Canada' then cannot be taken as a given. It is obviously a construction, a set of representations, embodying certain types of political and cultural communities and their operations. These communities were themselves constructed in agreement with certain ideas regarding skin colour, history, language (English/French), and other cultural signifiers – all of which may be subsumed under the category 'White.' A 'Canada' constructed on this basis contains certain notions of nation, state formation, and economy. Europeanness as 'whiteness' thus translates into 'Canada' and provides it with its 'imagined community.' (1997, 24)

Constance Backhouse, a white feminist legal scholar, is critical of the Canadian mythology of being 'raceless' and of the 'stupendous innocence' that pervades this notion. 'Despite remarkable evidence to the contrary, despite legislation that articulated racial distinctions and barriers, despite lawyers and judges who used racial constructs to assess legal rights and responsibilities, the Canadian legal system borrowed heavily from this mythology, and contributed to the fostering of the ideology of Canada as a "raceless" nation' (Backhouse 1999, 13). The racialized terms that were used in legal discourse before World War II included 'Orientals,' 'Chinese,' 'Japanese,' 'Hindu,' 'half-breed,' 'Indians,' 'Negroes,' as well as the more elusive terms 'Caucasian' and 'whites' (14). The ideas of 'racial purity' facilitated the entry of northern Europeans into Canada and barred the entry of anyone Chinese or 'Hindu' (as Indian women were incorrectly referred to) in the early 1900s. Such racialization constructed Canada as a white nation and produced literature referring to white women as 'mothers of the race.' The common belief was that women transmit and produce culture and thus a nation. Legislation and governmental sponsorship helped white women immigrate to Canada in the late nineteenth century, but others were excluded. After all, racists asked, how could Asian women participate in such a nation-building exercise? (Perry 2004; Dua 2000, 2004). In this volume, Creese argues that racialized women who have recently migrated to Canada have to negotiate complex and contradictory processes of belonging to a nation that has been predominantly defined as white. Canadian identity, she argues, is a bordered space that only partially admits racialized immigrants.

Voice and Authority

'Coming to voice' is a metaphor for overcoming oppression and for the ability, however hesitant and insecure at first, to articulate that experience. When individuals speak out and articulate a 'truth' from a perspective that is in opposition to established knowledge, the result is often social change, but it may also create vulnerability. Such 'truths' may be deemed suspect and critiqued for being inadequate or simply not credible. To avoid such potential problems, Smith's chapter in this book extensively documents his 'truth' that blacks and those of Arab descent are facing additional harassment in Canada under the guise of the war against terrorism.

Speaking out is a responsibility and a duty for those who care about a just society and social order, and such articulations of injustice, however enunciated, bring immediate rewards to the individual. Resistance lies in recognizing and identifying the hegemonic ideology embedded in knowledge and by engaging with its seemingly normative discourse from an oppositional standpoint (hooks 2003; Collins 2000). Questioning knowledge about Canada, whether from a historical or contemporary perspective, makes visible the axes of power and authority and enables us to challenge them. Mohanty writes: 'Who we are, how we act, what we think and what stories we tell become more intelligible within an epistemological framework that begins by recognizing existing hegemonic histories ... Resistance lies in self-conscious engagement with dominant, normative discourses and representations and in active creation of oppositional analytic and cultural spaces' (Mohanty 1994). But as Montoya notes, 'Speaking out assumes prerogative. Speaking out is an exercise of privilege. Speaking out takes practice. Silence ensures invisibility. Silence provides protection. Silence masks' (Montoya 1995).

Identity and experience have become particularly significant in scholarship and politics in the last few decades. The neutral author and his or her objective understanding is a chimera. Rather, our identity and subjectivity determine our perspectives and scholarship. The question of who has the authority to speak on behalf of a group of people has become an intensely contested issue. Thus, if we argue that only black people can speak for other blacks, does it imply a pregiven identity as a 'natural' basis for politics? Furthermore, if subjectivity is discursively produced, fluid, and changing, does it always coincide perfectly with identity? Do racialized individuals need to create a 'safe space' in Canadian universities at the present time through excluding white individuals, as contended by some critical race theorists? Would such exclusionary politics be simply retaliation or would they be racism? What is the role of white people in antiracism?

Identity is important because it creates an understanding that the 'personal is political,' or that the phenomena that we experience in our everyday lives and accept as natural, normal, and routine have been constructed by the power relations of society. Identity politics, at one level, simply means that identity is important and relevant to one's politics and makes a difference that must be taken into account. Such politics 'focus on the affirmation of common identities by groups of mobilizing individuals' (Andermahr, Lovell, and Wolkowitz 2000, 124).

The black consciousness movement and white feminism used identity as an organizing tool to build cohesive and vocal political communities and to forge solidarity among them in the 1960s and 1970s. 'A traditional identity politics defines itself in terms of an absolute, undivided commitment to, and identification with, a particular community; a group which presents a united front through an exclusion of others' (Procter 2004, 118). Identity politics were criticized in the 1980s for an overemphasis on identity that was thought to erode progressive politics. Further postmodern post-structuralist formulations of identity and subjectivity have overturned some of the earlier working assumptions.

Postmodern thought considers the concept of a fixed stable self as dubious. Rather, it argues that a set of values is imposed on a 'fluid and open ended subjectivity [which] aids in making subjects of the state more susceptible to dominant ideologies and disciplinary techniques' (Code 2000, 264). Subjectivity is discursively produced; that is, it is created through a process. It is the effect of conscious and unconscious forces, embodied. It is also an expression (or an effect) of power (398). In the late 1980s and 1990s, Stuart Hall, in light of postmodern theorizations of identity as fragmented, transitional, fluid, and changing, rethought his earlier stance and redefined the politics of identity by 'emphasizing difference over homogeneity, the local and transnational over the national, "contingent" positions over pure, fixed origins' (Procter 2004, 117). Hall defined the alternative identity politics as follows:

The recognition ... of the impossibility of 'identity' in its fully unified meaning, does, of course, transform our sense of what identity politics is about. It transforms the nature of political commitment. Hundred-and-one percent commitment is no longer possible ... Looking at new conceptions of identity requires us also to look at redefinitions of the forms of politics which follow that: the politics of difference, the politics of self-reflectivity, a politics that is open to contingency but still able to act. (qtd in Procter 2004, 119)

Hall's politics of identity focuses on three specific terms: difference, self-reflectivity, and contingency. Difference involves the recognition of many identities rather than one definitive or normative identity, and a rejection of clear-cut binaries such as black/white. Self-reflectivity requires the individual to reveal what is relevant about her or his own identity. Contingency involves a sense of dependency on other events and contexts and recognizes that the political positions we take up are not set in stone, that we may need to reposition ourselves over time and in different circumstances (Procter 2004, 119). The practice of self-reflectivity requires an examination of the subject position and its value for political action, but we should do so in a manner that does not 'paralyze the subject as knower' (Castagna and Dei 2000, 29).

Black scholars such as bell hooks and Patricia Collins have struggled with the theories of identity and subjectivity to overcome the biological argument of race and yet give some primacy to the racialized individual who has personal experience and insight into racism (hooks 2003; Collins 2000). They argue that the situated scholar has some insights that may elude those who are outside that category of oppression, but I ask whether it must necessarily be so. The situation of Frances Henry, a white scholar who has studied racism against blacks, is a case in point.

Conclusion

Newspapers and magazines sometimes glibly report that Toronto is a multicultural and multiracial city. However, I live in a neighbourhood that is predominantly white, and the non-whites who also make it their home are, with some very few exceptions, women who perform housekeeping and childcare services for my neighbours. In the summertime, I walk along the tree-lined sidewalks and quietly admire the lush, aesthetically laid-out gardens full of blossoms. I am a familiar figure, for I have lived in this neighbourhood for twenty years, mostly contentedly. On my walks, I pass by the house of a white male, a distinguished member of the legal profession, a churchgoer, and he will beckon me from afar and engage me in small talk while standing on the sidewalk. He has on many occasions told me about his secretary, an Anglo-Indian (a term used in India for those who are of mixed race), whom he likes and with whom he has had a very good working relationship for several years.

Yet every time he mentions this woman, my guard goes up, for I know from experience it is a prelude to some racist remark. In discussing his courtroom, he said, 'All the blacks who come to my courts are pimps.' When his son's relationship with a South Asian Muslim woman ended (both his son and the woman are lawyers), he said gleefully and without recognizing to whom he was speaking, 'Thank God, he has come to his senses. Now he is dating a woman of his own kind.' 'His own kind,' presumably, did not refer to a lawyer or a male – he meant race. The sting of a racist remark or act always hurts.

Racism has been with us for centuries in myriad guises and continues at the present time; it is chameleonlike, and its power lies in its 'ambiguity, its mutability, its parasitism' (Holt 2000, 119). Few are as pessimistic and despairing as Derek Bell, who has argued that racism is permanent (1992). Racialized individuals live under its shadow, but they are not defeatists. Rather, they have developed a range of strategies for resisting racism. At times, it might involve confronting individuals at a one-to-one level. At other times, it might mean engaging in organized, antiracist activities of the type documented in this volume by McDonald. Hagey, Turrittin, and Das Gupta (also in this volume) suggest that adopting 'relational accountability' can improve working relationships and understanding between black nurses and their white patients. Ostow observes how memorializing the past by establishing a Jewish Museum in Berlin has allowed a sense of reconciliation and hope to emerge. Racism, history teaches us, can be challenged, and its intensity and severity can change. In the pre–September 11 period, reflections on Canadian history would have suggested that racism was decreasing, however slow the pace of change might be. The picture is grimmer now, and there are more allegations of racism, particularly against Muslim males (commonly referred to as 'Islamophobia').

Niggling doubts and feelings of vulnerability can nevertheless cause anguished questioning and a search for answers among racialized individuals. Such questions may simply refer to the everyday experience of racism: when individuals ask themselves whether they should make a point or ignore a racist remark or slur, when they wonder how to best pick their battles over racism or whether they ought to challenge racism every time they encounter it. How should individuals cope with racially motivated injustices, such as denied promotions and opportunities at work? But more poignant and difficult are questions that relate to children. How should the family and community foster confidence, self-esteem, and respect in children, teaching them to protect their inner selves from the racial slur and the racist act? How to teach children courage and perseverance so that they may realize their human potential, despite racism? How can children avoid the scourge of racism that plagues them and their opportunities? Racism causes anxiety and leads to feelings of physical and psychological insecurity.

Holt advises that racialized individuals should live as if it were possible to change the world. Such a dream of the future does not mean negating one's racial identity or history. Rather, it means struggling to imagine ourselves in images of our own choosing. Holt would advise his young daughter thus:

> Like many who have gone before you must struggle against injustice with all your might. You must refuse to be racialized or to racialize others. But at the same time you must also live as if the world were otherwise. You must reach out and claim it as your own. I know that it is a lot to ask. It will certainly require a difficult heroism and a subtle resistance, as well as exposure to the risk of being misunderstood by your peers and elders. But perhaps ... just perhaps ... when enough people do as you do, racism will indeed have no future. (2000, 123)

Themes of this book

This book is divided into four parts. Part One, entitled 'Border Policies: Immigration, Refugees, and Asylum Seekers,' shows that although Canada has promoted immigration, both historically and in contemporary times, the issue of who gains entry and under what conditions remains contentious. The chapters of Part One document the racialization of discourses of immigration and immigrants and show that although 'the text of the law and legal discourse in the area of immigration has evolved from its explicitly racist orientation to one of "objective" discrimination, racism in its less obvious, systemic forms has persisted' (Aiken in this volume). Although some individuals are excluded by immigration laws, they may nevertheless gain entry through subterfuge and live in Canada. Even though they are deemed 'illegal,' their cause has been championed by anti-racist activists who have raised questions about formal, substantive, and (in Étienne Balibar's concept) 'active' citizenship.

Part Two discusses systemic and everyday racism under the title 'Race, Work, and Workplace.' Racism in employment has been widely practised despite legislation to counteract such biases. It continues to bedevil the life chances of racialized men and women. This section presents case studies of Chinese immigrants, black nurses, and Canadian-born racialized groups. These studies demonstrate that despite the heterogeneity of their origins and characteristics, Chinese immigrants experience racist discrimination at work as evidenced by their lower earnings. Such income penalty is borne not only by immigrants, but also by racialized Canadian-born and Canadian-educated individuals. Case studies such as these raise the question of whether Canada needs more anti-discriminatory legislations and public policies to counteract racism. One answer may be to look beyond legislations and instead hold individuals accountable for everyday racisms that lead to personal harm and professional inequities.

Part Three, entitled 'Nation and Identity,' takes the debate of race and racism into a broader international context and into the post–September 11 period. The need to be vigilant against terrorism has led to the tightening of national borders and has given rise to new dilemmas for racialized populations. Racial profiling victimizes black people and Arab-Canadians, but their situation is not exceptional; rather, it is replicated in the United States as well. A specific social and political context has been created by the events of September 11, yet the racism of the present time finds strong overtones in similar treatment of Japanese-Americans during World War II. What lessons have we learnt from history about racializing and victimizing individuals and groups? Is there a possibility for hope and reconciliation? An innovative answer is to be found in Germany's creation of museums that address the anti-Semitism of the past and seek to fill in the voids of history.

Race and racialization alienates those who are its victims, and although they survive by resisting, they come to question who they are and with whom they belong. Socially constructed identity thus includes and excludes individuals in public policies, anti-racist activism, and in interpersonal social relations. Part Four, entitled 'Nation, Citizenship, and Belonging,' deals with struggles against exclusions, whether they are systemic or interpersonal, and exposes the roadblocks to inclusionary policies and behaviour. The contention is not over the entitlement to formal equality guaranteed by Canadian citizenship; rather, the struggle is to give this entitlement substance by eliminating the invidious distinctions based on class, race, and gender, and their many intersections. The realization of substantive citizenship will lead to a sense of belonging, creating hope for a future where individuals of all hues and varieties can believe that together, they all belong to the Canadian nation.

References

Agnew, Vijay. 1996. *Resisting discrimination: Women from Asia, Africa, and the Caribbean and the women's movement in Canada*. Toronto: University of Toronto Press.

Andermahr, Sonya, Terry Lovell, and Carol Wolkowitz. 2000. *A glossary of feminist theory*. London: Arnold.

Anderson, Kay. 1991. *Vancouver's Chinatown: Racial discourse in Canada, 1875–1980*. Montreal: McGill-Queen's University Press.

Appiah, Kwame Anthony. 2005. *The ethics of identity*. Princeton: Princeton University Press.

Backhouse, Constance. 1999. *Colour-coded: A legal history of racism in Canada, 1900–1950*. Toronto: Osgoode Society for Canadian Legal History and University of Toronto Press.

Bannerji, Himani. 1997. Geography lessons: On being insider/outsider to the Canadian nation. In *Dangerous territories: Struggles for difference and equality in education*, ed. Leslie Roman and Linda Eyre, 23–42. New York: Routledge.

Baldwin, James. 1976. *The devil finds work*. New York: Dell. Quoted in Lipsitz 1998, 47.

Balibar, Étienne. 1991. Is there a neo-racism? In *Race, Nation and Class: Ambiguous Identities*, ed. Étienne Balibar and Immanuel Wallerstein. London: Verso. Quoted in Torres, Miron, and Inda 1999, 9.

Bell, Derek. 1992. *Faces at the bottom of the well: The permanence of racism*. New York: Harper Collins.

Blum, Lawrence. 2004. What do accounts of 'racism' do? In *Racism in mind*, ed. Michael Levine and Tamas Pataki, 56–77. Ithaca: Cornell University Press.

Castagna, Maria, and George Sefa Dei. 2000. An historical overview of the application of the race concept in social practice. In *Anti-racist feminism: Critical race and gender studies*, ed. Agnes Calliste and George Sefa Dei, 19–38. Halifax: Fernwood.

Code, Lorraine. 2000. *Encyclopedia of feminist theories*. New York: Routledge.

Collins, Patricia. 2000. *Black feminist thought: Knowledge, consciousness, and the politics of empowerment*. New York: Routledge.

Commission on Systemic Racism in the Ontario Criminal Justice System. 1995. Co-chairs D. Cole and M. Gittens. Toronto: Queen's Printer. Quoted in Ontario Human Rights Commission 2005, 9.

Davis, Angela. 1983. *Woman, race, and class.* New York: Vintage.

Dua, Enakshi. 2000. 'The Hindu woman question': Canadian nation building and the social construction of gender for South Asian–Canadian women. In *Anti-racist feminism: Critical race and gender studies,* ed. Agnes Calliste and George Sefa Dei, 55–72. Halifax: Fernwood.

– 2004. Racializing imperial Canada: Indian women and the making of an ethnic community. In *Sisters or strangers? Immigrant, ethnic, and racialized women in Canadian history,* ed. Marlene Epp, Franca Iacovetta, and Frances Swyripa, 71–88. Toronto: University of Toronto Press.

Dunlop, Rishma, and Priscilla Uppal, eds. 2004. *Red silk: An anthology of South Asian Canadian women poets.* Toronto: Mansfield.

Fleras, Augie. 2004. Racializing culture/culturalizing race: Multicultural racism in a multicultural Canada. In *Racism, eh? A critical inter-disciplinary anthology of race and racism in Canada,* ed. Camille Nelson and Charmaine Nelson, 429–43. Concord, ON: Captus.

Frankenberg, Ruth. 1993. *The social construction of whiteness: White women, race matters.* Minneapolis: University of Minnesota Press.

Fredrickson, George. 2002. *Racism: A short history.* Princeton, NJ: Princeton University Press.

Goldberg, David Theo. 1990. *Anatomy of racism.* Minneapolis: University of Minnesota Press. Quoted in Blum 2004, 58–9.

Hacking, Ian. 1986. Making up people. In *Reconstructing individualism: Anatomy, individuality, and the self in Western thought,* ed. Thomas Heller, Morton Sosna, and David Wellbery. Stanford: Stanford University Press. Quoted in Appiah 2005, 65.

Hall, Stuart. 1980. Race, articulation and societies structured in dominance. In *Sociological theories: Race and colonialism.* Paris: UNESCO. Quoted in Holt 2000, 21.

Harding, Sandra. 1990. Feminism, science, and the anti-enlightenment critiques. In *Feminism/postmodernism,* ed. Linda Nicholson, 83–106. New York: Routledge.

Hartigan, John. 1999. Establishing the fact of whiteness. In Torres, Miron, and Inda 1999, 183–99.

Henry, Frances, and Carol Tator. 2002. *Discourses of domination: Racial bias in the Canadian English-language press.* Toronto: University of Toronto Press.

Holt, Thomas. 2000. *The problem of race in the 21st century.* Cambridge, MA: Harvard University Press.

hooks, bell. 2003. *Teaching community: A pedagogy of hope.* New York: Routledge.

Hurtado, Aida. 1999. The trickster's play: Whiteness in the subordination and liberation process. In Torres, Miron, and Inda 1999, 225–44.

James, Carl, ed. 2000. *Experiencing difference.* Halifax: Fernwood.

Khilnani, Sunil. 1998. *The idea of India.* London: Penguin.

Li, Peter. 2004. *Destination Canada.* Toronto: Oxford University Press.

Lipsitz, George. 1998. *The possessive investment in whiteness: How white people profit from identity politics.* Philadelphia: Temple University Press.

Miles, Robert. 1989. *Racism.* London: Routledge. Quoted in Torres, Miron, and Inda 1999, 7.

Mohanty, Chandra. 1991. Under Western eyes: Feminist scholarship and colonial discourses. In *Third World women and the politics of feminism,* ed. Chandra Mohanty, Ann Russo, and Lourdes Torres, 51–80. Bloomington: Indiana University Press.

– 1994. On race and voice: Challenges of liberal education in the 1990s. In *Between borders: Pedagogy and the politics of cultural studies,* ed. H. Giroux and P. McLaren, 145–166. New York: Routledge. Quoted in Srivastava 1997, 115.

Montaya, M. 1995. Un/masking the self while un/braiding Latin stories. In *Critical race theory: The cutting edge,* ed. R. Delgado, 529–39. Philadelphia: Temple University Press. Quoted in Srivastava 1997, 118.

Ontario Human Rights Commission. 2005. *Policy and guidelines on racism and racial discrimination.* Toronto: Ontario Human Rights Commission.

Perry, Adele. 2004. Whose sister and what eyes? White women, race, and immigration to British Columbia, 1849–1871. In *Sisters or strangers? Immigrant, ethnic, and racialized women in Canadian history,* ed. Marlene Epp, Franca Iacovetta, and Frances Swyripa, 71–88. Toronto: University of Toronto Press.

Pitman, Walter. 1977. *Now is not too late.* Report submitted to the Council of Metropolitan Toronto by the Task Force on Human Relations.

Procter, James. 2004. *Stuart Hall.* London: Routledge.

Razack, Sherene. 1998. *Looking white people in the eye: Gender, race, and culture in courtrooms and classrooms.* Toronto: University of Toronto Press.

Said, Edward. 1978. *Orientalism.* New York: Vintage.

Simmons, Alan. 1998. Racism in immigration policy. In *Racism and social inequality in Canada,* ed. Vic Satzewich, 87–114. Halifax: Fernwood.

Small, Stephen. 1999. The contours of racialization structures: Structures, representations, and resistance in the United States. In Torres, Miron, and Inda 1999, 47–64.

Srivastava, Aruna. 1997. Anti-racism inside and outside the classroom. In *Dangerous territories: Struggles for difference and equality,* ed. Leslie Roman and Linda Eyre, 113–26. New York: Routledge.

Torres, Rodolfo, Louis Miron, and Jonathan Inda, eds. 1999. *Race, identity, and citizenship: A reader.* Malden, MA: Blackwell.

PART ONE

Immigrants, Refugees, and Asylum Seekers

History provides us with many examples of people who were enticed by dreams of a better life for themselves and their families and voluntarily left their countries of birth for other, more prosperous geographical regions. Yet sometimes the necessity of leaving has been thrust upon people because of environmental disasters, political ideologies, ethnic cleansing, and civil wars. At times, the countries receiving these individuals have opened up their hearts and homes to the newcomers, perceiving them as fellow human beings and hoping to make a better and richer community and society together. But at other times, biases have intervened and societies have treated newcomers unequally, favouring immigrants and refugees of one country or identity over those of another. At the heart of discussions about immigrants, refugees, and asylum seekers is the vision that citizens have articulated about who they are as a nation, the values and norms that motivate them, and the ideals that they wish to uphold individually and collectively.

When Canadian policies relating to immigrants and refugees are measured against enunciated ideals of equality and non-discrimination, scholars find a gap between ideals and practice. Questioning the policies and rhetoric of immigration reveals the racism that is embedded in its discourse and thus in its intent. Canada has been compassionate and humanitarian in accepting individuals fleeing persecution because of race, ethnicity, religion, and political beliefs, but scholars ask if their countries have done enough according to present moral and ethical standards. Have the persecuted been treated fairly and equally, particularly with regard to their gender and race, by the receiving countries? Refugees, asylum seekers, and immigrants are not passive victims who are acted upon by others; rather, they organize to resist oppression. Some scholars are skeptical about the receiving countries' rhetoric of compassion and humanitarianism. Canada, they argue, has prioritized the well-being of its own society and has not been overwhelmingly generous in relieving the distress of refugees. A discussion of refugees in Canada illuminates strategies that have worked well in the past and the possibilities for more egalitarian and humanitarian practices in the future.

In 'Contradictions of "Racial" Discourses,' Peter Li argues that the challenge in deconstructing racism in a democratic society is to explain how people attribute social significance to race in everyday life when the law disallows – and norms discourage – the use of race as grounds to differentiate people. This apparent contradiction is reconciled through the use of what Li calls a 'racial syntax,' which removes references to race and relies instead upon encoded concepts and messages to articulate racism. Thus, racial discourse represents a sophisticated way in which race is articulated in democratic societies through the use of an encoded language that gives the appearance of rejecting racism and advocating equality on the one hand, while still condoning racial signification on the other.

Immigration law and policy are informed by competing and often contradictory philosophies, argues Sharryn Aiken in 'From Slavery to Expulsion: Racism, Canadian Immigration Law, and the Unfulfilled Promise of Modern Constitutionalism.' Nevertheless, as the text of the law and legal discourse in the area of immigration have evolved from an explicitly racist orientation to one of 'objective' neutrality, racism in its less obvious, systemic forms has persisted. From slavery to expulsion, racialized people have been the victims of a legal system that has worked to disadvantage and oppress. This chapter elaborates on the meaning of race and racism and introduces critical race theory as both a lens and a foil against which the role of judicial review and constitutional adjudication of the claims asserted by non-citizens in Canada can be explored.

Aiken's central thesis is that reliance on the courts has failed to deliver the systemic changes required for a truly antiracist immigration program. A review of the defining features of immigration law and policy from the early 1990s to the present documents key components of the immigration program, including immigrant selection, the rules for refugees, 'humanitarian and compassionate' cases, as well as public danger and security provisions. Aiken analyses a number of recent judicial decisions to show that although racism in immigration law has been modified, the promise of transformative litigation remains unful-filled for non-citizens. Indeed, the appearance of change – the language of equity and fairness in the text of the law and in law talk – has served as a cover for preserving the status quo and sustaining systemic racism in the contemporary immigration program.

Jean McDonald addresses important issues of citizenship, identity, and space in 'Citizenship, Illegality, and Sanctuary.' She believes that refugees acquire de facto legality as they participate in civil society, as shown by the refusal of members of a Montreal-based organization to accept the 'illegal' label. The first part of this chapter describes how the Action Committee of Non-Status Algerians was formed and the ways in which members of this committee have emerged as 'active citizens,' thus reconfiguring citizenship as a collective practice. The Action Committee repudiates the social space of invisibility created in the process of illegalization by making claims on the state and by making demands through direct action.

The second part of this chapter recounts the targeting of Mohamed Cherfi, a member of the Action Committee, whose arrest inside a Quebec City church was a violation of church sanctuary for the first time in recorded Canadian history. McDonald demonstrates how the offering of sanctuary often enacts a challenge to state-produced boundaries, while at the same time ultimately legitimizing the categories put forward by the immigration system. The idea of 'sanctuary cities' presents another problem for the ideological and spatial enforcement of state borders. The chapter concludes with an exploration of this concept and a brief survey of the literature on cities as a strategic location for the practice of active citizenship.

1 Contradictions of 'Racial' Discourse

PETER S. LI

As ideologies, liberal democracy and racism are contradictory because the former rejects the relevance of 'race' in determining the worth of human beings and the latter thrives on the signification of individuals and groups based on 'racial' and other superficial features.[1] Liberal democracy is premised upon the principle of equality, under which all human beings are equal. Racism, on the other hand, posits essential differences between peoples, produced either by heredity or by adaptation, which in turn produce further differences in human capacity and achievement. These two ideologies create another contradictory phenomenon. Despite the wide acceptance of the principle of equality and non-discrimination under liberal democracy, 'race' remains a meaningful concept that some people use to signify 'otherness' and to make sense of everyday life and social relations. As well, 'race' as a socially constructed concept continues to affect the life chances of people. In short, the significance of 'race' persists as cultural representation and social reality in democratic societies. The purpose of this chapter is to explain how the discourse of 'race' in Canada provides a representational framework based on constructed 'racial' features of people, by which 'racial' signification and 'racism' can be articulated without making them appear offensive to democratic principles. In this way, the signification of 'race' and the construction of 'otherness' become acceptable and, indeed, natural; at the same time, the normative integrity of liberal democracy is preserved.

Theories of 'Race'

Goldberg (1992) has suggested that theories of 'race' tend to be reductionistic in treating 'race' as an a priori concept, either in the biological sense of a genetically based subspecies or in the social sense of phantom social categories. The former conception links 'racial' differences to genetic causes and interprets 'racial' hierarchy as a permanent feature of nature. The second conception sees 'race' as a false ideological formulation with no reality in social relations. 'Race' so conceived is static, and the concept leaves little room to explain why racial formation is different during different times. The theoretical challenge for Goldberg is to view 'race' as having an adaptive capacity that needs to be explained. Goldberg's notion that 'race' mutates, subject to history and historical moments, points to the importance of understanding 'racial' formation as a variable social outcome. The fluid and hybrid nature of 'race' does not mean that there is no minimal significance that can be ascertained. As Goldberg puts it, 'race both establishes and rationalizes the order of difference as a law of nature' (1992, 559–60). But it does so in different ways during different times. Hence, under liberal democracy, the deconstruction of 'race' necessarily involves what Winant calls addressing 'the persistence of racial classification and stratification in an era officially committed to racial equity and multiculturalism' (2000, 180).

At a minimal level, racism involves the evaluation and hierarchical ranking of individuals and groups, based on some phenotypic or genotypic features deemed 'race' based. Thus, racism presupposes the signification of 'race' and its ability to classify human beings. But the precise content and significance attributed to 'race' vary throughout history. As Goldberg points out, there are 'corrections between the historically specific connotations of 'race' and the broad forms of racist expressions' (1992, 558). Historically, specific 'racial' connotations give new life to different forms of 'racial' expressions, but they in themselves are parts of the cultural frameworks with which people make sense of their times. Cultural frameworks, or regimes of representation in a culture, constitute but also reflect the social world (Hall 1996). Thus, cultural representations of 'race' both reflect 'race' relations in the social world and, at the same time, influence 'race' relations by injecting meanings to them to give them a rational appearance. Hence, deconstructing 'racial' discourse necessarily involves unravelling the unequal relations embedded in the discourse itself (see Caldas-Coulthard and Coulthard 1996; van Dijk 1993, 2001; Mills 1997; Henry and Tator 2002).

One way to study the representation of 'race' at a given time is to see how 'race' is articulated in 'racial' discourses. In short, the construction of ideas of 'race' requires its discursive representations in concepts, ideas, and syntax with which meanings of 'race' are encoded and decoded. The study of 'race' at any historical moment necessitates understanding how it is represented by concepts and codes in the cultural frameworks of people and how these discursive tools are used to construct and attribute meanings to phenomena deemed 'racial.' Foucault points out that linguistic discourse is governed by what he calls 'rules of exclusion,' which specify the right to speak or not to speak of a particular subject in a certain way (1972, 216). Thus, deconstructing 'racial' discourse also involves understanding the discursive policies or rules that govern the production of such a discourse, and the embedded differential power in being able to set and influence such rules.

In order to appreciate how 'racial' discourse helps to resolve normative inconsistencies under liberal democracy, it is helpful to review how such inconsistencies are articulated in Canadian society.

Normative Inconsistencies in Canada

Many public opinion polls indicate that Canadians strongly endorse a policy of multiculturalism and an ideology of 'racial' and ethnic equality (Angus Reid Group 1991; Jedwab and Baker 2003; Jedwab 2002a, 2002b). Yet these same polls also indicate that people do not find it objectionable to express an opinion on the social desirability of immigrants and 'racial' minorities based on superficial features, such as skin colour. Indeed, Canada seems to be confronted with two sets of values that on the surface are difficult to reconcile. On the one hand, there are strong values of democracy, justice, and equality, and yet on the other hand, 'race' and 'racial' differences remain meaningful and alive in the ideas, values, and indeed the normative system of Canada.

There is now substantial evidence to show that normative inconsistencies regarding democratic principles and the signification of 'race' comfortably coexist in the ideas of Canadians. For example, the Department of Multiculturalism and Citizenship commissioned Angus Reid to do a study of Canadian attitudes towards multiculturalism in 1991. The results indicated strong support for 'racial' and cultural diversity as well as a prevailing opinion reflecting 'racial' preferences. Over 60 per cent of the respondents from the national sample indicated support for the federal policy of multiculturalism; as many as 76 per cent of the respondents agreed with the policy in its recognition of cultural and 'racial' diversity as a fundamental characteristic of Canada; and 79 per cent supported a policy to ensure that organizations and institutions reflect and respect the cultural and 'racial' diversity of Canadians (Angus Reid Group 1991). It would appear that equality, respect for diversity, and multiculturalism are well engrained in the minds of Canadians. Yet at the same time, respondents had no difficulty in answering questions to indicate that they would be more comfortable with immigrants of European origin than with those of Asian, Arab, or West Indian origins (Angus Reid Group 1991). In short, in the minds of pollsters and respondents, the origin or implied 'colour' of people does become a legitimate basis upon which people can attribute a level of comfort, as though people can justifiably pass judgments on human quality and human worth based on the very features that the Canadian Charter says cannot be used as grounds for discrimination. How could the same respondents who overwhelmingly support the recognition of diversity articulate a social preference for immigrants based on origin? How could the same respondents who endorse multiculturalism artic- ulate a comfort level based on 'racial' features? How could the same respondents who accept diversity as a fundamental characteristic of Canada find it unobjectionable to respond to pollsters' questions about comfort levels towards people that are based on nothing other than ori- gin or implied 'colour'?

The same normative inconsistencies can be seen in the reports of the national public consultation on immigration in the mid-1990s. A report of Citizenship and Immigration Canada in 1994 highlighted the contra- dictory tendencies: 'Many Canadians considered diversity as a source of strength for Canada, and at the same time, there was a growing con- cern over the fragmenting impact of immigration and citizenship poli- cies on the values, traditions, and cohesion of Canada' (Citizenship and Immigration Canada 1994, 10). How could the same Canadians who consider 'racial' and cultural diversity a source of strength also con- sider it a source of fragmentation?

Many public opinion polls commissioned by the Association for Canadian Studies and conducted by Environics Research Group also reflect the normative inconsistencies of Canadians (Jedwab and Baker 2003; Jedwab 2002a). Several opinion polls gathered in 2002 and 2003 confirmed that Canadians overwhelmingly considered multicultural- ism to be important to Canadian identity. They also agreed that the pres- ervation and enhancement of Canada's multicultural heritage promotes the sharing of common values and enhances Canadian citizenship (Jedwab and Baker 2003; Jedwab 2002a). Yet in another 2002 poll, 43 per cent of respondents thought there were too many immigrants from

Arab countries; 40 per cent thought there were too many from Asian countries; and 24 per cent thought there were too many from African countries (Jedwab 2002b). Meanwhile, 39 per cent of the respondents said the number of immigrants coming each year was right, and another 14 per cent said the number was too low (Jedwab 2002b; Baxter 2002). In short, it would appear that many Canadians have little trouble accepting the democratic values of multiculturalism and diversity on the one hand while supporting policy choices premised upon colour or origin on the other. Canadians' endorsement of multiculturalism and diversity implies a rejection of superficial phenotypic features of 'race' to signify 'others' – that is, those deemed less desirable. Yet polling results persistently indicate that the Canadian public attaches significance to colour and origin as grounds for evaluating the social desirability of prospective new Canadians. How can these normative inconsistencies be reconciled?

Racial Discourse

Canada's liberal democratic system protects individual rights based on the principles of equality, justice, and non-discrimination. For example, the Charter clearly guarantees equality rights as follows: 'Every individual is equal before and under the law and has the right to the equal protection and equal benefit of the law without discrimination based on race, national or ethnic origin, colour, religion, sex, age or mental or physical disability' (Canadian Charter of Rights and Freedoms, s.15.1). In short, the principle of equality negates signification based on 'race,' origin, and colour – features that are often made significant when groups or individuals are being racialized. In contrast, racialization involves attributing significance to superficial phenotypic or genotypic features of people as though these characteristics constitute unbridgeable and therefore natural differences that are primordial in origin (Henry and Tator 2002; Li 1999; Miles 1982; Satzewich 1991). Racialization encourages signification based on 'race,' colour, origin, and other essentialized features; liberal democracy rejects such signification due to the principle of equality that recognizes congenital and primordial features as having no relevance in determining the dignity, capacity, and social worth of individuals.

It becomes clear that under liberal democracy, there is little legal space for 'racial' articulation because the principle of equality provides sufficient checks and bounds to limit the explicit use of 'race' as a feature of importance in everyday life. But the articulation of 'race' is well protected under the principle of freedom of expression if the 'racial' discourse is subtle, implicit, and rational (Li 1995).

'Racial' discourse operates within the margins of liberal democracy. In so doing, it helps to resolve what otherwise would be normative contradictions in everyday life. 'Racial' discourse may be defined as the adoption of a language form that uses encoded concepts, hidden subtexts, and a coherent syntax that, taken together, provide a logical apparatus for individuals to signify 'race' and 'racial' differences without having to abandon the democratic principles of equality and justice. 'Racial' discourse is at the heart of what Henry and Tator (2002, 23) call 'democratic racism' – an ideology that reconciles democratic principles of equality and justice with negative feelings about minorities and discrimination against them. In short, 'racial' discourse provides the means by which people can articulate 'race' comfortably in a democratic society without contravening the principle of equality and justice. In turn, 'racial' discourse becomes an integral part of the normative structure of Canada; that is, the widely shared system of prescriptive understanding that provides guidance for individual actions. This structure supplies concrete meanings for 'race' and sustains its social import, without tarnishing the image of Canada as an open and tolerant society. Thus, 'racial' discourse is contradictory in that it facilitates the articulation of 'race' and yet at the same time preserves the normative integrity of democratic society.

Even prior to the entrenchment of the Canadian Charter, political debates about immigration often resorted to the use of language techniques in order to soften policies that differentiate on the grounds of 'origin' or 'race' and to demonstrate that Canada did not engage in 'racial' discrimination. For example, Mackenzie King, the prime minister of Canada, made a widely-quoted statement on immigration in 1947 to stress the need for Canada to maintain a high level of immigration but at the same time be selective of prospective immigrants to ensure they fit Canada's social fabric:

> The government is strongly of the view that our immigration policy should be devised in a positive sense, with the definite objective, as I have already stated, of enlarging the population of the country ... With regard to the selection of immigrants, much has been said about discrimination. I wish to make it quite clear that Canada is perfectly within her rights in selecting the persons whom we regard as desirable future citizens ... There

will, I am sure, be general agreement with the view that the people of Canada do not wish, as a result of immigration, to make a fundamental alteration in the character of our population. Large-scale immigration from the orient would change the fundamental compositions of the Canadian population ... The government, therefore, has no thought of making any change in immigration regulations which would have consequences of the kind. (Canada, House of Commons, 1947, 2645–6)

This quote makes it clear that Canada wanted to enlarge its population through immigration by selecting immigrants who would not change the fundamental composition of Canada's population. Accordingly, given Canada's population of predominantly European origin, a large immigration from Asia would pose a threat to Canada's population composition. The logical policy to follow was not to make any change that would bring such an 'undesirable' consequence. Furthermore, given Canada's undeniable right to select its immigrants, it would not be 'racial' discrimination if Canada chose not to select large numbers of Asian immigrants in light of its European tradition. The above discourse represents a carefully crafted message that uses coded concepts and a developed rationale to justify why Canada should not open its door to large-scale immigration from Asia, and to further rationalize why such an origin-based policy was necessary and justifiable.

'Racial' discourse in a democratic society often resorts to discursive techniques that camouflage the offensive nature of racist ideas by using encoded concepts, a specially constructed syntax, and rationalization. The reason for using encoded concepts is to disguise the dark side of the message in order to make it appear more palatable, but it has to be done in such a way that the message being encoded can be readily decoded. Thus, encoding and decoding 'racial' messages involves a common normative structure that provides people with certain linguistic cues to represent 'race' or 'racial' differences.

At times, 'racial' discourse can be explicit and direct, providing it furnishes a convincing rationale to justify the articulation, such as dwelling on the undesirability of vulgarized cultural practices, using extenuating circumstances to show that the public good is being threatened, or appealing to nativism – the right of the resident population to protect its heritage and tradition from unwelcome intrusion by outsiders. By relying on a well-grounded rationale and using a balanced language that does not appear to be excessive, the discourse can make the articulation of 'race' reasonable and acceptable in a democratic society.

'Racial' discourse can also make it possible to trivialize and essentialize cultural differences without appearing 'racist,' provided the discourse is cast in a positive light as though it is showcasing genuine 'racial' differences in a multicultural society. In the following section, several examples are provided to demonstrate how discursive techniques work in public discourse by using encoded concepts and constructed syntax as well as by relying on a rationale that dwells on implied 'racial' differences in order to protect public interest.

Coded Concepts in Racial Discourse

The racial discourse in Canada often adopts encoded terms that appear to be neutral to signify 'racial' categories based on implied colour. These terms enable 'race' to be discussed in the political arena without signalling that 'colour' is of social significance. The use of encoded terms or codes suggests that there are hidden messages being conveyed, and that there is a common understanding of codes being shared by people encoding and decoding the messages. The following example, taken from a report entitled *Immigration to Canada: Issues for Discussion* and distributed by·the Department of Employment and Immigration in 1989, shows how an implied message about 'race' can be conveyed without resorting to the concept of 'race':

> More and more in public discussions of immigration issues people are drawing attention to the fact that Canada's immigration is coming from 'non-traditional' parts of the world. Thirty years ago, more than 80 per cent of Canada's immigrants came from Europe or countries of European heritage, whereas 70 per cent now come from Asia, Africa, and Latin America, with 43 per cent coming from Asia alone ... As a result, many Canadians are concerned that the country is in danger of losing a sense of national identity. (Employment and Immigration 1989, 8–9)

In the above text, the phrase 'non-traditional parts of the world' stands for 'non-white' countries. The term 'race' or 'colour' is not used, but the 'racial' implication is clear. The changing influx of immigrants from 'non-traditional parts of the world' or 'non-white' countries triggers the concern of many Canadians who fear their national identity will be lost as non-white immigrants transform the country. It is apparent that Canada's 'national identity,' as the term is used in the above context, refers to the European tradition of white Canada, which is seen as being undermined by 'non-traditional' immigrants from Asia, Africa, and Latin America. It should be pointed out there are striking parallels between certain terms used above, such as 'non-traditional parts of the world' and 'sense of national identity,' and those used in Mackenzie King's statement cited earlier, such as 'immigration from the orient' and 'fundamental alteration in the character of our population.' The only difference is that the more recent statement tends to be more subtle and elusive, especially regarding references to 'racial' origin.

In the mid-1990s, the Government of Canada conducted a nationwide public consultation about immigration. There were many reports that summarized the public discourse on immigration, and the use of encoded concepts to represent 'racial' problems of immigration was rampant. For example, a report entitled *Talking about Immigration*, prepared by the Democratic Education Network and distributed by the Immigration Consultations Task Force of the Department of Citizenship and Immigration in 1994, states the following: 'The Department asked Canadians what vision of Canada they wished to support. Many participants were asking another question: what vision of Canada is possible if its citizens are invisible? How can immigrants belong to a country that no longer belongs to Canadians? ... Just as participants were struggling to assert their ownership as democratic citizens, they were also wrestling with the dilemmas of diversity' (Democratic Education Network 1994, 2). The report never explains what 'the dilemmas of diversity' are, but the term *diversity* refers unmistakably to non-white immigrants and to the substantial differences they are deemed to have brought to Canada, differences that undermine a Canada that should rightfully belong to majority Canadians. The term *Canadians*, as used here, clearly means European or white Canadians, as opposed to the term *diversity*, which stands for non-white newcomers. In short, through carefully constructed syntax, apparently neutral terms like *diversity* and *Canadians* assume a clearly racial overtone without making the message seem 'race specific.'

A discussion paper distributed by the Department of Citizenship and Immigration in 1994 also resorts to many encoded terms to convey a message when it notes that 'changes in immigration source countries may make some Canadians feel uncomfortable. They may see the influx of new cultures to Canada as contributing to an erosion of our traditional values. In fact, some observers argue that social tensions are an inevitable result of immigration and diversity' (Citizenship and Immigration 1994). The phrases 'changes in immigration source countries,' 'new cultures,' and 'diversity' are used here to refer to non-white immigrants who are responsible for increasing social tensions because their influx contributes to the erosion of 'traditional values' – a surrogate term that stands for European values.

Over time, terms like *diversity* and *non-traditional source countries* become encoded concepts that signify non-white immigrants and the problems and tensions that they have brought and continue to bring to Canada. In contrast, the term *traditional values* when used in conjunction with *diversity* means 'conventional European values in Canada' that have been romanticized as enduring features of good old Canada now under siege.

Sometimes the encoded terms in 'racial' discourse can be borrowed from a benign source such that the terms in themselves are commonly used and accepted. However, in the context in which they are used, these terms become 'racially' charged, but the objectionable nature of their usage is camouflaged because the original terms are innocent or noble when first created. For example, a question that has been typically asked in opinion polls to gauge the public's view on immigration levels is framed as follows: 'Forgetting about the overall number of immigrants coming to Canada, of those who come would you say there are too many, too few, or the right amount who are members of the visible minorities?' (Li 2001, 86). What the term *visible minorities* means is unambiguous to the pollsters and the respondents of surveys as well as to anyone reading the findings of these surveys in media reports. This term has been developed in employment equity policy to refer to target populations of non-white origin for the purpose of inclusion in employment. Thus, its use in employment equity legislation designates groups historically marginalized in order to include them for remedial actions. In the context of opinion polls on immigration, the term *visible minorities* is hijacked out of context and used as a substitute for otherwise offensive terms like *non-whites* or *the coloured*, and respondents are asked to place a value on prospective immigrants based on nothing except colour. Thus, the use of the term *visible minorities* in this context obfuscates the real intention behind asking the question and camouflages the offensive nature of asking respondents to evaluate immigrants by colour. Another neutral-appearing phrase sometimes used in opinion polls is 'people who are different from most Canadians' (Li 2001, 87). The following question has also been used: 'How do you view the increase in the number of immigrants arriving in Canada from Asia, the West Indies and other, mainly Third World countries?' (Wood

1993, 4). Once again, the phrase 'immigrants arriving ... from Asia, the West Indies and other, mainly Third World countries' is an encoded way of asking respondents to evaluate the social worth of immigrants based on colour. Indeed, pollsters have little trouble drawing conclusions from answers to the above question that reflect how the public attributes the idea of a 'bad' or 'very bad' thing to the increase in the number of non-white immigrants (Wood 1993). The repeated reliance on these encoded terms popularizes their usage in otherwise offensive contexts and makes them appear increasingly justifiable. The encoded terms hide the objectionable practice of evaluating immigrants by colour in a democratic society, thus making such an activity palatable and over time, natural. The very fact that encoded concepts are needed suggests that the phenomena they represent and the messages they seek to convey are not benign or innocent. 'Racial' codes permit the underlying 'racial' messages to be encoded and decoded in the public discourse without the word 'race' ever being explicitly used.

Constructed Syntax of Racial Discourse

Encoded concepts provide the basic tools by which 'race,' 'colour,' and other 'race'-based features of people can be liberally articulated in the public arena without the ideological burden of specifying 'race.' But 'racial' discourse also relies on the use of carefully constructed syntax and rationalization to justify why the signification of 'race' is acceptable and proper in a democratic society.

Racial discourse becomes unobjectionable if it is premised upon objectionable or vulgarized behaviours believed to be 'race' based. For example, a propensity for criminal action is sometimes linked to certain 'racial' groups, and by implication, controlling the admission of these groups to Canada becomes a necessary policy to control serious crimes. In her book *Immigration: The Economic Case*, Diane Francis asks the following questions at the beginning of a chapter entitled 'The Abdication of Protection': 'What criminal or terrorist problems do immigrants and refugees visit upon Canada? How many have we let in who should have been screened out? What proportion of crimes committed in Canada are by refugees or immigrants? Are they more likely to break the law than native-born Canadians? If so, which groups are most undesirable in terms of criminality?' (2002, 125). Among the examples cited in her book is the case of what Francis calls 'Tamil terrorists.' Under this heading, she describes the growth of the Tamil community in Canada and quotes a source that refers to Tamil Tigers and their accomplices as having been 'involved in a wide range of criminal activities in this country ... [including] drug trafficking, migrant smuggling, passport forgery, and fraud' (145). There are additional descriptions, as follows: 'They have also been a major factor in the spawning of Tamil street gangs in Toronto, which have accounted for 40 shootings in the past three years and five unresolved homicides' (145).

This discourse clearly associates the Tamil community with violent and serious crimes in Canada and blames the lax immigration system for allowing criminals from other countries to terrorize Canada. The notion of 'Asian gangs' has been popularly accepted in public discourse, and the term is used liberally to refer to any violent and criminal behaviours committed by Asians in Canada to signify that such behaviours are always organized, as opposed to individually based, and that they are features of certain cultural minorities. For example, in 1991 a feature article in *Maclean's* was entitled 'Terror in the streets: Ruthless Asian gangs bring a new wave of violence to Canadian cities' (Kaihla 1991). Based on several incidents, mostly in Toronto, the article stated that the killings have established what it called a 'new threshold in a surge of Asian violence sweeping the country' (Kaihla 1991). Terms like *Asian gangs* and *Asian violence* clearly racialize criminal behaviours and criminalize 'racial' groups, but nevertheless the use of the word *Asian* is widely accepted in this context. In their analysis of racial discourse in the print media, Henry and Tator (2002, 201) point out that the media often make stereotypic assumptions about Asian immigrant communities as violent and gang-infected, thus elevating crimes committed by individuals to the level of collective features of the communities. In other words, racial discourse constructs a syntax that points to the implied conclusion that certain 'racial' groups are violent and harmful to Canada. The reference to 'race' in such a context is subtle and therefore acceptable because it is made in the context of serious crimes of a violent nature that are supposedly perpetrated by those of foreign origins. It can be seen that over time, concerns about violent crimes can be easily associated with certain 'racial' groups that are supposedly linked to a high propensity for crime. In this sense, the 'racial' discourse criminalizes 'racial' groups and makes the reference to 'race' justifiable because it is used as the pretext for crime prevention.

The syntax of 'racial' discourse is also premised upon extenuating circumstances under which the reference to 'race' becomes acceptable and, indeed, necessary. The pretext of the country or the public under siege – whether the threat is national security, public health, the environment, or a conventional way of life – constitutes an extenuating circumstance. The articulation of 'race' is then acceptable, especially when the threat to public good is deemed to have come from a 'race'-based foreign source.

In the public debate about 'monster houses' in Vancouver in the 1990s, wealthy Hong Kong immigrants were blamed for putting up large, bulky houses that overshadowed the traditional homes in WASP neighbourhoods (Li 1994). Even though officials tried to keep 'race' out of the debate, by the late 1980s and early 1990s, the term 'monster house' had assumed an unmistakable 'racial' connotation that referred to the undesirable impact on urban development, housing architecture, and graceful neighbourhoods brought about by Hong Kong immigrants. The media contributed to racializing the 'monster houses' debate by using sensational headlines and claims with 'racial' overtones. For example, a columnist wrote in the *Vancouver Sun*: 'The influx of Asian money is not only driving up the cost of housing in Vancouver but is also reshaping our neighbourhoods as small, older houses are replaced by near-mansions that often appear garish to Canadian tastes' (Rossiter 1988, 38). Another reporter wrote a front-page article in the *Vancouver Sun* entitled 'Hong Kong connection: How Asian Money Fuels Housing Market,' in which she said that 'on the streets of Kerrisdale, once a WASP bastion, bilingual English-Chinese signs are springing up' (Bramham 1989). Private letters to the city council were more blatant. One letter from a west-side resident said: 'Has anyone stopped to consider that the huge new dwellings being built to replace the older family homes are well beyond the financial reach of almost all Canadians and that we're selling out to wealthy foreigners who have little knowledge of, interest in, or concern for a Canadian way of life?' (cited in Stanbury and Todd 1990, 47). In the end, the racialization of 'monster houses' took on features of a crusade to save the environment, protect conventional neighbourhoods, and defend a romanticized Canadian way of life. In the process, foreign cultural tastes were essentialized as they were cast as opposites to the aesthetic values of Canada. The 'monster houses' controversy shows that when 'racial' differences are believed to be a threat to a Canadian way of life, racialization of the social issue is condoned, sometimes in the form of a crusading passion in defence of a noble cause.

The aftermath of September 11 provides an example of another extenuating context that makes the public more willing to condone 'racial' profiling as a measure to defend national security. An opinion poll commissioned by *Maclean's*, Global TV, and Southam News in 2002 indicates that 44 per cent of the respondents of a national sample approved 'restricting the number of immigrants that come to Canada from Muslim countries' (Strategic Counsel 2002), as compared to another similar survey a year earlier in which 49 per cent approved such a restriction. The *National Post* used the headline 'Limit Muslim Immigration, 44% Say,' and the *Times Colonist* ran the headline 'Keep Muslims Out, Poll Says – Nearly Half of Canadians Want Immigration Crackdown' (Blanchfield 2002a; 2002b). Another poll conducted in 2002 also found that 43 per cent of the respondents said Canada accepts too many immigrants from Arab countries (Baxter 2002). The terror of September 11 and the concern for national security have created the extenuating circumstance that allows pollsters to be openly 'race' specific in opinion surveys, respondents to accept 'race'-based questions as natural and proper, and the media to be 'racially' explicit in reporting the results. As Michael Sullivan, a pollster, put it, 'Has this [11 September] allowed, somehow, some of our more intolerant feelings to become more socially acceptable? Are we more comfortable voicing them?' (Blanchfield 2002a).

There are many other examples of extenuating circumstances under which direct and blatant 'racial' discourse becomes acceptable in a democratic society. For example, when 599 Chinese migrants came to the Vancouver coast in several boats in 1999, they were seen as a threat to Canada's security. A minister referred to the Chinese migrants as 'law-breakers' who abused Canada's generosity and caused an anti-immigration backlash in Canada (Rudowski 1999). As a result, respondents in Canadian opinion polls were particularly critical of immigrants and Canada took extraordinary measures to incarcerate the migrants. In their analysis of the media's reporting of the Chinese arrival, Hier and Greenberg (2002) argue that a racialized moral panic was created in Canada – one that exaggerated the actual danger to the public and played on the public fear of 'racialized' foreigners.

Sometimes racialized health panics are created, during which time linking 'racial' origin to health hazards becomes acceptable in the public discourse. For example, in a 2002 article entitled 'Immigration Fuels Soaring TB Rate,' a reporter in the *Times Colonist* wrote that 'most of the immigrants who come to B.C. arrive from countries where TB is rampant – India, China, the Philippines and Vietnam' (Fayerman 2002). The paper also reprinted the comment of Dr Kevin Elwood, director of TB control for the BC Centre for Disease Control, as follows: 'The Chinese immigrants are particularly not interested in preventable drugs' (Fayerman 2002). The discourse depicts certain 'races' as more likely to be disease infected and also disinterested in prevention, thus implying that they pose greater dangers to Canada than other groups.

The notion that extenuating circumstances justify explicit 'racial' targeting is evident in an Ontario opinion poll commissioned by CanWest News Service and Global Television in 2003. The poll shows that most Ontario residents regard 'racial' profiling as a legitimate tool to fight crime, international terrorism, and the spread of infectious diseases like SARS (Duffy 2003). In short, the use of 'race' and the attributing of undesirable connotations to 'race' become normal and natural as long as they are constructed in the context of preventing public danger and upholding public good.

Concluding Remarks

The challenge in deconstructing racism in a democratic society is to explain how people attribute social significance to 'race' in everyday life when the law disallows and norms discourage its use to differentiate and exclude people. The apparent contradiction is reconciled in everyday life through 'racial' discourse that relies on codified concepts and messages to articulate 'race,' as well as on carefully constructed syntax and rationalizations to justify the signification of 'race.' The use of encoded concepts implies that the underlying messages are 'racially' offensive, and that codes are needed to obfuscate and sanitize the 'racial' appearance. The successful use of such 'racial' codes in a democratic society like Canada implies that there are sufficient understandings in the cultural framework of people to enable them to encode and decode 'racial' messages based on cues. The development of 'racial' discourse also suggests that there are pre-existing social relations based on 'race' and on cultural representations of such relationships. In turn, 'racial' discourse furthers these relations and their representations by making them appear justifiable and natural.

'Racial' discourse does not necessarily have to be subtle all the time. It can be direct and explicit about 'race' if the syntax is properly constructed to provide a convincing rationalization. Such a rationalization may be based on the undesirability of vulgarized cultural practices or extenuating circumstances when the public good is being threatened. By relying on codified concepts, a well-constructed syntax, a well-grounded rationalization, and reasonable language that does not appear to be excessive, the discourse can make the articulation of 'race' reasonable and acceptable in a democratic society. Thus, 'racial' discourse represents a sophisticated way of articulating 'race' in democratic societies, one that gives the appearance of rejecting racism and advocating equality on the one hand while condoning 'racial' signification on the other. The successful use of 'racial' discourse also implies that there are well-developed rules and guidelines, albeit unspoken, in shaping how the discourse is to be framed and when it is to be articulated.

'Racial' discourse is contradictory because it enables the signification of 'others' based on 'colour' without undermining the principles of equality, justice, and fairness. In the long run, 'racial' discourse also naturalizes 'race' relations by providing a linguistic and cultural framework to articulate and to justify the meaning of 'race.'

Note

This paper is based on research supported by research grants from the Social Sciences and Humanities Research Council of Canada and the Prairie Centre of Excellence for Research on Immigration and Integration.

1 Terms like 'race' and 'racial' are contested concepts because there are no scientific grounds for using these concepts to refer to human types as though they are primordially constituted. Nevertheless, these terms are used in everyday life and they remain meaningful to many people. Thus, a convention in the literature is to use quotation marks around them to designate the problematic nature of these concepts and to stress the point that references to these terms in academic discussions do not represent accepting their scientific legitimacy. The choice of not using quotation marks would give an unwitting endorsement of these concepts as though they are unproblematic. Furthermore, the repeated usage of these terms without quotation marks conditions readers to accept them as conceptually valid and socially proper.

References

Angus Reid·Group. 1991. *Multiculturalism and Canadians: Attitude study 1991.* Submitted to Multiculturalism and Citizenship Canada.
Baxter, James. 2002. Asian, Arab immigrants least favoured, poll finds: Canadi-

ans more open to accepting newcomers from Europe, Latin America and Africa. *Ottawa Citizen*, 12 September.

Blanchfield, Mike. 2002a. Limit Muslim immigration, 44% say: most say refugees should be locked up pending approval. *National Post*, 21 December.

– 2002b. Keep Muslims out, poll says: Nearly half of Canadians want immigration crackdown. *Times Colonist*, 21 December.

Bramham, Daphne. 1989. Race relations deemed healthy. *Vancouver Sun*, 18 February.

Caldas-Coulthard, Carmen Rosa, and Malcolm Couthard, eds. 1996. *Texts and practices: Readings in critical discourse analysis*. London: Routledge.

Canada, House of Commons. 1947. Debates. 23 Session – 20th Parliament, Vol. 3, 14 April 1947–12 May 1947, pp. 2644–49.

Canadian Charter of Rights and Freedoms. 1982. Part I of the *Constitution Act* [En. by the *Canada Act* 1982 (U.K.), c.11].

Citizenship and Immigration Canada. 1994. *Into the 21st century: A strategy for immigration and citizenship*. Ottawa: Minister of Supply and Services.

Democratic Education Network. 1994. *Talking about immigration: The study circles of the future of immigration policy.*

Duffy, Andrew. 2003. Ontarians approve racial profiling, poll suggests. *National Post*, 24 May.

Employment and Immigration Canada. 1989. *Immigration to Canada: Issues for discussion*. IM 061/11/89. Ottawa: Employment and Immigration Canada.

Fayerman, Pamela. 2002. Immigration fuels soaring TB Rate: Disease increases 35 per cent in B.C. to nearly twice the rate across Canada. *Times Colonist*, 21 November.

Foucault, Michel. 1972. *The archaeology of knowledge and the discourse on language*. New York: Pantheon.

Francis, Diane. 2002. *Immigration: The economic case*. Toronto: Key Porter.

Goldberg, David Theo. 1992. The semantics of race. *Ethnic and racial Studies* 15 (4): 543–69.

Hall, Stuart. 1996. Cultural studies and its theoretical legacies. In *Critical dialogues in cultural studies*, ed. David Morley and Kuan-Hsing Chen, 262–75. London and New York: Routledge.

Henry, Frances, and Carol Tator. 2002. *Discourses of domination: Racial bias in the Canadian English-language press*. Toronto: University of Toronto Press.

Hier, Sean, and Joshua Greenberg. 2002. News discourse and the problematization of Chinese migration to Canada. In Henry and Tator 2002, 138–62.

Jedwab, Jack. 2002a. *Thirty years of multiculturalism in Canada, 1971–2001*. Montreal: Association for Canadian Studies.

– 2002b. *The impact of September 11th on immigration*. Montreal: Association for Canadian Studies.

Jedwab, Jack, and Chris Baker. 2003. *Canadian identity: Bilingualism, multiculturalism and the Charter of Rights*. Montreal: Association for Canadian Studies.

Kaihla, Paul. 1991. Terror in the streets: Ruthless Asian gangs bring a new wave of violence to Canadian cities. *Maclean's*, 25 March.

Li, Peter S. 1994. Unneighbourly houses or unwelcome Chinese: The social construction of race in the battle over 'monster homes' in Vancouver, Canada. *International Journal of Comparative Race and Ethnic Studies* 1 (1): 47–66.

– 1995. Racial supremacism under social democracy. *Canadian Ethnic Studies* 27 (1): 1-17.

– 1999. Race and ethnicity. In *Race and Ethnic Relations in Canada*, ed. Peter S. Li, 3–20. Toronto: Oxford University Press.

– 2001. The racial subtext in Canada's immigration discourse. *Journal of International Migration and Integration* 2 (1): 77–97.

Miles, Robert. 1982. *Racism and migrant labour*. London: Routledge and Kegan Paul.

Mills, Sara, 1997. *Discourse*. London: Routledge.

Rossiter, Sean. 1988. Big houses. *Western Living*, November, 31–41.

Rudowski, Ray. 1999. Minister condemns smuggling of humans. *National Post*, 3 September.

Satzewich, Vic. 1991. *Racism and the incorporation of foreign labour*. London: Routledge.

Stanbury, W.T., and John D. Todd. 1990. *The housing crisis: The effects of local government regulation*. Vancouver: The Laurier Institute.

Strategic Counsel. 2002. Public opinion poll conducted November 1–12 by telephone survey.

van Dijk, Teun A. 1993. *Elite discourse and racism*. Newbury Park, CA: Sage.

– 2001. Critical discourse analysis. In *The handbook of discourse analysis*, ed. Deborah Schiffrin, Deborah Tannen, and Heidi E. Hamilton, 352–71. Oxford: Blackwell.

Winant, Howard. 2000. Race and race theory. *Annual Review of Sociology* 26: 169–85.

Wood, Nancy. 1993. A reluctant welcome. *Maclean's*, 4 January.

2 From Slavery to Expulsion: Racism, Canadian Immigration Law, and the Unfulfilled Promise of Modern Constitutionalism

SHARRYN J. AIKEN

And yet we live in the era of progress, don't we? I suppose progress is like a newly discovered land; a flourishing colonial system on the coast, the interior still wilderness, steppe, prairie. The thing about progress is that it appears much greater than it actually is.

Johann Nestroy, *Der Schutzling*

For the master's tools will never dismantle the master's house. They may allow us temporarily to beat him at his own game, but they will never enable us to bring about genuine change.

Audre Lorde, *Sister Outsider*

The primary goal of pre-Confederation Canadian immigration policy was to divest the indigenous population of their sparsely populated 'wild lands' and render those lands productive as quickly as possible (Tie 1995). For this reason, the early British and French settlers permitted unrestricted admission to their North American colonies. According to various accounts, the first non-white immigrant to arrive in Canada directly from Africa was a black slave by the name of Oliver LeJeune. He was brought to New France as a six-year-old child in 1628 (Winks 1971, 1). In 1689, the French colonizers in New France received the authorization of Louis XIV to import African slaves to work in agriculture. With the conquest of New France in 1760, the British legalized slavery under the Quebec Act and it continued under British rule in Quebec, Nova Scotia, New Brunswick, and Ontario until the early nineteenth century. Although slavery as a labour system did not develop on the large scale that it did in the United States, slavery produced an inferior status for black people that had profound consequences for their place in Canada long after its abolition (Bolaria and Li 1988, 204). Indeed, numerous authors have documented how the objective of building a white Canada translated into an explicitly racist immigration policy and how immigration law and its underlying ideology continue to exclude or restrict the admission of racialized persons today (Matas 1996; Jakubowski 1997; Walker 1997; Simmons 1998; Arat-Koc 1999; Li 2003; Preston 2003; Sharma 2005). As Stasiulus and Yuval-Davis observe, immigration laws have been utilized in settler societies to encourage 'desirable' immigrants – that is, those of the hegemonic white 'race' – to settle in the country and to exclude the 'undesirable' ones (1995, 23–4).

Replicating a paradigm that was created and sustained by European imperialism, Canadian immigration law imposed admission restrictions based on 'race.' People of African, Chinese, Japanese, Indian, Jewish, and Caribbean ancestry were among the groups subjected to discriminatory treatment in post-Confederation Canada. The exclusion of black people from subsidized settlement opportunities in western Canada, the exorbitant head tax imposed on Chinese migrants from 1885–1923, the continuous-journey rule that turned away the *Komagata Maru* from Vancouver Harbour in 1914, together with 'preferred country' lists that restricted admission to all but Europeans: these are merely a few examples of the stains on Canada's historical record. Throughout this exclusionary period in Canadian history the courts largely reinforced the policies of the day (Bolaria and Li 1988; Knowles 1997; Kelley and Trebilcock 1998; Kelley 2004).

The content and objectives of Canadian immigration law and policy have been shaped by a multiplicity of factors, including economic and demographic objectives, ideological and political considerations, as well as concerns about public safety and security (Elliott and Fleras 1996, 290; Jakubowski 1999, 100). The relationship among these factors is exceedingly complex, particularly now with the ascendancy of the post–September 11 security agenda. In the contemporary context, immigration law and policy are informed by competing and often contradictory impulses (Dauvergne 2003). With the acceleration of economic globalization and transnationalism, international boundaries have declined in significance. Capital and information, together with the elites that generate them, circulate in a 'borderless world' in which economies and societies are becoming increasingly integrated and networked (Castells 1997). In opposition to this trend, however, the state continues to play the most important role in immigration policy development and implementation. Immigration law remains an important (albeit contested) site for states to exercise their sovereign power over markets and people. In a world that is characterized by growing economic cleavages, in which poor nations and their peoples have been and continue to be exploited by the rich, migration flows from the South to the North and West have intensified (Lister 1997, 42–65; IOM 2003). Canada is one of just a few countries that actively plans and promotes immigration, but managing and controlling who gets in remains central to the government's agenda. Immigration is characterized as a privilege rather than a right, and immigration regulation becomes a means of both inclusion and exclusion, of differentiating who may belong to the nation and who is 'alien.' Subject to some limited exceptions for refugees, the basic supposition that continues to underpin Canadian law and policy is that states have an absolute right of control over their borders and territories and a corresponding prerogative to adopt discriminatory admissions policies. In this regard, immigration law is consistent with both liberal and communitarian views of the world that defend the legitimacy of the state's gatekeeping function as critical for the preservation of the rights and interests of its members (Rawls 1993; Walzer 1983). As articulated by Justice John Sopinka of the Supreme Court, 'the most fundamental principle of immigration law is that non-citizens do not have an unqualified right to enter or remain in the country ...' (*Chiarelli* 1992). Immigration law in Canada – with the endorsement of the courts – continues to expressly exclude immigrants on the basis of poor health or disability as well as income. Criminality and security measures operate as further technologies of control.[1] Once admitted, the status of immigrants as non-citizens is also seen as a legitimate basis for restricting the scope of human rights protections afforded by the law. Canadian citizenship and immigration laws foster a hierarchical ordering of 'insiders' and 'outsiders' living and working *within* Canadian society (Sharma 2005, 13). As the text of the law and legal discourse in the area of immigration has evolved from its explicitly racist orientation to one of 'objective' discrimination, racism in its less obvious, systemic forms has persisted. From slavery to expulsion, racialized people have been the victims of a legal system that has worked to disadvantage and oppress.

One of the central myths of our national identity is that Canada is an egalitarian, pluralist society free from the scourge of racism that exists in the United States and throughout most Western societies. The Commission on Systemic Racism in the Ontario Criminal Justice System noted that racism has 'a long history in Canada' and remains a defining feature of Canadian society. While the primary focus of the provincial study was the criminal justice system, the commissioners emphasized that 'racism has shaped immigration to this country and settlement within it' (Commission 1995, ii). Notwithstanding the scholarship and even the judicial notice of the problem of racism in Canada, there has been relatively little focus on racism and immigration law by constitutional theorists.[2]

The purpose of my chapter is to address this important lacuna with a view to deconstructing our collective mythology concerning 'race,' immigration law, and the role of modern constitutionalism. Harris (1982) and Hartog (1987) define constitutionalism in terms of the reliance on words as a touchstone for shaping governing practices. I am using the concept in a somewhat broader sense to connote the supremacy of a legal rights discourse as the basis for practising democratic politics. I will attempt to demonstrate that use of this discourse has failed to deliver the systemic changes required for a truly antiracist immigration program. Evaluating the success of legal mobilization strategies can be difficult. Even unfavourable decisions can exert a positive influence on the policy climate or may serve to strengthen the social movements that organized around the litigation (Manfredi 2004, 12, 150). The important, if limited, contributions of constitutionalism to the development of progressive legal doctrine as well as policy reform in certain areas has been charted by others (Schneiderman and Sutherland 1997; Manfredi 2001; Jhappan 2002). I contend, however, that for immigrants and refugees the promise of transformative litigation remains wholly unfulfilled.

The chapter begins with an analysis of the meaning of 'race' and racism and a brief introduction to critical race theory as a lens through which my central thesis concerning constitutionalism and immigration can be explored. At the outset, a note on the terms race and racialized: the word race has been placed in quotation marks throughout this paper in acknowledgment of its meaninglessness as a biological category. I am using the term racialized to emphasize that irrespective of the racial identities that may be affirmatively embraced by individuals and groups, 'race' does not exist in the absence of its social construction (Appiah and Gutmann 1996, 71–4; Walker 1997, 303–5). The balance of the chapter examines key elements of contemporary immigration law and policy. A number of recent judgments will be analysed to illuminate the extent to which the norms embedded in immigration law are so predominant that the basic concepts of constitutionalism are interpreted in agreement with them (Tully 1995, 9). Indeed, the appearance of change – the language of equity and fairness in the text of the law and in law talk – has served as a cover for preserving the status quo and sustaining systemic racism in the contemporary immigration program.

'Race' and Racism: Constructing the Other

In 'Equality: Beyond Dualism and Oppression,' Hodge suggests that the many forms of oppression, including racism and sexism, are sustained by a framework that codifies the world in terms of the struggle between the forces of good and evil. As Hodge states, 'The dualism of good and evil contains assumptions that enable those accepting it to believe that they have greater moral worth than those they oppress. Their victims, on the other hand, are seen as bad or as motivated by evil. The treatment of their victims is not viewed as oppression at all, but instead is believed to be justified as the victory of good over evil. Dualism helps create and sustain oppression by appearing to be rational' (Hodge 1990, 89). Derrida emphasizes that since the Enlightenment, the use of binary oppositions has formed the basis of Western thinking and language. Inherent in the idea of binary opposition is the notion of hierarchy or privilege of one over the other. Derrida maintains that this domination produces fear of the other: 'Absolute fear would then be the first encounter of the other as other: as other than I and other than itself. I can answer the threat of the other as other (than I) by transforming it into another (than itself), through altering it in my imagination, my fear, or my desire' (Derrida 1976, 277). In most societies, dualism has been the organizing principle and key justification for the creation and maintenance of all forms of violence and oppression. It is the basis for organizing our social experience in terms of 'us' and 'them' and for the view that one's own group (family, generation, gender, class, etc.) is better than 'them' or the other (Essed 1990). Similarly, the notion of 'race' as a device for conceptualizing differences between persons and groups is a clear manifestation of dualistic thinking. It was not until the eighteenth century, however, that the concept of 'race' was used to signify certain physical or biological features that were believed to distinguish between various categories of human beings through the logic of a *natural* hierarchy (Outlaw 1990, 62). 'Blackness' became associated with whatever was evil, ugly, filthy, and depraved while 'whiteness' became associated with whatever was pure, clean, virtuous, and beautiful (Vizkelety 1987, 67). With the aid of science, skin colour became a potent rationale for slavery, a practice that emerged from the material quest of the European colonizers for a cheap source of labour to clear the lands and work the fields in the colonies. The colonizers initially perceived the Africans as other or unlike themselves, primarily because they were 'heathen' – that is, not Christian. As the practice of slavery became institutionalized through the market forces of capitalist production, however, racism was the result. The colonizers came to essentialize and dehumanize the Africans whom they enslaved on the basis of their blackness. At the beginning of this century, a prominent English scholar, Gilbert Murray, encapsulated the prevailing imperialist view about 'race': 'There is in the world a hierarchy of races ... [Some] will direct and rule the others, and the lower work of the world will tend in the long run to be done by the lower breeds of men. This much we of the ruling colour will no doubt accept as obvious' (qtd in Walker 1997, 12). The view that the population of the world was divided into different 'races' and that these 'races' could be ranked in a hierarchy of biological superiority and inferiority has been wholly discredited (Anthias and Yuval-Davis 1993, 1). It is generally understood that there are no scientific grounds to use phenotype or biological heredity as an explanation of social inequality (Bolaria and Li 1988, 17). In the mid-nineteenth century, Marx commented on the role that capital assumed in defining the social relations between persons: 'A negro is a negro. In certain circumstances he becomes a slave. A cotton-spinning jenny is a machine for spinning cotton. It becomes *capital* only in certain relations. Torn from these relationships it is no more capital than gold in itself is *money* or sugar is the price of sugar' (Marx 1847, 207). The essential meaning conveyed by Marx was prescient. Sociologists today speak of 'race' as relational and historically specific. As both Li and Satzewitch explain, 'race' is a socially constructed concept used to describe certain patterns of physical and other superficial difference (Li 2006, 1; Satzewitch 1998, 27). To the extent that 'race' is a meaningful category in the law, it is the concrete expression of social discourse. Racism is both the symptom and the result of a social process in which unequal relationships between dominant and subordinate groups are defined, socially organized, and maintained on racial grounds. There are different types of racisms, and they may be understood as 'modes of exclusion, inferiorization, subordination and exploitation that present specific and different characters in different social and historical contexts ... There is not a unitary system of signification that can be labelled racist nor is there a unitary perpetrator or victim' (Anthias and Yuval-Davis 1993, 2).

Researchers from a variety of theoretical traditions emphasize the importance of addressing the ways in which categories of racialized difference and exclusion intersect (or 'interlock') with class, gender, and other variables, thereby particularizing the experience and outcomes of racism (Ng 1993; Crenshaw 1993; Anthias and Yuval-Davis 1993; Agnew 1996; Brewer 1997; Razack 1998). There are divergent views in the academic literature with regard to how to conceptualize the interrelationship and significance of these categories. Informed by a political economy perspective, some scholars have suggested that racial injustice is derivative of economic exploitation. For example, Miles has argued that 'race' should be considered in the context of class relations under capitalism. Miles identifies coloured labour as the racialized fraction of the working class and suggests that the process of racial categorization 'can then be viewed as affecting the allocation of persons to different positions in the production process and the allocation of material and other rewards and disadvantages to groups so categorized within the class boundaries established by the dominant mode of production' (Miles 1982, 159). For Miles, the goal would be to dismantle the national and transnational structures of capital accumulation and distribution, thereby ameliorating the disparities between the rich and the poor and eradicating racism from its roots. History certainly confirms that racism originated with the drive – in both colonial societies and capitalist states – to reproduce cheap sources of labour (Bolaria and Li 1988, 19). Yet this analysis fails to account for the fact that injustice continues to afflict individuals because of their skin colour, assumed ancestry, and the corresponding racial identity that is imputed to these characteristics, regardless of their material conditions or class (Appiah and Gutmann 1996, 110). The early work of Stuart Hall also emphasizes the importance of class but acknowledges that socially constructed definitions of 'race' are the 'modalities' and the 'medium' through which social and economic class relations are lived and experienced (Hall et al. 1978).[3] Étienne Balibar considers the articulation between racism and nationalism and emphasizes the role of state institutions in mediating and sustaining racism (Balibar 1991).

In the Canadian context, it is clear that racism is not the only cause of inequality and injustice in society and, more specifically, in the immigration program. Indeed, racism may be more accurately understood as a manifestation of unequal relationships in a society in which salient sources of discrimination include 'race,' income, and class, as well as gender, sexual orientation, and age. Nevertheless, 'race' continues to influence the opportunities and experience of racialized groups in North America, even after controlling for other factors.[4] Despite the divergence of theories with regard to the causes of racism, there is consistent support for the view that racism is a significant factor in informing public discourse and, in turn, the behaviour of individuals and social institutions in settler societies. Depending on the context, institutional racism can be manifested in the form of explicitly racist policies in which the state directly reinforces existing racist biases in society, or it can be found in a systemic form ('systemic racism') and concealed in systems, practices, policies, and laws that appear neutral and universal on their face but disadvantage racialized persons.

Critical race theory examines the meaning of 'race' and racism in the specific context of legal theory and practice. Informed by critical sociology, neo-Marxism, and postmodern philosophy, the critical race theory movement emerged in the late 1970s with the work of Derrick Bell, Alan Freeman, and other American scholars (Bell 2004; Delgado and Stefancic 2000). The movement was a reaction to the failure of Marxism and liberal pluralism to account for the social reality of racism and the role that the law plays as both product and promoter of racism. In conceptual terms, the focus of inquiry for critical race theorists is the privileging of whiteness as an invisible norm and societal organizing tool. On the one hand, the movement has stressed the importance of contextual analysis, examining racism from the perspective of those who experience it (Yamamoto 1997). It has also insisted on critical race praxis – the need for theory to incorporate pragmatic solutions to the problems identified. In this regard, some critical race theorists have sought to reconstruct rights discourse and litigation strategies premised on this discourse to shift the way in which 'race' is articulated in the law and before the courts (Matsuda 1996, 22). On the other hand, these theorists, along with many other American legal scholars, have been less sanguine about the actual effectiveness of recourse to the courts as a means of achieving social justice. In the face of the widely acknowledged failures of the American civil rights movement and growing empirical evidence that decades of rights-based litigation in the United States have not generated appreciable improvements in social conditions or life opportunities for racialized people, many scholars are bringing rights down from their pedestal and assessing their impact in the context of everyday social and political experiences (Goldberg-Hiller 2002, 339). In the Canadian context, critical race theorists and other scholars remain divided about the transformative potential of legal mobilization and constitutionalism in particular. The dearth of judgments that have incorporated a 'race-sensitive' lens is seen by some as evidence of the need for more effective and coordinated legal strategies, rather than a retreat (Aylward 1999; St Lewis 2001).

In contrast, socialist, postmodernist, and certain feminist scholars have emphasized the limitations of constitutional judicial review as an agent of progressive social and economic change (Mandel 1994; Glasbeek 1990; Turpel 1989–90; Smart 1989; Fitzpatrick 1990). More recently and with specific reference to Canada, a rare empirical study of the concrete, real-life effects of the Canadian Charter of Rights and Freedoms (the 'Charter') as experienced by its intended beneficiaries concludes that contemporary constitutionalism has not changed Canada much, if at all (Arthurs and Arnold, forthcoming, 2).

It is not my intent to trivialize or underestimate the significance of a positive court decision in the lives of successful litigants. I support the drive for judicial appointments that better reflect the diversity of Canadian society and for more focused judicial and legal education on 'race' and racism. Nevertheless, this chapter seeks to demonstrate that over twenty years of Charter litigation have failed to diminish systemic racism in immigration law and policy. Carol Smart's admonition concerning the paradoxical effect of legal intervention – that in 'exercising law, we may produce effects that make conditions worse' – offers an important analytic lens for my inquiry (Smart 1989, 16).

Questions of democratic legitimacy and the appropriate relationship between Parliament and the courts have been the subject of much debate since the Charter's inception.[5] I agree with Mandel's thesis concerning the dangers of over-reliance on the courts as a means of disrupting existing structures of oppression. At the same time, I do not share the view, most commonly espoused by both leftists and social conservatives, that Parliament is an inherently more democratic or even trustworthy site for advocacy. Rather, I argue that neo-liberal resistance to progressive reform ensures that individual legal victories seldom translate into substantive gains in equality and justice for non-citizens. Litigation strategies predicated on rights claims may serve an important role in the redress of discrete cases of unfairness and prejudice. Nevertheless, they have been ineffective in attacking the embedded discriminatory premises of immigration law and utterly impotent in addressing the deeper root causes of inequality in society (Bakan 1997, 62). To paraphrase Marx, the political instrument of enslavement cannot serve as the political instrument of emancipation (Marx 1871, 147). Audre Lorde's more contemporary caution about the perils of attempting to dismantle the master's house with the master's tools is my starting point (Lorde 1984).

Before proceeding further I believe it is important to address the question of my subject position. The project of critical scholarship requires the writer to identify her conceptual vantage point – the voice in which the story is being told (Brodkey 1987). I am clearly outside the 'epistemic privilege' acquired by the experience of everyday racism.[6] At the same time, my understanding of what it means to live in this country as a racialized person is shaped by the interconnected personal and social spaces of my life. I have been involved as counsel or advisor in a number of the more recent cases that serve as the basis of my study. In *Looking White People in the Eye*, Razack underscores the importance of exposing how we are implicated in the systems and processes of oppression that we aim to critically evaluate. Razack states that 'we need to examine how we explain to ourselves the social hierarchies that surround us. We need to ask: Where am I in this picture? Am I positioning myself as the saviour of less fortunate peoples? as the progressive one? as more subordinated? as innocent? These are the moves of superiority and we need to reach beyond them ... Accountability begins with tracing relations of privilege and penalty' (Razack 1998, 170). Razack expresses concern that the white female gaze often sustains rather than disrupts white supremacy. Critical race theory asks us to look at the law from the perspective of people adversely affected by racism and allow our analysis to be informed by this perspective (Aylward 1999, 173). I am a white, Jewish academic and immigration lawyer. In this regard, the fact of my whiteness demands the exercise of methodological humility in approaching a study of immigration law and policy as a product and promoter of racism. From the position of ally, both insider and outsider, my primary objective is to contribute to the transformation of the structures of disadvantage that perpetuate the injustice of racialized borders.

Racism in Contemporary Immigration: Law, Policy, and Constitutional Adjudication

The Charter of Rights and Freedoms was formally entrenched in the Canadian Constitution in 1982 with a signing ceremony on Parliament

Hill. In a celebratory statement launching the Charter, Justice Minister Jean Chrétien expressed a popular expectation when he said, 'Now it is not just the politicians who will defend our rights, it will also be the courts. That is better because politicians tend to just go with the wind. Now, due to the Charter, it is possible to think about those issues in the courts away from the arena of political debate and where emotions and votes cannot influence you' (Chrétien 1986, 10). Optimistic predictions suggested that the Charter would fundamentally alter the Canadian legal and political landscape and that its guarantees would 'offer minorities a place to stand, a ground to defend, and the means for others to come to their aid' (Berger 1984, 83).[7] With the implementation of the Charter, Canada became a constitutional democracy. Section 52 of the Charter explicitly established the supremacy of the Constitution, thereby imposing a new constraint on the powers of government and cementing the judicial review role of the courts. When legislation or regulations violated constitutional rights and the government could not defend the violation as a 'reasonable limit that is demonstrably justified in a free and democratic society,' the law could be declared invalid – 'read down' to narrow its scope – or the offending portion of the legislation could be severed. In cases where the law itself raised no constitutional objections but protected rights were violated through the exercise of law enforcement discretion, section 24 of the Charter offered a broad range of remedies, including stays of proceedings, damages, declarations, and even injunctions in exceptional circumstances. The Charter sought to protect a broad catalogue of civil and political rights. Most pertinent to immigration matters are the rights to life, liberty, and security of the person and the right not to be deprived thereof except in accordance with the principles of fundamental justice (section 7), the right not to be subjected to cruel and unusual treatment or punishment (section 12), the right to equality before and under the law, and the right to equal protection and benefit of the law without discrimination (section 15). The Charter makes an explicit distinction between citizens and non-citizens, according mobility rights to permanent residents and citizens exclusively and affirming that only citizens have the right to enter, remain in, and leave Canada (section 6).

The adoption of the Charter was preceded by positive changes to immigration law. As early as 1962, nondiscriminatory immigration regulations were implemented, marking a significant shift from the 'white Canada' policy in which immigrant selection was explicitly predicated on 'race,' ethnicity, and nationality to a more 'objective' assessment system that was formally colour blind. In 1976, a new Immigration Act was introduced, offering an express commitment to values of universalism and equality. This Act, together with the possibility of a constitutional judicial review based on an entrenched catalogue of rights, appeared to introduce a 'new paradigm into the interpretation of rights and the judicial function' (Walker 1997, 324–5). Canadian immigration law and practice would be informed by principles of fairness and respect for the equality rights of the immigrants and refugees to whom the reach of the law and its administration extended. The prospect of Charter challenges would offer an important mechanism of accountability, with the courts providing aggrieved individuals direct access to public decisions affecting their lives and an opportunity to challenge laws, independent of government law reform agendas (Russell 1983, 49).

Since the early 1980s, thousands of racialized immigrants and refugees from 'nontraditional source countries' in Africa, Asia, and the Americas have been admitted to Canada. By 1992, the shift in immigration source countries was clearly reflected in the fact that approximately 81 per cent of new immigrants were persons of colour (CIC 1994a, 22). These immigrants were from precisely those groups that the government had historically discriminated against on the basis of their 'race,' national or ethnic origin, and colour (Tie 1995, 71). It would be misleading, however, to attribute the shift in immigration demographics to the influence of the Charter or even the legislative changes of 1978. In this regard, the dynamics of global capitalism have played a significant role in the changing face of Canadian immigration. For at least the past two decades, prospective immigrants from Europe have been less inclined to view Canada as a desirable destination. Relatively high levels of taxation combined with significant barriers in terms of access to trades and professions have fuelled the transformation of Canada's immigration and refugee programs. As economic factors have compelled a radical reorientation in the demographics of immigrant selection, the government has sought to maintain its grip on the program by retaining control of who gets in. As suggested by Simmons, the government shifted from a neo-colonial, racist immigration strategy to one that could be described as 'neo-racist'; that is, one that 'reveals significant racist influences and outcomes within a framework that claims to be entirely nonracist' (Simmons 1998, 91). High-income earners with the skills to contribute to Canada's knowledge economy have been effectively 'deracialized,' while neo-racism remains embedded in core elements of immigration law and practice. Affluent business immigrants can pur-

Figure 2.1. Foreign-born population in Canada 1901–2001

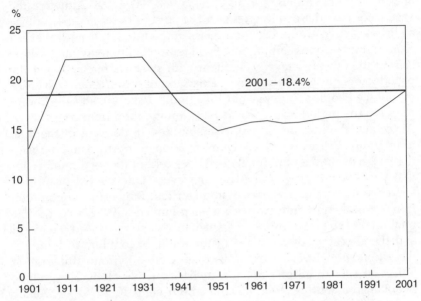

Source: Statistics Canada, *2001 Census*

chase a visa, while immigration policies reinforce inequalities based in gender and race that intersect with and constitute class (Preston 2003). The courts and the Charter in particular have not shifted the balance of power in favour of racialized immigrants and refugees nor, as Mandel has observed, have they posed any serious obstacle to Canada's repressive immigration policies (Mandel 1994, 257). The following sections will examine some of the salient indicators of racism in the contemporary immigration program and take a closer look at the role of constitutionalism in sustaining that which it claims to counteract.

The Demographics of Immigration and Immigrant Admissions

Foreign-born persons constitute a growing proportion of Canada's population. According to the 2001 Census, they reached 5.1 million or about 18.4 per cent of the country's total population. The graph in figure 2.1 represents the changing percentage of foreign-born individuals in Canada over the course of the twentieth century.

For 2005, the federal government planned to bring between 220,000 and 245,000 new immigrants to Canada (CIC 2004, 19). Although the vast majority of these immigrants will be persons of colour, they will be a fairly selective group. Economic class immigration (primarily skilled workers and business immigrants) will represent approximately 60 per cent of the overall intake. Consistent with statistics for well over the past decade, most will come from a handful of countries in Asia – primarily the People's Republic of China, India, Pakistan, and the Philippines. In the period from 1991 to 1996, immigration from countries in Africa and the Middle East represented only 16 per cent of the total immigration to Canada. By 2004, immigration from Africa and the Middle East had climbed minimally to 21 per cent of the total number for that year. No country from Africa has ever made the list of top ten source countries for all classes of immigration. Targets for immigration from Central and South America remain limited at 9.2 per cent of the total intake. The distribution of Canadian visa posts around the world and the allocation of resources to these offices continue to reinforce these trends. In 1998, for example, there were only four immigration offices to service all of sub-Saharan Africa while Hong Kong alone maintained a staffing level of eighteen officers (CIC 1998, 6–8; Kelley and Treblicock 1998, 411). The chart in table 2.1 identifies the distribution of permanent residents according to immigration category and source region for the years 1995–2004.

In addition to the distribution of visa posts, other factors that contribute to the under-representation of certain racialized groups in current immigration demographics include the continuing role of discretion under the *Immigration and Refugee Protection Act* (IRPA) and Regulations implemented in 2002, the selection criteria and associated income requirements, and processing fees. An immigrant's admission to Canada as a 'skilled worker' depends on how many points she or he receives on a scale that attempts to gauge her or his economic potential in terms of six selection factors: education, language ability (English or French), skills, work experience, age, and adaptability. Additional points are allocated for prospective immigrants with arranged employment. Although the discretionary category of 'personal suitability' was eliminated with recent reforms, immigration officers are still permitted to override the points system altogether to either accept or refuse an applicant on the basis that the rating does not reflect the 'immigrant's chances of becoming successfully established.' The continued role of discretion in overseas immigration decision-making permits individual, biased immigration officers to make discriminatory decisions, and it allows the law, more broadly, to act as a tool for perpetuating racism (Jakubowski 1999, 111).

Revamped in 2002, the methodology embedded in the points system favours immigrants with flexible skills that offer a significant economic benefit to Canada's knowledge economy (RIAS 2001). It admits only those tradespersons with significant certification and bars most service personnel below the managerial level. The selection grid effectively precludes both domestic and agricultural workers from successful consideration as skilled workers, since childcare and farm labour are simply not included in the list of eligible occupations.[8] In the face of chronic labour shortages in these sectors, the federal government continues to rely on temporary worker programs.[9] Numerous scholars and advocacy organizations have documented how the precarious status of these workers, the requirement that caregivers and agricultural workers live in the homes or on the farms of their employers, and the ever-present threat of deportation reinforces their subordination and vulnerability to all forms of abuse (Macklin 1992; Arat-Koc 1999; Li Wai Suen 2000; Sharma and Baines 2002; Basok 2002; Cook 2004). In the words of Noreen, a domestic worker from the island of St Vincent: 'It's just the treatment that people dish out to you, you know they treat you worse than how they treat their dog or cat ... You know sometimes I feel like a slave, sometimes I dream about freedom' ('Noreen' in Silvera 1983, 20). In a similar vein, a farm worker from central Mexico explains, 'They treat us worse than animals ... in my mind slavery has not yet disappeared' (farm worker in Lee 2003).

As Sharma and others have suggested, the use of temporary work visas has facilitated significant growth in the temporary, low-wage labour sector while inhibiting the permanency of a resident non-white working class (Sharma 2005, 12; Simmons 1998, 106). In correlation with the barriers many workers face in qualifying under the selection criteria, a significant number of workers – particularly women who have less access to education, money, and information than men – are electing to migrate illegally (Langevin and Belleau 2000). Estimates of the actual numbers of undocumented workers living in the country vary widely, but it is clear that many sectors of the Canadian economy, including food and services, manufacturing, construction, garment making, childcare, and cleaning, rely heavily on non-status labour. The health and social services available to these workers are limited. In general, people without status are not entitled to access hospital treatment

Table 2.1. Canada – Permanent residents by category and source area

Source area	1995	1996	1997	1998	1999	2000	2001	2002	2003	2004
					Number					
African and the Middle East	7,499	7,174	6,061	5,163	5,831	7,055	7,805	6,384	7,461	7,892
Asia and Pacific	44,151	37,292	32,423	27,377	29,601	32,532	35,263	36,630	38,649	34,038
South and Central America	13,951	11,743	10,356	8,025	8,753	8,742	10,038	7,831	7,381	7,437
United States	2,780	3,158	2,495	2,603	2,953	3,179	3,614	2,786	2,966	3,690
Europe and the United Kingdom	8,996	8,990	8,641	7,725	8,124	9,095	10,046	8,638	8,583	9,069
Source area not stated	9	2	3	5	15	11	28	30	84	120
Family class	77,386	68,359	59,979	50,898	55,277	60,614	66,794	62,299	65,124	62,246
African and the Middle East	18,249	20,234	23,121	19,284	18,996	23,411	30,705	30,604	25,386	27,590
Asia and Pacific	58,446	75,477	75,317	49,008	59,061	78,658	87,726	71,209	62,244	66,480
South and Central America	4,406	4,456	4,932	4,425	4,993	5,959	7,473	8,041	7,313	8,454
United States	2,361	2,591	2,470	2,103	2,544	2,575	2,242	1,938	1,703	2,977
Europe and the United Kingdom	23,148	22,606	22,511	23,077	23,629	25,683	27,551	26,058	24,403	28,240
Source area not stated	25	6	0	16	38	13	22	10	1	5
Economic immigrants	106,635	125,370	128,351	97,913	109,261	136,299	155,719	137,860	121,050	133,746
African and the Middle East	7,143	8,665	7,975	7,661	8,499	10,338	9,662	8,823	9,536	12,593
Asia and Pacific	9,608	8,977	7,201	6,218	7,260	9,323	9,858	10,197	10,166	12,158
South and Central America	2,087	2,450	1,752	1,329	1,417	2,220	2,657	2,842	3,712	4,597
United States	53	90	54	57	30	69	55	33	45	132
Europe and the United Kingdom	9,195	8,295	7,321	7,576	7,182	8,138	5,684	3,219	2,523	3,172
Source area not stated	1	1	5	1	9	4	3	6	2	34
Refugees	28,087	28,478	24,308	22,842	24,397	30,092	27,919	25,120	25,984	32,686

Table 2.1. (concluded)

Source area	1995	1996	1997	1998	1999	2000	2001	2002	2003	2004
					Number					
African and the Middle East	38	422	642	488	222	101	61	526	1,294	1,445
Asia and Pacific	689	3,071	2,159	1,616	643	224	99	998	2,639	1,869
South and Central America	21	228	386	267	113	85	40	752	1,935	1,760
United States	1	11	11	13	5	4	0	536	1,278	695
Europe and the United Kingdom	12	133	202	163	48	46	5	949	2,050	1,367
Source area not stated	0	0	0	0	0	0	0	0	0	10
Other immigrants	761	3,865	3,400	2,547	1,031	460	205	3,761	9,196	7,146
African and the Middle East	32,929	36,495	37,799	32,596	33,548	40,905	48,233	46,337	43,677	49,520
Asia and Pacific	112,894	124,817	117,100	84,219	96,565	120,737	132,946	119,034	113,698	114,545
South and Central America	20,465	18,877	17,426	14,046	15,276	17,006	20,208	19,466	20,341	22,248
United States	5,195	5,850	5,030	4,776	5,532	5,827	5,911	5,293	5,992	7,494
Europe and the United Kingdom	41,351	40,024	38,675	38,541	38,983	42,962	43,286	38,864	37,559	41,848
Source area not stated	35	9	8	22	62	28	53	46	87	169
Category not stated	0	1	0	0	0	0	1	0	1	0
Total	212,869	226,073	216,038	174,200	189,966	227,465	250,638	229,040	221,355	235,824

Source: CIC, *Facts and Figures 2004: Immigration Overview – Permanent and Temporary Residents.*

and the children of non-status parents are often denied the right to an education. Fearing that any contact with authorities might lead to deportation, undocumented workers are particularly vulnerable to exploitation in the workplace and at home (Khandor et al. 2004, 6).

For immigrants who qualify as skilled workers under the points system, a further hurdle of providing evidence of adequate 'settlement funds' must be met. Current guidelines require approximately $10,000 per adult. Highly skilled individuals with strong employment prospects can be turned down on the basis that they have insufficient settlement funds. Even in cases where discretion may be exercised positively to waive or at least adjust the requirement for 'settlement funds,' all immigrants must pay a $975 Right of Landing Fee together with a nonrefundable $550 processing fee. These fees, resonant of the head tax imposed on Chinese migrants in the earlier part of the last century, have been defended by the government as 'a small price to pay to come to the best country in the world' and necessary to offset at least some of the costs of settlement programs (the success of the government's deficit-reduction strategy over the past several years makes this argument less persuasive). The government claims that the fees are not discriminatory because they apply to everyone. Yet given the disparities between Canadian currency and currencies in the South as well as between the rich and the poor in most countries of the world, the fees amount to a regressive flat tax that violates fiscal fairness. Among those disproportionately affected by this modern-day head tax are racialized immigrants from the South, where the fees very often represent up to three years of salary (CCR 1997).

Income restrictions have been an increasing feature of family sponsorship rules as well. Regulations require family members to meet minimum income levels when applying to sponsor relatives other than their spouse and dependent children. New rules impose an absolute bar on family reunification for sponsors in receipt of social assistance for reasons other than disability. Although family unity is recognized as a fundamental right in a range of international and regional human rights treaties to which Canada is signatory, the notion that family reunification is a privilege one has to pay for has been incorporated in Canadian immigration law since the 1950s. Over the past decade, just as studies were confirming that racialized persons are over- represented among those who live in poverty and that the marginalization of immigrants has worsened across Canada, immigration policy has been imposing more rigid income requirements for family sponsorship.

Although today's immigrants arrive with more education and skills than their predecessors, persistent barriers to accessing the trades and professions for which they have been chosen have resulted in increasing unemployment and underemployment for newcomers (Ornstein 2000; Worswick 2004). Clustered in low-wage work, today's immigrants suffer greater economic disadvantage relative to other Canadians than they did in the decades prior to the introduction of the Charter (Campaign 2000, 2005; Galabuzi 2001; Arthurs and Arnold, forthcoming). It is now taking university-educated immigrants at least ten years to achieve the employment earnings of comparably educated Canadians (RIAS 2001). During this difficult transition, immigrants find themselves increasingly isolated and alone, without the support and assistance of their families. For sponsors who are single parents unable to afford accessible childcare while working, the arrival of a spouse or other relative enables one or both parents to work outside the home, generate income, and either terminate welfare payments or increase family income beyond the minimum cut-offs. Immigration law's one-dimensional construction of family in terms of economic dependency reinforces exclusionary policies that have a disproportionate impact on racialized single parents – primarily women (Macklin 2002). Indeed, family-class immigration has declined dramatically from the largest component of the overall annual immigration intake to approximately 24 per cent for 2004–05 (CIC 2004, 19). Reducing the number and proportion of family class immigrants in favour of preferred economic migrants has been an explicit policy goal of the federal government since 1994 (CIC 1994b, 21). Financial eligibility requirements, along with a range of bureaucratic obstacles, have been intentionally structured to stall family reunification for months or years, if not indefinitely (Macklin 2002).

Relatively few cases have reached the Supreme Court that have directly challenged the intersecting forms of discrimination inherent in current immigration laws and policies. In an early Charter case, *Andrews v. Law Society of British Columbia*, the Supreme Court observed that 'non-citizens are an example without parallel of a group of persons who are relatively powerless politically, and whose interests are likely to be compromised by legislative decisions.' Justice Gérard La Forest went on to note that 'discrimination on the basis of nationality has from early times been an inseparable companion of discrimination on the basis of race and national or ethnic origin' (*Andrews* 1989, 195). It deserves mention that Mark David Andrews was a permanent resident who enjoyed a relatively privileged position in society as a white male lawyer. Three years after the decision in *Andrews*, the Supreme Court issued its ruling in *Chiarelli* (which stated that non-citizens do not have an inherent right to enter or remain in Canada). The ideological contradiction between these two decisions is a good indication of the tensions that characterize current thinking in the area of immigration. Quite apart from the question of the right to enter or the right to remain in a country – principles which international law actually supports in varying degrees – all persons, regardless of their citizenship status, 'race,' or national origin have a fundamental claim to be treated with dignity and accorded full equality as human beings. Yet until 2002, in decisions taken pursuant to the former immigration act, the Charter was held not to apply to the actions of visa officers outside of Canada (*Deol* 2003; *Lee* 1997; *Ruparel* 1990; see also Tie 1998). This reading of the Charter was upheld by the Federal Court, even in the face of a contradictory ruling by the Supreme Court that the Charter had extraterritorial application in the context of the criminal law, extending to Canadian police investigations undertaken in the United States (*Cook* 1998). Thus, the Department of Citizenship and Immigration's most significant sphere of activity was immune from Charter review. Section 3(3)(d) of the *Immigration and Refugee Protection Act* (IRPA) provides that the new law is to be construed in a manner that 'ensures that decisions under this act are consistent with the Canadian Charter of Rights and Freedoms, including its principles of equality and freedom from discrimination.' Prospects for successful equality challenges do not appear promising. Jurisprudence confirms that admissions criteria that draw distinctions on the basis of the *actual* circumstances of each visa applicant rather than ascribed, stereotypical characteristics do not constitute unconstitutional discrimination (*Deol* 2003, 327).

In addition, practical deterrents remain to using the courts to challenge the basic underpinnings of the admissions scheme. These include the difficulty of finding plaintiffs outside Canada and sustaining their commitment to lengthy litigation with an uncertain outcome, the residual uncertainty regarding their status vis-à-vis the Charter, and the fact that once inside Canada, they may fear the risk that litigation could pose to their already vulnerable status as well as to their future in the country. The prospect of serious delays in resolving their cases, together with the exorbitant costs associated with litigation and the limited availability of legal aid in most provinces, serve as further deterrents. After the federal government adopted the Right of Landing

Fee in 1995, a Toronto-based coalition attempted to launch a Charter challenge of the fee. For three years, however, not a single client could be identified who was willing to risk the delays associated with raising a constitutional challenge and the prospect, even if successful at the first instance, of defending against further appeals to the Federal Court of Appeal and then the Supreme Court. In those cases that do go forward, resort to the courts has led to the quashing of admissions decisions that were made unfairly or in a discriminatory manner but has rarely generated any fundamental changes to the inequities of the legislative scheme itself.

Refugees

In 1979, Canada played a leading role in resettling tens of thousands of Vietnamese refugees in the aftermath of a decades-long war. While the government condemned the interception and piracy of Vietnamese boats on the high seas, it was forging innovative partnerships with private groups across the country to receive and support the refugees. As a result of these efforts, the United Nations awarded the people of Canada the prestigious Nansen Medal 'in recognition of their major and substantial contribution to the cause of refugees.' Nevertheless, Canada's record of compliance with international human rights standards and the UN Refugee Convention in particular has been uneven. The government's responsiveness to refugee crises around the world has frequently been informed by racism as well as geopolitical and economic considerations, rather than respect for international legal obligations and the spirit of humanitarianism that both the former Immigration Act and IRPA allegedly enshrine. During the past decade, in the face of massive human rights atrocities in Sudan, Rwanda, and Burundi, and more recently in Sierra Leone and the Ivory Coast, only Somalia and the Democratic Republic of Congo ranked in the list of top ten source countries for refugees by source area for more than one year.

For 2005, Canada's projected refugee intake was approximately 13 per cent of total immigration, consisting of 7,500 government-assisted and 3,400 to 4,000 privately sponsored refugees, as well as between 14,500 to 16,500 'self-selected' refugees who will arrive in Canada on their own and successfully proceed through the in-land determination system (CIC 2004, 19, 25). The current rules for selecting refugees from abroad make use of establishment criteria modified from the points system for immigrants. With exceptions for urgent or 'special needs' cases, applicants must convince a visa officer that they will be able to adapt to life in Canada and will be able to successfully establish themselves within three years of arrival, in addition to demonstrating that they are at risk of persecution as a Convention refugee or are facing a refugee-like situation.[10] While the criteria are to be applied with an emphasis on social rather than strictly economic factors, subjective and highly discretionary considerations with regard to the refugee's 'personal suitability' continue to supplant the assessment of the refugee's need for protection. Canadian visa officers frequently overrule the advice of legal officers from the United Nations High Commissioner for Refugees with regard to deserving cases. Despite widespread criticism of the government's refugee resettlement model, officials have refused to eliminate the establishment criteria from overseas selection (Giles 1996, 45; Casasola 2001, 81).

For reasons explained in the previous section, the Charter has not afforded overseas applicants any prospects for challenging refusals. Even ordinary judicial review applications challenging visa officer decisions are relatively rare, given the constraints faced by refugees living in precarious conditions in camps or in other circumstances where local integration is not possible. For in-land refugee claimants, the courts have had occasion to consider the scope of Charter protections and the leading cases will be considered in turn below.

In 1985, the Supreme Court released its decision in *Re Singh and Minister of Employment and Immigration and 6 other appeals*. It stated that where a serious issue of credibility is involved, fundamental justice requires that credibility be determined on the basis of an oral hearing. Justice Bertha Wilson found that the system for determining refugee status inside Canada failed to meet the procedural guarantees of section 7 of the Charter. Prior to *Singh*, refugee claimants did not have an oral hearing or an opportunity to address the evidence the government might have with respect to their claim. Instead, they recounted the events that led to their departure from their country of origin in an examination under oath with an immigration officer, who then forwarded the transcript of that examination to the Refugee Status Advisory Committee, which made a decision on the claim without ever hearing from the claimant. Three of the six justices in the Supreme Court's ruling in *Singh* confirmed that everyone present in Canada as well as anyone seeking admission at a port of entry was entitled to the protection of the Charter.[11] Refugee advocates and lawyers celebrated the decision and each year commemorate the date of the decision's release in April as 'Refugee Rights Day' across the country.

In the short term, the implications of *Singh* were quite dramatic. The government had to spend millions of dollars to set up a refugee-determination system that included procedures for a full oral hearing and the right to counsel. By 1989 the Immigration and Refugee Board had been established, affording refugee claimants inside Canada a 'quality' status determination by an independent, quasi-judicial tribunal. Developments in the wake of *Singh*, however, clearly demonstrate the extent to which legal victories so easily slide into irrelevance. In the aftermath of the decision, the government took swift steps to limit access to the refugee-determination system by limiting the appeal rights of claimants in Canada and increasing measures of interdiction to ensure that fewer refugees actually reached Canada in the first place. Introduced in 1987, Bill C-84, known as the *Deterrents and Detention Act*, authorized the government to turn away ships in the internal waters of Canada, the territorial seas, or twelve miles beyond the outer limit of the territorial waters when there are 'reasonable grounds' for believing the vessels are transporting anyone in contravention of the act. Another provision of the bill made it an offence to assist anyone to come to Canada who was not in possession of proper travel documents, whether that person was a bona fide refugee or not. Transportation companies were subject to fines (or technically, levied administration fees) if they brought any improperly documented passenger into Canada. Since 1990, the government has been expanding its interdiction efforts through its support for a network of immigration control officers (recently renamed as 'migration integrity officers') stationed around the world to prevent migrants without proper documents from reaching Canada. Little is known about the circumstances of the approximately 6,000 persons whom these officers 'successfully' intercept each year, but reports surface very occasionally of refugees who have suffered serious human rights violations upon return to their countries of origin (Aiken 2001, 47–8; AI 1998).

By 1992, the Supreme Court had narrowed the application of *Singh* in the case of a permanent resident seeking to challenge the constitutionality of provisions that imposed deportation for serious criminal offences and denied an appeal to residents suspected of engaging in organized criminal activity (*Chiarelli* 1992). Joseph Chiarelli, who had come to Canada with his parents as a teenager, was facing deportation as a result of two criminal convictions as well as allegations that he would engage in organized crime. The Court assumed, without deciding, that section 7 could apply to the case but found that the provisions in question did not constitute a violation of fundamental justice. The judgment noted that Parliament had the 'right to adopt an immigration policy and to enact legislation prescribing the conditions under which non-citizens will be permitted to enter and remain in Canada.' The conditions imposed by Parliament on a permanent resident's right to remain in the country represented 'a legitimate, non-arbitrary choice' (*Chiarelli* 1992, 735).[12] Although not a refugee case, the Supreme Court's decision in *Chiarelli* was extended to refugees facing similar circumstances. A year later, in *Nguyen v. Canada*, the Federal Court considered a constitutional challenge to provisions of the *Immigration Act* that rendered individuals convicted of serious crimes ineligible to make a refugee claim. The Court held that 'a foreigner has no absolute right to be recognized as a political refugee under either the common law or any international convention to which Canada has adhered. It follows that ... to deny dangerous criminals the right, generally conceded to immigrants who flee persecution, to seek refuge in Canada certainly cannot be seen as a form of illegitimate discrimination ...'(*Nguyen* 1993, 704). In *Dehghani v. Canada*, the Supreme Court reinforced the citizen/non-citizen distinction in holding that the questioning of a refugee claimant in a 'secondary examination' at the border was equivalent to the routine procedures to which any non-citizen seeking entry was subject. Consequently, the implied compulsion and questioning did not constitute detention within the meaning of the Charter and did not attract any procedural rights to due process or the right to counsel. As a result of this ruling, statements made by refugee claimants at the port of entry in the absence of counsel were increasingly introduced in the initial 'credible basis' hearing as evidence of prior inconsistent statements with a view to denying the claimant the right to proceed to the second stage, which is a hearing on the merits of their claim. More generally, the prospects that the Charter could be used in aid of refugees seeking to challenge any aspect of their treatment by immigration law, policy, or practice had been restricted to the narrowest of grounds (Kelley 2004, 268).

In 1993 new legislative amendments to the *Immigration Act* (Bill C-86) that centred on abuses to the system by outsiders were introduced. Included in the package of amendments was a provision that required Convention refugees to produce 'satisfactory' identity documents in order to be landed.[13] Prior to the passage of Bill C-86, the *Immigration Act* exempted Convention refugees from the requirement to provide identity documents. Somali refugees were among those disproportionately affected by the new requirement. Since the collapse in 1991 of the Siyad Barre regime in Somalia, there has been no central government and thus no institutions to issue identity documents. The last legal Somali passports were issued in 1989 and by 1994 all valid Somali passports had expired. Even before the collapse of the government, however, a large majority of the population did not register their births, marriages, or divorces, a cultural reality that is shared by many other countries, especially those in Africa (Brouwer 1999, 4). Three years after Bill C-86 was implemented, in a professed effort to address community concerns, the government set up the Undocumented Convention Refugee in Canada Class (UCRCC), imposing a mandatory five-year waiting period on all Somali refugees seeking permanent residence.[14] The five-year period (reduced to three years in 1999) was calculated from the date of receiving a positive decision from the Immigration and Refugee Board, with the result that the total period of time that 'undocumented' refugees have to wait prior to landing is at least seven years. By 1999 there were approximately 13,000 refugees, primarily Somali women and children, and a comparatively smaller group of Afghans, in legal limbo as a direct result of the identity document requirement (Brouwer 1999). Several years after adoption of the UCRCC only 38 per cent of the original group of refugees in limbo had been landed (Maytree 2002, 7; Brouwer 1999, 5). While protected from removal, refugees without landed status are unable to leave the country for the purpose of a temporary visit to another country or to be reunited with family members whom they would have otherwise been able to sponsor. Due to the age restrictions of the family class sponsorship program (subject to a few, narrow exceptions, the former Immigration Act stipulated that dependent children could only be sponsored when they were under nineteen years of age), parents who may have been forced to leave children behind in refugee camps in an effort to secure safety for themselves and their family in Canada were never able to sponsor any child who was over the age of eleven years when left behind. In addition, refugees in the UCRCC were denied access to postsecondary education, professional training programs, and bank loans for small businesses. As holders of temporary work permits, many refugees were forced to rely upon social assistance as employers were often unwilling to hire them. Many of the Somali refugees reported discrimination in the housing market, where landlords were reluctant to rent to racialized women on social assistance who were also newcomers with large families (Murdie 2002; Preston 2003). These restrictions produced the social marginalization of an entire community.

The government justified the identity document requirement for refugees and later the Undocumented Convention Refugee in Canada Class by using the rhetoric of maintaining the safety of Canadian society, suggesting that without identity documents, there was no way to confirm whether or not the refugee was a war criminal or a terrorist. Former citizenship and immigration minister Lucienne Robillard stated somewhat equivocally that these measures were about 'balancing risk to Canada against compassion.' Yet there was no evidence of widespread danger. The refugee hearing itself affords an opportunity for extensive examination of identity issues. Refugee applications are routinely turned down if it is found that the individual is not who she or he claims to be. Prior to landing, every refugee is subjected to a security screening process conducted by the Canadian Security Intelligence Service. For the few who have managed to obtain refugee status on the basis of misrepresentation or concealment of any material fact, proceedings could be initiated against the particular individual pursuant to existing immigration provisions.

A Charter challenge to the identity document requirements initiated by eleven Somali refugees in Ottawa in 1996 was successfully settled with a government commitment to accept affidavit evidence concerning a refugee's identity in lieu of identity documents (Maytree 2002). The IRPA subsequently inscribed into law administrative guidelines adopted in the wake of the settlement, which permit refugees with few or no identity documents to submit statutory declarations attesting to their identity. For those unable to obtain a credible organization or individual who can vouch for their identity, an Undocumented Protected Persons in Canada class has been maintained, with a waiting period of three years and all the attendant hardships. As Razack suggests, the identity documents rule acquires its coherence in the context of 'a national story of white innocence and the duplicity and cunning of people of colour' (Razack 2000, 187). The rule is difficult to account for in any other terms, given the fact that verifying identity continues to be a central issue in protection hearings.

The IRPA reinforces and extends the government's preoccupation with refugees as queue-jumpers and dangerous outlaws. Underpinning current policy is the myth that refugee claimants who travel with forged documents (often the only feasible way for an individual to escape a situation of danger and travel to a country of asylum) or 'unsatisfactory' documents (i.e., documents that do not conform to Western standards) are not genuine refugees.[15] A series of new measures have been adopted, aimed at addressing the 'problem' of undocumented refugees. These measures include enhanced interdiction to intercept 'improperly documented' people before they arrive in Canada, increased disembarkation checks as passengers leave aircraft, collaboration with other countries to develop a system of data collection on illegal migration, and the prospect of detention for refugee claimants who refuse to 'cooperate' in establishing their identity. The legislation also expands the grounds for denying refugee claimants access to the refugee determination process of the Immigration and Refugee Board and imposes an absolute bar on repeat claims, regardless of the length of time that has passed or the extent to which conditions in the refugee's country of origin may have worsened.[16] Denied access to a hearing, 'ineligible' claimants are only entitled to request relief from removal through a 'pre-removal risk assessment' by way of a written application to the minister. With a fairly consistent acceptance rate of less than 5 per cent, most advocates consider this administrative remedy to be an exceedingly poor substitute for a hearing.[17] In the introduction to the white paper that preceded the IRPA, the government asserted: 'In reaffirming its commitment to an open immigration system and to the protection of refugees, the government wishes to ensure a sound immigration and refugee system that is not open to abuse. Canada, together with other major Western industrialized countries, has committed to developing a multidisciplinary and comprehensive strategy to address the common problem of illegal migration (CIC 1999, 46). Despite the rhetoric of 'open immigration' and a stated commitment to refugee protection, the government's agenda for reform has been predicated on stereotypes of refugees as criminals and threats to Canada's security.

Within days of the attacks on the World Trade Center and the Pentagon in September 2001, Prime Minister Jean Chrétien indicated that tougher requirements for would-be refugee claimants would be part of a package of reforms to respond to the new global realities (Harper 2001). In fact, no changes were made before the bill was hurriedly proclaimed on 1 November 2001; new enforcement measures had already been included in earlier versions of the bill, well before September 11. On 3 December 2001, American Attorney General John Ashcroft, Immigration Minister Elinor Caplan, and Solicitor General Laurence MacAulay initialed an important new policy document – a Joint Statement on Border Security and Regional Migration Issues. The statement focused on 'deterrence, detection and prosecution of security threats, the disruption of illegal migration and the efficient management of legitimate travel.' It outlined a series of new measures, including joint border patrols, a policy review on visitor visas, and information sharing on high-risk visa applications, an increase in the number of migration integrity officers overseas, as well as the development of common biometric identifiers for documents (CIC 2001). A short time later, these measures were codified in a Smart Border Declaration with an accompanying thirty-point Action Plan. For refugee advocates, the most controversial part of the border accord was the proposed Safe Third Country Agreement. Implemented in late 2004, the agreement requires, with limited exceptions, all refugee claimants arriving at a Canadian land border from the United States to pursue their asylum claim in the United States, and vice versa. Given the more limited availability of direct flights to Canada than to the United States, dramatically higher numbers of refugees arrive in the United States as their first destination. Indeed in 2003, approximately 11,000 refugee claimants made claims at Canadian ports of entry at the land border while the flow from Canada to the United States was barely a few hundred. The refugee populations that will be most disadvantaged by the agreement are likely to be racialized people from the global South, who lack the financial means to fly directly from their country of origin. In her discussion of the 1992 amendments to Canada's immigration law, which permitted the designation of 'safe countries,' Jakubowski compares the safe country provisions to the Continuous Journey Stipulation of 1908, which refused entry to immigrants who came to Canada other than by way of a single, uninterrupted passage. The genesis of the continuous journey rule was the policy goal of curtailing immigration from India. As Jakubowski suggests, without ever mentioning the word 'race,' the ultimate effect of these provisions is 'to control a particular dimension of the refugee population – developing world refugees, the majority of whom are classified by the government as visible minorities' (Jakubowski 1997, 85–6).

Canadian officials justify the Safe Third Country Agreement on the premise that protection will be readily available in the United States and that this is a measure simply aimed at 'burden sharing' of international refugee flows. The implicit objective of the agreement, however, is simply to reduce the number of refugees who can claim refugee protection in Canada. The experience of similar accords in Europe suggests that the agreement may actually have the perverse effect of encouraging asylum seekers to cross Canadian land borders illegally and then pursue their claims inland (Canada 2002).[18] Refugees have every reason to assume those risks, given the lower standards of due process protection available in the United States with respect to refugee hearings, the greater prospect of detention and deportation in expedited removal procedures, as well as differing (and detrimental) U.S. interpretations of international refugee law. A Charter challenge of the agreement is currently being planned by a coalition of Toronto-based lawyers. Arguably, however, the importance of the agreement has become less significant as increasing resources are being allocated to interceptions overseas – far from any Canadian land border. In support of this contention is the fact that the numbers of refugee claimants arriving in Canada have plummeted in the past three years, with overall numbers at their lowest point since 1994 (UNHCR 2004).

Existing immigration law and practice with regard to refugee admissions, rules on identity documents, and the Safe Third Country Agreement represent classic examples of systemic racism. By using the logic of sanitary coding (the law is framed in neutral, objective language) and the technique of equivocation (the rationale for the law is framed in terms of keeping out system abusers while at the same time upholding the principles of the Constitution and international law), the government has been able to avoid any accountability for the adverse effects on racialized refugees of its efforts to manage the immigration program (Jakubowski 1999, 120). Viewed through the lens of recent experience, the due process guarantees achieved through the *Singh* decision have failed to protect substantive rights for most refugees. Indeed, many features of current legislation draw directly from the Supreme Court's jurisprudence, to the detriment of non-citizens and refugees in particular (Kelley 2004, 283). As increasingly fewer refugees are able to access a protection hearing in Canada, Canada's overall contribution to international refugee protection remains paltry in relative terms. Canada continues to host less than one-quarter of one per cent of all the world's refugees (UNHCR 2004). The perception that the in-land status determination system established in response to the Supreme Court's ruling in *Singh* is an unacceptable drain on public resources appears be to rising (Simpson 2003, 2005; Jiménez 2005), reinforcing a neo-racist, anti-refugee policy agenda.

'Humanitarian and Compassionate' Cases

Immigration law has long provided a residual authority to the Minister of Citizenship and Immigration to exempt anyone from any of the requirements of the act or otherwise facilitate their admission to the country, based on 'compassionate or humanitarian considerations.' Neither the IRPA nor the regulations provide any indication of the meaning to be ascribed to 'humanitarian or compassionate,' nor of the procedures applicable to an individual seeking such an exemption. Administrative guidelines have been developed and are contained in the *Immigration Manual*. A series of changes were introduced to these guidelines in 1999 and again with implementation of the IRPA. The newest version suffers from the same lack of transparency and inconsistent application as the older versions. Current guidelines indicate that applicants bear the burden of satisfying the decision-maker that their personal circumstances are such that the hardship of having to obtain a visa outside Canada in the normal manner would be (i) unusual and undeserved; or (ii) disproportionate. In practice, applications are rarely given favourable consideration unless the applicant can demonstrate successful establishment in Canada in addition to whatever hardship might be suffered by returning to their home country. A request for humanitarian and compassionate consideration can be made in the context of any application to the department, but arises most frequently in the cases of individuals already in Canada and seeking special consideration to remain. For failed refugee claimants, this procedure is frequently the only safety net available to ensure that there will be some consideration of the reasons why they may be at risk, if returned to their country of origin. The program provides for the possibility of spouses and other members of the family class to remain in the country with their family rather than endure the hardship of the lengthy separation of overseas sponsorship. In the past, the policy guidelines also included a special category for 'illegal de facto residents' who had established themselves in Canada after a period of many years and sought to regularize their status. This category was the only remedy available for many racialized women who came to Canada to take up positions as domestic workers outside legal channels. The underlying policy rationale for this category seemed to be a recognition that people who have severed ties with their home country and demonstrated an ability to be self-sufficient in Canada over a significant period of time should not be subject to an indefinite penalty for gaining illegal admission to the country. Current guidelines, however, specifically proscribe such recognition, noting instead that favourable consideration may be warranted when individuals have been in Canada for a prolonged period of time due to 'circumstances beyond their control.'[19] The language of the guidelines does not appear to translate easily to a situation where someone has been 'underground' and seeks to regularize her or his status. A humanitarian and compassionate application is processed as an administrative review. There is no right to a hearing, although the person concerned may be requested to attend an interview. For many years, the courts refused to accept that an applicant seeking judicial review of an immigration officer's decision was entitled to anything more than minimal fairness in what was otherwise characterized as a wholly discretionary decision (*Shah* 1994).

In 1999, the Supreme Court rendered its decision in *Baker v. Minister of Citizenship and Immigration*, a case concerning the rights of Canadian-born children in the context of their parent's immigration proceedings. Mavis Baker is a woman from Jamaica who came to Canada and over-stayed her visit. She supported herself as a live-in domestic worker for eleven years and was self-sufficient until she suffered an attack of post-partum psychosis following the birth of her youngest child. While undergoing treatment, two of her children were placed in the custody of their father, a citizen of Canada, and the other two went into foster care. As her health improved, the two children placed in foster care returned to live with Ms Baker. The other two remained with their father, but Ms Baker and her former partner maintained a hybrid family in which the children visited back and forth between the two homes. Ms Baker's humanitarian and compassionate application was turned down by the immigration officer who reviewed her case, with the following explanation in his notes:

> This case is a catastrophy [sic] ... The PC is a paranoid schizophrenic and on welfare. She has no qualifications other than as a domestic. She has FOUR CHILDREN IN JAMAICA AND ANOTHER FOUR BORN HERE. She will of course be a tremendous strain on our social welfare systems for (probably) the rest of her life. There are no H&C factors other than her FOUR CANADIAN-BORN CHILDREN. Do we let her stay because of that? I am of the opinion that Canada can no longer afford that sort of generosity. (*Baker* 1999, para. 5)

Justice Claire L'Heureux-Dubé, writing for five justices of the Court, found among other things that the immigration officer's comments gave rise to a reasonable apprehension of bias, noting as 'most unfortunate' the link made between Ms. Baker's mental illness, her training as a domestic worker, the fact that she has several children, and the conclusion that she would be a strain on our social welfare system for the rest of her life. She stated that the officer's notes and the manner in which they were written 'do not disclose an open mind or a weighing of the particular circumstances of the case free from stereotypes.' In addressing the rights of the children, the Court noted that international human rights law was a 'critical influence' on the interpretation of the scope of the rights included in the Charter. Yet the court did not address any of the underlying problems with the discretionary decision-making scheme. Although constitutional issues were raised, they were side-stepped by the court when it rendered a decision that rested primarily on administrative law principles. Mavis Baker, like a number of other people whose applications were rejected in a similar manner, won the right to have her application reconsidered. After a lengthy delay, Baker eventually received permanent residence, and the standard of review applicable to humanitarian and compassionate cases has been clarified as 'simple reasonableness,' a threshold that provides a little more lati-tude for judicial intervention.

On the one hand, the *Baker* case has been quite significant in terms of its impact on administrative law doctrines relating to standard of review. It has opened up the possibility of subjecting a range of discre-tionary administrative decisions that had been otherwise beyond the reach of the courts to judicial scrutiny. On the other hand, in the several years since the court's ruling it has become increasingly clear that the decision has meant relatively little to migrants in circumstances similar to Baker's.[20] Officers' notes no longer reflect in so transparent a manner any hint of racism or stereotyping. The children's interests are more carefully weighed, rather than so abruptly dismissed. While the *Baker* ruling may provide somewhat easier access to the courts for judicial review and, in this sense, widen the scope of procedural or due process rights for all categories of migrants, the barriers to justice for racialized women like Mavis Baker are significant and the remedy more hypo-thetical than real. At best, this small legal victory has resulted in one person at a time being allowed to stay in the country and even then, perhaps only for a limited time (Sterett 1997, 13). The Court overlooked the question of racism in society, its relationship to poverty, and the sys-temic problems associated with the humanitarian review process. The judgment reflected little of the analysis urged upon the Court through interventions by the Charter Committee on Poverty Issues, the Cana-dian Council of Churches and the joint submissions of the Canadian Council for Refugees, the Canadian Foundation for Children, Youth and the Law, and the Defence for Children International–Canada.[21] With the implementation of the current guidelines, it is even less likely that racialized women who have contributed their labour as domestic workers, permitting middle-class Canadians the benefits of two incomes and someone to care for their children, will be afforded any recognition by the immigration system. Proof of this contention was readily available in the court of public opinion in the wake of the decision's release. An editorial in the *Globe and Mail* suggested that Mavis Baker was the 'author of her own misfortunes' and that when her case was considered again, she should be deported because the 'integrity of the immigration principles demands it.' Similarly, an editorial in the *National Post* intoned that if Mavis Baker 'truly believes the welfare of her children is paramount, she would return to Jamaica and reconcile her two sets of children.'

Francis (Litigation guardian of) v. Canada (Minster of Citizenship and Immigration) was a direct constitutional challenge to the humanitarian and compassionate decision-making structure. By the time her case reached the Ontario Court of Appeal, Maria Francis had been living in Canada without status for eleven years. She had two Canadian-born children; her eldest son, born in Grenada, was ordered deported with her. When the Federal Court denied their application for a stay of the removal, the Canadian-born children filed an application in the Ontario Court on the grounds that deportation of their mother would violate their Charter rights, and that the Department had failed to properly consider their best interests before ordering the deportation of their mother and brother. A broad coalition including the African Canadian Legal Clinic, the Women's Legal Education and Action Fund, the Congress of Black Women, the National Action Committee on the Status of Women, the Metro Toronto Chinese and Southeast Asian Legal Clinic, and the Coalition of Visible Minority Women intervened to address issues of racism. The coalition argued that fundamental justice in the context of a humanitarian and compassionate review should necessarily include the right of both Francis and her children to a fair hearing, one that was not influenced by systemic discrimination or by myths about racialized Caribbean women who immigrate to Canada. Although the children's application had been successful at the first instance, the government's appeal was allowed by the Ontario Court of Appeal on the basis that the ruling in *Baker* afforded adequate instructions to immigration officers to ensure that the children's interests were considered in deportation proceedings. While the Court allowed Francis and her son to remain in Canada to pursue a new humanitarian review, none of the issues raised by the coalition appeared to inform the Court's judgment. In the face of a political determination to preserve the integrity of immigration control and eradicate any incentives for 'abusers,' the courts and the government have been mutually reinforcing. Drawing on the judgment in *Baker*, section 25 of the IRPA sets out the general authority for humanitarian and compassionate applications and indicates that the Minister's discretion to exempt an individual from the usual requirements of the Act should take account of the 'best interests of the child.' Similarly, the current humanitarian guidelines, which were not applicable to either the *Baker* or *Francis* cases, actually make reference to international human rights standards and indicate that the applicant's submissions *may* (emphasis added) be considered in light of these standards.[22] Arguably, such references will serve to ensure that immigration officers seeking to refuse particular applicants will now do so using the language of human rights standards, without importing human rights reasoning into the substance of their decisions.

Expulsion of African-Canadian Residents

On 5 April 1994, twenty-three-year-old Georgina Leimonis was killed during a late-night robbery of Just Desserts, a café in Toronto. A few months later, in June 1994, police constable Todd Baylis was killed. Both deaths were the result of shootings alleged to have been committed by Jamaican immigrants already under deportation orders. Some of the men charged had been in Canada since they were children but had, like many other Caribbean immigrants, neglected to apply for Canadian citizenship as soon as they became eligible (Pratt and Valverde 2002, 145). Both deaths were embraced by the media as potent symbols of a deeply flawed immigration system that, had it been functioning effectively, could have prevented the deaths of two innocent victims. Responding to Canadians' worries about their personal safety came to be seen as a key priority by the federal government. The notion that more effective legal tools were needed to improve 'system integrity' swiftly acquired currency in the Canadian policy arena. Within a year, in a climate of rising public hysteria about 'immigrant criminals,' the government accomplished the swift passage of Bill C-44, a set of amendments to the *Immigration Act* (Noorani and Wright 1995). Bill C-44 introduced significant changes to the rights of refugees and long-term permanent residents in Canada. Individuals classified as a 'danger to the public' could be arrested and held indefinitely, pending deportation from Canada under an opinion issued by the minister. The right to an oral hearing was replaced by a paper process in which the minister was both adversary and decision-maker, and the person concerned was provided with a scant fifteen days in which to respond to the minister's submissions.

Williams v. Canada was a decision involving a challenge of the public danger provisions by a Jamaican-Canadian man who was facing deportation as a non-citizen. Jeffrey Williams had resided in Canada for over twenty years, having arrived as a child at the age of ten. As a young man he was convicted of a number of narcotics offences and one offence of assault. The Federal Court of Appeal's ruling confirmed that the danger opinion process met minimum common-law requirements for procedural fairness and that 'liberty' did not include the right of personal choice for permanent residents to stay in Canada where they had 'deliberately violated an essential condition under which they were permitted to remain in Canada' (*Minister of Citizenship and Immigration v. Williams* 1997, para. 26). In a subsequent judgment, the Court refused to accept that a permanent resident with family and deep roots in Canada should be accorded an independent Charter-based right to be considered a citizen and protected from deportation (*Solis* 2000). As Kelley points out, until 1976 most grounds of deportation only applied to persons with less than five years residence. With the 1976 *Immigration Act* the concept of 'domicile' was removed, permitting the deportation of long-term permanent residents but providing a right to appeal their removal on compassionate grounds, except when a security certificate had been issued against them. The combined result of *Chiarelli* and the more recent judgments in *Williams* and *Solis* was that what a non-citizen could expect from the Charter was actually less than what had been provided by immigration legislation before the Charter was adopted (Kelley 2004, 266–8). Most Canadians would enjoy greater rights of appeal in relation to minor traffic violations than long-term permanent residents had in relation to decisions depriving them of their liberty and separating them from family members and the only home they know.

Between 1995 and 2000, the Department sought and issued danger certificates in an estimated 2,000 cases, a number that did not conform with an expressed intention of limiting the use of the process to exceptional cases where appeals would be manifestly without merit. In a discussion paper on the implementation and impact of the public danger provisions, the African Canadian Legal Clinic documented that the common denominator among persons who have been subject to removal based on a public danger opinion is that they are members of racialized groups, including 'an overwhelming number of persons of African descent with previous drug-related offences' (ACLC 1999, 3). The department's own statistics confirm that two years after Bill C-44 had been implemented, nearly 40 per cent of the total public danger removals executed in Ontario were deportations to Jamaica, constituting more than five times the number of the next-highest recipient country of Trinidad and Tobago, and more than the total number of deportees to all of Europe, the United States, and South America (CIC 1997). The subjective nature of the danger opinion process often led to lengthy litigation, thwarting the policy intent of removing dangerous criminals from Canada as quickly as possible. It also led to charges by some that the public danger scheme was reinforcing systemic racism in the immigration program and that the removal of long-term permanent residents offended both the Charter and international human rights norms. In a brief to the UN World Conference on Racism held in 2001, the African Canadian Legal Clinic submitted that 'while Blacks have difficulty migrating to Canada, they are also the group that is being expelled most frequently. Racist anti-immigration sentiment has fuelled the mass expulsion of long-term African Canadian residents from Canada. For example, while African Canadians comprise only 3% of the population of the Province of Ontario, approximately 60% of the people deported from the Ontario Region since 1995 have been people of African descent, many of whom have lived in Canada since childhood as permanent residents' (ACLC 2001). Strong support for the clinic's concerns may be found in evidence of the unequal treatment of racialized persons in the criminal justice system (Commission 1995, 191, 262, 284). The reliance on the criminal background of a person as the rationale for expulsion without due regard for the other circumstances of their life perpetuates the effects of systemic racism in the combined apparatus of criminal justice and immigration control.

The IRPA replaced the danger opinion process by statutorily defining 'serious criminal' as a permanent resident or foreign national who has been convicted of an offence punishable by a sentence of at least ten years or more or has been convicted of an offence for which a term of imprisonment of more than six months has been imposed. The consequences of a 'serious criminal' designation is significantly extended, permitting immigration officers to issue removal orders supported only by the fact of a conviction, denying permanent residents any right of appeal on legal or equitable grounds and denying access to humanitarian and compassionate applications. In the context of the concerns raised with regard to the public danger process under the former act, the measures contained in the IRPA represent a further indication of the extent to which public stereotypes concerning the foreign and immigrant nature of Canadian crime have entered into immigration policy discourse and law.[23]

Racial Profiling and National Security post–September 11

While various definitions of racial profiling have been advanced by scholars and policy makers over the years, the Ontario Human Rights Commission has offered a useful starting point. The Commission defines racial profiling broadly to include 'any action undertaken for reasons of safety, security or public protection that relies on stereotypes about race, colour, ethnicity, ancestry, religion, or place of origin rather than on reasonable suspicion to single out an individual for greater scrutiny or different treatment' (OHRC 2003, 6). Racial profiling, the report explains, differs from criminal profiling, which is not based on stereotypes but rather relies on actual behaviour or on information about suspected activity by someone who meets the description of a specific individual. In other words, criminal profiling is not the same as racial profiling since the former is based on objective evidence of wrongful behaviour while racial profiling is based on stereotypical assumptions. As the commission suggests, 'while it may be somewhat natural for humans to engage in stereotyping, it is nevertheless wrong. And, it is a particular concern when people act on their stereotypical views in a way that affects others. This is what leads to profiling' (OHRC 2003, 6). In the context of Canada's war on terrorism, legal scholars have emphasized that racial profiling entails the use of race as a proxy for assessing the security risk posed by individuals (Bahdi 2003, 295; Choudhry 2001, 372).

None of the national security measures in the IRPA have anything to say about racial profiling. They neither explicitly condone nor prohibit racial profiling. However, as Bahdi notes, 'the lack of explicit endorsement of racial profiling ... does not mean that it does not take place in Canada ... the silence of the legislature regarding the practice, at best, fails to effectively check racial profiling and, at worst, creates opportunities for racial profiling' (Bahdi 2003, 297). As in other manifestations of systemic discrimination, racial profiling is embodied in the exercise of discretionary powers by officials enforcing apparently neutral laws.

Well before September 11, the Canadian Council for Refugees had documented the extent to which certain refugee communities seemed to be
particularly targeted under immigration security provisions, including
Iranians associated with the Mujahedin-E-Khalq movement, Kurds, Sri
Lankan Tamils, Sikhs, Algerians, and Palestinians, while other groups
were not subjected to the same levels of security scrutiny (CCR 2001). In
the wake of September 11, ample anecdotal evidence suggests that refugees and even naturalized citizens of Arab and Muslim descent have
been the targets of increased surveillance and security scrutiny by
immigration officials (CCR 2004; Bahdi 2003; ICLMG 2003).

According to national security exclusions in the IRPA (and the former
Immigration Act), refugees and prospective immigrants are 'inadmissible' where there are reasonable grounds to believe they will 'engage in
terrorism' or are 'members of an organization that there are reasonable
grounds to believe will ... engage in terrorism.' An additional subsection provides that persons are inadmissible if they engaged in terrorism
in the past or are 'members of an organization that was engaged in terrorism' unless they can satisfy the minister that their admission would
not be detrimental to the national interest. As 'terrorism' and 'membership' are undefined in the law, these largely indeterminate concepts
have afforded both immigration officers and the judges who reviewed
their decisions the broadest possible discretion. Non-citizens may be
barred from entering Canada on the basis of security inadmissibility, or
once inside the country, they may be subject to removal at the conclusion of an immigration inquiry or a 'security certificate' procedure.

With implementation of the IRPA in June 2002 and the availability of
greater revenue allocated for immigration enforcement pursuant to the
federal government's multi-pronged 'Anti-Terrorism Plan,' there has
been an increase in the overall numbers of non-citizens, including refugee claimants, subject to preventive immigration detention (CBSA
2004, Dench 2004). When confronted with the raw statistics, it is often
difficult to interpret the data. Is the use of detention on the rise because
more dangerous people have turned up at our borders? Or is it a tangi-
ble result of a moral panic about security in the wake of September 11?
The numbers alone reveal little about the circumstances of the detainees, but one recent and fairly high-profile case drew media attention
and suggests at least a partial answer to these questions.

In August 2003, a group of twenty-three South Asian men were
arrested and detained on security grounds as a result of 'Operation
Thread,' a joint investigation by the RCMP and Citizenship and Immigration Canada. Twenty-two of the young men were from Pakistan

while one was from India. Initial reports splashed across Canadian newspapers identified the group as an al-Qaeda sleeper cell. The incriminating allegations, which department officials were unable to substantiate, included a plot to destroy the CN Tower, a student pilot with a flight course over the Pickering nuclear plant, several young men living together in sparsely furnished apartments, the setting off of a smoke alarm in a kitchen (supposedly a sign of testing explosives), and one man who knew someone with an al-Qaeda connection (Jiménez, Freeze, and Burnett 2003; Khan 2004). Officials very quickly backed away from their initial claim that the men posed a threat to national security as the cases devolved into simple immigration fraud with an illegitimate Scarborough business college at the centre. The aftershocks of the investigation, however, cast a long shadow over the men's lives. Marked as terrorists, many of the men continue to face harassment and unemployment back in Pakistan (Shephard and Verma 2003; Verma 2004). Department officials may have had a reasonable basis for pursuing investigations in at least some of the 'Operation Thread' cases – namely the visa violations – but the decision to detain the men as security risks appears to have been a blatant example of racial profiling.

For non-citizens subject to the security-certificate procedure, the decision made by a single, designated judge in a review of the reasonableness – but not the merits – of the ministerial security opinion is considered conclusive proof of the allegations against the individual and cannot be appealed. The certificate process allows the government to arrest, detain, and deport non-citizens after secret hearings without the person or her counsel being present. In 1996 a Charter challenge of these procedures was unsuccessful (*Ahani* 1996). With the implementation of the IRPA, the entitlement of permanent residents (in contrast to other non-citizens) subject to an adverse security report to have their case investigated by the Security Intelligence Review Committee with direct recourse to an administrative hearing was clawed back. Now all non-citizens are offered only an 'informal and expeditious' Federal Court review with diminished due process guarantees Although fewer than thirty security certificates have been issued since 1991, the procedure and related preventive detention provisions have continued to draw criticism from a wide range of observers and advocates (IACHR 2000; Aiken and Brouwer 2004; Jackman 2005; AI 2005).

Manickavasagam Suresh is a Tamil man of Sri Lankan origin who was recognized as a Convention refugee in Canada in 1991. His involvement as a coordinator for two Toronto-based agencies which the

Canadian Security Intelligence Service alleged to be fronts for the Liberation Tigers of Tamil Eelam (LTTE) resulted in the filing of a security
certificate against him on grounds that he engaged in terrorism and
was a member of organizations engaged in terrorism. The Federal
Court upheld the reasonableness of the security certificate, emphasizing that terrorism 'must be seen through the eyes of a Canadian' and
that 'the term "terrorism" or "terrorist act" ... must receive a wide and
unrestricted interpretation' (*Re Suresh* 1997, para. 29).[24] Subsequently,
Suresh lodged a wide-ranging constitutional challenge of the Immigration Act's anti-terrorism provisions along with the specific sections
that authorized the deportation of Convention refugees deemed to
be threats to the security of Canada. In a unanimous judgment, the
Supreme Court ruled that fundamental justice required that Suresh
should not be removed without a more careful review of the risk of torture he might face upon return to Sri Lanka. The Court's ruling was a
clear victory for Suresh. The judgment, however, reinforced a number
of disturbing doctrinal and policy trends. In holding that heightened
due process was required only in cases where there was a 'prima facie
risk' of torture, the Court accorded the Minister considerable latitude
to determine when such protections apply. Apparently grave harm
that falls short of torture would not even be entitled to the same level
of protection afforded to Mavis Baker. Further, in ruling that the Minister retained the discretion to deport a refugee to face torture in 'exceptional circumstances,' the judges flouted the absolute prohibition
incorporated in the UN Convention against Torture and endorsed the
Minister's prerogative to interpret the ambit of such exceptional circumstances in a largely unfettered manner. Neither the appellant nor
any of the eight separate public-interest interveners succeeded in per-
suading the Court that the legislation's failure to define 'terrorism' or
'membership' was unconstitutional (*Suresh* 2002; Kelley 2004, 276–82).

The Supreme Court released its decision in *Suresh* in early 2002. On
the very same day, the Court authorized the deportation of another
Convention refugee, Mansour Ahani, on the basis that his case failed to
disclose a prima facie risk of torture (*Ahani* 2002).[25] By 2005, five Muslim men were facing deportation to countries where Amnesty International has indicated they face a risk of torture (Egypt, Algeria, Morocco,
and Syria). All had been named threats to national security pursuant to
ministerial certificates issued between 1999 and 2003, and all five had
been jailed – with one man, Adil Charkaoui, recently released under
stringent bail conditions (AI 2005).

Hassan Almrei, one of the four currently jailed on a security certifi-cate, is a refugee who fears return to his native Syria. Government law-yers, arguing against a stay of his deportation order, suggested in Federal Court that Almrei faced no personal risk of torture if returned to Syria, just when human rights monitors and even the U.S. Department of State had documented that torture in detention was routine in Syria and that members and associates of the Muslim Brotherhood, such as Almrei, were at particular risk. The lawyers offered an alternative argument as well: in the event that a risk of torture could be substanti-ated, the 'exceptional' danger posed by Almrei justified deportation. Although most of the evidence upon which this assessment was based has not been disclosed on national security grounds, the essence of the government's case appears to be that Almrei 'is a member of an inter-national network of extremist individuals who support the Islamic extremist ideals espoused by Osama Bin Laden and that Almrei is involved in a forgery ring with international connections that produces false documents' (Re Almrei 2001). In a candid affidavit, Almrei has offered convincing explanations of his activities, including time spent as a teenager in a weapons training camp in pre-Taliban Afghanistan with anti-Soviet factions (Freeze and Abbate 2003). Without access to the clas-sified evidence, a thorough analysis is impossible. It can be stated with certainty, however, that unlike Suresh, Almrei was not even alleged to have played an important role with an organization directly or indi-rectly affiliated with terrorist activities. To the extent that exceptional circumstances could not justify Suresh's deportation, it is hard to ratio-nalize the exercise of such extraordinary discretion in Almrei's case. On what basis, then, have federal officials decided to invoke these special security measures? The government could have elected to deny Alm-rei's permanent residence application on grounds of security inadmis-sibility and either sought to deport him at that stage or simply permitted him to remain in Canada in limbo and under close surveillance, as it had elected to do in the cases of many other Convention refugees through-out the 1990s (Aiken 2001). Equally possible would be the prospect of prosecuting Almrei under the antiterrorism amendments of the Crimi-nal Code. None of these options were pursued. The government seems to be sending a clear signal that when it comes to non-citizens, being Muslim with some unseemly associations may be all that is necessary to justify the invocation of secret hearings and mandatory, indefinite detention in unacceptable conditions.

At the time of writing, Almrei has been detained in solitary confinement in a 'transitory' detention facility for over three-and-a-half years. His lawyers were forced to seek a judicial order to afford him the right to wear shoes on the cold concrete floor of his jail cell (*Almrei* 2003). In a separate case, the constitutionality of the indefinite detention regime pursuant to which Almrei was detained has been upheld. The Federal Court of Appeal was satisfied that the detention provisions had 'a close and direct relationship to the objectives of the IRPA, the obligation to ensure the protection of national security and the *right of the Parliament of Canada to control the access to and sojourn in Canada of permanent residents'* (*Charkaoui* 2004: para. 130; emphasis added). Reinforcing the Supreme Court's reasoning in *Chiarelli*, the status of an individual as a non-citizen is seen by the Court as a relevant factor in determining whether someone can remain in the country. The notion that someone's status, in itself, should be the primary lens for assessing the fairness or constitutionality of the procedures invoked to detain that person is perverse (Jackman 2005, 9). Meanwhile, the Federal Court of Appeal has given Almrei a temporary reprieve from deportation, ordering that his case be reconsidered by another delegate with regard to the risk he faces upon return to Syria as well as the risk he poses to the security of Canada. The Court declined to consider a constitutional challenge of the provisions that permit removal to torture, a matter that is currently the subject of ongoing litigation and may yet return to the Supreme Court (*Almrei* 2005).

Conclusion

Reva Siegel has observed that history can serve many purposes in law, but most often it functions to preserve the authority of the past (Siegel 1997, 1146). In advancing rights-based claims in the courts today, however, advocates are assuming a distinctive stance towards the past. Rather than turning to the past as a source of legitimation, constitutional argument often seeks to deconstruct and repudiate traditional practices. In the American context, Siegel demonstrates how repudiating past practices has both preservative and transformative effects: it facilitates continuity as well as rupture (Siegel 1997). The act of repudiating past practices can exculpate present practices if we characterize the wrongs of the past narrowly enough to differentiate them from current regulatory forms.

In the United States, early constitutionalism legalized slavery. In the nineteenth century, slavery was abolished on constitutional grounds and a regime of segregation and lynching was produced, usurping slavery as a new form of racial injustice. In the 1950s, the American Supreme Court dismantled segregation in the landmark decision of *Brown v. Board of Education*, but its swift adoption of the 'discriminatory purpose' doctrine (which requires plaintiffs to demonstrate that those acting on behalf of the state intended to discriminate, in order to successfully challenge apparently neutral state actions alleged to discriminate on the basis of 'race') continues to sustain racial stratification in America today. While constitutionalism in Canada is distinct from the United States, the American experience offers an interesting vantage from which to evaluate our own struggles with law and justice. Through a contemporary lens, we can easily condemn the 'race'-based classifications in the earlier immigration laws and practices just as we repudiate an appellate court's reasoning in *Munshi Singh* concerning a challenge to the continuous journey rule and the grounding of the *Komagata Maru* in 1914: 'Better that peoples of non-assimilative – and by nature properly non-assimilative – race should not come to Canada, but rather, that they should remain of residence in their country of origin and there do their share, as they have in the past, in the preservation and development of the Empire' (*Re The Immigration Act and Munshi Singh* 1914).

Yet Siegel challenges us to inquire into whether we have really broken decisively with our past or whether we have merely adopted a new rule structure to legitimate the same substantive inequalities. Despite significant changes in Canadian immigration law over the past thirty years, we can still see the continuity of historic racism in the neo-racist stratification that remains embedded in the fabric of the law. With the exception of the admission and mobility guarantees of section 6, the text of the Charter appears to apply to 'everyone' regardless of status or location. Yet historically and today, judges, policy makers, and parliamentarians operate on the contrary assumption that non-citizens, by reference to their status alone, are to be accorded diminished forms of both substantive rights and due process. In the area of immigration, constitutionalism has not only failed to dismantle the discriminatory policy and practice of border control, it has perpetuated injustice and subverted our attention from the wider terrain of conflict. Charter litigation may have achieved limited gains for certain sectors in Canadian society but there is little evidence that any dents have been made with regard to systemic racism (Herman 1997, 213). As I have attempted to demonstrate in this chapter, constitutional challenges of immigration law and policy may occasionally redress some of the manifestations of racism, but they can only do so in an incremental and individualized manner.

Constitutionalism or 'the judicialization of politics' has been steadily expanding throughout the world (Tate and Vallinder 1995, 5). In South Africa, for example, the new anti-apartheid regime moved swiftly to adopt a constitution with entrenched equality guarantees and a prominent role for the courts. Yet the structures of racism are deeply embedded in South African society, and the Constitution has failed to deliver the promise of social transformation. The liberation struggle in South Africa originated in the ideal of anti-apartheid combined with socialism: that is, in the sense of a radical project of equality. Instead, what has been achieved is anti-apartheid within the structures of globalized capitalism – a system that is predicated on racism and inequality. Similarly, here in Canada, constitutionalism, even in the context of litigation informed by critical race theory, is not competent to disrupt the structures of racism and exclusion that underpin the federal immigration program. As Fitzpatrick suggests, law by its very nature is unable to counter racism because 'racism marks the constitutive boundaries of law,' placing 'persistent limits on its competence and scope' (Fitzpatrick 1990, 250). Thus, the task of forging truly antiracist immigration laws has to be a profoundly political struggle that should be inseparable from a larger project of social justice and grounded in a fundamental transformation of individual and collective consciousness as well as social institutions.

Notes

I am grateful to R. Cheran, Harry Arthurs, Sherene Razack, and Emily Carasco for helpful comments on earlier drafts of this paper.

1 These exclusions are found in sections 33–42 of the IRPA.
2 One notable exception is Michael Mandel's analysis (1994, 240–57), which was the inspiration for my own interest in this area. For the British context, see also Susan Sterett (1997, 183–95) and Stephen H. Legomsky (1987).
3 Hall's more recent writing, informed by strands of postmodernist theory, emphasizes cultural constructions of 'race' but does not deny the importance of political economy. See, for example, his 'New Ethnicities' (1996).
4 In his introduction to *Color Conscious* (Appiah and Gutmann 1996), Wilkins

comments on the picture painted by advocates of 'class, not race,' noting that in the United States black middle-class workers are nearly twice as likely as their white counterparts to become unemployed.

5 For an excellent review of the contours of this debate in Canada, see Kent Roach (2001).

6 Uma Narayan suggests that the feminist notion of the 'epistemic privilege of the oppressed' means that outsiders must sensitize themselves to the fact that insiders may have more subtle and complex understanding of the ways in which oppression operates and is experienced (Narayan 1988).

7 Harry Arthurs and Brent Arnold offer an instructive review of the range of positive Charter-related commentary generated by judges and lawyers as well as by social activists and equality-seeking groups in the 1980s (Arthurs and Arnold, forthcoming).

8 While farmers and farm managers are included in the National Occupation List used as the basis for skilled-worker selection, only owners or individuals with significant managerial experience are awarded points. The government *may* even require a college diploma in agriculture as a condition of admission.

9 The Live-in Care Giver program permits workers to apply for permanent residence after completing two years of employment within a three-year period. In contrast, the Seasonal Agricultural Worker program is premised on workers returning home upon completion of temporary contracts. In the past few years, the federal government has piloted other temporary work programs including a software pilot project and CREWS – the Construction Recruitment External Workers Services Program.

10 Section 139(1)(g) of the *Immigration and Refugee Protection Regulations* indicates that 'successful establishment' will take account of the following factors: (i) the refugee's 'resourcefulness and other similar qualities that assist in integration in a new society, (ii) the presence of their relatives, including the relatives of a spouse or a common-law partner, or their sponsor in the expected community of resettlement, (iii) their potential for employment in Canada, given their education, work experience and skills, and (iv) their ability to learn to communicate in one of the official languages of Canada.' According to section 139 (2) these criteria do not apply to refugees who have been determined by an officer to be vulnerable or in urgent need of protection. In the case of refugees destined for Quebec, different rules apply [s. 139(1)(h)].

11 This was the view of Justices Wilson, Dickson, and Lamer. Although the court was unanimous in result, it was split on the question of the Charter's applicability to the case. Nevertheless, Justice Wilson's reasoning soon

became the accepted point of departure for the Court in terms of refugee cases.

12 For an analysis of the *Chiarelli* decision, see Eliadis 1993.

13 Section 46.04 (8) of the former Immigration Act stated: 'An immigration officer shall not grant landing either to an applicant under subsection (1) or to any dependent of the applicant until the applicant is in possession of a valid and subsisting passport or travel document or a satisfactory identity document.'

14 The Undocumented Convention Refugee in Canada Class also applied to Afghan refugees.

15 In 2000, an estimated 60 per cent of refugee claimants arrived in Canada without adequate documents or false documents (Office of the Auditor General 2003, chapter 5, section 5.95).

16 Section 101 of the IRPA provides that a claim is ineligible to be referred to the Refugee Protection Division of the Immigration and Refugee Board where a prior refugee claim has been made; where the claimant has Convention refugee status in another country and can be returned to that country; where the claimant could have sought protection in a country prescribed by the regulations as 'safe' before arriving in Canada; and where the claimant has been determined to be inadmissible on grounds of security, violating human or international rights, serious criminality, or organized criminality.

17 In 2004 only 2.7 per cent of decisions from this procedure were positive (Janet Dench, email to CCRList, 23 April 2005). See also CCR 2005.

18 In testimony before a parliamentary committee in 2002, Judith Kumin, former representative of the United Nations High Commissioner for Refugees in Canada, cited the example of Germany. When refugee claims became illegal at German land borders after adoption of a safe third country rule in 1993, the claims received at land borders dropped from 100,000 annually to zero almost overnight. Since then, the overall numbers shot back up to previous levels with all claims being pursued inland (Canada 2002). See also Hayter 2004.

19 See CIC 2005, IP-5, section 5.21. The former policy was contained in Employment and Immigration Canada *Examination and Enforcement, IE-9*. Section 9.06 of IE-9 set out the 'public policy' grounds which would warrant favourable consideration and included the category of 'illegal de facto residents.'

20 For example, in *Selliah v. Canada* 2004, the Court found that an immigration officer's decision concerning the risk faced by a child if removed to Sri

Lanka was not unreasonable because the officer had duly considered the child's application separately from his parents, considered his young age, that he had not attended school, and that he had limited integration in Canadian society. Application of the *Baker* principles has failed to offer overseas visa applicants much beyond the barest form of due process: see *Khairoodin v. Canada* 1999 and *Hayama v. Canada* 2003.

21 The Court denied the intervention request of a coalition consisting of the African Canadian Legal Clinic, the Congress of Black Women of Canada and the Jamaican Canadian Association (*Baker v. Canada*, [1997]). The Coalition had sought to introduce a critical race analysis into the case.

22 CIC 2005, IP-5, section 12.10, Separation of parents and children.

23 Although 2003–04 statistics on removals with country of destination information were unavailable at the time of writing, Marie Chen, litigation lawyer with the African Canadian Legal Clinic, indicates that the clinic has continued to see through their work 'a disturbing number of deportations of Black men to Caribbean countries, many of whom have lived in Canada since their childhood' (email to author, 18 April 2005).

24 See also the more recent cases of *Canada v. Mahjoub* and *Re Harkat* for similar reasoning.

25 For commentary on the Convention against Torture, its status in domestic law and the judgments in the *Suresh* and *Ahani* cases, see Heckman 2003.

References

ACLC. 1999. *No clear and present danger: The expulsion of African Canadian residents from Canada*. Toronto: African Canadian Legal Clinic.
– 2001. *Eliminating racism: Linking local and global strategies for change, immigration and refugee issues: Promoting full participation and reversing the tide of criminalization and expulsion*. Brief to UN World Conference Against Racism. Toronto: African Canadian Legal Clinic. http://www.aclc.net/un_conference/report10.html.
Agnew, Vijay. 1996. *Resisting discrimination: Women from Asia, Africa, and the Caribbean and the women's movement in Canada*. Toronto: University of Toronto Press.
AI. 1998. Amnesty International Index, ASA 37/19/1998; ASA 37/21/98.
– 2005. *Security certificates: Time for reform*. Take Action, Amnesty International Canada, March. http://www.amnesty.ca/take_action/actCertificates_300305.php.

Aiken, Sharryn J. 2001. Of gods and monsters: National security and Canadian refugee policy. *Revue Québécoise de Droit International* 14 (2): 1–51.

Aiken, Sharryn J., and Andrew Brouwer. 2004. The stroke of a pen. *Globe and Mail*, 14 October.

Anthias, Floya, and Nira Yuval-Davis. 1993. *Racialized boundaries: Race, nation, gender, colour and class and the anti-racist struggle*. London: Routledge.

Appiah, K. Anthony, and Amy Gutmann. 1996. *Color conscious: The political morality of race*. Princeton: Princeton University Press.

Arat-Koc, Sedef. 1999. 'Good enough to work but not good enough to stay': Foreign domestic workers and the law. In *Locating Law, Race/Class/Gender Connections*, ed. E. Comack and Sedef Arat-Koc, 125–6. Halifax: Fernwood.

Arthurs, Harry, and Brent Arnold. Forthcoming. Does the Charter matter? *Review of Constitutional Studies*.

Aylward, Carol. 1999. *Canadian critical race theory: Racism and the law*. Halifax: Fernwood.

Bahdi, Reem. 2003. No exit: Racial profiling and Canada's war against terrorism. *Osgoode Hall Law Journal* 41 (2, 3): 293–317.

Bakan, Joel. 1997. *Just words: Constitutional rights and social wrongs*. Toronto: University of Toronto Press.

Balibar, Étienne. 1991. Es gibt keinen Staat in Europa: Racism and politics in Europe today. *New Left Review* 186 (March–April): 5–19.

Basok, Tanya. 2002. *Tortillas and tomatoes: Transmigrant Mexican harvesters in Canada*. Montreal: McGill-Queen's University Press.

Bell, Derrick. 2004. *Race, racism and American law*. 5th ed. New York: Aspen.

Berger, Thomas R. 1984. Towards the regime of tolerance. In *Political thought in Canada: Contemporary perspectives*, ed. S. Brooks, 83–96. Toronto: Irwin Publishing.

Bolaria, B. Singh, and Peter S. Li. 1988. *Racial oppression in Canada*. 2nd ed. Toronto: Garamond.

Brewer, Rose M. 1997. Theorizing race, class, and gender: The new scholarship of black feminist intellectuals and black women's labour. In *Materialist feminism: A reader in class, difference, and women's lives*, ed. R. Hennessy and C. Ingraham, 236–47. London: Routledge.

Brodkey, Linda.1987. Writing critical ethnographic narratives. *Anthropology and Education Quarterly* 18:67–76.

Brouwer, Andrew. 1999. *What's in a name? Identity documents and convention refugees*. Ottawa: Caledon Institute of Social Policy.

Campaign 2000. 2005. *Decision time for Canada: Let's make poverty history.* 2005

Report card on child poverty in Canada. http://www. campaign2000.ca/rc/
    rc05/index.html.
Canada. 2002. 37th Parliament, 2nd Session, Standing Committee on Citizen-
    ship and Immigration. *Evidence*, 19 November.
Casasola, Michael. 2001. Current trends and new challenges for Canada's reset-
    tlement program. *Refuge* 19 (4): 76–83.
Castells, Manuel. 1997. *The rise of the network society.* Cambridge: Blackwell.
CBSA. 2004. Departmental performance report, 2003–2004. Ottawa: Canada
    Border Services Agency.
CCR. 1997. *Impact of the right of landing fee.* Montreal: Canadian Council for Ref-
    ugees, February. http://www.web.net/~ccr/doceng.htm.
– 2001. Revised 2002. *Refugees and security.* Montreal: Canadian Council for
    Refugees. http://www.web.net/~ccr/doceng.htm.
– 2004. *Anti-terrorism and the security agenda: Impacts on rights, freedoms and
    democracy.* Forum of the International Civil Liberties Monitoring Group,
    Canadian Council for Refugees. http://www.web.net/~ccr/fronteng.htm.
– 2005. *The refugee appeal: Is no one listening?* Montreal: Canadian Council for
    Refugees, 31 March. http://www.web.ca/~ccr/refugeeappeal.pdf.
Choudhry, Sujit. 2001. Equality in the face of terror: Ethnic and racial profiling
    and the Charter. In *The security of freedom: Essays on Canada's anti-terrorism
    bill*, ed. R. Daniels, P. Macklem, and K. Roach, 367–82. Toronto: University of
    Toronto Press.
Chrétien, J. 1986. The negotiation of the Charter: The federal government per-
    spective. In *Litigating the values of a nation: The Canadian Charter of Rights and
    Freedoms*, ed. J.M. Weiler and R.M. Elliot. Toronto: Carswell.
CIC. 1994a. *Immigration statistics 1992.* Ottawa: Citizenship and Immigration
    Canada.
– 1994b. *A broader vision: Immigration and citizenship plan 1995–2000.* Annual
    Report to Parliament. Ottawa: Citizenship and Immigration Canada.
– Ontario Region. 1997. Ontario region danger to the public removals: Statis-
    tics provided to the African Canadian Legal Clinic. Toronto: Citizenship and
    Immigration Canada. 16 September.
– 1998. *A stronger Canada: 1998 Annual immigration plan.* Ottawa: Citizenship
    and Immigration Canada.
– 1999. *Building a strong foundation for the 21st century: New directions for immi-
    gration and refugee policy and legislation.* Ottawa: Citizenship and Immigration
    Canada.
– 2001. Canada–United States issue statement on common security issues.
    News Release. Ottawa: Citizenship and Immigration Canada. 3 December.

– 2004. *Report on plans and priorities, 2004–2005 estimates.* Ottawa: Citizenship and Immigration Canada.
– 2005. *Immigrant Applications in Canada Made on Humanitarian or Compassionate Grounds.* Ottawa: Citizenship and Immigration Canada. Available from http://www.cic.gc.ca/manuals-guides/english/ip/index.html.
Commission. 1995. *Report of the Commission on Systemic Racism in the Ontario criminal justice system.* Toronto: Queen's Printer.
Cook, Verda. 2004. Workers of colour within a global economy: CLC research paper on migrant workers. Ottawa: Canadian Labour Congress. December.
Crenshaw, Kimberlé. 1993. Demarginalizing the intersection of race and sex: A black feminist critique of antidiscrimination doctrine, feminist theory, and antiracist politics. In *Feminist legal theory: Foundations,* ed. D. Kelly Weisberg, 383–98. Philadelphia: Temple University Press.
Dauvergne, Catherine. 2003. Evaluating Canada's new immigration and refugee protection act in its global context. *Alberta Law Review* 41:725–44.
Delgado, Richard, and Jean Stefancic, eds. 2000. *Critical race theory: The cutting edge.* 2nd ed. Philadelphia: Temple University Press.
Dench, Janet. 2004. Detention statistics. Email to Canadian Council for Refugees email list, 23 March.
Derrida, Jacques. 1976. *Of grammatology.* Trans. A. Bass. Chicago: University of Chicago Press.
Eliadis, Pearl. 1993. The swing from Singh: The narrowing application of the Charter in immigration law. 26 Imm. L.R. (2d) 130.
Elliott, Jean Leonard, and Augie Fleras. 1996. *Unequal relations: An introduction to race and ethnic and aboriginal dynamics in Canada.* 2nd ed. Scarborough, ON: Prentice-Hall.
Employment and Immigration Canada. n.d. *Examination and Enforcement.*
Essed, Philomena. 1990. *Everyday racism: Reports from women of two cultures.* California: Hunter House.
Fitzpatrick, Peter. 1990. Racism and the innocence of law. In *Anatomy of racism,* ed. D.T. Goldberg, 247–62. Minneapolis: University of Minnesota Press.
Freeze, Colin, and Gay Abbate. 2003. Almrei reveals 'terror' résumé. *Globe and Mail,* 27 November.
Galabuzi, Grace-Edward. 2001. *Canada's creeping economic apartheid.* Toronto: Canadian Centre for Social Justice Foundation for Research and Education.
Giles, Wenona. 1996. Aid recipients or citizens? In *Development and diaspora: Gender and the refugee experience,* ed. W. Giles, H. Moussa, P. Van Esterik, and V. Foote, 44–59. Dundas, ON: Artemis.

Glasbeek, Harry. 1990. From constitutional rights to 'real' rights. *Windsor Yearbook of Access to Justice* 10:468.

Grewal, San. 2001. Prejudice, yes, but fear? *Toronto Star*, 17 September.

Hall, Stuart. 1996. New ethnicities. In *Stuart Hall: Critical dialogues in cultural studies*, ed. David Morley and Kuang-Hsin Chen, 441–9. London: Routledge.

Hall, Stuart, Charles Critcher, Tony Jefferson, John Clarke, and Brian Robert. 1978. *Policing the crisis: Mugging, the state, and law and order*. London: Macmillan.

Harper, Tim. 2001. Chrétien pledges battle over global terror threat. *Toronto Star*, 18 September.

Harris II, William F. 1982. Bonding word and polity: The logic of American constitutionalism. *American Political Science Review* 76:34–45.

Hartog, Hendrik. 1987. The constitution of aspiration and the rights that belong to us all. *Journal of American History* 74:1013–34.

Hayter, Teresa. 2004. *Open borders: The case against immigration controls*. 2nd ed. London: Pluto.

Heckman, Gerald. 2003. International human rights law norms and discretionary powers: Recent developments. *Canadian Journal of Administrative Law and Practice* 16:31.

Herman, Didi. 1997. The good, the bad, and the smugly: Sexual orientation and perspectives on the Charter. In Schneiderman and Sutherland 1997, 200–17.

Hodge, John L. 1990. Equality: Beyond dualism and oppression. In *Anatomy of racism*, ed. D.T. Goldberg, 89–107. Minneapolis: University of Minnesota Press.

IACHR. 2000. *Report on the situation of human rights of asylum seekers within the Canadian refugee determination system*. Inter-American Commission on Human Rights, OEA/Ser.L./V/II.106/Doc.40 rev., paras. 143–57. http://www.cidh.org./countryrep/Canada2000en/table-of-contents.

ICLMG. 2003. *In the shadow of the law: A report by the International Civil Liberties Monitoring Group (ICLMG) in Response to Justice Canada's 1st Annual Report on the Application of the Anti-Terrorist Act (Bill C-36)*. http://www.interpares.ca/en/publications/pdf/shadow_of_the_law.pdf.

IOM. 2003. Facts and figures on international migration. *Migration Policy Issues* 2 (March). International Organization for Migration. http://www.iom.int/iomwebsite/Publication/ServletSearchPublication?event=detail&id=2213.

Jackman, Barbara. 2005. One measure of justice in Canada: Judicial protection for non-citizens. Paper presented at the Canadian Bar Association Annual Conference, Banff, Alberta.

Jakubowski, Lisa Marie. 1997. *Immigration and the legalization of racism.* Halifax: Fernwood.

– 1999. 'Managing' Canadian immigration: Racism, ethnic selectivity, and the law. In *Locating law: race/class/gender connections,* ed. E. Comack and Sedef Arat-Koc, 98–104. Halifax: Fernwood.

Jhappan, Radha, ed. 2002. *Women's legal strategies in Canada.* Toronto: University of Toronto Press, 2002.

Jiminéz, Marina, Colin Freeze, and Victoria Burnett. 2003. Case of 19 terrorists unravelling. *Globe and Mail,* 30 August.

Jiminéz, Marina. 2005. Canada's welcome mat frayed and unravelling. *Globe and Mail,* 16 April.

Kelley, Ninette. 2004. Rights in the balance: Non-citizens and state sovereignty under the Charter. In *The unity of public law,* ed. D. Dyzenhaus, 253–88. Oxford: Hart.

Kelley, Ninette, and Michael Trebilcock. 1998. *The making of the mosaic: A history of Canadian immigration policy.* Toronto: University of Toronto Press.

Khan, Sami. 2004. Shattering the fantasy of multiculturalism: 'Project thread' and Canada's secret war on immigrants. *Samar* 17 (Summer).

Khandor, Erika et al. 2004. The regularization of non-status immigrants in Canada 1960–2004: Past policies, current perspectives, active campaigns. Ontario Council of Agencies Serving Immigrants. http://www.ocasi.org/status/Regularization_booklet.pdf.

Knowles, Valerie. 1997. *Strangers at our gates: Canadian immigration and immigration policy, 1540–1997.* Toronto: Dundurn.

Langevin, Louise, and Marie-Claire Belleau. 2000. *Trafficking in women in Canada: A critical analysis of the legal framework concerning immigrant live-in caregivers and mail-order brides.* Ottawa: Status of Women Canada.

Lee, Min Sook, director and writer. 2003. *El contrato.* Montreal: National Film Board of Canada.

Legomsky, Stephen H. 1987. *Immigration and the judiciary: Law and politics in Britain and America.* Oxford: Clarendon.

Li, Peter S. 2003. *Destination Canada: Immigration debates and issues.* Don Mills, ON: Oxford University Press.

Li Wai Suen, Rachel. 2000. You sure know how to pick'em: Human rights and migrant farm workers in Canada. *Georgetown Immigration Law Journal* 16 (Fall): 199–227.

Lister, Ruth. 1997. *Citizenship: Feminist perspectives.* New York: New York University Press.

Macklin, Audrey. 1992. Foreign domestic workers: Surrogate housewives or imported servants? *McGill Law Journal* 37:681–760.

– 2002. Public entrance/private member. In *Privatization, law, and the challenge of feminism*, ed. B. Cossman and J. Fudge, 218–64. Toronto: University of Toronto Press.

Mandel, Michael. 1994. *The Charter of Rights and the legalization of politics in Canada*. Toronto: Thomson Educational.

Manfredi, Christopher P. 2001. *Judicial power and the Charter: Canada and the paradox of liberal constitutionalism*. 2nd ed. Toronto: Oxford University Press.

– 2004. *Feminist activism in the Supreme Court: Legal mobilization and the Women's Legal Education and Action Fund*. Vancouver: UBC Press.

Marx, Karl. 1847, 1891. Wage labour and capital. In *The Marx-Engels reader*, 2nd ed., 1978, ed. R.C. Tucker, 203–17. New York: Norton.

– 1871. The Civil War in France, second draft. In *Readings from Karl Marx*, 1989, ed. D. Sayer. London: Routledge.

Matas, David. 1996. Racism in Canadian immigration policy. In *Perspectives on racism and the human services sector*, ed. C. James, 93–103. Toronto: University of Toronto Press.

Matsuda, Mari. 1996. *Where is your body? And other essays on race, gender, and the law*. Boston: Beacon.

Maytree Foundation. 2002. Brief to the Standing Committee on Citizenship and Immigration regarding proposed immigration and refugee protection regulations. 31 January.

Miles, Robert. 1982. *Racism and migrant labour*. Boston: Routledge and Kegan Paul.

Murdie, Robert A. 2002. The housing careers of Polish and Somali newcomers in Toronto's rental market. *Housing Studies* 17:365–80.

Narayan, Uma. 1988. Working together across difference: Some considerations on emotions and political practice. *Hypatia* 3 (2).

Noorani, Arif, and Cynthia Wright. 1995. They believed the hype. *This Magazine* 28 (5).

Ng, Roxanna. 1993. Racism, sexism, and immigrant women. In *Changing patterns: Women in Canada*, 2nd ed., ed. S. Burt, L. Code, and L. Dorney, 184–203. Toronto: McClelland and Stewart.

Office of the Auditor General. 2003. Report of the Auditor General of Canada.

OHRC. 2003. *Paying the price: The human cost of racial profiling*. Inquiry Report. Toronto: Ontario Human Rights Commission.

Ornstein, Michael. 2000. *Ethno-racial inequality in the City of Toronto: An analysis of the 1996 census*. Toronto: City of Toronto, Access and Equity Unit, Strategic and Corporate Policy Division, Chief Administrator's Office.

Outlaw, Lucius. 1990. Toward a critical theory of 'race.' In *Anatomy of racism*, ed. D.T. Goldberg, 58–82. Minneapolis: University of Minnesota Press.

Pratt, Anna, and Mariana Valverde. 2002. From deserving victim to 'masters of confusion': Redefining refugees in the 1990s. *Canadian Journal of Sociology* 27 (2): 135–62.

Preston, Valerie. 2003. Gender, inequality and borders. *ACME: An International E-Journal for Critical Geographies* 2 (2): 183–7. http://www.acme-journal.org.

Rawls, John. 1993. *Political liberalism*. New York: Columbia University Press.

Razack, Sherene. 1998. *Looking white people in the eye: Gender, race, and culture in courtrooms and classrooms*. Toronto: University of Toronto Press.

– 2000. 'Simple logic': Race, the identity documents rule, and the story of a nation besieged and betrayed. *Journal of Law and Social Policy* 15:181–209.

Roach, Kent. 2001. *The Supreme Court on trial: Judicial activism or democratic dialogue*. Toronto: Irwin Law.

Russell, Peter. 1983. The political purposes of the Canadian Charter of Rights and Freedoms. *Canadian Bar Review* 6:30.

Satzewich, Vic, ed. 1998. *Racism and social inequality in Canada: Concepts, controversies and strategies of resistance*. Toronto: Thompson Educational.

Schneiderman, D., and K. Sutherland, eds. 1997. *Charting the consequences: The impact of charter rights on Canadian law and politics*. Toronto: University of Toronto Press.

Sharma, Nandita. 2005. White nationalism, illegality and imperialism: Border controls as ideology. In *(En) Gendering the war on terror: War stories and camouflaged politics*, ed. K. Hunt and K. Rygiel, 117–39. Aldershot: Ashgate.

Sharma, Nandita, and Donna Baines. 2002. Migrant workers as non-citizens: The case against citizenship as a social policy concept. *Studies in Political Economy* 69 (Autumn): 442–66.

Shephard, Michelle, and Sonia Verma. 2003. They only arrested the Muhammads. *Toronto Star*, 30 November.

Siegel, Reva. 1997. Why equal protection law no longer protects: The evolving forms of status enforcing state action. *Stanford Law Review* 49:1111.

Silvera, Makeda. 1983. *Silenced: Makeda Silvera talks with working class West Indian women about their lives and struggles as domestic workers in Canada*. Toronto: Williams-Wallace.

Simmons, Alan. 1998. Racism and immigration policy. In *Racism and social inequality in Canada: Concepts, controversies & strategies of resistance*, ed. Vic Satzewich, 87–114. Toronto: Thompson Educational.

Smart, Carol. 1989. *Feminism and the power of law*. London: Routledge.

Stasiulis, Daiva, and Nira Yuval-Davis, eds. 1995. *Unsettling settler societies: Articulations of gender, race, ethnicity and class*. London: Sage.

Sterett, Susan. 1997. *Creating constitutionalism? The politics of legal expertise and administrative law in England and Wales*. Ann Arbor: University of Michigan Press.

St Lewis, Joanne. 2001. Canadian critical race theory and the law: An overview. Presentation to Regional Lawyers' Meetings 27 January and 3 March. In *Consultation Report*, ed. F. Niemi. Montreal: Center for Research–Action on Race Relations.

Tate, C. Neal, and Torbjörn Vallinder, eds. 1995. *The global expansion of judicial power*. New York: New York University Press.

Tie, Chantal. 1995. Immigrant selection and section 15 of the Charter: A study of the equality rights of applicants for admission to Canada. LLM thesis, University of Ottawa, Faculty of Law.

– 1998. Only discriminating visa officers need apply: Visa officer decisions, the Charter and *Lee v. Canada (Minister of Citizenship and Immigration)* Imm. L.R. 2d. 42:197–209.

Tully, James. 1995. *Strange multiplicity: Constitutionalism in an age of diversity*. Cambridge: Cambridge University Press.

Turpel, Mary Ellen. 1989–90. Aboriginal peoples and the Canadian Charter: Interpretive monopolies, cultural differences. *Canadian Human Rights Yearbook* 3.

UNHCR. 2004. *2003 global refugee trends*. Geneva: United Nations High Commissioner for Refugees.

Verma, Sonia. 2004. Our dreams are now dust. *Toronto Star*, 8 February.

Vizkelety, Béatrice. 1987. *Proving discrimination in Canada*. Toronto: Carswell.

Walker, James W.St.G. 1997. *'Race,' rights and the law in the Supreme Court of Canada: Historical Case Studies*. Waterloo, ON: Wilfred Laurier University Press, Osgoode Society for Canadian Legal History.

Walzer, Michael. 1983. *Spheres of justice: A defense of pluralism and equality*. New York: Basic.

Winks, Robin W. 1971. *The blacks in Canada: A history*. Montreal: McGill-Queen's University Press.

Worswick, Christopher. 2004. Immigrants' declining earnings: Reasons and remedies. C.D. Howe Institute *Backgrounder* 81 (April): 1–11.

Yamamoto, Eric. 1997. Critical race praxis: race theory and political lawyering practice in post-civil rights America. *Michigan Law Review* 95:821.

Legislation and Case Law

Ahani v. Canada (1996), 201 N.R. 233 (Fed. C.A.), leave to appeal to the S.C.C. dismissed [1996] S.C.C.A. No. 496.

Ahani v. Canada (Minister of Citizenship and Immigration), [2002] 1 S.C.R. 72.
Almrei v. Canada (Attorney General), [2003] O.J. No. 5198.
Almrei v. Canada (Minister of Citizenship and Immigration), [2005] F.C.J. No. 213
    (Fed. C.A.) leave to appeal to the S.C.C. pending.
Andrews v. Law Society of British Columbia, [1989] 1 S.C.R. 143.
Baker v. Canada, [1997] S.C.C.A. No. 85.
Baker v. Canada (Minister of Citizenship and Immigration), [1999] 2 S.C.R. 817.
Canada v. Mahjoub, [2001] F.C.J. No.1483 (Fed. T.D.).
Canadian Charter of Rights and Freedoms. 1982. Part I of the *Constitution Act*,
    being Schedule B to the *Canada Act 1982* (U.K.), 1982, c. 11.
Charkaoui v. Canada (Minister of Citizenship and Immigration), [2004] F.C.J. No.
    2060 (C.A.), leave to appeal to the S.C.C. pending.
Chiarelli v. Canada (Minister of Citizenship and Immigration), [1992] 1 S.C.R. 711.
Dehghani v. Canada (Minister of Employment and Immigration, [1993] 1 S.C.R.
    1053.
Deol v. Canada (Minister of Citizenship and Immigration), [2003] 1 F.C. 301 (C.A.).
Francis (Litigation guardian of) v. Canada (Minster of Citizenship and Immigration)
    (1999), 49 O.R. (3d) 136 (Ont. C.A.), leave to appeal to the S.C.C. granted
    S.C.C. Bulletin 2000, p. 1018, motion to quash granted [1999] S.C.C.A. No.
    558.
Hayama v. Canada (Minister of Citizenship and Immigration) (2003), 33 Imm. L.R.
    (3d) 89 (Fed. T.D.).
IRPA. 2001. *Immigration and Refugee Protection Act*, S.C. 2001, c. 27.
Khairoodin v. Canada, [1999] F.C.J. No. 1256 (T.D.).
Lee v. Canada (Minister of Citizenship and Immigration) (1997), 126 F.T.R. 229.
Minister of Citizenship and Immigration v. Williams, [1997] F.C.J. No. 393 (C.A.),
    leave to appeal to the S.C.C. refused, [1997] S.C.C.A. No. 332.
Nguyen v. Canada (Minister of Employment and Immigration, [1993] 1 F.C. 696
    (C.A.).
RIAS. 2001. *Immigration and Refugee Protection Regulations, Regulatory Impact
    Analysis Statement. Canada Gazette*. 135 (50).
R. v. Cook, [1998] 2 S.C.R. 597.
Re Almrei, [2001] F.C.J. No. 1772 (T.D.).
Re Harkat, [2005] F.C.J. No. 481 (T.D.).
Re Singh and Minister of Employment and Immigration, [1985] 1 S.C.R. 177.
Re Suresh (1997), 40 Imm. L.R. (2d) 247 (Fed.T.D.).
Re The Immigration Act and Munshi Singh, [1914] 6 W.W.R. 1347.
Ruparel v. Canada (Minister of Employment and Immigration) (1990), 11 Imm. L.R.
    (2d) 190 (Fed. T.D.).

Selliah v. Canada (Minister of Citizenship and Immigration), [2004] F.C.J. No. 1134.
Shah v. Minister of Employment and Immigration (1994), 170 N.R. 238 (Fed. C.A.).
Solis v. Canada (Minister of Citizenship and Immigration) (2000), 4 Imm. L.R. (3d) 189 (Fed. C.A.).
Suresh v. Canada (Minister of Citizenship and Immigration), [2002] 1 S.C.R. 3.

3 Citizenship, Illegality, and Sanctuary

JEAN MCDONALD

Formal citizenship, according to James Holston, refers to membership within a nation-state (1998, 50). Substantive citizenship, on the other hand, comprises a variety of rights – civil, political and / or social, which may or may not be accessed through formal citizenship. Formal citizenship, scholars suggest in recent studies, is no longer an integral factor in securing substantive citizenship (Holston and Appadurai 1999; Soysal 1999). Yet studies of illegality in the context of immigration demonstrate the difficulties of exercising substantive citizenship without full legal status or permanent residency in a country. Scholars have examined the ways in which migrants are made illegal, calling attention to the processes of illegalization in the context of immigration (Balibar 2003, 2000; De Genova 2002; Lowry and Nyers 2003; Ong 2003; Sharma 2001, 2002; Walters 2002; Wright 2003). For example, discriminatory requirements of immigration policies, migrant worker programs, and refugee determination practices are identified as some of the political processes that make refugees and migrants 'illegal.' Threats of detention and deportation leave non-status immigrants extremely vulnerable to exploitation by employers, spouses, landlords, community workers, and authority figures such as police or immigration officers. Canada's immigration policies are no longer overtly racist, yet institutional racism thrives in a system that divides people into separate classes of deserving and undeserving.

In this chapter, I draw upon the idea of substantive citizenship, along with Étienne Balibar's notion of 'active citizenship' (used to describe the *sans-papiers* movement in France), to examine citizenship in Canada as a collective practice rather than one of status alone. Through an examination of three central examples, I argue that in Canada, formal citizenship, or full legal status, remains a key component in accessing substantive citizen rights. First, I look at the ways in which the Action Committee of Non-Status Algerians/Comité d'action des sans-statuts algériens (CASSA) in Montreal, Quebec, has activated citizenship through its demand for full legal status for non-status immigrants living in Canada. Second, through the case of Mohamed Cherfi, a member of CASSA, I explore how an emerging sanctuary movement in Canada recreates the categories of 'deserving' and 'undeserving' immigrants. Third, in the example of the Don't Ask, Don't Tell Campaign in Toronto, Ontario, I examine the idea of sanctuary cities.

In many parts of the world, being a member of society means being a 'rights-bearing citizen of a territorial nation-state' (Holston and Appadurai 1999, 1). Nation-states work to establish citizenship as the identity that subsumes all others, with the symbolic intent of creating a 'universal citizen.' As a result, local stratifications and privileges are eroded in favour of equal rights. Yet the political mobilization of those who are excluded from the ideal of universal equality calls into question beliefs about democracy and citizenship (1–2). Holston and Appadurai argue that 'formal membership in the nation-state is increasingly neither a necessary nor a sufficient condition for substantive citizenship' (4). Although there is some acceptance of this premise by scholars, I contend nevertheless that full legal status continues to be critical to the exercise of substantive citizenship. The struggle of non-status immigrants reveals the significant roles that illegality and the threat of deportation play in the lives of people without full legal status in Canada, in the process demonstrating the ways in which citizenship is reconfigured.

Citizenship, both formal and substantive, is intricately connected with nationalism and racism. Citizenship is manifested through processes that include and exclude; it is a practice and a status, and becomes an indicator of the Othering necessary to the creation and reproduction of the nation-state. Citizenship is a marker of belonging within the community of the nation. Historically, as Lee argues in this volume in her discussion of Japanese-Americans and Arab-Americans, racism appears in the guise of nationalism, particularly during war, to establish the boundaries of who does or does not belong to the nation. Creese, also in this volume, shows how factors such as accent, language, physical appearance, and dress create boundaries for women who immigrate to Canada from Africa, thereby excluding and robbing them of a sense of belonging to the Canadian nation. The connection between racism and nationalism is one of mutual conditioning rather than a perversion of nationalism. The nation is constituted and homogenized as an imagined social space with a specific body politic, and that can only occur, writes Torfing, through the simultaneous construction of 'enemies of the nation' (1999, 193). In Canada, people who are denied legal immigration status are often constructed as 'unlawful' or 'deviant,' and considered 'outsiders' to the Canadian nation, thus legitimizing their detention and deportation. In contemporary times, racism frequently manifests itself as culturalism or cultural racism.[1] Bannerji notes that the 'official multiculturalism' of the Canadian nation rests upon the positioning of 'Canadian culture' against 'multicultures.' She points out that 'an element of whiteness quietly enters into cultural definitions, marking the difference between a core cultural group and other groups who are represented as cultural fragments' (2000, 10). Racism, Torfing argues, is a necessary supplement to the production of a homogenous national body (1999, 202). Nationalist assumptions such as 'assimilation' and 'integration,' which have historically guided immigration policies, have conveniently allowed the entry of middle- to high-income white Europeans and Americans while becoming barriers to lower- to middle- income people of colour from the global South, as well as people from eastern Europe. Certain groups have become racialized, creating the Other in relation to the Canadian national body.[2] In Canada, the 'imagined nation' has involved the production, differentiation, and stigmatization of Others; thus, nationalism and racism have become intertwined in discourses that racialize some individuals and groups, as discussed in this volume by Li and Lee. Similarly, in the previous chapter Aiken discusses how immigration rules disadvantage racialized immigrants. The majority of people living without full legal status in Canada are racialized individuals from poorer countries. Members of CASSA, as racialized immigrants in Canada, experience discriminatory treatment from the Canadian immigration system and are stigmatized as being 'illegal.'

This chapter challenges the concept of illegality as 'unlawfulness' or 'deviance' as applied to non-status immigrants. CASSA and its supporters have questioned the ways by which a person comes to be classified as illegal and consequences for their citizenship rights. Since its inception, the committee has worked closely with an allied organization that mobilizes under the banner 'No One Is Illegal' (No One Is Illegal–Toronto, 25 April 2004). Similar to members of the 'No Borders' movement in Europe, activists in Canada reject processes that deny the legal personhood of non-status immigrants and construct people as illegal, instead embracing a 'no borders' or 'no one is illegal' framework. Through this political manoeuvre, immigrant-rights advocates avoid legitimizing the production of borders and the construction of illegality. A 'no one is illegal' framework challenges the sovereignty of the Canadian nation-state while recognizing indigenous sovereignty and rights to self-determination.

Reconfiguring Citizenship

In Montreal, a reconfiguration of citizenship as an active, collective practice has taken place through the struggles and resistance of CASSA. The committee came together in April 2002, when a moratorium on deportations to Algeria, originally set in place in March 1997, was lifted by the Canadian state. By pointing out the necessity of formal citizenship (full legal status) to substantive citizenship, members of the committee have remade citizenship as a collective practice, in ways similar to the *sans-papiers* movement in France. Members of CASSA have refused the category of illegality through their formulation of new claims on society and state. Like the *sans-papiers* in France, they have 'ceased to simply play the victims in order to become the actors of democratic politics' (Balibar 2000, 43). As a result, committee members have become visible, demanding rights and recognition from the Canadian state. Their campaign has made them political actors who reject the social space of illegality that erases their legal personhood. This may at first seem to be a paradox: that the demand for full legal status has resulted in active citizenship. Yet this assertion of active citizenship makes possible the demand for formal citizenship, while at the same time demonstrating the importance of legal status in securing substantive citizenship.

Since 1997, failed refugee claimants from Algeria have lived in limbo while finding employment, creating homes, sending their children to school, and settling into communities. Yet as Soumya Boussouf, a member of CASSA, points out in Lowry's and Nyers's Round Table Report, this seemingly normal life is fraught with everyday reminders that she does not have full legal rights in Canada. She states:

It's biding time: you start to work, you start to have friends. After a year, two years, you are involved in many things. When you really realize that you don't have status is when you decide, for example, to take action and, let's say, study. For example, you go to university. I personally did. I was very proud of myself and I said, 'Okay, I am going to get a certificate in accounting because I like it.' I went to McGill University and the person there said to me, 'I am really sorry but it says on your work permit that you have no rights at all to study here. If you want to study, then you have to apply for a study permit at Immigration Canada.' If they give it to you, then you have to pay foreign fees, which is [sic] much more. (2003, 67)

In April 2002, however, this state of normalized limbo abruptly came to a halt. At this time, the Canadian government's moratorium on deportations to Algeria was lifted. Interestingly, the removal of the moratorium coincided with Prime Minister Jean Chrétien's trade mission to Algeria, which resulted in a lucrative trade deal between the two countries involving millions of dollars. It seems that Canada's moratorium on deportations to Algeria would have imperilled the image of the government in this profitable free-trade deal. Over one thousand failed refugee claimants from Algeria were suddenly faced with imminent removal (Lowry and Nyers 2003, 66). Through word of mouth and community networks, the Comité d'action des sans-statut algériens (CASSA) was formed, setting a precedent and an example for other predominantly non-status groups in the Montreal area, such as the Coalition Against the Deportation of Palestinian Refugees and the Action Committee of Pakistanis Against Racial Profiling. The three initial demands of CASSA included an end to deportations to Algeria; a reinstatement of the moratorium on deportations to Algeria; and the regularization of all non-status people in Canada (Wright 2003, 8). CASSA's first set of demands focused specifically on the issues facing non-status Algerians and later broadened to include all non-status immigrants in Canada.

At the height of the committee's initial campaign, the case of Yakout Seddiki, Mourad Bourouisa, and their two-year-old Canadian-born son, Ahmed, became a central rallying point for the committee and its supporters. Support was generated when CASSA created a Women's Committee, which became an integral part of the campaign work and direct action initiatives. It was the Women's Committee that mobilized a delegation of women to visit Immigration Canada's offices in Montreal in support of Seddiki and Bourouisa, and subsequently organized a Women's March in downtown Montreal on 12 October 2002 (STATUS Coalition, 31 January 2003). Facing imminent deportation, the Seddiki-Bourouisa family took sanctuary in a Montreal church in November

2002, making international headlines (Lowry and Nyers 2003, 66). Eleven days after the family's entrance into sanctuary, the Canadian and Quebec governments responded: a ninety-day stay on all deportations to Algeria was granted, and many non-status Algerians were allowed the opportunity to apply for permanent residency through a special regularization procedure (66–7). This regularization, however, fell short of a general amnesty for non-status Algerians – over one hundred were excluded through the strict criteria of the application. Barred from the application process were potential applicants who lived outside the province of Quebec, along with those who had already been served with a deportation order or had already been deported, anyone who had a criminal record of any sort, and/or those who were not able to afford to pay the exorbitant application fees ($550 per adult, $150 per child) (67). Furthermore, those persons permitted to submit an application were then evaluated according to their so-called record of integration (STATUS Coalition, 31 January 2003).[3]

The struggle of CASSA for a regularization procedure demonstrates its members' refusal to accept their illegal status, as well as the importance of full legal status. Legal status is integral to social inclusion, because it shapes the range of rights and entitlements to which a person has access. The threat of detention, the risk of deportation, and the surveillance of their activities are critical issues facing non-status immigrants (Wright 2003). People without full legal status live, work, and pay taxes in Canada, yet they are denied any claims within society and state (Sharma 2002). Practical problems encountered by non-status immigrants include a lack of access to legal support, education, health care, social services, and basic personal security, as well as exposure to exploitative working conditions (Sharma 2001). As Jacqueline Bhabha argues, 'The power of the state as an enforcer of individual rights and as a conduit to entitlements, political, economic or social, is still unrivalled' (1999, 12). While CASSA has mounted a considerable challenge to the Canadian state and has fought for and won a substantial victory in terms of the special regularization procedure, members of the committee have faced significant barriers as well – for example, increasing repression in their daily lives and in their activism. At the same time, they have had to deal with many of the everyday pressures that all non-status immigrants in Canada generally face. Prominent members of the committee have been targeted by immigration-enforcement officials and the police, and their claims for refugee and/or legal status have been denied.

Processes of subjectification, Aihwa Ong notes, involve the social construction of identities and at the same time, the exercise of human agency or conscious action of those who are so constructed (2003, 12). Through this theoretical framework, the processes that define a person as 'illegal' can be understood as created by the state as well as by the technologies of government. These technologies include 'the policies, codes, and practices (unbounded by the concept of culture) that attempt to instill in citizen-subjects particular values (including: self-reliance, freedom, individualism, calculation, or flexibility) in a variety of domains' (6). Michel Foucault has called this governmentality. Who should be governing, who is governed, and how they need to be governed all become explicable through the practices of social institutions and through an examination of official state policy. These technologies of governmentality can be rejected, adjusted or altered by those so targeted and by those who represent authority, such as government officials, immigration officers, and settlement workers. A variety of social services – refugee agencies, community health centres, and welfare offices – construct new immigrants as specific types of clients. In turn, immigrants use a variety of strategies to access the resources they need. In this dual process, subjects and subjectivities are not being constructed unilaterally by those in power, but by immigrant clients participating in defining their personhood within a system of governmentality (Ong 2003, 16–19).

This system of governmentality includes 'techniques of power' designed to study, survey, manipulate, and control the behaviour of individuals located within institutions of various sorts (Gordon 1991, 3–4). In the context of immigration and the processes of illegalization, these institutions range from detention centres, prisons, airports, and immigration offices to schools, hospitals, social housing agencies, and welfare offices. The refusal of CASSA to be labelled illegal has challenged the state and its subject-making ability. CASSA rejects the label of 'illegal' and 'unlawful' and thus, 'deviant.'

One of the techniques of power in this regime of governmentality is the categorization of deviance in opposition to 'normal' status-bearing members of society. The illegality of a person is thus perceived through various technologies of government that define and rationalize the categorization of deserving migrants versus those deemed undesirable or undeserving. As De Genova notes, illegalization itself is a sociopolitical process, one that is 'constituted and regimented by the law' (2002, 424). Regularization procedures, through which non-status immigrants are able to apply for legal status, do not eliminate illegality; instead, illegality is redefined and reconstituted (429). This is demonstrated by the criteria used in the December 2002 special regularization procedure for failed refugee claimants from Algeria living in Quebec, which created new categories of illegality. Before the special regularization procedure came into force, all failed refugee claimants from Algeria were considered illegal by the Canadian state. Although over one thousand applicants were granted permanent residency, over one hundred were denied status and faced deportation. Thus, the process of regularization did not eliminate the category of illegality; rather, it simply reconfigured it.

Regularization reconstitutes illegality, and 'illegal' migrations continue to be produced through state practices of increased border controls and stricter immigration policies. This has further intensified in the post–September 11 period, as Smith documents in this volume. A significant consequence of policies that reproduce illegalization is that non-status immigrants are 'socially include[d] under imposed conditions of enforced and protracted vulnerability ... The social space of "illegality" is an erasure of legal personhood – a space of forced invisibility, exclusion, subjugation, and repression' (De Genova 2002, 427–9). Illegality, then, is a spatialized condition that reproduces the physical borders of the nation-state in the everyday lives of racialized immigrants in countless locations. The *Toronto Star* reports, for example, that when women without full legal immigration status in Canada attempt to press charges on abusive partners, they often subsequently face detention and deportation (Keung 2004). This occurs because city police regularly pass details of the legal status of non-status women on to immigration enforcement officials. In this sense, borders are not only physical boundaries of a nation-state, they are also ideological, and they resurface to impose the social space of illegality on non-status immigrants in a variety of ways. Physical borders and entry points (such as airports) into a nation-state thus expand to include social-housing cooperatives, health centres, schools, food banks, welfare offices, and police stations, among others places. As such, physical and ideological borders affect not only the individual's legal and political rights, but are also implicated in notions of who belongs and who does not (Sharma 2001, 416).

CASSA, through its refusal to be silent and invisible, has exposed as problematic the processes that make people illegal and relegate non-status immigrants to social spaces of invisibility. In making their demands for formal citizenship, its members are rejecting illegality and are becoming active citizens, as defined by Balibar. As Mohamed Cherfi points out, the actions of the committee – distributing flyers, holding rallies, and speaking at conferences, among other activities – have led to greater visibility for non-status people living in Canada. He states: 'It might not be that people know the details, but at least they know that non-status people exist as a result of this activity' (2004, 69). The actions of the committee have challenged the nationalist practice of viewing 'the Self as insider and the Other as foreigner or outsider' (Sharma 2001, 416). In addition, CASSA has exposed the unjust nature of the state's allocation of citizenship to some and not to others. For example, they have challenged the policies of the current immigration system by their ongoing campaign for an inclusive regularization program. The Special Regularization Procedure for Algerians excluded applicants with serious medical conditions and those who did not fit the arbitrary criteria of 'integration.' This is demonstrated in the highly publicized case of Mohamed Cherfi, which is outlined in the next section. For the politically appointed members of the Immigrant and Refugee Board (IRB), there is no well-articulated or standardized measure of what integration entails, thus allowing individual board members to arbitrarily decide who is or is not integrated into Canadian society. Members of CASSA also demonstrated that the IRB did not take into account the situation of several non-status Algerians, including Cherfi, who would face persecution and incarceration in Algeria because of their refusal to serve in the armed forces. In ceasing to be relegated to the social and political spaces allotted to them, members of the committee have rejected the role of passive victimhood. Through this rejection, they have demonstrated the necessity and significance of full status in securing substantive citizenship.

Sanctuary and Multiple Governmentalities

Mohamed Cherfi, a well-respected and outspoken member of the Comité d'action des sans-statuts Algériens, took refuge in Saint-Pierre United Church in Quebec City on 10 February 2004. He decided to seek sanctuary to avoid the detention and subsequent deportation he would surely have faced had he presented himself at the offices of Immigration Canada in Montreal for his appointment on 10 February 2004 to receive the results of his Pre-Removal Risk Assessment (PRRA). Like other members of CASSA, Cherfi is a failed refugee claimant who has resided in Canada for many years, having lived in Montreal since 1997. Cherfi applied for permanent residency under the special regularization for non-status Algerians living in Quebec. On 22 January 2004, however, immigration officers refused Cherfi's application on the basis that he was not fully 'integrated' into Canadian society. Cherfi writes:

> This process [the special regularization procedure] was based on the process of selection, and not on the assurance of protection from deportation to a country in conflict. Moreover, the selection process was based on criteria linked to an evaluation of our ability to 'integrate' into Quebec society, a *very ambiguous and arbitrary process*, in particular for war refugees who have lived for years without status and with the continual anxiety of being eventually deported. (Cherfi 2004; my emphases)

Cherfi's supporters argued that immigration laws can be applied in an arbitrary manner, and that the discretion given to officers in applying the law has led to the unfair decision to not grant him permanent status. Cherfi, his supporters contended, was penalized for his outspoken activism (No One Is Illegal–Toronto, 19 February 2004). After taking sanctuary in the church, Cherfi was forcibly arrested by Sûreté du Québec police officers at approximately 12:30 p.m. on Friday, 5 March 2004. The officers had a warrant for his arrest for breaking previous bail conditions for failing to give notice of a change of address. This charge was immediately dropped upon his arrest, and Cherfi was promptly delivered to the newly established Canadian Border Security Agency. Very soon thereafter, he was deported to the United States and locked in a jail cell at the Batavia Detention Center near Buffalo, New York by 6:30 p.m. – less than six hours after his initial arrest (No One Is Illegal–Toronto, 5 March 2004). Supporters in cities across Canada quickly mobilized, and on Tuesday, 9 March, demonstrations were held in Quebec City, Montreal, Ottawa, Toronto, Guelph, Winnipeg, Edmonton, and Vancouver. One speaker at the Toronto demonstration, held outside then immigration minister Judy Sgro's home, suggested that if claiming sanctuary was now an illegal act, the sanctuary movement was following in an honourable history of illegality – a history that includes those courageous persons who acted 'unlawfully' by helping slaves free themselves and escape the American South, and those who hid Jews in Nazi Germany.

Cherfi's arrest and deportation emphasized the Canadian state's intent to penalize, by whatever means necessary, those who challenge and expose the political and arbitrary ways in which formal citizenship is allocated. Cherfi was deported to the United States rather than directly to Algeria, due to Canada's policy of 'direct backs.' This policy ensures that failed refugee claimants who arrive via the United States are returned to the United States rather than to their country of origin.[4] They can then apply for refugee status from the Immigration and Naturalization Service in the United States. Cherfi, like many failed refugee claimants, is in terrible danger and faces severe hardship if he is forced to return to Algeria. Having left Algeria as a conscientious objector to mandatory military service, he will be subject to five years' imprisonment for this alone under Article 254 of Algeria's Code of Military Justice. In Canada, Cherfi has become a prominent political activist whose criticisms of the Algerian government are widely known. Amnesty International has condemned Cherfi's deportation from Canada, as well as the rejection of his refugee claim and application for permanent residency, and the negative decision on his PRRA. In their June 2003 report, Amnesty International recognized that in Algeria, 'real or presumed opponents of the political system and human rights defenders risk becoming victims of violations to their fundamental rights.' The report goes on to note: 'The motives for persecution can be linked not only to activities, opinions, or membership in groups, but also to political activities, the defence of human rights, or other activities, conducted abroad' (Amnesty International 2004). On 7 April 2004, Cherfi appeared before an immigration judge who denied his application for release on bail (No One Is Illegal–Toronto, 9 April 2004). After a year-and-a-half-long campaign to have Cherfi returned to Canada, he was finally released from U.S. custody in July 2005. His application for refugee status in the United States is pending, and supporters continue to request that Quebec and Canadian immigration authorities issue Cherfi the appropriate documents so that he can return to his home in Montreal (Solidarity Committee for Mohamed Cherfi 2005). The Canadian state, by arresting and deporting Cherfi to the United States (despite the considerable threats he will face if returned to Algeria), clearly targeted this political activist and at the same time violated the tradition of sanctuary for the first time in Canadian history.

In North America, the practice of sanctuary is centuries old. Churches provided a safe resting place for slaves travelling along the Underground Railroad from the American South. During the Vietnam War, when conscientious objectors fled mandatory military service in the

United States, Canadian churches gave them shelter. In Europe, under Nazi rule, churches sometimes provided sanctuary to Jews fleeing Nazi persecution. More recently, churches in Canada (on a limited scale) have been opening their doors to failed refugee claimants. Reverend Brian Burch, a historian of the sanctuary movement, notes that in general, only a minority of Christians in the past and today have offered sanctuary to those in need of a place of refuge (Burch 2003). As immigrant-rights activists have pointed out, there is at present no 'sanctuary movement' per se in Canada. Instead, there are only a small number of generally isolated cases of churches offering sanctuary across the country (Singh and McDonald 2004). Yet mobilization towards a sanctuary movement seems to be building: an information and organizing meeting on the topic was held in Toronto on 22 April 2004. Furthermore, a number of recent cases in Montreal and Quebec City, including that of Mohamed Cherfi, have generated widespread support for the idea and practice of sanctuary.

The Canadian immigration system creates categories of deserving and undeserving immigrants, separating those who 'belong' from those who do not. Ironically, the process of offering sanctuary also creates its own definitions of deserving versus undeserving immigrants and refugees. Most often, when a church congregation decides to provide sanctuary, it will do so for a failed refugee claimant where a mistake by immigration officials is presumed to have occurred. Michael Creal, chair of the Southern Ontario Sanctuary Coalition, offered advice to congregations at a conference entitled 'Community, Solidarity, Sanctuary,' organized in Toronto by No One Is Illegal. Creal advised congregations to be very sure that the failed claimant was really a refugee under the terms set out by the United Nations Convention on Refugees, and that immigration officials who had denied the claim had made a mistake in refusing the person's right to refuge within Canada's territorial boundaries (Creal 2003). If proponents of the sanctuary movement do not oppose the categorization of people into deserving versus undeserving immigrants and refugees, the offering of sanctuary will not pose a substantial challenge to the immigration system. Instead, sanctuary becomes a space where 'mistakes' can be corrected and the legitimacy of the immigration system upheld, albeit indirectly. Despite this, offering sanctuary redefines the spaces of the nation-state and illegality, and as such it is a significant act.

By demonstrating that the state can make mistakes in its adjudication of refugee claims, the burgeoning sanctuary movement draws attention to shortcomings in the refugee-determination process in Canada. In the case of the Ayoub family, who entered into sanctuary in February 2004 in the Notre-Dame-de-Grâce church in Montreal, members of the congregation feel that the family members have been wrongfully denied refugee status.[5] Supporters of the Ayoubs point out that like many other stateless Palestinians facing deportation, if denied legal immigration status, the family would be returned to a refugee camp in Lebanon or occupied Palestine (No One Is Illegal–Toronto, 9 February 2005).

The practice of sanctuary in Canada has generally been associated with larger political movements challenging specific flaws in the immigration system. For instance, one of the major recognized flaws of the Immigrant and Refugee Board (IRB), the governmental bureaucracy that makes decisions on claims for permanent residency based on humanitarian and compassionate grounds and for refugee status, is the lack of an 'in-person' appeals process for refugee claims. This is despite the fact that under the 2002 Immigration Act the implementation of a Refugee Appeals Division is required by law. As well, refugee claims are often heard and adjudicated by one IRB member alone, making the process vulnerable to personal biases and mistakes. Immigrant-rights activists have also questioned the efficacy of using politically appointed IRB members rather than trained professionals knowledgeable in refugee issues.

The provision of church sanctuary is understood and rationalized by congregations, particularly in the absence of a viable process of appeal, as fixing a flaw in the system. For example, Reverend Gerald Doré, the minister of the church in which Cherfi took sanctuary, stated: 'The United Church, on whose ground Mohamed Cherfi had taken refuge, considers it a moral duty to offer asylum to any person whose life is endangered if the State does not fulfill its responsibilities' (Solidarity Committee for Mohamed Cherfi 2004). For Doré, the goal of sanctuary is to fulfill the responsibilities that the state neglects; in this case, to offer asylum to persons whose lives are in danger. By making refused refugee claimants *deserving* through discourses of mistakes and flaws within the IRB, the sanctuary movement can challenge the ways in which the Canadian state has defined deserving versus undeserving migrants.

Sanctuary, then, can present a challenge to the governmental regime of the state and become a space in which state definitions of 'illegality' and 'refugee' are reconfigured. Congregations that provide sanctuary to failed refugee claimants reject the ideological reproduction of the state's physical borders by refusing to recognize the state-defined illegality of select persons. At the same time, however, congregations produce modes of governmentality specific to the practice of sanctuary when they, like government agencies, decide who may enter church sanctuary. In this way, the sanctuary movement reconstitutes state definitions of illegality through the creation of new categories of deserving and undeserving immigrants but does not challenge the notion that persons can be illegal. The Canadian state, through its violent traversing of the boundaries of church sanctuary, has demonstrated that the defiance of its borders and boundaries through the practice of church sanctuary will not always be tolerated. The arrest of Mohamed Cherfi inside a church shows the Canadian state's desire to enforce its spatial and ideological borders and to reinforce its definition of 'illegality.'

When Sûreté du Québec police officers, federal and provincial immigration officers, ministers of Quebec Immigration, Public Safety and Emergency Preparedness, and Citizenship and Immigration Canada came together to plan and ensure the swift arrest, detention, and deportation of Cherfi on 5 March 2003,[6] they dramatically reconfigured the space of sanctuary in Canada, making church sanctuary no longer a space of safety. Before this date, entering into sanctuary was a last measure that select non-status immigrants, usually failed refugee claimants, could use as a means to avoid deportation. To take sanctuary is, in many ways, a choice to enter into incarceration and as such, is generally only a temporary stage in a larger struggle to gain landed status. While some sanctuary cases are kept out of the public domain to respect the wishes of the congregation or the individual or family in sanctuary, a few prominent cases, such as that of Cherfi, are chosen for their potential ability to mobilize a larger political campaign for immigrant and refugee rights. However, with the arrest and deportation of Cherfi, such cases will no longer be understood as having the same protection under church sanctuary that they once had. For many individuals and families choosing to enter into sanctuary, the choice to 'go public' with their case may be a very difficult one to make – one that may result in their violent removal from a safe haven. The practice of sanctuary and the case of Mohamed Cherfi demonstrate the importance of full legal status in garnering substantive citizen rights. Although churches at times provide sanctuary for people living without full legal status, sanctuary is not a solution but rather a means towards gaining legal status. Cherfi's case shows that the Canadian state is willing to violate sanctuary in order to enforce their practice of determining access to formal citizenship, thus remaining the primary arbiter of rights and enforcer of immigration law.

Sanctuary Cities

Scholars of citizenship have identified the city as a strategic site for an emergent and active citizenship (Isin 2002; Sassen 1998; Holston and Appadurai 1999; Holston 1998). The assertion of active citizenship within cities at times presents a challenge to state definitions of illegality and the spatial and ideological borders that reinforce and reproduce processes of illegalization. For example, many cities across the United States have adopted resolutions that challenge federal immigration laws, often referring to themselves as 'sanctuary cities' or 'safety zones.' Over fifty cities have passed legislation that forbids the use of municipal funds, resources, and workers for the enforcement of federal immigration laws. Other cities, such as Los Angeles, Chicago, Portland, Seattle, New York City, and Minneapolis, have taken more proactive roles, putting into place legislation that bars city workers from inquiring into and/or disseminating immigration information regarding persons using city services. Resolutions passed in Baltimore, Austin, Cambridge, and other cities affirm that no city service will be denied on the basis of formal citizenship status (National Immigration Law Center 2004). These changes in municipal policy were not simply granted by municipalities; rather, immigrants, refugees, and their allies won these transformations through research, networking, advocacy, and direct action. Municipal policies that assert the right of access to city services to all residents of the city, regardless of formal legal status and without the sharing of immigration information with federal immigration enforcement officials, enable a double reconfiguration of citizenship practices. First, the potential of cities as spaces that facilitate substantive citizenship is reaffirmed. Second, practices of active citizenship are enabled. The social space of illegality, while certainly not abolished, is remade through the establishment of porous city boundaries.

In Toronto, a broad-based coalition is mobilizing a campaign for a municipal 'Don't Ask, Don't Tell' policy that would affirm access to services for non-status immigrants. This coalition includes unions, women's shelters, anti-poverty organizations, immigrant-rights groups, the Law Union of Ontario, neighbourhood centres, legal clinics, and community health centres.[7] Access to public services such as health care, emergency care, police services, social housing, and education plays a crucial role in substantive citizenship. Currently, access to such services in Toronto is often allocated on the basis of formal citizenship. Municipal policies that affirm the right of all members of the metropolis to use public services pose an important challenge to state definitions of 'illegality.' As noted above, the physical borders of the nation-state are ideologically reproduced in countless scenarios within the national territory. One example includes people being turned away from services based on their lack of full legal status. A municipal policy that prohibits questions about immigration status circumvents racism and discrimination in many situations – attending school, going to the hospital, applying for social housing, accessing emergency shelter services, and calling for police assistance. Sassen argues that the denationalization of urban space, along with the formation of new claims made by transnational actors, raises the question 'Whose city is it?' (1998, xx). The idea of a 'sanctuary city' provides one answer to this question: the city belongs to all who inhabit it, and its residents belong in the city.

Holston and Appadurai note that cities have been and remain a key strategic arena for the development of active citizenship, pointing out that with their 'concentrations of the nonlocal, the strange, the mixed, and the public, cities engage most palpably the tumult of citizenship' (1999, 2). Holston notes in his critique of modernist urban planning that the state is not the only source of legitimate citizenship; he argues instead that the city is potentially a space in which 'insurgent citizenship' can become manifest and legitimate (1998, 39). Sassen points out that the city has emerged as a space in which new claims are being formulated (1998, xx). For Sassen, 'the global city is a strategic site for disempowered actors because it enables them to gain presence, to emerge as subjects, even when they do not gain direct power' (xxi). Citizenship for these scholars is not defined as formal legal status but rather in broader, more practice-based terms.

In a sense, active citizenship is a process, one that is engaged and enabled through various social practices including (but not limited to) formal legal status, access to social services, the right to use to public spaces, social and political obligations, and the ability to make claims on state and society. Although non-status immigrants are denied the right to make claims on the state, many refuse to accept that this prevents them from participating in society. Political activism enables an active citizenship. This is similar to the experience of the *sans-papiers* movement within France, about which Balibar notes that *droit de cité* and citizenship are not primarily 'granted or conceded from above but are, in an essential respect, constructed from below' (2003, 48). For Holston, an insurgent citizenship refers to new and non-state sources of citizenship (1998, 39). This idea of an insurgent or 'active' citizenship can be used to describe the political activism of CASSA in Montreal and the work of municipal campaigns such as the Don't Ask, Don't Tell Campaign in Toronto. Members of CASSA have refused the social spaces of illegality allotted to them through their demand for legal citizenship. The Don't Ask, Don't Tell Campaign, on the other hand, circumvents the reconfiguration of illegality that a regularization would entail by demanding that substantive citizenship be accessible to all city residents in the form of public services such as social housing and community health care.

In many instances the illegality of a person surfaces when their lack of state-issued documentation exposes them as 'outsiders' and bars them from necessary services. Consequently, everyday forms of surveillance and repression based upon the 'heightened policing directed at the bodies, movements, and spaces of the poor' (De Genova 2002, 438) and racialized have a significant impact on the daily lives of people without full legal status in Canada. Indeed, many of the women incarcerated at the Toronto Immigrant Holding Centre, also known as the Heritage Inn detention centre (formerly at the Celebrity Inn) have been detained after calling police in instances of domestic abuse and sexual assault. Others have been exposed through minor infractions such as a traffic ticket or a motor vehicle accident, or when an employer, landlord, or neighbour reports their illegal status to police. According to many women who have been incarcerated at the detention centre, racism has played a major role in their arrest by police, who inquired into their immigration status most likely because they were not white. Immigrant rights advocates have pointed out that non-status immigrants and refugees, despite their outsider status, constitute a large, exploitable labour force that bolsters the Canadian economy (McDonald 2004). The condition of deportability or the threat of deportation ensures that the labour of non-status immigrants remains a distinctly cheap and easily replaceable commodity. When undocumented workers are targeted for deportation, the effect is the intimidation of the majority, forcing them to remain in disposable and exploitable conditions (De Genova 2002, 439).

Holston and Appadurai argue that in a globalized world, formal citizenship is no longer a requisite for access to substantive rights and social inclusion (1999, 4). Yasemin Soysal, in her discussion of member states of the European Union, makes a similar point: 'Access to a formal nationality status is not the main indicator for inclusion or exclusion in today's Europe. Rights, membership and participation are increasingly matters beyond the vocabulary of national citizenship' (1999, 12). Verena Stolcke, on the other hand, argues that as intra-European borders are becoming more porous, external borders are becoming more fortified and impermeable (1995, 2). In the Canadian context, the Canadian Border Security Agency (CBSA) was established following September 11 in order to increase security against illegal infiltration. Coordination with American counterparts took place at the Great Lakes Security Summit, held in Toronto in April 2003. Increased security measures are not only in effect at physical borders. Tom Godfrey reports in the *Toronto Sun* that the Greater Toronto Enforcement Centre (GTEC) has issued mandatory orders to appear, many of which will lead to deportation and to failed refugee claimants living in the GTA (Godfrey 2005). While in some cases national citizenship may no longer be necessary for 'rights, membership, and participation,' the fundamental flaw in the arguments of Holston and Appadurai and Soysal is that they homogenize the category of 'immigrant.' These scholars do not give adequate importance to practices of exclusion and inclusion in immigration policy that are based on multiple factors, including gender, race, class, and ability. Migrants, unfortunately, are not equally received and accepted in all nation-states in which they live. In Canada, this is clearly shown through the example of failed refugee claimants who have become non-status immigrants, such as the members of CASSA in Montreal and those targeted by GTEC in Toronto. The notion of 'sanctuary cities' affirms the right of all residents of the city, even non-citizens, to access city services. Yet it is clear that without formal legal status, non-status immigrants face insecurities that make active citizenship extremely difficult. Even within a city that provides access to city services regardless of formal citizenship, federal authorities such as the CBSA and GTEC are not barred from enforcing federal immigration laws – arresting, incarcerating, and deporting those persons deemed not acceptable within the national body politic.

Conclusions

As demonstrated through the examples discussed in this chapter, full legal status continues to be an integral component in realizing substantive citizenship in the Canadian context. The continuous threat of detention and deportation marginalizes non-status people, making them vulnerable to exploitation while maintaining a large, disposable labour force that supports the Canadian economy. The CASSA, by refusing the social space of illegality, has exposed the arbitrary and political nature of processes of illegalization as imposed by the state and through governmental institutions. Through their political activism, they have reconfigured citizenship in important and far-reaching ways. CASSA members, by mobilizing and organizing support, have enacted citizenship as a collective practice – an active citizenship. Processes of illegalization are implicated in various 'technologies of governmentality,' creating and defining categories of inclusion and exclusion such as citizen, permanent resident, migrant worker, refugee claimant, visa-holder, and illegal immigrant. The racist practices and policies of Citizenship and Immigration Canada (CIC), along with other discriminatory practices such as sexism and ableism, work to reproduce a homogenized national body politic, and through this nationalist enterprise further entrench processes of illegalization.

The Canadian state is not the sole arbiter of rights and entitlements but it is the primary authority and the central enforcer of state laws, as was demonstrated in this chapter. Although elsewhere formal citizenship (legal status as defined by the state) is becoming less necessary in securing substantive citizenship (rights and entitlements), such is not the case in Canada. The practice of church sanctuary defies the physical borders of the nation-state and, like regularization, reconstitutes illegality and spatial borders in new ways. Yet like CIC, the sanctuary movement is implicated within processes of illegalization because it creates and defines categories of inclusion and exclusion through the selection of non-status immigrants deserving of sanctuary.

The global city has recently emerged within citizenship studies as a denationalized space, opening up possibilities for the production of new forms of active and substantive citizenship. An example is the emergence of 'sanctuary cities,' which ensure that access to city services is not dependent upon immigration status. In this sense, a city's (permeable) boundaries allow the social space of illegality to be remade in new ways. Furthermore, access to social services and the use of public spaces are two vital aspects within the practice of active citizenship. Full legal status is another integral aspect of citizenship. Even when able to access city services, non-status immigrants and those without full legal status continue to be subject to the violence of detention and deportation. A hierarchical system of rights and belonging based on citizenship status denies the legal personhood of non-status immigrants and degrades the humanity of those who are considered to be illegal. For this reason, the Comité d'action des sans-statuts algériens demands the regularization of all non-status people in Canada. Paradoxically, the demand for formal citizenship has enabled an active citizenship for members of CASSA. In Toronto, the Don't Ask, Don't Tell Campaign demands access access to city services for all residents, opening up possibilities for substantive citizen rights for people without full legal status. Nevertheless, the continued exploitation, marginalization, and deportability of non-status immigrants reinforces the necessity for formal citizenship within the Canadian context.

Notes

1 For a discussion of culturalism and cultural racism, see Agnew, Introduction, and Lee, chapter 8, this volume.
2 Racism in the Canadian immigration system is not new, as is extensively documented by Aiken in the previous chapter of this volume. One can easily argue that the immigration system has been founded upon racist practices since its inception. A few historic examples: the Chinese Head Tax from 1885–1923, the incident of the *Komagata Maru* in 1914, the denial of refuge to Jews fleeing Nazism in the 1920s and 1930s, and the exclusion of Caribbean migrants in the 1950s (despite being British subjects). More recent examples include the Right of Landing Fee, the Safe Third Country Agreement, the denial of refuge to Palestinians fleeing Israeli persecution, the Live-In Caregiver Program, and the Migrant Farm Worker Program. These latter examples may be tacit in their racism, but the effect of their programs and policies is no less racist.
3 At present, the only option available to non-status persons in Canada to obtain permanent residency is to file a claim based upon humanitarian and compassionate grounds. This application is based primarily upon criteria of 'integration,' economic independence and stability – provided the applicant passes a medical examination and a criminal check. With a 5 per cent success rate, the Humanitarian and Compassionate application is far from adequate.
4 For many rejected claimants, the policy of 'direct backs' only results in further incarceration for themselves and their families, as the U.S. immigration system is in many ways more stringent than that of Canada. In a recent case in Toronto, a woman from Argentina facing deportation along with her three children had to fight back and mobilize support in order to convince immi-

gration officials that she should be able to purchase her own ticket to Argentina rather than languish in a U.S. detention prison for months with her children (No One Is Illegal–Toronto, 6 April 2004). In January 2005, Canadian immigration officials adopted the Safe Third Country Agreement to replace the current policy of 'direct backs.' The passing of this agreement means that anyone arriving in Canada via the United States who wishes to apply for refugee status in Canada would no longer be able to do so. They would be immediately sent to the United States, a so-called safe country, to make their claims.

5 The Ayoub family's application for permanent residency on humanitarian and compassionate grounds was accepted by Citizenship and Immigration Canada in February 2005, more than one year after they first entered church sanctuary, marking a significant victory for non-status and sanctuary movements in Canada (CBC News, 27 February 2005).

6 Supporters of Cherfi from across Canada denounced the actions of these ministries and pointed out that without prior knowledge and planning, the rapid deportation of Cherfi to the United States could not have occurred. In a 6 March 2004 article in the *Montreal Gazette*, however, the ministries denied involvement with Cherfi's initial arrest (Hanes 2004).

7 See http://www.dadttoronto.org.

References

Amnesty International. 2004. Open letter re: Mohamed Cherfi. 12 March.
Balibar, Étienne. 2000. 'What we owe to the *sans-papiers*.' In *Social insecurity*, ed. Len Guenther and Cornelius Heesters, 42–3. Toronto: Anansi.
– 2003. *We, the people of Europe? Reflections on transnational citizenship*. Princeton: Princeton University Press.
Bannerji, Himani. 2000. *The dark side of the nation: Essays on multiculturalism, nationalism, and gender*. Toronto: Canadian Scholars Press.
Bhabha, Jacqueline. 1999. Belonging in Europe: Citizenship and post-national rights. *International Social Science Journal* 51 (1): 11–23.
Burch, Brian. 2003. A brief history of sanctuary. Paper presented at Community, Solidarity, Sanctuary conference organized by No One Is Illegal–Toronto, 29 November.
Cherfi, Mohamed. 2004. Open statement, Saint-Pierre United Church, Quebec City, 18 February 2004.
Creal, Michael. 2003. On sanctuary. Paper presented at Community, Solidarity, Sanctuary conference organized by No One Is Illegal–Toronto, 29 November.

De Genova, Nicholas P. 2002. Migrant 'illegality' and deportability in everyday life. *Annual Review of Anthropology* 31:419–47.

Godfrey, Tom. 2005. Failed refugees told: Start packing. *Toronto Sun*, 7 December.

Gordon, Colin. 1991. Governmental rationality: An introduction. In *The Foucault effect*, ed. G. Burchell et al., 1–53. Chicago: University of Chicago Press.

Hanes, Allison. 2004. Cops storm church, nab asylum-seeker in Quebec City. *Montreal Gazette*, 6 March.

Holston, James. 1998. Spaces of insurgent citizenship. In *Making the invisible visible: A multicultural planning history*, ed. L. Sandercock, 37–49. Berkeley: University of California Press.

Holston, James, and Arjun Appadurai. 1999. Cities and citizenship. In *Cities and citizenship*, ed. J. Holston, 1–18. Durham, NC: Duke University Press.

Isin, Engin. 2002. *Being political: Genealogies of citizenship.* Minneapolis: University of Minnesota Press.

Keung, Nicholas. 2004. Women face dilemma: Abuse or deportation? *Toronto Star*, 3 August.

Lowry, Michelle, and Peter Nyers. 2003. Round table report: 'No one is illegal': The fight for refugee and migrant rights in Canada. *Refuge* 21 (3): 66–74.

McDonald, Jean. 2004. Immigration activism in Toronto. Paper presented at Beyond Borders, Beyond Fear conference of the Student Christian Movement, 4 March.

National Immigration Law Center. 2004. Annotated chart of laws, resolutions and policies instituted across the U.S. against state and local police enforcement of immigration laws. http://www.nilc.org/immlawpolicy/LocalLaw/Local_Law_Enforement_Chart_FINAL.pdf. Last updated 27 February 2004.

No One is Illegal – Toronto email list. http://groups.yahoo.com/groups/noone is illegal.

Ong, Aihwa. 2003. *Buddha is hiding: Refugees, citizenship, the new America.* Berkeley: University of California Press.

Sassen, Saskia. 1998. *Globalization and its discontents.* New York: New Press.

Sharma, Nandita. 2001. On being not Canadian: The social organization of 'migrant workers' in Canada. *Canadian Review of Sociology and Anthropology* 38 (4): 415–40.

– 2002. Immigrant and migrant workers in Canada: Labour movements, racism and the expansion of globalization. *Canadian Woman Studies* 21 (4): 18–26.

Singh, Jaggi, and Jean McDonald. 2004. Question period at Beyond Borders, Beyond Fear conference of the Student Christian Movement, 4 March.

Solidarity Committee for Mohamed Cherfi. 2005. Mohamed released! Statement, 24 July.

– 2004. It's not too late! Bring Mohamed home! Press release, 6 March.

Soysal, Yasemin Nuhoglu. 1999. Citizenship and identity: Living in diasporas in post-war Europe? *Ethnic and Racial Studies* 23 (1): 1–15.

STATUS Coalition email list. http://ca.groups.yahoo.com/groups/statuscoalition/?yguid=189341884.

Stolcke, Verena. 1995. Talking culture: New boundaries, new rhetorics of exclusion in Europe. *Current Anthropology* 36 (1): 1–24.

Torfing, Jacob. 1999. *New theories of discourse.* Oxford: Blackwell.

Walkom, Thomas. 2003. Immigrants rap Tory plan. *Toronto Star,* 4 September.

Walters, William. 2002. Deportation, expulsion, and the international police of aliens. *Citizenship Studies* 6 (3): 265–92.

Wright, Cynthia. 2003. Moments of emergence: organizing by and with undocumented and non-citizen people in Canada after September 11. *Refuge* 21 (3): 5–16.

PART TWO

Race, Work, and Workplace

Racism and racist ideologies are fluid rather than static: they change their contours over time and place, embedding themselves in institutions and in our everyday interactions. Sometimes racism is so natural a part of our everyday life that it seems normal and routine, acceptable rather than contemptible behaviour. Racism based on skin colour is now widely condemned as being misguided and plain wrong. Yet biases associated with the identity of some people continue, with social and psychological repercussions for their well-being. One of the most significant aspects of racism is that it leads to discrimination in employment. Discrimination can manifest itself when educational and professional credentials obtained in Third World countries are not recognized or when individuals are unable to locate a job on the basis of demonstrated merit and work experience. At times, racialized individuals are compelled to work in environments that are inhospitable, chilly, and alienating. The documentation of racism in its various manifestations has led to some changes and resulted in policies that seek to mitigate some of its deleterious consequences. Yet problems still remain. As Pendakur and Pendakur and Wang and Lo demonstrate, despite many changes in legislation and in attitudes, Canadian society still attributes unequal social value to racialized individuals, and this, in turn, substantially impacts their income.

In 'Colour My World: Have Earnings Gaps for Canadian-Born Ethnic Minorities Changed over Time?' Krishna Pendakur and Ravi Pendakur use the census databases from 1971 through 1996 to estimate earnings equations for Canadian-born female and male workers and assess the earnings differentials between white and visible minority workers. These databases allow Pendakur and Pendakur to focus on the small populations of Canadian-born visible minority and Aboriginal workers across Canada and in eight large Canadian metropolitan areas. Earnings differentials are also examined according to birth cohort and across twenty-six subgroups within the white and visible-minority categories. Pendakur and Pendakur find that in general, differentials narrowed through the 1970s, were stable through the 1980s, and grew between 1991 and 1996.

Shuguang Wang and Lucia Lo use landing records and tax data as the basis for their research in 'What Does It Take to Achieve Full Integration? Economic (Under)Performance of Chinese Immigrants in Canada.' Their research documents that the source countries for Chinese immigrants have changed over the last two decades and that more individuals come as economic immigrants than from any other category. The more recent immigrants have better educational qualifications and are more proficient in the English language. Yet despite their increased human capital, they still experience very different economic outcomes in the labour market compared to members of the general population. For example, Chinese immigrants have much lower employment and self-employment income than the general population, and earnings differentials are found in all groups irrespective of age, gender, or country of origin. Although some of these new immigrants have come to Canada as investors, entrepreneurs, or self-employed business owners, they still earn less than salaried workers in the general population. Wang and Lo conclude from such data that Canadian-specific educational credentials are better remunerated than those acquired in the immigrants' countries of origin, and that it would take more than twenty years to close the earnings gap between Chinese immigrants and the general population.

Considering the long history of racism in its innumerable forms leads to questions about its staying power and permanence. Is there hope that we as a society can overcome racial difference to enhance individual and collective well-being? In 'Racialized Discrimination in Nursing,' Rebecca Hagey, Jane Turrittin, and Tania Das Gupta observe that the nursing profession in Canada is beginning to pay attention to the everyday racism that nurses face. This chapter is based on qualitative interviews with fourteen nurses who completed a survey on racism in nursing. The authors juxtapose concepts based on Maureen Walker's relational/cultural theory with examples of testimony by racialized women to develop situation-specific 'best practices' for navigating the race hierarchies of the Canadian health care system. According to

Statistics Canada, nurses of colour in Ontario have barely half the chance of being promoted to management levels compared to their white counterparts. Past experience shows, however, that documenting and contesting such discriminations have not resulted in desired changes. Thus as an alternative strategy, the authors suggest dialogue within the profession to ensure equity for racialized nurses.

4 Colour My World: Have Earnings Gaps for Canadian-Born Ethnic Minorities Changed over Time?

KRISHNA PENDAKUR AND RAVI PENDAKUR

The last decade and a half has witnessed a growing flow of research devoted to examining the degree to which people from ethnic minorities are subject to labour-market discrimination in Canada (Akbari 1992a; Howland and Sakellariou 1993; Stelcner and Kyriazis 1995; Christofides and Swidinsky 1994; Baker and Benjamin 1997; Hum and Simpson 1998; Pendakur and Pendakur 1998; Lian and Matthews 1998). While these authors have generally concluded that immigrant groups often face significant labour-market disadvantage, there is debate over the degree to which people from minority groups who were born in Canada are subject to a similar disadvantage compared to white workers (Stelcner 2000). This debate is frustrated somewhat by the variety of empirical approaches, datasets, and time periods used to evaluate such discrepancies experienced by Aboriginal people and those from visible minorities born in Canada. In this chapter, we evaluate the scope of labour-market disadvantage with five specially created micro-datasets that contain all the 'long form' records collected by Statistics Canada for the 1971, 1981, 1986, 1991, and 1996 censuses. These datasets are very large and allow consistent definitions of variables over the period 1971–96; they also allow the assessment of earnings differentials facing ethnic minorities in the Canadian-born population. We concentrate on the Canadian-born population because while immigrants may face earnings differentials related to such things as language or accent penalties, non-recognition of credentials, or loss of work related networks, these issues are not faced by ethnic minorities born in Canada.

Specifically, we estimate log-earnings equations for Canadian-born workers conditional on a variety of personal characteristics, including age and education, to assess the size of white–Aboriginal and white–

visible-minority earnings differentials in Canada as a whole and in eight large Canadian cities across five census years. The novelty of our empirical work lies in two extensions to the literature, both of which are made possible by the very large size of the census micro-databases. The long-form data used are from 33 per cent of Canadian households in 1971 and from 20 per cent of Canadian households in 1981, 1986, 1991, and 1996. These yield usable samples of several hundred thousand Canadian-born working-age labour-force participants in each sample year, and in each usable sample there are at least 6,000 Aboriginal and visible-minority persons. The first extension is that we are able to look at Canadian-born minority workers as far back as 1971 and examine changes over the five census periods. Thus, direct immigration effects do not 'pollute' our results on ethnicity effects. The second extension is that we are able to treat each of eight large Canadian metropolitan areas as local labour markets – and therefore as separate regression equations – with different white–Aboriginal and white–visible-minority earnings differentials in each city. We then go on to look at differences among twenty-six ethnic groups within the white and visible-minority categories in order to examine heterogeneity of earnings differentials within the aggregate categories. This level of analysis is conducted for Canada as a whole, and for the metropolitan areas of Montreal, Toronto, and Vancouver.

Generally, we find a pattern of stable or narrowing earnings differentials through the 1970s, stability through the 1980s, and enlargement of the earnings differentials between 1991 and 1996. This is the case among both men and women, for most birth cohorts, and for most of the ethnic groups constituting the white and visible-minority categories.

The Literature

In the past few years, there has been a surge of interest among both economists and sociologists in labour-market discrimination against Aboriginal people and visible minority groups in Canada. Researchers have used a variety of empirical approaches together with public-use data to assess the existence and magnitude of wage and earnings differentials facing ethnic minorities in Canada. Much of this literature has also focused on immigration effects, but here we will limit our discussion to material relating to Canadian-born ethnic minorities. In particular, we focus on a three-way classification of ethnic origin for the Canadian-born population: Aboriginal, visible-minority, and white.

Aboriginal people are defined as those who report at least one Aboriginal ethnic origin in their ancestry. Visible minorities are defined as non-Aboriginals who report at least one non-European ethnic origin in their ancestry. White people are defined as non-Aboriginals who report only European ethnic origins in their ancestry.

Previous research on data from the 1980s suggests that during this period, Aboriginal people and those from visible minorities faced substantial earnings differentials at the Canada-wide level. For example, Stelcner and Kyriazis (1995) use 1981 census data to examine earnings differentials across two visible-minority and fourteen white ethnic groups; Howland and Sakellariou (1993) use 1986 census data to examine earnings differentials across three visible-minority ethnic groups, and Akbari (1992b) uses 1986 census data to examine earnings differentials among a variety of white and visible-minority ethnic groups. These three papers find that earnings gaps exist for a number of ethnic groups in Canada, especially visible-minority ethnic groups.

Research that uses data from the 1990s shows less unanimity. Three papers using 1991 census public-use micro-data find substantial and significant differences between British-origin workers and workers in a number of visible-minority ethnic groups (Pendakur and Pendakur 1998; Lian and Matthews 1998; Baker and Benjamin 1997). Similarly, Christofides and Swidinsky (1994) use the 1989 Labour Market Activity Survey (LMAS) and find that visible-minority workers face a large wage gap compared to their white counterparts.

In contrast to these results, de Silva and Dougherty (1996) and Hum and Simpson (1998) use the 1993 Survey of Labour and Income Dynamics (SLID) and find that while a gap exists for Canadian-born black men, it does not exist for other visible-minority ethnic groups. Similarly, Kelly (1995) studies the occupation distribution of workers using 1991 census data and argues that visible minorities are well represented in managerial occupations and thus not subject to labour-market disadvantage.

Work on the earnings of Aboriginal people in Canada has been sparse, but George and Kuhn (1994) use 1986 census data and find that Aboriginal men and women have wages 8 per cent and 6 per cent lower, respectively, than white men and women with similar characteristics. However, de Silva (1999) uses 1991 census data and concludes that Aboriginal–white wage differentials are mainly attributable to differences in personal characteristics rather than to labour market discrimination.

In the context of visible-minority–white earnings differentials, some of the variation in findings of various researchers can be explained by differences in the data used. The public-use databases for the Census of Canada are comparatively large, but have relatively short variable lists. In contrast, the 1989 LMAS and 1993 SLID offer far smaller samples, but more and better control variables. For example, the SLID and LMAS both include measures of job tenure, and the SLID provides information on full- and part-time labour-market experience. The census databases offer little information related to these important control variables but does offer sample size. Since visible-minority individuals born in Canada and Aboriginal people each make up at most 3 per cent of the Canadian-born population, small samples are problematic because the associated large confidence bands around parameter estimates may lead researchers to not reject false hypotheses. Similarly, since labour-market experience has an important effect on earnings independent of age, better control lists are important because missing variable bias will cause the effects of left-out correlates of ethnic origin to be attributed to ethnic origin. We believe it is impossible to determine which data problem is more damaging, but since non-census data sources with high-quality control variables and consistent ethnic-origin variables are not available prior to 1986 (the first wave of the LMAS), we use five census datasets to investigate the pattern over time of earnings differentials across ethnic groups.

There is at least one additional argument in favour of using census data for this type of investigation. The public-use LMAS and SLID datasets do not provide information on the name or size of the respondent's city of residence.[1] Since visible-minority groups are over-represented and Aboriginal people under-represented in Canada's large cities, and since earnings are on average higher in large cities than in smaller cities and towns, leaving out information on the city of residence – at least its size – potentially biases estimates in favour of smaller earnings differentials for visible minorities and larger earnings differentials for Aboriginal people. Thus, the fact that census data include city of residence is helpful in estimating Canada-wide earnings differentials. Since our datasets are so large, and since Pendakur and Pendakur (1998) show evidence that earnings differentials vary from city to city in Canada, we estimate earnings differentials across ethnic groups separately for eight Census Metropolitan Areas (CMAs)[2] in Canada, thus effectively treating them as eight separate labour markets.

Discrimination in Labour Markets

In what sense can the presence of a significant earnings differential between white and visible-minority workers or between white and Aboriginal workers point to discrimination against minorities in labour markets? The differentials we report control for a variety of personal characteristics, including age and education, but do not control for any job characteristics, such as occupation, industry, or work hours. Thus, even if all workers in the same occupation and industry groupings receive the same earnings regardless of their ethnicity, our empirical strategy might find earnings differentials due to the greater concentration of white workers than non-white workers in higher-paying occupations and industries.

We believe that the job characteristics of workers – such as occupation and industry – are at least as susceptible to ethnic discrimination as the wages paid to workers. In fact, the case is made by Becker (1996) and others that in competitive labour markets, ethnic discrimination by employers, workers, or customers results not in wage differentials for workers in identical jobs but in segregation of workers into different jobs by ethnicity. With competitive product and labour markets, this segregation leads to a 'separate-but-equal' type of world where ethnic discrimination divides the economy into sub-economies composed of single ethnic groups, with identical wage and earnings outcomes across sub-economies.

If either of these competitive assumptions is relaxed, the 'separate-but-equal' conclusions do not follow. For example, if product markets are not competitive, so that some firms make excess profits that are partially shared with (possibly unionized) workers, then workers in those firms make more money than seemingly identical workers in other firms with fewer excess profits (see for example Dickens and Lang 1992). If ethnic discrimination on the part of employers, workers, or customers results in white workers ending up in the high-profit firms and non-white workers ending up in the low-profit firms, then the segregation of workers across firms by ethnicity results in differential outcomes. An alternative example may be seen by relaxing the restriction that labour markets are competitive (see Shapiro and Stiglitz 1984). For example, consider the occupation of investment banker. This career pays well, perhaps because investors' expectations are also high. Since this occupation performs well financially relative to others, there are more workers who want such jobs than there are openings. If white workers have a better chance of getting these 'good jobs' than non-white workers, occupation segregation results in earnings differentials between white and non-white workers. However, these earnings differentials will only be observed if the researcher does *not* control for job characteristics such as occupation and industry, because these are the very factors affected by ethnic discrimination.

Thus, to the extent that ethnic discrimination may manifest itself *both* in the allocation of workers to jobs and in the remuneration commensurate with those jobs, it seems to us prudent to estimate models that do not control for job characteristics.[3] A second reason to exclude job characteristics is that the occupational coding in the census main bases changed dramatically between 1981 and 1996. A consistent occupational coding structure usable across all the census periods would capture only about 40 per cent of workers – the other 60 per cent would be in a category called 'other occupations.'

Pendakur and Pendakur (1998) provides evidence from the 1991 census public-use sample that controlling for job characteristics (occupation, industry, weeks worked, and full-time/part-time status) shrinks but does not eliminate earnings differentials across ethnic groups in Canada. The 1971 to 1996 data do not support consistent controls for occupation and industry, but do allow consistent controls for weeks worked and full-time/part-time status. Although we do not report results using them, the models below have been run with these variables added to the control list. The results are essentially similar to those presented – estimated earnings differentials with additional controls are somewhat smaller in absolute value, but follow similar patterns. These findings reassure us that our estimation results are meaningful.

Data and Method

Our data consist of five customized micro-data files that initially contained information from all the long-form records collected for the Census of Canada in the years 1971, 1981, 1986, 1991, and 1996.[4] The population examined consists of all Canadian-born residents of Canada twenty-five to sixty-four years of age whose primary source of income is from wages and salaries. People without any schooling were dropped from the sample, as were those who did not report any income.

Table 4.1 shows weighted counts for our sample by geographic area, sex, and ethnic origin. As per Statistics Canada guidelines, we are unable to release exact counts, but we note that weighted counts are approximately five times the actual number of observations for 1981 to 1996 and three and one-third times the actual number of observations for 1971. The key feature of table 4.1 is that it shows the very large size of the datasets at our disposal.

Our analysis is divided into three parts. The first part uses a Canada-wide sample and then looks separately at eight CMAs (Halifax, Montreal, Ottawa, Toronto, Winnipeg, Calgary, Edmonton, and Vancouver) in each of the five census periods. The second part is a quasi-cohort analysis that pools all the data and interacts Aboriginal/visible-minority status with birth cohorts. The third part breaks the three groups into twenty-six ethnic subgroups (six visible-minority groups, nineteen white groups, and one Aboriginal category). The differentials compared to British-origin men and women are examined for Canada as a whole and for the three largest CMAs (Montreal, Toronto, and Vancouver).

The dependent variable in all regressions is the natural logarithm of earnings from wages and salaries. The logarithmic function de-skews the distribution of earnings, which is useful because it decreases the influence of very-high-earnings reporters. However, it also increases the influence of very-low-earnings reporters. We note that regression runs dropping all observations with less than $100 in annual earnings yield qualitatively identical results.

We use a variety of independent variables to control for the personal characteristics of workers in our samples:

Age	Eight age cohorts as dummy variables (ages 25–29, 30–34, 35–39, 40–44, 45– 49, 50–54, 55–59, and 60–64). Age 25–29 is the left-out dummy variable.
Schooling	Twelve levels of schooling as dummy variables (less than 5 years of school, 5–8 years of school, 9–10 years of school, more than 10 years of school [includes high-school graduates], some post-secondary schooling without a certificate, post-secondary certificate, trades certificate, some university without a certificate, some university with a trades or other certificate, a university diploma below the BA level, bachelors degree, first professional degree, master's degree, or PhD).[5] Less than 5 years of schooling is the left-out dummy variable.

Table 4.1. Weighted frequency counts of ethnic group by sex and selected geographic area, 1971 to 1996

Sex	Region	Group	1971	1981	1986	1991	1996
females	Canada	White	1,505,455	2,522,035	3,028,740	3,323,710	3,781,420
		Visible minorities	9,680	16,910	28,655	40,455	46,675
		Aboriginal persons	10,870	47,770	73,140	119,800	109,060
	Halifax	White	20,465	37,090	45,305	50,495	57,570
		Visible minorities	220	555	1,165	1,845	1,955
		Aboriginal persons	25	270	525	1,070	480
	Montreal	White	207,795	321,215	376,905	428,225	470,550
		Visible minorities	1,125	1,345	2,125	3,585	3,455
		Aboriginal persons	670	2,375	3,990	8,285	2,865
	Ottawa-Hull	White	57,290	95,470	122,570	137,925	155,315
		Visible minorities	200	455	865	1,755	1,725
		Aboriginal persons	125	960	2,520	5,630	3,065
	Toronto	White	187,985	268,395	350,010	356,915	391,710
		Visible minorities	2,545	4,000	7,205	10,185	12,905
		Aboriginal persons	695	2,540	5,845	6,885	3,545
	Winnipeg	White	50,175	70,710	80,965	79,465	90,615
		Visible minorities	275	485	810	1,010	1,055
		Aboriginal persons	370	2,010	3,365	4,855	6,290
	Calgary	White	33,615	69,615	92,880	96,690	114,515
		Visible minorities	220	745	1,230	1,820	2,215
		Aboriginal persons	175	1,160	2,150	3,405	3,120
	Edmonton	White	40,695	75,765	103,165	102,615	117,760
		Visible minorities	270	500	1,015	1,440	1,785
		Aboriginal persons	360	2,000	3,245	5,145	4,705
	Vancouver	White	81,975	127,970	147,690	161,770	189,135
		Visible minorities	1,880	3,540	5,340	7,720	9,950
		Aboriginal persons	565	2,385	4,305	6,120	5,300

Table 4.1. (concluded)

Sex	Region	Group	1971	1981	1986	1991	1996
Males	Canada	White	2,837,325	3,419,815	3,696,510	3,723,390	4,068,945
		Visible minorities	16,375	21,160	33,260	43,000	49,125
		Aboriginal persons	27,560	73,630	90,385	128,970	118,515
	Halifax	White	37,660	49,050	54,485	56,035	60,285
		Visible minorities	400	695	1,340	1,665	1,515
		Aboriginal persons	55	410	745	1,090	515
	Montreal	White	412,600	431,350	455,340	459,575	486,435
		Visible minorities	1,700	1,475	2,195	3,415	3,650
		Aboriginal persons	1,515	3,420	4,370	7,750	3,395
	Ottawa-Hull	White	95,245	119,180	141,475	147,135	160,300
		Visible minorities	410	650	1,190	1,915	1,820
		Aboriginal persons	220	1,150	2,510	5,230	2,915
	Halifax	White	286,425	307,230	377,750	367,000	387,260
		Visible minorities	3,960	4,515	7,555	10,195	12,885
		Aboriginal persons	900	3,020	5,765	6,280	3,500
	Winnipeg	White	76,305	84,490	92,085	83,975	94,370
		Visible minorities	510	715	900	1,075	1,040
		Aboriginal persons	600	2,615	3,460	5,000	6,775
	Calgary	White	54,695	89,245	105,750	107,795	125,070
		Visible minorities	360	870	1,505	2,135	2,425
		Aboriginal persons	265	1,705	2,125	3,475	2,760
	Edmonton	White	66,780	95,250	119,520	114,185	126,340
		Visible minorities	390	755	1,235	1,765	1,760
		Aboriginal persons	535	2,615	3,485	4,745	4,980
	Vancouver	White	134,085	156,360	169,750	176,995	200,730
		Visible minorities	2,810	4,220	5,885	7,935	10,610
		Aboriginal persons	800	3,050	4,070	6,135	4,820

Source: 1971, 1981, 1986, 1991 and 1996 census mainbase.
Selection: All Canadian-born residents of Canada, 25 to 64 years of age, whose primary source of income is from wages and salaries.
            People without any schooling were dropped from the sample as were those without any earnings.

Marital status	Five dummy variables indicating marital status (single – never married, married, separated, divorced, widowed). Single is the left-out dummy variable.
Household size	A dummy variable indicating a single-person household and a continuous variable indicating the number of family members for other households.
Official language	Three dummy variables (English, French, bilingual – English and French). English is the left-out dummy variable. We note that because our sample is entirely Canadian-born, every observation reports the speaking of either English or French. This also eliminates much of the variation in quality of language knowledge that plagues the estimation of earnings differentials across ethnic groups.
CMA	In regressions that pool all the cities together, we use 11 dummy variables indicating the Census Metropolitan Area/Region (Halifax, Montreal, Ottawa, Toronto, Hamilton, Winnipeg, Calgary, Edmonton, Vancouver, Victoria, and a flag for not living in one of the 10 listed CMAs). Toronto is the left-out dummy variable.
Group status	Three dummy variables indicating group status (white, visible minority, Aboriginal). White is the left-out dummy variable.

Group status (white, visible minority, or Aboriginal) is the primary independent variable of interest.[6] These three groups are quite coarse, and are chosen because of their use in federal employment-equity policy. There are at least two possible issues arising from the use of such broadly defined groups. First, as noted in Pendakur and Pendakur (1998), coarse groupings may mask important within-group heterogeneity. Not all white ethnic groups are advantaged, and not all visible-minority groups are disadvantaged. We explore this issue below by breaking group status into twenty-two single-origin ethnic categories and assessing how earnings differentials evolved across these ethnic groups over time. Second, since multiple-origin people have become much more numerous over time, their treatment in these broad categories merits assessment. That is, is the treatment of a person with one British-origin parent and one Caribbean-black parent similar to that of a white or visible-minority person? Pendakur and Pendakur (1998) found some evidence that multiple-origin men with one visible-minority parent were about as disadvantaged as 'full' visible-minority men. We assess this issue below by evaluating the pattern of earnings for multiple-origin people over time.

Discussion

Table 4.2 shows results from ninety separate regressions. A separate model was run for Canada as a whole and for eight CMAs in each of five census periods for each of two genders. The coefficients are approximately equal to the percentage difference in annual wages and salaries between Canadian-born white and Aboriginal or visible-minority persons, holding personal characteristics constant. For large coefficients (especially those larger in absolute value than 0.10), this approximation will overestimate the percentage difference for negative coefficients and underestimate the percentage difference for positive coefficients.

Results for Females

ABORIGINAL WOMEN

Looking first at the results for Aboriginal women (top panel of table 4.2), the coefficient for the Canada-wide regression in 1971 is –0.20. This suggests that on average, an Aboriginal woman could expect to receive annual earnings from wages and salaries 20 per cent lower than a white woman of similar age, official language ability, schooling, and marital-status characteristics.[7] By 1996, this differential had shrunk somewhat to about 16 per cent (and the hypothesis that the difference across those years is zero is rejected at the 1 per cent level of significance). We see that the gap decreased greatly between 1971 and 1986 but then reversed direction after 1986, almost reaching its 1971 high point. In the urban areas, the picture is somewhat different. Regardless of census period, the confidence intervals are substantially wider, suggesting that the point estimate is not tight. Furthermore, in 1971 only in the western CMAs are the estimates significantly different from zero (ranging from –32 per cent in Edmonton to –18 per cent in Winnipeg). In the period 1971–96, the point estimates for all the CMAs held at about the same magnitude, but the confidence intervals tighten up over time. By 1996, the gaps are large and statistically significant in all regions (ranging from –14 per cent in Ottawa-Hull to –41 per cent in Edmonton).

Table 4.2. Selected coefficients from log-earnings regression models, with ethnicity dummies, 1971 to 1996

Sex	Group	City	Year				
			1971	1981	1986	1991	1996
Females	Aboriginal	Canada	-0.20***	-0.10***	-0.09***	-0.17***	-0.16***
		Halifax	-0.42	-0.01	-0.01	-0.10	-0.23*
		Montreal	-0.09	-0.04	-0.13***	-0.13***	-0.32***
		Ottawa-Hull	-0.19	-0.02	-0.01	-0.06**	-0.14***
		Toronto	-0.09	-0.24***	-0.13***	-0.11***	-0.16***
		Winnipeg	-0.18**	-0.27***	-0.25***	-0.34***	-0.29***
		Calgary	-0.24*	-0.24***	-0.22***	-0.26***	-0.37***
		Edmonton	-0.32***	-0.31***	-0.25***	-0.36***	-0.41***
		Vancouver	-0.19***	-0.15***	-0.11***	-0.24***	-0.37***
	Visible minority	Canada	0.09***	0.07***	0.04***	0.00	-0.06***
		Halifax	-0.33***	-0.05	-0.17**	-0.16***	-0.14
		Montreal	0.11**	-0.03	0.03	-0.06*	-0.19***
		Ottawa-Hull	0.21*	-0.16	0.03	-0.19***	-0.15***
		Toronto	0.08**	-0.03	0.02	-0.01	-0.12***
		Winnipeg	0.10	0.08	-0.02	0.04	-0.12*
		Calgary	0.03	0.17**	0.17***	0.06	0.02
		Edmonton	0.05	0.12	0.07	0.07	-0.04
		Vancouver	0.14***	0.19***	0.13***	0.09***	0.10***

Table 4.2. (concluded)

Sex	Group	City	Year				
			1971	1981	1986	1991	1996
Males	Aboriginal	Canada	-0.48***	-0.37***	-0.44***	-0.48***	-0.57***
		Halifax	0.15	-0.23***	-0.23***	-0.03	-0.35***
		Montreal	-0.13***	-0.06**	-0.14***	-0.10***	-0.27***
		Ottawa-Hull	-0.05	-0.09**	-0.14***	-0.10***	-0.27***
		Toronto	-0.24***	-0.16***	-0.13***	-0.16***	-0.49***
		Winnipeg	-0.36***	-0.37***	-0.39***	-0.42***	-0.55***
		Calgary	-0.24***	-0.26***	-0.30***	-0.34***	-0.35***
		Edmonton	-0.41***	-0.19***	-0.36***	-0.51***	-0.63***
		Vancouver	-0.40***	-0.12***	-0.26***	-0.32***	-0.52***
	Visible minority	Canada	-0.05***	-0.03***	-0.07***	-0.06***	-0.15***
		Halifax	-0.17***	-0.30***	-0.41***	-0.19***	-0.24***
		Montreal	-0.11***	-0.12***	-0.10***	-0.21***	-0.21***
		Ottawa-Hull	0.02	0.03	-0.03	-0.08**	-0.08*
		Toronto	-0.11***	-0.09***	-0.08***	-0.11***	-0.17***
		Winnipeg	-0.08*	0.01	-0.06	-0.08	-0.16***
		Calgary	-0.04	0.04	-0.10**	0.10**	-0.18***
		Edmonton	-0.09	-0.01	-0.11**	-0.08*	-0.16***
		Vancouver	-0.10***	-0.08***	-0.04	0.00	-0.06***

Variables in model include: 8 age cohorts, 12 dummys for schooling, 5 dummys for marital status, 3 dummys for official language ability, and 3 for group status. The Canada wide regression includes 13 dummies for region (10 CMAs, a small CMA identifier, and non-CMA identifier.

Source: 1971, 1981, 1986, 1991 and 1996 census mainbase.

Selection: All Canadian-born residents of Canada, 25 to 64 years of age, whose primary source of income is from wages and salaries. People without any schooling were dropped from the sample as were those without any earnings.

Significance: ***: 0.01, **: 0.05, *: 0.1

VISIBLE-MINORITY WOMEN

The picture for visible-minority women is very different. At the Canada-wide level (table 4.2, lower panel of females) in 1971 among Canadian-born women, visible minorities earned about 9 per cent *more* than white women with similar age, marital status, official language, and education characteristics. This pattern of positive (or at least non-negative) earnings differentials also holds for all of the CMAs examined except Halifax.

By 1981, however, much of the earnings advantage for visible-minority women had disappeared. Although the point estimates are still positive, in about half the cases they are insignificant, which implies that for many cities, we cannot reject the hypothesis that white and visible-minority women earned the same amount. Only in Calgary and Vancouver did visible-minority women enjoy a significant earnings advantage in comparison to white women.

From 1986 to 1996 we see a pattern for visible-minority women that can be described as 'losing ground.' In 1996, only in Vancouver did visible-minority women enjoy a statistically significant earnings advantage. In all other CMAs, visible-minority women had earnings either insignificantly different from or significantly less than the earnings of white women. For example, in Montreal and Toronto, visible-minority women earned 19 per cent and 12 per cent less, respectively, than white women with identical personal characteristics.

Patterns over time for specific cities are illuminating. In Halifax, the negative earnings differential faced by visible-minority women in comparison with white women was fairly stable over the later years, equal to about 15 per cent in 1986, 1991, and 1996. In contrast, the earnings differential in Montreal changed fairly smoothly from an earnings advantage of 11 per cent in 1971, to an amount insignificantly different from 0 per cent in 1986, to an earnings disadvantage of 19 per cent less in 1996. Toronto shows a pattern similar to that of Montreal, but Vancouver stands out as different. In Vancouver, visible-minority women earned significantly more than white women in each of the census years, varying from a 9 per cent earnings advantage in 1991 to a 19 per cent earnings advantage in 1981.

Overall, for non-white women, the period 1981 through 1996 was one of worsening relative earnings outcomes. Aboriginal women saw their fortunes going from bad to worse, while visible-minority women saw their position decline from one of earnings advantage over or parity with white women to one of overall earnings disadvantage.

Results for Men

ABORIGINAL MEN

For Canada as a whole, the results for Aboriginal men are similar to those for Aboriginal women (see table 4.2). However, the negative earnings differentials are much larger for men than for women. At the Canada-wide level in all of the census years, Aboriginal men received about half the earnings of white men with similar characteristics.

Because Aboriginal people are concentrated outside the CMAs and in a few of Canada's large CMAs, the situation in most of Canada's largest CMAs is not quite as bleak. In these places, the negative earnings differentials are neither as large nor as tightly estimated. In 1971, Aboriginal men living in Montreal, Toronto, or Vancouver, earned substantially less than white men with similar attributes. The coefficients for these three cities are –0.13, –0.24, and –0.40, respectively. In 1981, the earnings differentials shrank in these three large CMAs. However, by 1996, the negative earnings differentials faced by Aboriginal men in these CMAs had grown to be even larger than they were in 1971, with coefficients of –0.27 (Montreal), –0.49 (Toronto), and –0.52 (Vancouver) in 1996.

In the smaller CMAs a similar pattern of decline can be seen; however, the pattern is different across CMAs, with Aboriginal men facing relatively smaller negative earnings differentials in Ottawa-Hull and Halifax through the 1970s and 1980s, but then increasing through the 1990s. In the other CMAs, the negative earnings differentials are more consistent and remain lower. The pattern over time for Aboriginal men in Canada's labour markets is depressing. Although there was some improvement in their relative position between 1971 and 1981, this was entirely undone by declining relative performance in the 1980s and 1990s. By 1996, Aboriginal men again faced huge negative earnings differentials, earning as little as half of what white workers earned in some cities.

VISIBLE-MINORITY MEN

Table 4.2 shows the pattern of earnings differentials among Canadian-born men between whites and visible minorities with similar characteristics in different geographic areas from 1971 to 1996. For Canada as a whole in 1971, visible-minority workers faced a significant negative earnings differential of 5 per cent in comparison with white workers. This differential was between 3 per cent and 7 per cent through 1991.

However, the relative position of visible-minority men worsened in the early 1990s. By 1996, that negative earnings differential had grown to about 15 per cent.

Looking first at Montreal, Toronto, and Vancouver, we see that the 1970s and 1980s might be characterized by stability or improvement in the relative labour-market performance of visible-minority men in comparison with white men. In Montreal and Toronto, the negative earnings differentials were approximately –10 per cent in 1971, 1981, and 1986. In Vancouver, there was some improvement: the negative earnings differential shrank from –10 per cent in 1971 to an amount insignificantly different from zero in 1986. In contrast, the period after 1986 is one of decline in the relative performance of visible-minority men in all three CMAs. In Montreal and Toronto, the negative earnings differential grew by about 10 percentage points between 1986 and 1996, and in Vancouver, the insignificant earnings disadvantage found in 1986 turned to a significant negative earnings differential of –6 per cent in 1996.

In the smaller CMAs, the estimated earnings differentials are in most cases not as pronounced and do not vary to the same degree. The pattern of improvement in the relative earnings of visible-minority men is not as evident in the smaller CMAs as it is in the larger CMAs. In fact, the negative earnings differential in Halifax more than doubled between 1971 and 1986 and then decreased by 1996 to –24 per cent. However, the general pattern of declining relative earnings by visible minorities between 1991 and 1996 noted for the larger CMAs is strongly evident in the smaller CMAs.[8]

Overall, the pattern for non-white men (as was the case for non-white women) from 1981 to 1996 was one of worsening outcomes. The severe disadvantage for Aboriginal men got even worse, and the relatively small disadvantage for visible-minority men grew from –3 per cent in 1981 to –15 per cent in 1996.

Quasi-Cohort Analysis

Table 4.2 offers insight into the evolution of Aboriginal and visible-minority earnings differentials over time. Age is related to earnings because earnings typically increase with age up to a point and then decrease. As well, earnings tend to increase slowly over time with productivity growth. Thus, these two phenomena should be treated together. Ideally, we could address this by analysing a panel of individuals over time and asking whether or not their birth cohort and age affect the structure of the ethnic-origin differentials. However, our data do not permit exact-panel analysis. One solution is to use quasi-panel methods, which involve estimating ethnic-origin differentials for each birth cohort and age group in each period, and then drawing out the actual history of earnings differentials by age for different birth cohorts over time.

Quasi-cohort analysis has a big advantage if we are concerned about the generational composition of the Canadian-born visible-minority population. The immigration flow of visible minorities to Canada was relatively high in the late-nineteenth and early-twentieth centuries, low until the 1960s, and high thereafter (see Pendakur 2002). Thus, one might assume that working-age Canadian-born visible minorities in the 1970s were probably children of other Canadian-born visible minorities, but that working-age Canadian-born visible minorities in the 1990s were more likely to be children of immigrants. If immigration effects carry across the generations (Trejo 1998), then comparison of these populations is invalid. However, if we hold constant the birth cohort of Canadian-born working-age visible minorities, then we are implicitly holding constant the generational composition of these populations. Thus, if quasi-cohort analysis reveals the same patterns as the simple analysis in table 4.2, then the results are probably not driven by changes in the generational composition of the Canadian-born visible-minority population.

Figures 4.1 through 4.4 summarize results from log-earnings regressions by sex in which ethnic origin is interacted with five-year-wide age groups. For example, figure 4.1 shows how earnings differentials for Aboriginal women in six birth cohorts have evolved over time. The eldest cohort was born between 1932 and 1936, and women in this cohort faced a negative earnings differential of –8 per cent in 1971, –4 per cent in 1981, –1 per cent in 1986, –5 per cent in 1991 and a positive earnings differential of 3 per cent in 1996. This good-news story is characteristic of outcomes for the eldest cohorts. However, when we look at younger cohorts of Aboriginal women, we see the opposite pattern over time. For these Aboriginal women, negative earnings differentials shrank between 1971 and 1981 but then enlarged between 1986 and 1996.

For Aboriginal men, the wage disparities tend to be deeper. In 1971, Aboriginal men born in the 1930s could expect about half the earnings of their white male counterparts (see figure 4.2). Although there was some improvement during the 1970s, this was followed by a retrenchment of disparity during the 1980s and 1990s. The pattern for other birth cohorts is broadly similar.

Figure 4.1. Earnings differentials by age cohorts and year, Aboriginal females, Canada, 1971 to 1996

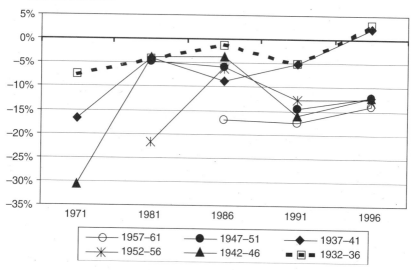

Figure 4.2. Earnings differentials by age cohorts and year, Aboriginal males, Canada, 1971 to 1996

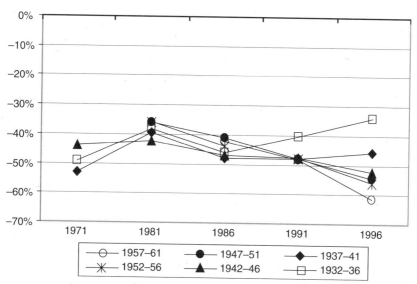

Figure 4.3. Earnings differentials by age cohorts and year, visible minority females, Canada, 1971 to 1996

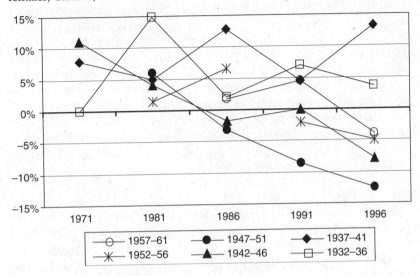

Figure 4.4. Earnings differentials by age cohorts and year, visible minority males, Canada, 1971 to 1996

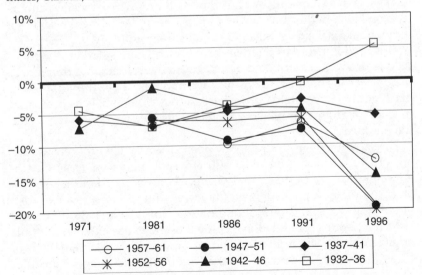

Visible-minority men and women tend to face smaller earnings differentials than Aboriginal workers regardless of age cohort (see figures 4.3 and 4.4). The other trend that is apparent is a general worsening of earnings differentials between 1991 and 1996 among men, regardless of cohort. Among women, there are a number of cohorts whose members actually make comparatively more than their white female counterparts. However, even here there was a decline in advantage between 1991 and 1996 for most visible-minority cohorts. That a decline in relative outcomes is observed for men and women for all birth cohorts suggests that compositional changes are not driving the decline seen in table 4.2, because composition does not change within a birth cohort.

Earnings Differentials by Detailed Group

So far the analysis suggests that as a group, Canadian-born visible-minority and Aboriginal peoples face a significant earnings penalty compared to whites, after controlling for personal characteristics. However, the visible-minority category is an amalgam of many distinct non-European groups, including Chinese, South Asian, and black. In the same way, the white grouping is the aggregate of all people of European origin. If there are substantial differences in the patterns of earnings differentials across subgroups, we may be overstating the size of the disadvantaged group – if, for example, the visible-minority disadvantage is driven mainly by one ethnic sub-group in the visible-minority aggregate. In this case, we would also be understating the earnings differential for the most disadvantaged sub-group(s).

This section explores the degree to which labour-market disadvantage is unevenly distributed across twenty-seven ethnic groups over the five census periods. In this way we may ask, for example, whether black groups have higher or lower earnings differentials as compared to Chinese groups, or whether there are disadvantaged groups within the European (white) category.

The selection of groups is largely determined by the 1971 census coding structure, which is the most restrictive and allows only a single ethnic origin to be reported. For 1971 and 1981, as noted earlier, single-origin ethnic groups are defined (nineteen white groups, seven visible-minority groups, and one Aboriginal category).[9] For 1986, 1991, and 1996, five groups are added to include those with more than one ethnic origin. Four of these multiple-origin groups consist of combinations of either British or French with another origin. A final category includes people with more than one origin other than British or French. Thus, coefficients are directly comparable between 1986 and 1996, but less comparable in 1971 and 1981 because of changes in data collection and coding.

Regressions are run separately for men and women, and the comparison group is males or females of British (single-origin) ancestry. As with previous analyses, controls include age groups, highest level of schooling, marital status, CMA, household size, and official language ability. In recognition of the fact that labour markets are local and that different groups may face varying levels of labour-market advantage or disadvantage depending on where they live, separate regressions are also run for Canada's largest three CMAs: Montreal, Toronto, and Vancouver.

This section contains a very large quantity of estimated coefficients, but we think they can be summarized fairly simply. In previous research (Pendakur and Pendakur 1998), we found that the white ethnic grouping contained substantial heterogeneity in labour-market outcomes using 1991 public-use data. In particular, we noted that southern European ethnic groups, especially Greeks, fared relatively poorly in Canadian labour markets. We saw less heterogeneity among the visible-minority ethnic groups in the 1991 public-use data. In particular, we concluded that the visible-minority ethnic groups for whom we had sufficient numbers of observations – blacks and Chinese – earned significantly less than British-origin men.

In this section, we show that the results we saw in the 1991 data for European ethnic groups are largely reproduced in the larger sample and in other census years. There is heterogeneity among European ethnic groups in their labour-market performance, but it seems to have little pattern over time, with one exception. Those with ethnic Spanish origins saw steadily worsening labour-market outcomes over the five census periods. It is notable that this group comprised almost entirely people of European origin in 1971, but by 1996 comprised a majority of Latin American-origin people.

We also show that the results we saw in the 1991 public-use data for visible-minority ethnic groups are largely reproduced in the larger sample and other census years. However, it seems that for most visible-minority groups, the negative earnings differential has grown in size between the 1980s and 1990s. A notable exception concerns those of ethnic Chinese origin, whose labour-market disadvantage had shrunk to essentially zero by 1996 at the Canada-wide level.

RESULTS FOR FEMALES

Table 4.3 shows estimated earnings differentials for twenty-seven ethnic groups at the Canada-wide level. Table 4.4 shows estimated earnings differentials for ten selected ethnic groups for each of Canada's three largest cities. Looking first at table 4.3, we see that among women in 1971, seven ethnic groups faced significant negative earnings differentials and nine enjoyed positive earnings differentials compared to British-origin women. Scandinavian, Dutch, Jewish, black, and Aboriginal women all experienced earnings disadvantages ranging from –3 per cent (for Scandinavian women) to –19 per cent (for Aboriginal women). Six European groups (French, Baltic, Polish, Italian, Balkan, and Ukrainian) and three visible-minority groups (Arab, Chinese, and Japanese) earned significantly more than British-origin women (ranging from 3 per cent more for French-origin women to 18 per cent more for Japanese-origin women).

In 1986, women in only a few ethnic groups had earnings significantly different from British-origin women. Jewish and Greek-origin women faced negative earnings differentials of –7 per cent and –19 per cent, respectively. Women in some ethnic groups fared better than British-origin women. French, German, Italian, and Japanese women earned between 4 per cent and 29 per cent more than British-origin women with similar credentials. Among people reporting more than one origin, those reporting British in combination with another origin experienced a significant earnings disadvantage.

The pattern of negative and positive earnings differentials in 1996 is similar to that in earlier years, but the differentials tend to be larger in magnitude. Among European-origin women, Jewish and Greek women faced significant negative earnings differentials of –11 per cent and –4 per cent, respectively. Among women of non-European origin, South Asian, black, and Aboriginal women saw earnings disadvantages ranging from –8 per cent to –35 per cent compared to British-origin women.

RESULTS FOR MALES

Earlier results for men suggested that the situation for visible-minority and Aboriginal males worsened steadily over the five census periods. This pattern is mirrored at the level of individual groups. In 1971, for example, of the six groups who earned less than British-origin men, three were from non-European origins. Chinese, black, and Aboriginal men faced earnings differentials of –12 per cent, –17 per cent, and –48 per cent, respectively. French, Portuguese, and Spanish-origin men also had lower earnings, facing earnings differentials of –3 per cent, –13 per cent, and –6 per cent, respectively. Notably, the disadvantaged visible-minority groups fared worse than the disadvantaged European groups in 1971. We see a very similar pattern of disadvantage across ethnic groups in 1986, with two new features: Japanese-origin men earned more than British-origin men, and Spanish-origin men earned about the same as British-origin men. Finally, the results for European groups in 1986 show that no European ethnic group was characterized by higher earnings than those of British-origin men.

By 1996, the pattern of earnings differentials across groups seems to have changed. Among European-origin men, many groups had higher earnings than men of British origin (French, Polish, Dutch, German, Czech/Slovak, Balkan, and Ukrainian). Two groups had substantially lower earnings: Greek and Spanish-origin men faced earnings differentials of –19 per cent and –17 per cent, respectively. The outcomes for Spanish-origin men seem to have worsened substantially over the twenty-five-year period.

Among visible-minority men, the relative labour-market performance of Chinese men improved substantially. By 1996, Chinese men earned about the same as British-origin men. Japanese men earned slightly more than British-origin men. However, outcomes for other visible-minority groups worsened between 1986 and 1996. Although Arab and South Asian men had earnings insignificantly different from British origin men prior to 1996, by 1996 these groups faced differentials of –6 per cent and –22 per cent, respectively. The relative earnings of black and Aboriginal men also declined in 1996, to the extent that they faced earnings differentials of –36 per cent and –63 per cent, respectively.

In previous research (Pendakur and Pendakur 2002), we found some evidence suggesting that earnings differentials related to ethnicity could be correlated with the ethnic composition of the local population. Different cities have different ethnic-group compositions, so we might expect to see varying patterns of earnings differentials across cities. In particular, our earlier research found that members of large ethnic communities in certain cities seemed to fare better than members of small ethnic communities in those same cities. In the next section, we try to assess how earnings differentials across ethnic groups vary across Canada's largest cities over the twenty-five-year period.

FEMALES IN MONTREAL, TORONTO, AND VANCOUVER

Table 4.4 shows estimated earnings differentials for ten selected ethnic groups in Canada's three largest CMAs for 1971, 1986, and 1996. First, consider earnings differentials among women in Montreal. In 1971,

Table 4.3. Earnings differentials by detailed ethnic origin, Canada, 1986 to 1996

Sex	Group	1971	1981	1986	1991	1996
Females	French	0.03***	0.06***	0.04***	0.04***	0.03***
	Scandinavian	-0.03***	0.01	0.02	0.01	0.01
	Baltic	0.11**	0.08*	-0.07	0.03	0.03
	Polish	0.09***	0.08***	0.01	0.04***	0.06***
	Dutch	-0.06***	-0.03**	-0.02	-0.02*	0.00
	German	-0.01*	0.03***	0.08**	0.01*	0.02**
	Russian	-0.02	0.04	-0.15	-0.02	0.01
	Hungarian	0.04	0.06**	-0.15*	0.02	0.06**
	Czech / Slovak	0.05*	0.04	-0.03	0.07**	0.02
	Jewish	-0.05***	-0.09***	-0.07***	-0.06***	-0.11***
	Portuguese	-0.10	0.05	0.24	0.11***	0.07**
	Italian	0.06***	0.07***	0.10***	0.07***	0.06***
	Greek	-0.02	-0.04	-0.19**	-0.10***	-0.04*
	Balkan	0.09**	0.15***	0.10	0.10***	0.09***
	Ukrainian	0.09***	0.09***	0.04	0.07***	0.06***
	Spanish	-0.05	0.11	0.25	-0.06	0.01
	Arab	0.10**	0.04	0.17*	0.01	-0.01
	Japanese	0.18***	0.17***	0.29**	0.15***	0.14***
	Chinese	0.10***	0.10**	0.03	0.14***	0.10***
	South Asian	0.04	0.10	0.09	0.00	-0.08**
	Black	-0.10**	0.03	0.02	-0.11***	-0.22***
	Aboriginal origins	-0.19***	-0.10***	-0.04	-0.19***	-0.15***
	Br. Fr. & other			-0.09***	-0.07***	-0.05***
	British & French			-0.01	-0.02***	0.00
	British & other			-0.07***	-0.03***	-0.01**
	French & other			-0.01	-0.02*	-0.03***

Table 4.3. (concluded)

Sex	Group	1971	1981	1986	1991	1996
Males	French	-0.03***	0.00	-0.04***	-0.01**	0.00
	Scandinavian	0.04***	0.09***	-0.04	0.05***	0.04***
	Baltic	0.03	-0.06**	0.01	0.04	0.04
	Polish	0.01	0.03***	-0.01	0.04***	0.06***
	Dutch	0.00	0.02**	-0.03	0.08***	0.08***
	German	0.01***	0.05***	-0.02	0.04***	0.06***
	Russian	-0.01	0.05***	-0.02	0.02	0.01
	Hungarian	-0.02*	0.05***	-0.04	0.01	0.01
	Czech / Slovak	0.05***	0.08***	0.08	0.09***	0.08***
	Jewish	0.08***	-0.01	0.01	0.05***	0.00
	Portuguese	-0.13***	0.08	-0.40***	-0.02	-0.01
	Italian	0.02***	0.05***	-0.03*	0.03***	0.01
	Greek	0.00	-0.10***	-0.14**	-0.17***	-0.19***
	Balkan	0.07***	0.02	0.01	0.06***	0.08***
	Ukrainian	0.00	0.04***	0.00	0.05***	0.02**
	Spanish	-0.06**	-0.06	0.06	-0.14***	-0.17***
	Arab	0.02	0.02	0.07	-0.03	-0.06*
	Japanese	0.00	0.09***	0.22***	0.10***	0.06**
	Chinese	-0.12***	-0.07***	-0.17**	-0.05***	0.00
	South Asian	0.04	-0.07	-0.16	-0.10**	-0.22***
	Black	-0.17***	-0.22***	-0.16**	-0.25***	-0.36***
	Aboriginal origins	-0.48***	-0.51***	-0.45***	-0.64***	-0.63***
	Br. Fr. & other			-0.15***	-0.03***	-0.02***
	British & French			-0.07***	-0.01	-0.02***
	British & other			-0.05***	0.02***	0.01
	French & other			-0.07***	-0.03***	-0.07***

Controls include: Age groups, schooling, marital status, census metropolitan area, household size, and official language ability.

Note: Canadian, other European, other Asian, other single origins, and other multiple origins were included as controls but have been omitted from the table.

Significance: ***: 0.01, **: 0.05, *: 0.1

Table 4.4. Earnings differentials by CMA and year, for selected ethnic groups in Montreal, Toronto, and Vancouver; 1971, 1986, 1996

Sex	Group	Montreal			Toronto			Vancouver		
		1971 Coef sig	1986 Coef sig	1996 Coef sig	1971 Coef sig	1986 Coef sig	1996 Coef sig	1971 Coef sig	1986 Coef sig	1996 Coef sig
Female	French	0.02*	0.03**	0.04**	0.00	0.07***	0.03	0.01	0.01	-0.03
	Dutch	0.07	-0.03	0.02	-0.06	-0.07*	-0.01	0.00	0.05	0.00
	Jewish	-0.03	-0.06**	-0.07**	-0.06***	-0.10***	-0.10***	0.02	0.03	-0.05
	Portuguese	0.25	0.18	-0.05	-0.56***	0.15	0.00	-0.01	0.04	0.05
	Italian	0.08***	0.08**	0.01	-0.05*	0.10***	0.02	0.04	0.15***	0.09**
	Greek	-0.15*	-0.19**	-0.18***	0.05	-0.07	0.01	0.04	-0.32*	0.02
	Chinese	0.09	0.21	0.12	-0.06	0.09	0.00	0.12*	0.24***	0.15***
	S. Asian	0.28	0.26	-0.21	-0.14	0.00	-0.21**	0.18	0.14	0.04
	Black	0.03	-0.03	-0.26***	-0.01	-0.08	-0.27***	-0.40*	.03	-0.08
	Aboriginal	-0.08	-0.09	-0.29***	-0.10	-0.24***	-0.17**	-0.19**	-0.07	-0.46***
Male	French	-0.09***	-0.03***	0.01	-0.04***	-0.05***	0.00	-0.03**	-0.05*	-0.03
	Dutch	0.02	-0.15*	0.16	-0.01	-0.04	0.06*	0.00	-0.01	0.08**
	Jewish	0.09***	0.05*	0.02	0.01	-0.05***	-0.05**	0.04	-0.05	-0.08
	Portuguese	-0.22***	-0.19	-0.08	-0.33***	0.06	-0.03	0.04	-0.35*	0.01
	Italian	-0.10***	-0.02	-0.07***	-0.04***	0.04**	-0.03**	0.05*	0.05	0.05
	Greek	-0.09**	-0.24***	-0.27***	-0.11***	-0.10*	-0.18***	0.04	0.04	-0.14
	Chinese	-0.32***	-0.24**	-0.19*	-0.25***	-0.22***	-0.09***	-0.17***	-0.08**	0.01
	S. Asian	-0.41***	0.40	-0.44**	-0.07	-0.49***	-0.30***	-0.06	-0.02	-0.20***
	Black	-0.28***	-0.27***	-0.41***	-0.14***	-0.36***	-0.41***	-0.21*	-0.31***	-0.19**
	Aboriginal	-0.19***	-0.14***	-0.18***	-0.25***	-0.34***	-0.87***	-0.41***	-0.40***	-0.68***

Variables in model include: 8 age cohorts, 12 dummys for schooling, 5 dummys for marital status, household size, and 3 dummys for official language ability.

Source: 1971, 1981, 1986, 1991, and 1996 census mainbase.

Significance: ***: 0.01, **: 0.05, *: 0.1

French and Italian women earned 2 per cent and 8 per cent more, respectively, than British women. In contrast, Greek women earned 15 per cent less than British women. By 1986, the pattern of differentials had changed little except that in this year, Jewish women also earned significantly less than British-origin women. By 1996, black and Aboriginal women were also facing a statistically significant earnings disadvantage.

A similar pattern can be seen in Toronto. In 1971, Jewish, Portuguese, and Italian women faced negative earnings differentials. In 1986, Aboriginal women joined the disadvantaged groups and in 1996, South Asian and black women also faced significant earnings disadvantage. Among European-origin women, only Jewish women earned less than British-origin women in 1996. Broadly speaking, for women in Montreal and Toronto, the disadvantaged ethnic groups became less European and more visible-minority in composition over time.

In Vancouver, the pattern over time is different. Aboriginal women earned much less than British-origin women in every year, but women in visible-minority ethnic groups did not (although the earnings differential for black women in 1971 is marginally significantly negative).

MALES IN MONTREAL, TORONTO, AND VANCOUVER

In Montreal, of the ten selected ethnic groups in 1971, only Jewish men earned significantly more than British-origin men. French men, men of southern European and non-European origins all earned significantly less than British-origin men. Portuguese, Italian, and Greek men saw earnings gaps of –22 per cent, –10 per cent, and –9 per cent, respectively. Chinese, South Asian, black, and Aboriginal men faced earnings gaps of –32 per cent, –41 per cent, –28 per cent and –19 per cent, respectively. Here, the visible minority and Aboriginal groups on the whole fared even worse than the disadvantaged European ethnic groups. These patterns in earnings differentials across ethnic groups in Montreal are fairly stable over time, except that the earnings gap faced by French men disappeared by 1996. It is also worth noting that over time, the earnings gap experienced by Chinese men shrinks, but that faced by black men grows.

In Toronto, we see broadly similar patterns. French men earned significantly less than British men in 1971, but earned the same by 1996. Italian and Greek men earned less than British men in all three years. Chinese men earned 25 per cent less than British men in 1971, but by 1996 earn only 9 per cent less. The opposite trend is evident for black men. In 1971, they faced an earnings differential of –14 per cent, which grew to –41 per cent by 1996. South Asians earned insignificantly less than British men in 1971, but by 1996 earned 30 per cent less. Outcomes for Aboriginal men deteriorated drastically: the estimated coefficient dropped from –0.25 in 1971 to –0.87 in 1996.

In Vancouver, the time trends for the different ethnic groups are similar to those observed in Montreal and Toronto, but the magnitude of earnings differentials are smaller. On the whole, European ethnic groups did not tend to face earnings gaps compared to British men. French men faced a –3 per cent earnings gap in 1971, but earned the same as British men by 1996. Among non-Europeans, we see some significant earnings differentials. Chinese men earned 17 per cent less than British men in 1971, but by 1996 faced no earnings gap. Black men earned significantly less than British men throughout the period, facing earnings gaps of approximately –20 per cent in both 1971 and 1996. Outcomes for South Asian and Aboriginal men deteriorated somewhat over the period. South Asian men faced no gap in 1971, but earned 20 per cent less than British men in 1996. The estimated coefficients for Aboriginal men in 1971 and 1996 are –0.41 and –0.68, respectively.

Assessing the Visible-Minority Category

As our analysis has shown, the aggregate categories of white, visible minority, and Aboriginal groups hide some variability across their constituent sub-groups. A number of European ethnic groups faced earnings gaps in each time period, a pattern that was hidden when examination was limited to looking at just the aggregate groups. Similarly, some visible-minority groups seem not to face labour-market disadvantage. For example, Japanese-origin workers did not earn less than British-origin workers in any year. We also find that different groups experience different degrees of earnings disadvantage depending on where they live. Thus, the groups that faced earnings gaps in Montreal are not necessarily the same as those that faced gaps in Vancouver.

Two questions emerge about the usefulness of the visible-minority category as an identifier of labour-market disadvantage: how does it change over time, and how does it vary across place? Considering the labour-market performance of groups comprising the visible-minority category first, we saw in table 4.3 that the pattern of disadvantage did change. In 1971, Arab, Japanese, and South Asian men were not disadvantaged at all. Spanish men were somewhat disadvantaged, and

Chinese and black men were very disadvantaged. At the time the *Employment Equity Act* was passed in 1986, Japanese-origin men earned more than British-origin men. However, by 1996, Arab and South Asian men had joined the disadvantaged groups, while Chinese-origin men faced no earnings disadvantage in Canada-wide labour statistics. Given that in 1986 almost half of the Canadian-born working-age visible minorities were of Chinese or Japanese origin, this suggests that the visible-minority category is somewhat blunt. On the other hand, South Asian and black men, who also comprise about half the population, faced very large earnings differentials.

For women, the pattern is similar, but the magnitudes are smaller and the starting point is one of higher rather than lower earnings. In 1971, only black women earned significantly less than white women, while Arab, Japanese, and Chinese women earned more. By 1996, Japanese and Chinese women continued earning more, but South Asian and black women earned significantly less than white women. This latter case may be evidence of a double negative.

One might think there is cause to develop a new categorization aimed at disadvantage that excludes workers of Japanese and Chinese origins. However, examination of earnings disadvantage across CMAs reveals that such a strategy may be ill-advised. In 1996, South Asian and black men faced substantial earnings disadvantage in Montreal, Toronto, and Vancouver. In contrast, Chinese men faced gaps in Montreal and Toronto, but not in Vancouver (where they are concentrated). Thus, the case for the bluntness of the category is partially driven by the heterogeneity of earnings differentials across cities. In Montreal and Toronto, the visible-minority category may adequately identify disadvantaged men while in Vancouver it may not. Considering that two-thirds of Canadian-born Chinese and Japanese workers are in Vancouver, this suggests to us that the ethnic composition of a city is important to the outcomes faced by minority workers (see also Pendakur and Pendakur 2001).

Conclusions

Previous research using data from the 1990s has shown that visible minorities and Aboriginals earn less than white workers, especially among men. Our goal in this chapter has been to show how these differentials have evolved over a long period of time by using a consistent dataset and econometric methodology. We find that for both broad ethnic categories studied – Aboriginal people and those from visible minorities – there was stasis or mild improvement in relative earnings compared to white workers between 1971 and 1981, stasis through 1991, followed by decline in relative earnings between 1991 and 1996. This finding is broadly true for Aboriginal and visible-minority persons, regardless of sex or city of residence.

We find some important differences across categories of sex. In particular, as noted in previous work (Baker and Benjamin 1997; Pendakur and Pendakur 1998), the pattern of earnings differentials among women is quite different from that among men. The earnings differentials faced by Aboriginal and visible-minority women in comparison with white women are smaller and sometimes positive. However, the pattern of erosion of relative standing over the 1990s is evident among both men and women. We also find some important differences across our broadly defined ethnic categories. In particular, among both men and women, Aboriginals fare less well than visible minorities. This reinforces results from previous research (George and Kuhn 1994; Pendakur and Pendakur 1998).

From a policy perspective, these findings are concerning. A decade after the implementation of employment-equity programming, inequity is on the rise at the same time as larger and larger numbers of Canadian-born minorities are entering the labour market. It appears that the labour market is neither colour blind nor moving towards that goal.

Notes

This chapter was previously published in *Canadian Public Policy/Analyse de Politiques* 28, no. 4 (2002): 489–512.

1 Researchers should note that the LMAS and SLID master files, which are available free of charge to academic researchers through the Research Data Centres, have much better geographical information than the public-use files.
2 A Census Metropolitan Area (CMA) is a very large urban area (known as the urban core), together with adjacent urban and rural areas (known as urban and rural fringes) that have a high degree of social and economic integration with the urban core. A CMA has an urban core population of at least 100,000, based on the previous census (Statistics Canada 1996).
3 For the same reason, we do not include hours of work, weeks of work, and full-time/part-time status.

4 The 1971 long form was given to 33 per cent of all households. In subsequent census periods, the long form data were collected from 20 per cent of households.

5 The 1971 census question on schooling does not include a flag for high school. We therefore combine the categories for ten years of high school or more for 1971 through to 1996.

6 For the purposes of the *Employment Equity Act*, Aboriginal persons are people who claim any Aboriginal origin, regardless of other origins claimed. Thus, someone claiming both British and North American Indian origin is an Aboriginal person. Bill C-32, which allowed people with Aboriginal ancestry to reclaim their Aboriginal rights, resulted in a substantial increase in Aboriginal reporting. Essentially, more people who would have reported European origins in 1986 reported Aboriginal origins in 1991 and 1996. In 1971, only a single-ethnic origin was collected from each respondent. We used this to define group status. Thus, the 1971 group-status definition is the most restrictive, yielding smaller proportions of visible-minority and Aboriginal persons. There are visible-minority flag variables on the 1981 to 1996 censuses. We note that Statistics Canada imputes visible-minority status based on ethnic origin as well as religion, mother tongue, home language, and place of birth.

7 We note that in 1971, only about 42 per cent of the women in our sample were labour-force participants. This rate rose greatly over the twenty-five-year period studied. Unfortunately, adequate treatment of the participation decision is not possible with these census data.

8 We also ran these regressions including controls for weeks worked and full-time/part-time status, which are the only job characteristics that permit consistent definitions over time. These results are presented in the tables below. Clearly, including these controls does make a difference to the estimated earnings differentials. For Aboriginal women, the earnings differentials that control for weeks and full-time status show a pattern of increased-earnings disadvantage over time, with the differential going from +2 per cent in 1971 to –2 per cent in 1981 to –6 per cent in 1996. Compared with the results from table 4.2, the pattern over the 1970s is different, but the pattern between 1981 and 1996 is similar, although smaller in magnitude. Turning to visible-minority women, the pattern of declining relative earnings outcomes over the entire period shows up even when these new controls are added. When we consider Aboriginal men, the pattern is that of large persistent earnings differentials even with these additional controls. However, the differentials are smaller in absolute size, suggesting that a part of the differentials faced by Aboriginal men is accounted for by differences in weeks and

hours worked. Finally, adding these additional controls makes essentially no difference for visible-minority men between 1971 and 1991, but the large increase in the differential in 1996 seen in table 4.2 is somewhat attenuated.
9 In 1971, only a single-ethnic origin was collected. In 1981, although only one ethnic origin was solicited, it was possible to provide two responses, both of which would be collected. Thus, 1981 represents a transition year for the collection of ethnic-origin data.

References

Akbari, A. 1992a. *Economics of immigration and racial discrimination: A literature survey (1970–1989)*. Ottawa: Multiculturalism and Citizenship.
– 1992b. *Ethnicity and earnings discrimination in Canadian labour markets: Some evidence from the 1986 census*. Ottawa: Multiculturalism and Citizenship.
Baker, M., and D. Benjamin. 1997. Ethnicity, foreign birth and earnings: A Canada/US comparison. In *Transition and structural change in the North American labour market*, ed. M. Abbott, C. Beach, and R. Chaykowski. Kingston, ON: IRC Press/ Industrial Relations Centre/ John Deutsch Institute for the Study of Economic Policy, Queen's University.
Becker, Gary S. 1996. *Accounting for tastes*. Cambridge, MA: Harvard University Press, 1996.
Christofides, L.N., and R. Swidinsky. 1994. Wage determination by gender and visible minority status: Evidence from the 1989 LMAS. *Canadian Public Policy/Analyse de Politiques* 20 (1): 34–51.
de Silva, A. 1992. *Earnings of immigrants: A comparative analysis*. Ottawa: Economic Council of Canada Working Paper Series.
– 1999. Wage discrimination against natives. *Canadian Public Policy /Analyse de Politiques* 25 (1): 65–85.
de Silva, A., and C. Dougherty. 1996. *Discrimination against visible minority men*. Ottawa: HRDC Applied Research Branch, Strategic Policy Document, W-96–6E.
Dickens, W., and K. Lang. 1992. Labor market segmentation theory: Reconsidering the evidence. In *Labor economics: Problems in analyzing labor markets*, ed. William Darity Jr, 141–80. Norwell, MA: Kluwer Academic.
George, P., and P. Kuhn. 1994. The size and structure of native-white differentials in Canada. *Canadian Journal of Economics* 27 (1): 20–42.
Howland, J., and C. Sakellariou. 1993. Wage discrimination, occupational segregation and visible minorities in Canada. *Applied Economics* 25:1413–22.
Hum, D., and W. Simpson. 1998. *Wage opportunities for visible minorities in Can-*

ada. Income and Labour Dynamics Working Paper Series. Ottawa: Statistics Canada.

Kelly, K. 1995. Visible minorities: A diverse group. *Canadian Social Trends* 37:2–8.

Lian, J., and D. Mathews. 1998. Does the vertical mosaic still exist? Ethnicity and income in 1991. *Canadian Review of Sociology and Anthropology* 35 (4): 461–82.

Pendakur, K., and R. Pendakur. 1998. The colour of money: Earnings differentials among ethnic groups in Canada. *Canadian Journal of Economics* 31 (3): 518–48.

– 2002. Speaking in tongues: Language as both human capital and ethnicity. *International Migration Review* 36 (1): 147–77.

Pendakur, R. 2001. *Immigrants and the labour force: Policy, regulation and impact.* Montreal: McGill-Queen's University Press.

Shapiro, C., and J.E. Stiglitz. 1984. Equilibrium unemployment as a worker discipline device. *American Economic Review* 74 (3): 433–44.

Statistics Canada. 1996. *1996 Census dictionary.* Ottawa: Statistics Canada.

Stelcner, M. 2000. Earnings differentials among ethnic groups in Canada: A review of the research. *Review of Social Economy* 58 (3): 295–317.

Stelcner, M., and N. Kyriazis. 1995. An empirical analysis of earnings among ethnic groups in Canada. *International Journal of Contemporary Sociology* 32 (1): 41–79.

Trejo, S. 1998. Intergenerational progress of Mexican-origin workers in the U.S. labor market. University of California, Santa Barbara, Working Papers in Economics 98/16.

5 What Does It Take to Achieve Full Integration? Economic (Under)Performance of Chinese Immigrants in Canada

SHUGUANG WANG AND LUCIA LO

The Chinese have become the largest group of immigrants in Canada, as both landing records and the 2001 census indicate. Between 1980 and 2000, nearly 800,000 Chinese immigrants landed in Canada (Citizenship and Immigration Canada 2001). They now account for 20 per cent of Canada's total immigration intake.

A number of factors have contributed to the accelerated emigration of the Chinese from various points of origin, particularly from Hong Kong, mainland China, Taiwan, and Vietnam (Lo and Wang 1997). Many Chinese immigrants are attracted by Canada's potential economic opportunities in both business and employment. Canada welcomes them, mainly because of their potential to contribute to the country's economic growth. Despite their high educational qualifications and proficiency in Canada's official languages, however, many new Chinese immigrants are disappointed and even frustrated, because their economic performance in the Canadian labour market has been unsatisfactory (Tian 2000; *World Journal* 2003; Yu 2002). The inability of these immigrants to succeed has also caused concern in all levels of government in Canada because it has serious implications for the goals of shared citizenship, social inclusion, and integration that Canada aims to achieve through its reformed immigration program.

Having come from distinct places that have varying political, social, and economic conditions, Chinese immigrants are by no means a uniform group, and significant internal differences can be expected to exist among them. Although immigrants from mainland China, Hong Kong, and Taiwan are all Chinese in ethnicity, their political tendencies, social values, and economic behaviour are markedly different. These background variations have differentiated them within the political, cultural, and economic realms in Canada.

In Toronto, there are many Chinese business, professional, and recreational associations. Those established or chartered before the 1990s were mostly organized around immigrants from Hong Kong. The Canadian Federation of Chinese Professionals, for example, consists of doctors, dentists, lawyers, engineers, accountants, and architects who emigrated primarily from Hong Kong and were trained in Canada. More recently, in 1992, immigrants from mainland China formed their own Chinese Professionals Association of Canada (CPAC). This association is now composed of several thousand members, all of whom hold university degrees.

In the commercial sector, the diversity of Toronto's Chinese immigrants is reflected geographically. Businesses in Toronto's central Chinatown are mostly owned and run by older immigrants from southern China (though this has been gradually changing), whereas business owners in Toronto's east Chinatown are predominantly Chinese from Vietnam. Those businesses owned by immigrants from Hong Kong are mostly located in newer suburban shopping centres. A shopping centre in Markham (named Metro Square) is occupied exclusively by Taiwanese immigrants, providing Taiwanese-style products and catering mainly to Mandarin-speaking Chinese.

Because Canada's recent Chinese immigrants have diverse backgrounds, they have experienced a variety of labour market conditions. In general, immigrants from Hong Kong have higher English-language proficiency than those of other origins, and the educational credentials and work experiences they obtained in Hong Kong are more likely to be recognized by Canadian employers. Those immigrants who acquired experience in mainland China and Taiwan are much less likely to have their qualifications recognized.

The above examples demonstrate the existence of significant internal differences among Chinese immigrants in Canada. Yet with the exception of Lo and Wang (2004), these differences have not been substantiated in the scholarly literature through any systematic analyses of relevant data. Many studies either lump all Chinese together or examine subgroups separately without cross comparisons, thus bypassing a consideration of the importance of diversity among subgroups of Chinese immigrants. For example, when Chinese immigrants are compared with other ethnic groups for labour market performance, they are often conveniently combined as a uniform group (see Reitz 1997; Swidinsky and Swidinsky 2002).

The focus of this chapter is twofold. First, we analyse the changing composition of the Chinese immigrants who were admitted to Canada in the last two decades to reveal their internal differences with regard to origin, immigration class, level of education, and official language proficiency, factors which often determine their differential human capital. We then examine their economic performance in Canada. Through this study, we intend to answer two important questions: What does it take for the Chinese immigrant to be on par with the average Canadian? And how much 'seniority' do they need to achieve full integration?

Integration is defined as the process by which newcomers become a part of the social, cultural, and institutional fabric of the host community or society while at the same time retaining their own cultural identity (Breton 1992; Henry and Tator 2005). In Canada, and in keeping with its Multiculturalism Policy (Canadian Heritage 2002), integration is preferred to assimilation because the former expects that adjustments are made by both newcomers and those already living in the country (Burstein and Duncan 2003), while the latter requires that newcomers eventually give up their cultural identity in order to become entitled to places in the already-established occupational and social structures of the host society (Harles 1997). Yet integration is not necessarily easy to achieve. There are two kinds of barriers to successful integration: the 'inability' of immigrants to adapt to the host society; and the systemic prejudice and racism that often exists in the host society.

According to the wealth-maximization thesis (Borjas 1988, 1993; Mueller 1999), migrants move to countries where economic returns to their human capital are higher than in their home country (except for refugees who move for political protection). When individuals migrate, most of them carry with them certain human capital, defined as educational attainment and work experience. These assets are usually obtained in their home countries, though some possess a combination of foreign and domestic credentials. It is commonly believed that the national origin of an individual's human capital is a critical determinant of its value (Friedberg 2000). Often, education and work experience acquired in less developed countries are valued significantly less than human capital obtained in more developed countries. In some instances, the former are not recognized at all. This seriously constrains immigrants' ability to integrate into the host society.

Racism can take various forms. Perhaps the most detrimental is institutional racism 'manifested in the policies, practices and procedures, which may, directly or indirectly, consciously or unwittingly, promote, sustain or entrench differential advantages or privileges for people of certain races' (Henry and Tator 2005, 53). Weinfeld (1990) has listed a large number of indicators of racism in all its forms. Among the economic indicators, he suggests that differences in income and discrimination in employment are direct consequences of employers' bias against hiring and promoting immigrant workers due to lack of recognition of foreign credentials.

Due to such credential constraints, newcomers either experience a period of non-employment or choose to work at a job below their qualifications (Green 1999). As a result, immigrants usually begin their working lives in the host economy with lower wages than native-born workers of similar education and age (Baker and Benjamin 1994; Borjas 1985; Chiswick 1986). They are often concentrated in the so-called tertiary labour market, where their human capital is not rewarded (James et al. 2002). As length of residence increases, the earning differentials narrow. The number of years it takes for immigrants to catch up to the earning levels of the native born can be described as the minimum 'seniority' needed to achieve full economic integration. Many studies examining immigrants' economic performance in Canada have shown that the time it takes for immigrants to integrate has become increasingly longer (Reitz 1997). Devoretz and Akbari estimated that new immigrants require ten to fifteen years to adjust (Campbell 1994; Preston et al. 2003). Recently, Statistics Canada (2003) also admitted that recent immigrants earn substantially less than their Canadian-born counterparts, even after ten years in the country. Sadly, this finding holds true both for immigrants with low levels of education and for those with a university degree.

While acknowledging that differences in human capital between immigrants and native-born workers do exist, Li (2000a) also argued that human capital is often evaluated differently from its holders, depending on their phenotypic characteristics (such as identifiable linguistic characteristics and racial features). In other words, systemic racism or economic discrimination may play a role in the Canadian labour market (Pendakur and Pendakur 1998; Baker and Benjamin 1997). This paper adds further, albeit indirect, evidence for the existence of institutional racism in Canada. In our examination of the internal differences among Chinese immigrants of different origins, we focus on the variations in their human capital as reflected by immigration class, educational attainment, and proficiency in Canada's official languages. As well, our analysis of their economic performance is conducted in close association with both their human capital and their length of residency (that is, their 'seniority') in Canada. Where data permits, we also compare their economic performance in Canada's three largest Census Metropolitan Areas (CMAs): Toronto, Vancouver, and Montreal.

Data Sources

Our research objectives were achieved through analysis of two administrative datasets in the Immigration Database (IMDB): the landed immigrant data system (LIDS) and tax data. The LIDS files consist of the landing records for all the immigrants who came to Canada between 1980 and 2000. This data system includes all the information that is part of an individual's landing papers, such as country of last permanent residence (CLPR), year of landing, immigration class, educational attainment at time of landing, Canadian official language ability, and intended destination in Canada.

Using the LIDS files, four variables have some potential use in identifying Chinese immigrants – country of birth (COB), citizenship, CLPR, and mother tongue – but none of them is perfect. We elected to use mother tongue as the defining factor because we believe it is more inclusive than the other three variables, as it captures Chinese immigrants from outside of mainland China, Hong Kong, and Taiwan. In this study, an immigrant was defined as Chinese if any of the following dialects was reported as his or her mother tongue: Cantonese, Mandarin, Chinese, Shanghai, Hakka, and other Chinese dialects. Using these criteria, a total of 797,653 Chinese immigrants were identified as having arrived in Canada between 1980 and 2000.[1]

The tax data were originally collected by the federal government from the immigrants' annual tax returns. For the purpose of this study, a special tabulation for Chinese immigrants was requested and received from Statistics Canada. This tabulation was for the 1999 tax year, the most current at the time of the study. In total, 343,890 Chinese immigrants who came to Canada between 1980 and 1999 and were fifteen years old or over in 1999 were captured in these files.[2] This accounts for 53 per cent of all the Chinese immigrants who came to Canada in the study period and were fifteen years or older in 1999. Of the 343,890 tax filers, 185,525 reported employment income, 31,620 reported self-employment income, and 174,495 reported investment income.[3] With these data, we were able to examine the economic performance of the Chinese immigrants using the various types of income as indicators.

This study differs from census-based studies in an important way.

Income derived from tax returns should be more accurate than that contained in the census, because the former is reported on T4, T4a, and T5 forms issued by employers and financial institutions, whereas the latter is self-reported. Because employment and self-employment are not defined as mutually exclusive activities, some tax filers report more than one type of income. Because the tax data were provided in aggregate form only (for reasons of confidentiality) and with no information about standard deviations, statistical tests cannot be performed when income is compared among subgroups of Chinese immigrants. It should also be pointed out that data from personal income tax returns are not a good source of information for studying the economic performance of investors and entrepreneurs. Since investment is usually long-term in nature, it may take many years to generate significant returns. In addition, corporate income, usually the largest part of investment return, is separated from personal income and thus not captured in the database used for this study.

Changes in Composition of Chinese Immigrants

By Origin and Intended Destination

Of the nearly 800,000 Chinese immigrants admitted to Canada between 1980 and 2000, an overwhelming majority (90 per cent) came from four places: Hong Kong (45.6 per cent), mainland China (27.7 per cent), Taiwan (11.8 per cent), and Vietnam (5.2 per cent). The remaining 10 per cent were from the rest of the world. For this reason, our analysis is focused on the Chinese immigrants from these four major origins.

Before 1997, Chinese immigrants from Hong Kong outnumbered those of all other origins. The peak occurred in 1994, with 43,300 arrivals (figure 5.1). The number of immigrants from mainland China has been on the rise since the late 1980s. In the early 1990s, the first sharp increase occurred, a consequence of the 1989 student movement in China. The second significant increase began in 1995, when Canada opened its doors to independent immigrants from mainland China (Wallis 1998). Between 1997 and 2000, the number of mainland Chinese immigrants nearly doubled from 18,400 a year to 36,600, making mainland China the largest single source of Chinese immigrants to Canada. In the meantime, the number of Hong Kong immigrants dwindled to less than one thousand. Between 1985 and 1997, immigrants from Taiwan also rose from less than one thousand to over 13,000. After 1997,

Figure 5.1. Chinese immigrants to Canada, 1980–2000

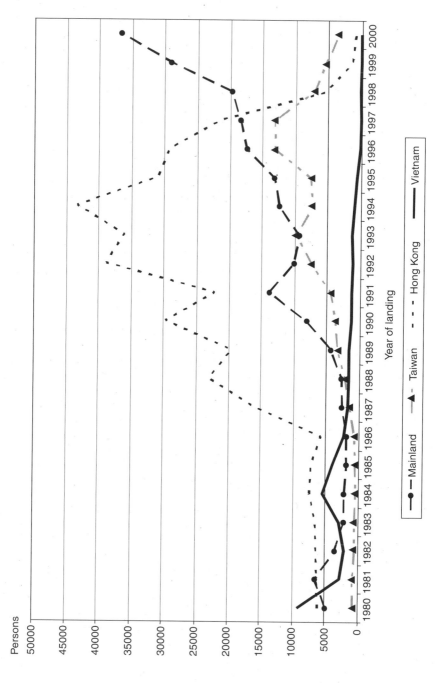

Persons

Year of landing

Mainland · · · Taiwan · · · Hong Kong Vietnam

however, their numbers also declined considerably. Most Chinese immigrants from Vietnam came to Canada in the early and mid-1980s, but their numbers diminished gradually after the mid-1990s.

Chinese immigrants to Canada highly favour large urban centres for settlement, with 95 per cent choosing one of fourteen large CMAs as their intended destination. This is 9 per cent higher than the rate at which members of the general immigrant population chose the same fourteen CMAs (86 per cent). In particular, 40 per cent of the Chinese immigrants chose Toronto and 31 per cent chose Vancouver as their intended destinations. Other favoured CMAs were Montreal (8 per cent), Calgary (4.4 per cent), Edmonton (4 per cent), and Ottawa (2.3 per cent).

By Immigration Class

Between 1980 and 2000, 54 per cent of the Chinese who came to Canada came as economic immigrants,[4] the class considered to be most able to participate in economic production and to contribute to the Canadian economy (see table 5.1). Another 42 per cent were accepted for family reunification, while only 5 per cent were admitted on humanitarian grounds. The considerable increase in economic immigrants among Chinese should also be noted. In the 1980s, only 43 per cent were economic immigrants; in the 1990s, this category increased to 58 per cent (very close to the new government quota of 60 per cent). Conversely, family immigrants declined from 47 per cent in the 1980s to 40 per cent in the 1990s (about 10 per cent higher than the new government quota). Humanitarian immigrants also decreased from 11 per cent to about 2 per cent (compared with the 10 per cent government quota), a trend many might find surprising in light of the high-profile news reports about illegal Chinese immigrants to Canada in the late 1990s (Langan 1997; Brooke 1999a, 1999b; Girard 1999a, 1999b; Thompson 1999).

Compared with the general immigrant population, Chinese immigrants during this period included a much higher proportion of economic immigrants (54 per cent versus 38 per cent). The proportion of entrepreneur-class and investor immigrants among the Chinese was also high, at 19 per cent as opposed to 7 per cent for the general immigrant population. On the other hand, the Chinese had a significantly lower proportion of humanitarian immigrants than was found among the general immigrant population during this period (5 per cent versus 16 per cent).

Table 5.1. Chinese immigrants in Canada by immigration class and origin, 1980–2000

Immigration class	Mainland China Number	%*	Hong Kong Number	%*	Taiwan Number	%*	Vietnam Number	%*	Total Chinese Number	%*	Total immigrants %*
Economic**	106400	48.2	206870	56.9	75653	80.1	110	0.3	430592	54.0	37.9
1980s	2252	6.9	65523	62.8	8008	77.8	73	0.2	91671	42.7	
1990s	104148	55.4	141347	54.5	67645	82.0	37	0.5	338921	58.1	
Skilled workers & professionals	97005	44.0	83847	23.0	25064	26.7	72	0.2	231049	29.0	27.2
Self-employed	1063	0.5	7517	2.1	3952	4.2	3	<0.1	14611	1.8	1.7
Entrepreneurs & investors	7765	3.5	89594	24.6	41938	44.7	2	<0.1	152124	19.1	6.8
Family	103050	46.7	156671	43.1	18099	19.3	22786	55.3	330763	41.5	46.2
1980s	30256	92.6	38576	37.0	3293	29.1	16431	48.6	100124	46.6	
1990s	72794	38.7	118095	45.5	14806	18.0	6355	86.3	230639	39.6	
Family members	78101	35.4	99275	27.3	8765	9.3	14450	35.1	220900	27.7	36.2
Assisted relatives	24949	11.3	57396	15.8	9334	10.0	8336	20.2	109863	13.8	10.0
Humanitarian	11195	5.1	334	0.1	23	<0.1	18279	44.4	36298	4.6	16.0
1980s	158	0.5	258	0.2	14	0.1	17311	51.2	22995	10.7	
1990s	11037	5.9	76	<0.1	9	<0.1	968	13.2	13303	2.3	
Refugee and DROC***	9978	4.5	54	<0.1	12	<0.1	280	0.7	10681	1.3	8.7
Designated class****	1217	0.6	280	0.1	11	<0.1	17999	43.7	25617	3.2	7.3

Source: Citizenship and Immigration Canada 2001.
****The percentage sum for the bolded items equals 100, as do the sums for 1980s and 1990s.
****Economic immigrants include retirees (32,446) and live-in caregivers (362), which are not listed separately in this table.
****DROC (Deferred Removal Order Class) refers to immigrants who at one time were ordered to leave Canada but subsequently had their deportation order cancelled. They are similar to refugees.
****Designated class consists of immigrants admitted under special government programs, usually in response to political upheavals in the home countries.

Variations by origin are also noteworthy. Immigrants from Taiwan had the highest proportion of economic immigrants, at 80 per cent of the total. Most economic immigrants from Taiwan were entrepreneurs and investors, accounting for 45 per cent of the total Taiwanese immigrants. The remaining economic immigrants were skilled workers or professionals (27 per cent).

Immigrants from Hong Kong also had a higher-than-average proportion of economic immigrants (57 per cent compared with 54 per cent for all Chinese immigrants). Of the economic immigrants, there were slightly more entrepreneurs and investors (25 per cent) than skilled workers and professionals (23 per cent). The remaining immigrants from Hong Kong were almost all family members and assisted relatives (43 per cent).

While immigrants from mainland China had a lower-than-average proportion of economic immigrants overall (48 per cent versus 54 per cent), their proportion increased dramatically from 7 per cent in the 1980s to 55 per cent in the 1990s, a 48 per cent difference in one decade. In sharp contrast to their counterparts from Taiwan and Hong Kong, the economic immigrants from the mainland were mostly skilled workers or professionals who accounted for 44 per cent of the total immigrants; only a small fraction (less than 4 per cent) were entrepreneurs and investors. There were approximately equal numbers of family-reunification immigrants and economic immigrants, but the proportion decreased by more than half during the period under consideration, from 93 per cent in the 1980s to 39 per cent in the 1990s.

The Chinese immigrants from Vietnam were a very different cohort. Only 0.3 per cent of them were economic immigrants. The rest were either family immigrants (55 per cent) or humanitarian immigrants (44 per cent). As the political situation in Vietnam stabilized and the last refugee camps in Southeast Asian countries were closed in the 1990s, humanitarian immigrants from Vietnam decreased significantly from 51 to 13 per cent, but the proportion of family immigrants increased, a consequence of the inflow of humanitarian immigrants in the 1980s.

The composition of Chinese immigrants by immigration class also varied among Canadian cities, especially between Toronto and Vancouver. More entrepreneurs and investors chose Vancouver over Toronto as their intended destination, with 42 per cent choosing the former and only 24 per cent choosing the latter. Conversely, more skilled workers and professionals chose Toronto (45 per cent) over Vancouver (29 per cent).

By Educational Qualifications and Canadian Official-Language Proficiency

Like many other immigrants to Canada, Chinese immigrants, especially those arriving in the 1990s, were well educated. Altogether, 19 per cent had some form of post-secondary education, such as a formal trade certificate, a college certificate or diploma, or some non-degree university education at the time of immigration (see table 5.2). Another 13 per cent already possessed a bachelor's degree, and 4 per cent had a master's degree. While only 1 per cent had a doctoral degree, this translated into 7,600 PhDs, a significant 'brain gain' for Canada. It should be pointed out that of the 88,000 Chinese immigrants who came to Canada in the 1980s and 1990s with no formal education, 63 per cent were actually pre-schoolers (0–6 years old) and another 11 per cent were 7–14 years old. Both of these age groups would acquire formal education and achieve full English or French proficiency through compulsory schooling in Canada.

Table 5.2 also shows that the Chinese immigrants who arrived in the 1990s possessed much higher educational qualifications than those who came during the previous decade. For instance, those with a bachelor's degree increased from 8 per cent in the 1980s to 15 per cent; those with a master's degree increased from less than 2 to more than 5 per cent. At the same time, those with secondary education or less decreased from 56 to 50 per cent.

Comparatively speaking, the immigrants from mainland China exhibited higher educational qualifications than those of other origins, primarily because of the enhanced qualifications brought to Canada by the 1990s arrivals. As table 5.2 shows, 21 per cent of the mainland Chinese immigrants had a bachelor's degree at the time of immigration, compared with 16 per cent of those from Taiwan, 9 per cent of those from Hong Kong, and less than 1 per cent of those from Vietnam. Furthermore, 9 per cent of the mainland immigrants had a master's degree, as opposed to 2 per cent of the Hong Kong immigrants and 5 per cent of the Taiwanese immigrants. The percentage of mainland Chinese immigrants with a PhD degree also was higher: 10 times higher than for those from Hong Kong and 2.5 times higher than those from Taiwan. The Chinese from Vietnam brought the least human capital as measured by their educational qualifications.

Overall, Chinese immigrants had similar educational qualifications to those possessed by the general immigrant population (see the last

Table 5.2. Chinese immigrants in Canada by education qualification and origin, 1980–2000

Education qualification	Mainland China		Hong Kong		Taiwan		Vietnam		Total Chinese		Total immigrants
	Number	%*	Number	%*	Number	%*	Number	%*	Number	%*	%*
No education	26119	11.8	35276	9.7	9256	9.9	6541	15.9	88032	11.0	11.9
1980s	5027	15.4	12257	11.7	1100	9.7	5722	16.9	29244	13.6	
1990s	21092	11.2	23019	8.9	8156	9.9	819	11.1	58788	10.1	
Some post-secondary (no degree)	87094	39.5	208229	57.2	45089	48.1	33358	81.1	413139	51.8	51.9
1980s	20199	61.9	50210	48.1	5611	49.6	26952	79.8	120901	56.3	
1990s	66895	35.6	158019	60.9	39478	47.9	6406	87.0	292238	50.1	
Trade certificate/ diploma/some univ. (no degree)	36505	16.5	79913	21.7	19199	20.5	1162	2.9	148099	18.6	18.8
1980s	5779	17.7	28704	27.4	2812	24.8	1039	3.1	43617	20.4	
1990s	30726	16.4	50209	19.4	16387	20	123	1.7	104482	17.9	
Bachelor's degree	46334	21.0	34146	9.3	14855	15.8	76	0.2	106275	13.3	13.3
1980s	1157	3.5	10781	10.3	1425	12.6	65	0.2	17015	8.0	
1990s	45177	24.0	23365	9.0	13430	16.3	11	0.1	89260	15.3	
Master's degree	19713	8.9	6646	1.8	4646	5.0	10	0	34363	4.3	3.2
1980s	295	0.9	2160	2.1	281	2.5	9	0	3255	1.5	
1990s	19418	10.3	4486	1.7	4365	5.3	1	0	31108	5.3	
Doctorate	4844	2.2	639	0.2	727	0.8	4	0	7599	1.0	0.9
1980s	185	0.6	226	0.2	83	0.7	4	0	631	0.3	
1990s	4659	2.5	413	0.2	644	0.8	0	0	6968	1.2	

Source: Citizenship and Immigration Canada 2001.
*The percentage sum for each level of education items equals 100, as do the sums for the 1980s and the 1990s.

two columns in table 5.2); however, their Canadian official language proficiency was lower than average. More than half (58 per cent) of the Chinese immigrants did not possess the required Canadian language skills at the time of immigration (see table 5.3), 14 per cent lower than the level of the general immigrant population. On the positive side, the proportion of Chinese possessing the required Canadian language skills has been increasing. In the 1980s, only 36 per cent could speak either English or French or both; in the 1990s, this increased to 45 per cent.

Not surprisingly, immigrants from Hong Kong had the highest English proficiency, with 49 per cent being able to speak English at the time of their arrival. The proportion of mainland Chinese immigrants with the required English proficiency was much lower (35 per cent), but it increased significantly in the 1990s, from only 9 per cent in the 1980s to 39 per cent in the 1990s. The proportion of Taiwanese immigrants with English proficiency was similar to that for those from mainland China: 36 versus 35 per cent. Those from Vietnam exhibited the lowest official language proficiency, with 95 per cent not meeting the language requirement at the time of landing. There was only a small improvement on this variable among the Vietnamese immigrants from the 1980s to the 1990s.

By Gender and Age

Of the 797,653 Chinese immigrants who came to Canada between 1980 and 2000, 52 per cent were females and 48 per cent were males. Similar gender differences existed for all age groups except the 0–14 cohort, where 49 per cent were females and 51 per cent were males. In general, the Chinese immigrants were relatively young, with three quarters between fifteen and sixty-four years of age. The dependency ratio among Chinese immigrants was thirty-two, which was much lower than the average of forty-six for the general population of Canada during this period. More specifically, 46 per cent of all Chinese immigrants were in their prime years (25–44) when they came to Canada (with more arrivals in this cohort in the 1990s than in the 1980s: 49 vs 37 per cent). Thus, Chinese immigrants represented a large pool of able workers ready to participate in the Canadian economy for at least twenty years. The proportion of mainland immigrants in this prime age group was much higher than the average for all Chinese immigrants, by a margin of 10 per cent.

Table 5.3. Chinese immigrants in Canada by Canadian languages proficiency and by origin, 1980–2000

Canadian language	Mainland China Number	%*	Hong Kong Number	%*	Taiwan Number	%*	Vietnam Number	%*	Total Chinese Number	%*	Total immigrants %*
English	76278	34.6	177416	48.8	33396	35.6	1901	4.6	332204	41.6	47.9
1980s	2947	9.0	50641	48.5	3603	31.8	1315	3.9	75445	35.1	
1990s	73331	39.0	126775	48.9	29793	36.1	586	8.0	256759	44.1	
French	638	0.3	258	0.1	70	0.1	224	0.5	2339	0.3	4.4
1980s	28	0.1	136	0.1	18	0.2	205	0.6	1043	0.5	
1990s	610	0.3	122	<0.1	52	0.1	19	0.3	1296	0.2	
English and French	1112	0.5	926	0.3	183	0.2	130	0.3	3750	0.5	3.7
1980s	74	0.2	338	0.3	46	0.4	111	0.3	1248	0.6	
1990s	1038	0.6	588	0.2	137	0.2	19	0.3	25.2	0.4	
Neither	142613	64.6	185266	50.9	60124	64.1	38915	94.5	459327	57.6	43.9
1980s	29613	90.7	53233	51.0	7646	67.6	32179	95.2	137021	63.8	
1990s	113000	60.1	132033	50.9	52478	63.6	6736	91.5	322306	55.3	

Source: Citizenship and Immigration Canada 2001.
*The percentage sum for breakdown by language equals 100, as do the sums for 1980s and the 1990s.

Economic Performance

With reference to the changing composition of Chinese immigrants, as established above, we will next consider their economic performance in Canada. This was examined by comparing four types of income: total income, employment income, self-employment income, and investment income. In 1999, the 343,890 tax filers who were captured in the special tabulation produced for this study reported total income of $5.15 billion, of which 80 per cent was employment income, 4.6 per cent was self-employment income, and 13.9 per cent was investment income.

In this analysis, we first compared Chinese immigrants with the general population of Canada, then examined subgroup variations. Unfortunately, comparisons with the general immigrant population cannot be made due to a lack of suitable data. It should be pointed out that total income is always lower than employment income because the former is calculated from a much larger group of Chinese immigrants, including non-salaried as well as salaried workers.

Chinese Immigrants vs the General Population of Canada

Compared with the general population of Canada, Chinese immigrants admitted between 1980 and 1999 had much lower incomes. In 1999, their average total income was slightly under $15,000, which represents only half of that earned by the general population (see table 5.4). Their employment income and self-employment income were $22,156 and $7,502, respectively, both of which were also lower than those for the general population, though with smaller margins: the former is 30 per cent less and the latter 16 per cent less. Only their investment income was higher, at 63 per cent more than that registered for the general population. Nevertheless, average investment income was only $4,000, making it by far the smallest source of income among the categories under consideration.

The above disparities hold true for all age groups across all types of earnings, with the exception of self-employment income for youths aged 15–19 years and for seniors aged 65 and above. It is not clear why Chinese youths had a self-employment income 15 per cent higher than their counterparts in the general population. For Chinese seniors, their higher self-employment income may mean that they still needed to work for a living due to insufficient savings and pensions. This was

Table 5.4. Average income of Chinese immigrants and as a percentage of income of the Canadian general population,* 1999 ($)

	Total income		Employment income		Self-employment income		Investment income	
	Chinese	% of general population	Chinese	% of general population	Chinese	% of general population	Chinese	% of general population
All ages and both sexes	14,974	49	22,156	70	7,502	84	4,088	163
By age groups								
15–19	2,964	42	4,019	77	4,626	115	2,161	278
20–24	7,417	52	10,532	84	4,194	87	2,419	419
25–44	18,765	57	24,438	83	7,836	78	2,817	288
45–64	15,804	41	22,782	66	7,390	57	5,218	223
65+	4,321	17	9,904	57	5,871	139	6,899	159
By sex								
male	17,922	47	25,518	77	8,267	78	4,269	178
female	12,046	52	18,334	87	6,406	98	3,920	153

Source: Statistics Canada 2002; Canada Customs and Revenue Agency 2001.
*Data for the general population of Canada are also for the 1999 tax year and were derived from Canada Customs and Revenue Agency 2001.

indicated by their extremely low total income, which was only $4,321, or just 17 per cent of that for all seniors in the general population.

The income disparities experienced by Chinese immigrants in comparison with the general Canadian population also hold true for both genders, but the gaps are consistently greater for Chinese male immigrants than for Chinese female immigrants. For example, male Chinese immigrants made 53 per cent less in total income than did the male population of Canada, 23 per cent less in employment income, and 22 per cent less in self-employment income. Female Chinese immigrants made 48 per cent less in total income, 13 per cent less in employment income, but only 2 per cent less in self-employment income than did the female population of Canada. That the income gap between Chinese male immigrants and the Canadian male population is larger than that between their female counterparts, especially in employment income, can be explained by the fact that more highly paid jobs (such as senior managerial positions) are held by native-born men than by native-born women.

By Immigration Class

The economic performance of Chinese immigrants by immigration class is shown in table 5.5. It should be pointed out that in LIDS, each class of immigrants includes not only the principal applicant but also their spouses and dependent children who were admitted at the same time but were not assessed by the points system. To examine more accurately the economic performance of the Chinese immigrants by immigration class, we focused on the principal applicants only.

Of the three broad categories of Chinese immigrants, the economic immigrants earned more than either family immigrants or humanitarian immigrants. Their total income was $20,453 (economic), $13,825 (family), and $17,743 (humanitarian); employment income was $28,897 (economic), $21,821 (family), and $23,262 (humanitarian). Economic immigrants also had the highest investment income at $4,991, compared to $3,570 for family immigrants and only $1,667 for humanitarian immigrants. Differences in self-employment income among the three categories of immigrants, however, were very small.

A closer look reveals that the high earnings for the economic immigrants were due to the high income of the skilled workers and professionals among this group, whose immigration applications were assessed on the sole basis of their human capital. In fact, this was the

Table 5.5. Average income of Chinese immigrants by immigration class, 1999 ($)

Immigration class	Total income	Employment income	Self-employment income	Investment income
Economic	20,453	28,897	7,768	4,991
Skilled workers/ professionals	24,939	31,678	8,056	2,699
Self-employed	13,107	19,009	8,136	5,482
Entrepreneurs/investors	13,005	18,017	7,100	7,395
Family	13,825	21,821	7,757	3,570
Family members	12,008	20,587	7,934	3,633
Assisted relatives	18,531	24,091	7,411	3,437
Humanitarian	17,743	23,262	6,452	1,667
Refugee/DROC*	12,275	14,914	6,084	1,464
Designated class**	20,891	28,100	6,838	1,778

Source: Statistics Canada 2002.
**DROC (Deferred Removal Order Class) refers to immigrants who at one time were ordered to leave Canada but subsequently had their deportation order cancelled. They are similar to refugees.
**Designated class consists of immigrants admitted under special government programs, usually in response to political upheavals in the home countries.

only class of immigrants who had achieved the same level of employment income by 1999 as the general population of Canada ($31,678 versus $31,712). The self-employed immigrants and the entrepreneurs and investors did not expect the same levels of employment income. Although self-employed immigrants did achieve the highest self-employment income ($8,136), and the entrepreneur/investor immigrants had the highest investment income ($7,395), neither type of income alone would be sufficient for one person to live above the poverty line in Canada.[5] Such incomes, therefore, must be supplemented either by other sources (such as employment income) or by savings in order to live above the poverty line.

In the category of family immigrants, assisted relatives performed much better than did immediate family members, displaying much higher total and employment incomes (54 and 17 per cent higher, respectively). These differences can be explained by the fact that the immediate family members were not assessed for their human capital at all at the time of admission, while the assisted relatives were partially assessed but received bonus points for having relatives in Canada. (For this reason, some researchers classify assisted relatives as economic immigrants.)

Similarly, there were significant differences between refugees and designated-class immigrants in terms of their economic performance. The latter group had much higher total and employment incomes than the former group (70 and 88 per cent higher, respectively). This indicates that they were two very different cohorts, even though both were admitted on humanitarian grounds and without reference to the customary points system. Usually, those admitted as refugees had little or no history of Canadian residency before their admission, while many designated-class immigrants had been in Canada for varying periods of time before they were granted landed immigrant status. The latter could not return to their place of origin due to the political upheavals in their home countries, such as the many mainland Chinese students who became landed immigrants after the 1989 Tien An Men Square incident. Their Canadian educational credentials and work experiences might have contributed to their better economic performance. In fact, the designated class as a whole was a group of high performers, next only to skilled workers and professionals. In contrast, the genuine refugees had the lowest income levels from all sources.

By Educational Qualifications and Canadian Official-Language Proficiency

It is clear that income, especially employment income, is positively correlated with the level of educational attainment at the time of landing (see table 5.6). On average, the immigrants with a doctoral degree had the highest incomes, at $34,656 for total income and $42,140 for employment income. This was followed by those with master's and bachelor's degrees: $26,322 and $19,743 for total income; and $34,141 and 27,621 for employment income. Those with secondary school education or less earned the least: $11,717 for total income and $17,936 for employment income. While this correlation is also true for self-employment income (with the exception of those with a master's degree), it does not apply to investment income. In fact, the immigrants with post-graduate degrees had the lowest investment incomes, suggesting that the most highly educated Chinese immigrants either did not invest as much as other immigrants did, or they did not have time to attend to the management of their investments. It is also possible that these individuals,

Table 5.6. Average income of Chinese immigrants by education qualification and Canadian languages ability, 1999 ($)

	Total income	Employment income	Self-employment income	Investment income
Education				
Secondary school or less	11,717	17,936	6,664	3,952
Some post-secondary education (with no degree)	16,936	24,129	7,519	4,534
Bachelor's degree	19,743	27,621	9,040	4,170
Master's degree	26,322	34,141	8,047	3,090
Doctorate	34,656	42,140	9,430	3,018
Languages ability				
English	19,879	27,136	8,175	4,186
French	18,463	24,125	9,119	2,864
English and French	25,894	31,816	13,178	2,982
Neither	10,901	17,097	6,363	4,014

Source: Statistics Canada 2002.

especially those from mainland China, did not come with as many assets or as much wealth to invest as did the business-class immigrants.

The economic performance of Chinese immigrants also corresponded positively with their Canadian language proficiency. Those who spoke both English and French had the highest incomes: $25,894 for total income, $31,816 for employment income, and $13,178 for self-employment income. Those who spoke English only did better than those who spoke only French. The immigrants who spoke neither official language had the lowest incomes (except for investment income). Compared with those who spoke English, these non-English-speaking Chinese immigrants earned 45 per cent less in total income and 37 per cent less in employment income.

By Length of Residence, Origin, and Intended Destination

In general, the economic performance of Chinese immigrants increased with their length of residence in Canada. As figures 5.2 and 5.3 illustrate, earlier immigrants displayed higher total and employment incomes than did the more recent immigrants. Undoubtedly, this is because salaries and wages are normally tied to work experience and

Figure 5.2. Comparison of total income among Chinese immigrants by origin, 1999

Income ($)

Canadian average $30,448

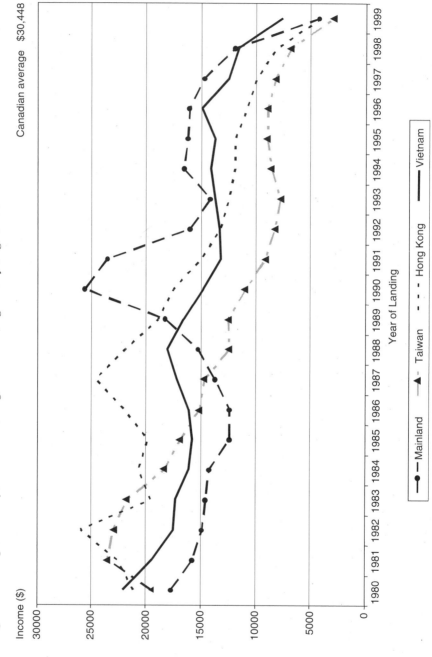

Year of Landing

—●— Mainland   —▲— Taiwan   - - - Hong Kong   —— Vietnam

Figure 5.3. Comparison of employment income among Chinese immigrants by origin, 1999

Income ($)

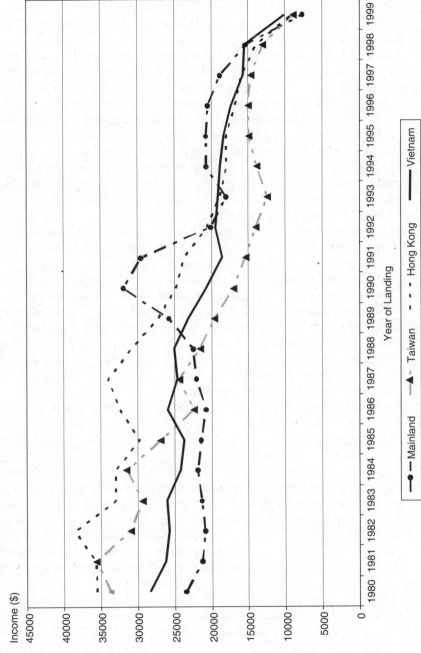

Year of Landing

●—●Mainland   ▲—▲ Taiwan   - - - Hong Kong   ——Vietnam

seniority, which accumulate over time. This pattern was most obvious for the Taiwanese immigrants and much less pronounced for the mainland Chinese.

Among the 1980s arrivals, the immigrants from Hong Kong had the highest earnings in both total income and employment income. Taiwanese immigrants who arrived in the first half of the 1980s also had higher incomes than those from Vietnam and mainland China. Immigrants from mainland China had the lowest earnings in both total and employment incomes. Surprisingly, their incomes were even lower than those of the Chinese immigrants from Vietnam – the group with a very high proportion of humanitarian immigrants and the least human capital to bring to Canada (that is, the fewest overall educational qualifications and the lowest Canadian language proficiency).

These patterns changed with the 1990s arrivals. The most significant difference was that the mainland Chinese began to outperform their counterparts from all other origins, which probably can be attributed to their higher educational qualifications. Figures 5.2 and 5.3 clearly show that those who landed in 1990 and 1991 were outstanding performers. These individuals were mostly visa students who were enrolled in graduate programs in Canadian universities and who were granted landed immigrant status after the Tien An Men Square incident. In other words, they already had Canadian human capital at the time they were granted landed immigrant status. The other major change during the 1990s was that the immigrants from Taiwan became the least successful economic performers, as measured by both total income and employment income. This can be explained by the high proportion of entrepreneurs and investors among the Taiwanese immigrants, who understandably reported low total and employment incomes on their income tax returns (see table 5.5).

Earnings differentials in self-employment income are barely discernible. Immigrants from both Vietnam and mainland China, however, had much lower investment incomes than those from Hong Kong and Taiwan. For instance, investment income for Taiwanese and Hong Kong immigrants was $5,362 and $5,244, respectively, while that for the mainland Chinese and the Chinese from Vietnam was only $1,995 and $1,658. This may be due to the low proportions of entrepreneurs and investors among the immigrants from mainland China and Vietnam.

Using more limited data, we were able to compare the economic performance of Chinese immigrants in the three largest CMAs: Toronto, Vancouver, and Montreal. As table 5.7 shows, Chinese immigrants in

Table 5.7. Average income of Chinese immigrants by destination, 1999 ($)

Destination	Total income	Employment income	Self-employment income	Investment income
Toronto	16,098	23,498	8,413	4,074
Vancouver	12,365	18,789	6,102	4,692
Montreal	10,872	16,766	7,008	2,665
Canada	14,974	22,150	7,502	4,088

Source: Statistics Canada 2002.

Toronto had the highest total incomes, employment incomes, and self-employment incomes. This was true for Chinese immigrants from all four origins, suggesting that Toronto indeed offers more economic opportunities than either Vancouver or Montreal, and has a more rewarding labour market. This may be why 45 per cent of all Chinese immigrants who were skilled workers and professionals chose Toronto as their settlement destination. In Vancouver, where a high proportion (42 per cent) of all entrepreneur and investor-class immigrants went, only investment income was the highest among the values for the three CMAs. Of Canada's three largest CMAs, Montreal seems to be the least rewarding place to make a living for the Chinese immigrants, of whom less than 1 per cent speak French (see table 5.3). In Montreal, only the self-employment income reported by Chinese immigrants was higher than it was in Vancouver.

Concluding Discussion and Policy Implications

The 2001 census points once again to the importance of immigration for Canada. It has been projected that there could be a deficit of one million skilled workers in Canada in the next ten to twenty years, despite the current intake of more than 200,000 immigrants each year (Thompson 2002; Tolley 2003). Without question, Chinese immigrants make an important contribution to fulfilling Canada's immigration goals and needs. In the past two decades, the number of Chinese immigrants to Canada increased significantly and their composition changed considerably. Since 1997, Hong Kong has no longer been a main point of origin, and the number of immigrants from both Taiwan and Vietnam has been in decline. In the meantime, arrivals from mainland China have been increasing steadily, making mainland China the largest single source of Chinese immigrants. In the near future, it is expected that most new Chinese immigrants to Canada will continue to come from mainland China.

In addition to shifts in origin, there have been other important changes in the composition of immigrants to Canada. Economic immigrants have been on the rise, while the proportions of both family immigrants and humanitarian immigrants have declined. The rising number and proportion of economic immigrants has been accompanied by an increase in both educational qualifications and Canadian language proficiency. Recent Chinese immigrants also have been younger, with nearly half in the age group of 25–44, the most productive years of their lives. All these changes have meant that recent Chinese immigrants have brought with them increased human capital and that Canada has been gaining higher-quality workers by admitting them into this country.

Economic performance is a significant indicator of how well integration is taking place in Canada. Despite their increased human capital, Chinese immigrants still experience unfavourable economic outcomes in the Canadian labour market compared with the general population of Canada. Our analysis shows this to be true wherever the Chinese immigrants have come from. Their average incomes have been much lower than those of the general population, and these earnings differentials exist for both genders and for all age groups. For many recent mainland Chinese immigrants who worked in the high-tech sector or held managerial positions in foreign-invested companies before immigration, economic returns to their human capital are even lower in Canada than in their home country. In a study of the Chinese enclave economy, Li and Li (1999) found that a Toronto-based Chinese newspaper devoted a substantial portion of its commercial advertisements to marketing professional services and major items such as real estate and automobiles. From this finding, they inferred that the Chinese enclave consumer market in Toronto was relatively affluent. Yet the present study has shown that the Chinese immigrants, who form the bulk of the enclave consumer market, are not as affluent as the general population of Canada, at least not according to their incomes. In Toronto, the average total income of Chinese immigrants in 1999 was $16,000 (see table 5.7), only three-quarters of that for the general Canadian population (see table 5.4). There was indeed a class of rich investors and entrepreneurs with high consumption powers in Toronto among the region's Chinese immigrants, but their cash was brought to Canada, not earned here, and their powers of consumption may not be sustainable.

The traditional upward-mobility thesis generalizes that new immigrants usually experience a transitional period of low income. Over time, however, they catch up or even outperform native-born workers. If this thesis is true, our findings suggest it will take more than twenty years for Chinese immigrants to catch up, because even those who have now been in Canada for twenty years have not closed the gap in total income between the general population of Canada and themselves (see figure 5.2). Apparently, much more 'seniority' is needed for Chinese immigrants to achieve full economic integration than that estimated by Devoretz and Akbari (Campbell 1994; Preston et al. 2003). In fact, it is not clear if complete integration will ever be achieved. Only the immigrants from Hong Kong who came to Canada in the 1980s have higher employment income than those in the general population (figure 5.3). Anecdotal evidence has it that many of them were former international students in Canadian universities.

The human capital theory assumes that in a fair and fully competitive market, individuals are rewarded on the basis of the societal value of their human capital (Becker 1964; Iceland 1999). Our research findings suggest that it would require the possession of a master's degree for a Chinese immigrant to earn an employment income higher than the average for the general population of Canada (see table 5.6 and figure 5.3). This is unfortunate because it indicates that the educational credentials of many Chinese immigrants have not been recognized, or at least have been discounted. More importantly, it leads to the conclusion that the Canadian labour market is not fully competitive, and that among other factors, economic discrimination and racism in the labour market may play a role in the underperformance of the Chinese immigrants.

As figure 5.3 shows, the mainland Chinese who landed in 1990 and 1991 (after the Tien An Men Square incident) outperformed all their peers, but as in the case of some Hong Kong immigrants who came in the 1980s, most individuals in this cohort were visa students enrolled in graduate programs in Canadian universities, and they possessed Canadian content in their bundle of human capital. The picture is considerably bleaker for those who possess only foreign-earned credentials. This is clear evidence that country-specific education and skills obtained in Canada are worth more than those acquired in China and are much better remunerated by Canadian employers. A survey of 102 mainland Chinese immigrants who landed in the 1990s revealed that only 15 per cent of them held jobs that were in line with their Chinese education and work experience; a further 22 per cent had a job that was close to their foreign education and work experience; and 52 per cent were working at a job that did not match their education and experience at all (Tian 2000). This suggests that new Chinese immigrants have indeed experienced great difficulties in accessing education-related professions and trades in Canada.

Many Chinese immigrants came to Canada as self-employed small business owners. Yet the business environment does not seem to have rewarded these immigrants either, because self-employment often yields fairly low monetary returns, a finding that seems to hold true not only for Chinese immigrants, but also for the general population of Canada (see table 5.4). The increased immigration of Chinese to Canada greatly expanded the Chinese enclave consumer market, especially in the large urban centres such as Toronto and Vancouver. This ethnic market, however, has not created more financially rewarding opportunities for the many self-employed immigrants, whose businesses mainly depend on their fellow Chinese consumers. Ironically, those who came as self-employed immigrants made less from self-employment than from working for others, as is evidenced by their higher employment income (see table 5.5). This finding is consistent with Li's study (2000b) of the general immigrant population in Canada. Li concluded that the self-employed are not better rewarded in the labour market than salaried workers. Indeed, a survey of Chinese business owners in the Toronto CMA revealed the existence of a variety of barriers to immigrant business development (Wang and Lo 2002).[6]

It should be reiterated that the data from personal income tax returns have never been a good source of information for studying the economic performance of investors and entrepreneurs. In the words of some observers, investors and business owners 'do not have' personal income, because they are better able to shelter their income in the form of re-investment. This may explain why the investor and entrepreneur classes of immigrants report low income, including investment income, on their tax returns. Another explanation is that some investors and entrepreneurs retain a significant portion of their capital and business in their home country. They may have moved their family members, especially school-aged children, to Canada while they themselves stayed behind or flew back and forth as 'astronauts,' spending the bulk of their time attending to business in their home countries (Wen 2003).

Their earnings made outside Canada might not have been reported in their personal income tax returns in Canada. In 1996, when the Canadian government proposed Bill C-92 (which was passed in 1998), making the declaration of overseas properties and reporting of foreign income mandatory, many Chinese business immigrants, particularly those in Vancouver, strongly objected to the proposal at first and then collectively lobbied for changes (Wu 1998).

The ability to use Canada's official languages, especially English, seems to be one of the most important determinants of the economic performance of Chinese immigrants in the Canadian labour market (see table 5.6). As table 5.3 reveals, 58 per cent of the Chinese immigrants who came to Canada in the 1980s and 1990s came without Canadian official language abilities. Our findings suggest that in addition to labour market discrimination, it may well be the lack of language and communication skills that prevents Chinese immigrants from utilizing their credentials and adapting themselves to the new, knowledge-based economy. An editorial column in a Toronto-based Chinese-language newspaper described the new immigrants who lack English proficiency as 'disabled persons' unable to fully participate in the Canadian labour market. The above suggestion is also based on the fact that until 2002, no standard test was applied to assess the communication skills of prospective immigrants. Instead, the assessment was conducted by an immigration officer during a face-to-face interview of the applicant simply by means of a conversation. This meant that a person who passed the conversation still might not have a good command of English or French, and that the 'official language ability' variable in LIDS may not be a reliable indicator of true communication skills. The present study should be supplemented by qualitative research, conducted by means of a survey and/or focus group discussions, to find out if and to what extent communication skills have been a factor in preventing Chinese immigrants from using their foreign-earned credentials and work experiences to achieve success in the Canadian labour market.

Like many other studies, our research findings reveal a troubling message about the experiences of Chinese immigrants in Canada and raise serious questions about the goals of inclusion and integration that are part of Canada's reformed immigration program. The inability to succeed in economic participation makes immigrants feel disadvantaged and excluded from equal access to the opportunities offered by societies and economies (Rodgers 1995). This results in alienation and distance from the mainstream society and may negatively affect immigrants' confidence about the merits of remaining in Canada to fulfill their immigration dream and commitment. An Internet survey of recent Chinese immigrants conducted by the Toronto-based North Chinese Community of Canada in 2002 found that only 20 per cent of the 1,345 survey participants indicated they would remain in Canada after obtaining Canadian citizenship (*World Journal* 2003).

If full integration is difficult to achieve, 'how much disparity must we accept as a trade-off for living in a pluralistic and free society? In general, how far should government interfere in the city's life or communities in order to protect the social good?' (Burstein and Duncan 2003, 373). Government can help in the integration process in a number of ways. To make full use of the talents and skills that Chinese immigrants possess, Canadian governments, both federal and provincial, should consider providing more assistance, or at the very least, improve the delivery of settlement services intended to help Chinese immigrants to adapt to and prosper in Canada. As the House of Commons Committee on Immigration has acknowledged, while the Canadian government enthusiastically recruits highly educated and skilled immigrants, it lacks adequate settlement services programs to help them adapt (*Toronto Metro* 2003). In the past, the Ontario arm of Citizenship and Immigration Canada (CIC–Ontario Region Settlement Directorate) contracted its Immigrant Settlement and Adaptation Program (ISAP) out to many agencies to deliver services to Chinese newcomers, but the settlement workers in these agencies were mainly Cantonese speakers, and most of them were familiar only with British and American lifestyles. This was largely because the former place of residence for most such settlement workers (Hong Kong) had British- or American-style civil services and bureaucracies and a capitalist market economy (Citizenship and Immigration Canada 2003).

In the summer of 2003, the CIC–Ontario Region Settlement Directorate issued a request for proposals from academic researchers to evaluate the relevance of existing service-delivery models to Mandarin-speaking newcomers from mainland China, and to recommend policy adjustments and improvements. This initiative signified that the Canadian government had begun to recognize the significant internal differences among the subgroups of Chinese immigrants with regard to their need for settlement services. Hopefully, such initiatives will lead to a real improvement in the delivery of settlement services for Chinese immigrants of different origins, which eventually will lead to increased levels of economic performance by Chinese immigrants. Such an outcome would benefit both the immigrants themselves and Canada.

Notes

A longer version of this chapter appeared in *International Migration* 43, no. 3 (2005), entitled 'Chinese immigrants in Canada: Their changing composition and economic performance.' The authors acknowledge the financial support of CERIS in the form of two research grants. The second author acknowledges the Social Science and Humanities Research Council of Canada for supporting the special data tabulation of this project. Both authors also thank Michael Doucet for his helpful comments.

1 The following dialects are listed in the decoding document for LIDS. The numbers of Chinese who speak each of the dialects are listed below:

Cantonese:	488,296	61.2%
Mandarin:	198,946	24.9%
Chinese:	68,035	8.5%
Hakka:	1,245	0.2%
Shanghai:	137	<0.1%
Other Chinese dialects:	40,994	5.1%
Total Chinese immigrants:	797,653	100%

2 The IMDB is created by a file linkage process, which matches individuals from LIDS to individuals on the personal income tax forms. Because the unique SIN (social insurance number) does not exist at time of landing and therefore is not available in the LIDS files, the IMDB linkage process uses four personal attributes: last name, first name, date of birth, and gender. All four attributes must be successfully matched in both files for an individual record to be captured in the new database. 'Fortunately, it has been observed that foreign-born tax filers have a strong tendency to use the name spelling recorded on their visas to fill out other official documents. It is because of this practice that the linkage and SIN assignment processes have been largely successful' (Badets and Langlois 1999).

3 Self-employment income corresponds to net income (i.e., gross income less any adjustment and expenses incurred but before personal income taxes are calculated) from the following sources: business income, professional income, commission income, farming income, and fishing income. Invest-

ment income is the total of bond and bank interest income from trusts and foreign income (Canada Customs and Revenue Agency 2001).

4 This includes the spouses and dependants of the principal applicants.

5 Statistics Canada calculates the poverty line for Canadian cities and rural areas using a formula that considers the cost of items such as food, clothing and footwear, shelter, and transportation. Using a reference family of four (two adults and two children), the poverty line for thirteen major cities ranges from $22,441 in Montreal to $27,791 in Vancouver (Mascoll 2003). Assuming each family has two wage earners, each needs to make at least $10,000 to $14,000 annually in order to be above the poverty line.

6 For a detailed analysis of the barriers faced by immigrant entrepreneurs in the Toronto area, see Lo, Teixeira, and Truelove (2002).

References

Badets, J., and C. Langlois. 1999. The challenges of using administrative data to support policy-relevant research: The example of the longitudinal immigration database (IMDB). Paper presented at the Statistics Canada Symposium 99: Combining Data from Different Sources.

Baker, M., and D. Benjamin. 1994. The performance of immigrants in the Canadian labour market. *Journal of Labour Economics* 12 (3): 369–405.

– 1997. Ethnicity, foreign birth and earnings: A Canadian/U.S. comparison. In *Transition and structural change in the North American labour market*, ed. M.G. Abbott et al., 281–313. Kingston, ON: IRC Press.

Becker, G.S. 1964. *Human capital.* New York: Columbia University Press.

Borjas, G.J. 1985. Assimilation, changes in cohort quality, and the earnings of immigrants. *Journal of Labour Economics* 3:463–89.

– 1988. *International differences in the labour market performance of immigrants.* Kalamzoo, MI: W.E. Upjohn Institute.

– 1993. Immigration policy, national origin, and immigrant skills: A comparison of Canada and the United States. In *Small differences that matter: Labour market and income maintenance in Canada and the United States*, ed. D. Card and R.B. Freeman, 21–43. Chicago: University of Chicago Press.

Breton, Raymond. 1992. Report of the academic advisory panel on the social and cultural impacts of immigration: Meeting on indicators of integration. Ottawa: Research Division, Strategic Planning and Research.

Brooke, J. 1999a. Vancouver is astir over Chinese abuse of immigration law. *New York Times*, 29 August.

– 1999b. Canada is taking a tough line with illegal Chinese migrants. *New York Times*, 30 September.

Burstein, M., and H. Duncan. 2003. Integrating community diversity in Toronto: On whose terms? In *The world in a city,* ed. P. Anisef and M. Lanphier, 373–456. Toronto: University of Toronto Press.

Campbell, C. 1994. When you hear of well-off immigrants, ask, when did they arrive. *Vancouver Sun,* 24 August.

Canada Customs and Revenue Agency. 2001. Income statistics. http://www.ccra-adrc.gc.ca/tax/individuals/stas/gb99.

Canadian Heritage. 2002. Annual report on the operation of the Canadian Multiculturalism Act 2001–2002. Ottawa.

Chiswick, B. 1986. Is the new immigration less skilled than the old? *Journal of Labour Economics* 4:168–92.

Citizenship and Immigration Canada. 2001. Landed immigrant data system. (Provided on CD.)

– 2003. Request for proposals: Recommendations for the delivery of ISAP services to Mandarin speaking immigrants from Mainland China. Toronto: CIC–Ontario Region Settlement Directorate.

Friedberg, R.M. 2000. You can't take it with you? Immigrant assimilation and the portability of human capital. *Journal of Labour Economics* 18 (2): 221–51.

Girard, D. 1999a. 159 Chinese seized off 4th smuggler ship after race with navy. *Toronto Star,* 11 September.

– 1999b. No free ride for smugglers, Immigration Canada says. *Toronto Star,* 11 September.

Green, D.A. 1999. Immigrant occupational attainment: Assimilation and mobility over time. *Journal of Labour Economics* 17 (1): 49–79.

Harles, J.C. 1997. Integration before assimilation: immigration, multiculturalism and the Canadian polity. *Canadian Journal of Political Science* 30 (4): 711–37.

Henry, F., and C. Tator. 2005. *The colour of democracy: Racism in Canadian society.* Toronto: Thomson Nelson.

Iceland, J. 1999. Earnings returns to occupational status: Are Asian Americans disadvantaged? *Social Sciences Research* 28:45–65.

James, F., J. Romine, and P.R. Terry. 2002. Big city labor markets and immigrant economic performance. *Policy Studies Journal* 30 (1): 107–31.

Langan, F. 1997. Canada's Chinese speakers on a roll as numbers rise third after English and French. *Christian Science Monitor,* 17 December.

Li, P. 2000a. Earning disparities between immigrants and native-born Canadians. *Canadian Review of Sociology and Anthropology* 37 (3): 289–311.

– 2000b. Economic returns of immigrants' self-employment. *Canadian Journal of Sociology* 25 (1): 1–34.

Li, P., and Y. Li. 1999. The consumer market of the enclave economy: A study of advertisements in a Chinese daily newspaper in Toronto. *Canadian Ethnic Studies* 2:43–60.

Lo, L., C. Teixeira, and M. Truelove. 2002. Cultural resources, ethnic strategies, and immigrant entrepreneurship: A comparative study of five immigrant groups in the Toronto CMA. Working Paper no. 21, Joint Centre of Excellence for Research on Immigration and Settlement–Toronto.

Lo, L., and S. Wang. 1997. Settlement patterns of Toronto's Chinese immigrants: convergence or divergence? *Canadian Journal of Regional Science* 1–2: 49–72.

Lo, L. and L. Wang. 2004. A political economy approach to understanding the economic incorporation of Chinese sub-ethnic groups. *Journal of International Migration and Integration* 5:107–40.

Mascoll, P. 2003. New light on poverty yardstick: Study measures cost of essential goods and services. *Toronto Star*, 28 March.

Mueller, R.E. 1999. Changes in the quality of immigrant flows between the United States and Canada in the 1980s. *American Review of Canadian Studies* 29 (4): 621.

Pendakur, K., and R. Pendakur. 1998. The colour of money: Earnings differentials among ethnic groups in Canada. *Canadian Journal of Economics* 31 (1): 518–48.

Preston, V., L. Lo, and S. Wang. 2003. Immigrants' economic status in Toronto: Stories of triumph and disappointment. In *The world in a city*, ed. P. Anisef and M. Lanphier, 192–262. Toronto: University of Toronto Press.

Reitz, J. 1997. Measuring down: The economic performance of new Canadians is declining. *Financial Post*, 8 November.

Rodgers, C. 1995. What is special about a social exclusion approach? In *Social exclusion: Rhetoric, reality, responses*, ed. C. Rodgers, C. Gore, and J. Figeiredo, 43–55. Geneva: International Labour Organization.

Statistics Canada. 2002. Special tabulation of 1999 income tax returns for Chinese immigrants. (Provided on CD.)

Statistics Canada. 2003. *The Daily*, 11 March.

Swidinsky, R., and M. Swidinsky. 2002. The relative earnings of visible minorities in Canada: New evidence from the 1996 census. *Relations Industrielles* 57 (4): 630–59.

Thompson, A. 1999. Hold illegals, report urged. *Toronto Star*, 11 September.

– 2002. Immigration in 2001 at the highest level in years. *Toronto Star*, 18 April.

Tian, G. 2000. Chinese refugees coping with stress in Toronto. In *Race and racism: Canada's challenge*, ed. L. Driedger and S. Halli, 253–75. Montreal: McGill-Queen's University Press.

Toronto Metro. 2003. Immigration policy blues. 6 June.

Tolley, E. 2003. The skilled worker class. *Canadian Issues* 5 (insert): 1–8.

Wallis, D. 1998. Beijing makes it happen. *Vis-à-vis* (The CIC magazine) (Fall): 4–7.

Wang, S., and L. Lo. 2002. Investigating policy barriers to immigrant business development: A Chinese case study in Toronto. Unpublished research paper.

Weinfeld, M. 1990. Racism in Canada: A multi-dimensional approach to measurement. Paper prepared for Conference on Race Relations in the United Kingdom and Canada, York University, ON.

Wen, B. 2003. Why do entrepreneurs emigrate from China? *Canadian Chinese Times*, 15 February.

World Journal. 2003. Nearly 80 per cent of recent Mainland Chinese immigrants are thinking of returning to China. 10 January.

Wu, X. 1998. Declaration of overseas properties becomes law. *World Weekly*, 18 October.

Yu, D. 2002. What happened to our fellow Chinese immigrants? *Chinese News*, 20 December.

6 Racial Discrimination in Nursing

REBECCA HAGEY, JANE TURRITTIN, AND
TANIA DAS GUPTA

Dedicated to the memory of Claudine Charley[1]

Racialized nurses are confronted with a dilemma every day of their working lives when they have to decide how to respond to racial discrimination from patients, colleagues, supervisors, and physicians (Das Gupta 2002). This chapter provides an interpretive reading of selective interpersonal strategies that nurses report having used to deal with the everyday racism they encounter at work. The data come from transcripts of taped qualitative interviews with fourteen racialized nurses, each of whom had previously filled out a survey on 'Racism in Nursing' (Das Gupta 2002). The survey was conducted in tandem with a participatory action research project in which more than 200 racialized nurses called for an investigation of the nursing profession by the Ontario Human Rights Commission under section 29(g) of the Ontario Human Rights Code (1981) ('the Code') to question and challenge systemic racism in the workplace (Hagey et al. 2005).

The term 'racialized' refers to the 'process and to the structures that accompany such a process which produce and construct meaning of race' (see Agnew, introduction to this volume). The Ontario Human Rights Commission defines racialization as 'the process by which societies construct races as real, different and unequal in ways that matter to economic, political, and social life' (Ontario Human Rights Commission 2005, 9). The use of the term racialization, as opposed to race and racism, emphasizes that meanings attached to race are fluid and change in different social contexts. Since whiteness is now acknowledged by scholars to also be a marker of race, albeit a privileged one, the term racialization could potentially refer to white people as well. However, the Ontario Human Rights Commission recommends using the term to refer to persons who require protection under the Code on grounds of race. In this chapter, we use the term 'racialized nurses' to refer to nurses of colour or from visible minorities.

When nurses encounter racial discrimination, they use a variety of strategies to maintain their working relationships with colleagues and patients. These strategies indicate that despite the discrimination racialized nurses experience at their workplace, they find ways to act professionally and with decorum and dignity. The situations reported by the nurses are examined using Maureen Walker's relational/cultural theory, which deals with concepts such as conflict in relations, courage in vulnerability, and relational accountability for responding to discrimination by racialized as well as non-racialized women (2002). The objective of this chapter is to contribute to the debate on how to dismantle everyday racism in Canada, particularly when a complaint of racism can bring backlash and reprisals to the individual so victimized (Calliste 1995, 1996; Hagey et al. 2005).

Racial Encounters in Nursing

Racial oppression, evidence suggests, is widely experienced by nurses. In other words, race, ethnicity, and colour are felt by the nurses so targeted to have an effect on relations in the workplace. In this chapter, we present findings from a pilot survey conducted by Tania Das Gupta. Of the sixty-two nurses who completed the questionnaire, thirty-eight identified themselves as Black/African Canadian, thirteen as Asian or South Asian Canadian, five as White/European Canadian, four as Other, one as Central/South American Canadian, and one gave no response (see table 6.1). There were fifty-seven women in the sample, along with three men and two respondents who did not specify gender.

Participants felt that race, ethnicity, and colour had an effect on various elements of their work (see table 6.2). Of the sixty-two nurses who participated, almost two-thirds reported that race, ethnicity, and colour had a significant effect on relations with patients (39 responses) and with colleagues (38). About half reported this effect on relations with managers (37 responses), on where they were assigned to work (33), and on access to training (30). One-third reported effects on performance reviews (21 responses), one-fourth on the experience of being disciplined (15), and one-fifth on sick leaves (12). As reported in table 6.3, fifty-six said they had been put down, insulted, or degraded as a nurse because of their race, colour, or ethnicity. Of these, thirty-eight said they had been denigrated by a patient, thirty-two by another

Table 6.1. Demographic overview of survey respondents (N = 62)

Ethnoracial identity	Number
Black/African Canadian	38
Asian or South Asian Canadian	13
Central/South American	1
White/European	5
Other	4
No response	1

Gender identity	Number
Female	57
Male	3
No response	2

Source: Information in Tables 6.1–6.4 from Tania Das Gupta's
survey of nurses in the Greater Toronto Area, November
2001–May 2002

Table 6.2. Impact of race, colour, or ethnicity reported by nurses

Area of employment	Effect	No effect	Don't know	No response
Hiring	30	25	2	5
Promotion	39	18	1	4
Relations with colleagues	38	17	0	7
Relations with management	37	17	1	7
Relations with patients	39	18	0	5
Assigned work location	33	14	0	15
Access to training	30	13	1	18
Response to disability	3	36	0	23*
Sick leave	12	40	0	10
Performance review	21	18	0	23*
Disciplinary review	15	34	0	13*

• includes not applicable
• non-inclusive categories

nurse, twenty-four by a manager, and nineteen by a doctor. Some respondents mentioned more than one offender.

Most of the fifty-six who had been harassed reported having been affected by the event, either emotionally (47), mentally (28), or physically (18). Several nurses noted more than one effect, and over half said

Table 6.3. Impact of racial discrimination in employment reported by nurses

Type of impact of race, colour, or ethnicity reported			Number
Made to feel uncomfortable as a nurse because of race, colour, or ethnicity			54
Felt put down, insulted or degraded because of race, colour, or ethnicity			56
By a doctor	19	By a patient	38
By manager	24	By another nurse	32

Table 6.4. Nurses' responses to racial discrimination in employment

Type of response reported	Number
Emotionally affected	47
Physically affected	18
Mentally affected	28
Took some action:	33
positive results	13
no results or negative result	16
ongoing	4
Did not take action	22
No response	7

(Non-exclusive categories)

that they had taken some action. Of those, sixteen had no results or unsatisfactory results, and thirteen had satisfactory results; four were in the midst of ongoing proceedings (see table 6.4).

The findings presented here are somewhat preliminary, since the goal of this pilot project was to assist Das Gupta in developing a questionnaire for a larger study. Nevertheless, we believe that this project provides substantial evidence that nurses experience significant levels of racism. These findings are further reinforced by a study commissioned by the Ontario Nurses Association, which documented that white nurses of European ancestry experience far fewer harmful effects of race, colour, or ethnicity than racialized nurses (Das Gupa 2002).

Marshall's analysis of the 1991 Census of Canada data for health-care professions showed that black people are under-represented in management positions (1966). Nestel, also using 1991 census figures, reported that visible-minority nurses in Ontario have only half the chance of their white counterparts to move into managerial positions (2000). Hagey and MacKay, who studied racist discourse in a nursing school, found that students were afraid of discussing racism. For example, one student said, '[Some] may perceive this as a threat, and it will come back on you in different ways' (Nestel 2000, 53; Hagey and MacKay 2000).

Methodology

The interviews were organized in conjunction with a participatory action research (PAR) project on 'Implementing Accountability for Equity and Ending Racial Backlash in Nursing' funded by the Canadian Race Relations Foundation. Interested participants were asked to complete a survey and some of the respondents were interviewed. All respondents identified themselves as racialized persons.

Of the fourteen nurses interviewed, seven identified themselves as black, two as South Asian, two as Asian (one born in the Philippines, one in Hong Kong), two as African Canadian, and one as a Caribbean Canadian. Seven had received all of their education in Canada, two outside Canada, and five had received some of their education outside Canada. Four had a diploma in nursing plus other certificates, six had a BScN, and two had a non-nursing degree with a master's degree in education near completion. Two had completed and two were working on a master's degree in nursing; two planned to pursue doctorates. The number of years of working in nursing ranged from twelve to forty years, with an average of twenty-two and a half years. One interviewee had worked in occupational health and safety (but not as a nurse) since 1991. Specialties included one nurse clinician, one union employee, three health educators, one school nurse, one clinical coordinator, one public-health nurse, one community nurse, and four staff nurses. Of the fourteen interviewed, five were born in the 1940s, four in the 1950s, and five in the 1960s. Country of birth was not surveyed.

The PAR research project on equity accountability did not have the specific goal of determining how nurses could best respond to racial encounters. The interviewer, an experienced black nurse manager enrolled in a master's program, asked questions such as: 'As a nurse, have you ever felt uncomfortable because of your race, colour, ethnicity, or accent?' 'Compared to a white nurse in the same situation, have you received different treatment?' 'Did you take action in any of these situations?' 'Do you feel that your race, colour, ethnicity, or accent has had an effect on your relations with colleagues?'

Although the PAR project was not aimed at discovering effective means of dealing with racial discrimination, a review of some of the transcribed interviews indicated to the research team that they might provide a rich set of data for documenting such strategies, as the following example suggests:

> One of my colleagues at work ... when people make racist comments ... has a very nice tact of calling them on that comment. She says, 'Now, let me ask you this question ... If this was your mother and this white person [did something inappropriate], would you do that?' And so, in a very nice way, she has that tact of calling them about it. So, I think that's the trait that I need to learn, 'cause I get very upset and I say, 'Why are you saying that? That is inappropriate...,' [and] the [other person] becomes defensive. Well, she does make them defensive, but she still calls them on it.

The team consequently decided to use interpretive, qualitative research methods, particularly the discourse theory of van Dijk (1993) and the widely adopted concept of everyday racism pioneered by Essed (1991), to identify strategies used by the nurses that also echoed Walker's recommendations (2002). Van Dijk's interpretive theory suggests ways of identifying the racialist arguments in discourse that signal who should have the advantage and who not, when racial lines segment the 'in' group from the 'out' group, and who is granted the capacity for ruling in a given situation. Essed documents educated black women's experiences of racial conflict and the strategies they use to struggle against it in a white-dominated society. The black women in her study described 'a continual battle against the denial of racism, against Whitecentrism, against automatic in-group preference among Whites, against constant impediments to their aspirations, against humiliations, against petty harassment and against denigrations of their cultures' (1991, 10). Essed provides a model of the ways that everyday racism is accomplished and legitimized (52):

1) Socialized racist notions are *integrated into meanings* that make practices immediately *definable and manageable*.
2) Practices with racist implications become in themselves *familiar and repetitive*.

3) Underlying racial and ethnic *relations are actualized and reinforced* through these routine or familiar practices in everyday situations.

By contrast, Walker's work in relational/cultural theory moves beyond noticing when a situation is racist to managing its meaning in ways that address human relationships and erase assumptions of racial dominance. Walker is a member of the Stone Center and Jean Baker Miller Training Institute at Wellesley College, Massachusetts, where relational/cultural theory is being developed. What makes this theory unique is its advocacy of a set of strategies that can be used to help build relationships. The theory is not a mere research aid for deconstructing aspects of social meaning that are structured by ruling practices in discourse, but rather a means for reconstructing the everyday realities of the taken-for-granted racial order. If all its elements are collectively put into practice, the approach has the potential to assert equity at every level of change, be it organizational and legislative or interpersonal and introspective.

Examples from our interview transcripts suggest possible ways of challenging everyday racism and provide insight into the effectiveness of relational/cultural theory as a strategy for resilience and for disarming those who condone or promote racism. The nurses' testimonies have the potential to increase sensitivity towards relational/cultural problems and their systemic nature, a consequence of a racist ideology that pervades our everyday lives (van Dijk 1993; Henry et al. 2000).

A review of the nurses' testimonies in light of Walker's ideas suggests ways of dealing with everyday racism (Turrittin et al. 2002).[2] As many antiracist scholars have documented, for racialized nurses and their colleagues the experiences of racism have a structure that is determined in part by racist ideologies and practices (Essed 1991). Depending on whether the situation is deemed to be safe or not, the nurses decide to process the experience either privately or in the context of the racist incident or situation (Hagey et al. 2005).

Power and Relational Strategies

Relational/cultural scholars define power as 'the capacity to produce change' and advocate for a more comprehensive understanding of relational power. Relational accountability is conceived as a requisite for being empowered rather than overpowered. Relational/cultural theory is an approach to therapy with women that emphasizes the development and healing of relationships as a way to personal growth and structural change (Miller and Stiver 1997).

As a preface to the presentation and discussion of the racialized nurses' accounts of their practices, we shall briefly review Walker's discussion of the concept of power as popularly understood versus that held by relational/cultural theory. Since relational/cultural theory advocates for a 'self in relation' approach to negotiating power relations, we present snippets of transcripts that provide insight into some of the nurses' perceptions of themselves in relation to others while confronting racial discrimination and its effects. And since the theory advises followers to be aware of their feelings in relationships, we include some of the emotional aspects of racial relations. The historical context of race-based dominance makes racial relations fundamentally conflictual, although this is seldom acknowledged. (Collins 1990). Historically, language and practices have provided an ever-lurking conflict situation where dominance is a privilege felt acutely by those dominated but probably not even noticed by those who dominate with impunity. One of the interviewees expressed this phenomenon as follows:

You know what? The strange thing is they don't realize that they are oppressing [us]. I don't believe [they do]. I could be wrong. Again, it's so systemic ... They are acting the way they feel they should act. It's just part of them.

In North America, a great deal of emphasis is placed on individualism and consequently, power is commonly viewed as an individual attribute. Popularly (but naively, says Walker), power is understood as 'the capacity to get others to do one's will.' In situations where individual A enjoys higher status than individual B – for example, in situations involving a supervisor and a nurse, a parent and a child, a teacher and a student, or a white and a black person – individual A has the capacity to make individual B act in accordance with the agenda defined and/or upheld by individual A. Since white people frequently enjoy higher social status, they can typically get black people or members of other racialized minority groups to conform to their will. When they are successful, white people may feel personally effective and good about themselves, while black or other racialized individuals may feel demeaned, 'like losers.' This popular definition of power – 'power over someone' – clearly reflects the ideology of radical individualism embraced by the socially advantaged that is widespread in capitalistic economies and encoded in North American cultural patterns (Walker 2002, 3).

Walker argues that the popular definition of power 'obscures the realities of relationships,' and that 'all power, including destructive power, is created by and depends upon relationship' (2002, 4). She notes that because the popular definition of power reflects the point of view of the socially advantaged, it is biased and erroneous. Since power emerges in relationships and is not an attribute of lone individuals, all parties to a relationship have social power. Moreover, suggests Walker, the capacity of certain individuals to get others to conform is an outcome of their authority's being linked to and backed up by a system; it is not because they possess particular attributes as individuals. Nursing supervisors, for example, carry out hospital policy; teachers enforce school rules; and parents enforce widely held moral values.

Roxanna Ng's definition of power as 'a dynamic relationship negotiated continuously in interactional settings' (2002, 92) is similar in orientation to that of Walker and her colleagues. Ng argues that we need to examine the 'way in which power operates to sustain existing forms of inequality in order to discover how to alter these relations' (91). She calls to our attention a distinction between power and authority that elucidates Walker's discussion. 'Power,' writes Ng, 'is a more individual property which is subject to negotiation interactionally,' while 'authority ... is formal power granted to individuals through institutional structures and relations' (92). Ng and Walker agree that individuals in positions of leadership are authoritative because they express, are backed by, and benefit from the rules, policies, and resources of institutional systems. Though authoritative, however, such individuals may not always be effective in using their personal power.

'Deterministic power obscures the realities of relationship. It affects the appearance of lone, individualistic action, when in fact action is supported by an entire system ... When we believe the lie of lone individualism, women – and all people who do not have access to the invisible supports – are left feeling deficient, or are somehow labeled less competent or less committed in systems where power distortions are the norm' (Walker 2002, 4). Ng's distinction between power and authority clarifies Walker's discussion of why a full understanding of power must encompass the points of view of both the disadvantaged and the advantaged if a non-victimizing, socially responsible approach to systemic change is to be created. The distinction is particularly helpful in interpreting the 'human accomplishments' of nurses who, when confronted with racism at work, activate their social power in constructive ways even though they lack formal authority.

Relational/cultural theory is not a species of victimology, but it does acknowledge victimhood, hopelessness, and helplessness, and it provides comprehensive strategies to achieve both individual and social responsibility. Our research found that antiracism theories and language were vigorously opposed by senior management because of the mistaken view that such theories encourage victimology (Hagey et al. 2005). Relational/cultural scholars have led the way in promoting an antiracism that practises relational responsibility both at an individual and an organizational level to bring about systemic change.

For Walker, power as 'the capacity to bring about change' necessitates making use of human capacities that differ from those we use when our actions are motivated by 'power over someone.' This occurs because there is a congruency between the definition of power and our social identities in relationships. The popular definition of power – the capacity to get others to conform to one's will – shores up the rugged individualist's sense of entitlement to take advantage and dominate others. In contrast, relational/cultural theory's definition of power enhances our capacities to facilitate mutuality and connection. Consequently, the definition of power in relational/cultural theory enables us to both more fully inhabit our experience of relationship and to make ourselves and others accountable for how we use our social power. 'Power ... is a basic human reality precisely because we are related to each other. If the goal of relationship is movement and creativity ... the option is to choose how to relate to and through the power that one has ... To envision an alternative paradigm is to reject the false dichotomies of the dominant paradigm in favor of a more complex, fully inhabited experience of relationship (Walker 2002, 3).

We can use our social power to 'move toward clarity and mutuality in relationship' (Walker 2002, 3). Relational/cultural theory is interested in the use of power in the service of 'zest, clarity, mutuality, and affirmation of connection to more fully inhabit our lives' (4). Considering the ways that people survive their disadvantage can lead to a fuller understanding of power (Brock 1993). Similarly, examining the experience of racialized nurses can teach us a great deal about power as 'the capacity to bring about change.'

Racialized Nurses' Self-Perceptions

In contrast to the notion of an autonomous, individual self, relational/

cultural theory conceives of the 'self in relation.' Miller and Stiver (1997) note that the great paradox practised by autonomous selves is to continually seek relationship while staying distant and avoiding affirmation of connection. Perceiving oneself in relationship to others is the beginning point for responsibility, where parties negotiate what's good for themselves and for the relationship. The following quotes indicate how some racialized nurses see themselves in relation to others:

> I am a person ... who belongs to the entire world, cause ... I travel quite a bit and I think I am an international citizen more than anybody else. But definitely I do know that my colour is ... identified very quickly ... People see it ... I don't care what they call it, but I know what I am, and I am an Indian.

> For [the] longest time, I thought they were better than me. I think I was made to feel that way. Right now, because of the education that I have ... you know, I think in a lot of ways I am better than they are ... I make a point that I am equal to them. I do not feel that they are any better. ... Don't become demoralized. Don't start doubting yourself, because once you are doubting yourself, they've won.

Several racialized nurses report having been taught from a young age that to be successful they have to be 'twice as good as members of the dominant group.' They learned from their parents and from their community that in order to contribute to society, it was important to get a good education. They learned to identify racial discrimination and believe that 'not to speak out is a way of participating in one's own oppression.'

> I am aware and more vocal ... now ... Before, it wouldn't bother me, but now every little thing I see, I kinda have to address it.

> At team meetings ... I challenge this type of behaviour because their individual behaviour is still part of the system. I think it ... get[s] to a point that people become more aware and more careful to make that type of comment in front of me.

> I am able to recognize discrimination behaviour processes a lot quicker [than before] and put a stop to it sooner ... I am able to come back with comments that would just squash it and comments that would [keep] my respect intact. And, I now know respect is extremely important.

Power as it is conceptualized in relational/cultural theory seeks to identify change within relationships. Nurses formulate their perceptions of the change process in this way:

> I feel that every single one of us experiences disempowerment ... but we also could find strategies to actually make changes. They're tiny, tiny, tiny, changes and there are days I just want to cry and cry and cry, but I think that power is also – could be – within reach if we [take] collective action.

> I think, when we look at race issues, we also need to look at each one of us as an agent ... because every time I experience something like that, because of my own inner strength, personality, or way of dealing with things, I would initially get really upset. But then afterwards, I would always think about strategies and share those experiences with other people and actually, you know, help my peers who experience the same thing ... answer those people.

> If you know that there's a discussion around unfairness and it involves people of colour, you really can't speak to it objectively because you're part of them ... so I usually stay very quiet. I may be asked, 'What is your opinion?' 'What are your perspectives?' And I would say ... well, I'd rather not share it.

Disillusionment causes some nurses to become despondent and come to believe that they cannot bring about social change:

> For the longest time, I thought, you know, you don't run. You try to change it. I've come to realize ... it ain't gonna change.

Emotions in Racial Conflict

Racial discrimination induces conflict and gives rise to powerful emotions. Consequently, maintaining control over one's emotions is one of the most difficult challenges an individual faces in responding effectively to discrimination. Several of the nurses interviewed in the PAR project reported becoming 'really upset' and 'very upset' when they realized they were being discriminated against. Elsewhere, we have reported the profound emotional and physical effects of prolonged racial conflict on racialized nurses (Hagey et al. 2005).

As members of a caring profession that must deal with a wide variety of difficult situations, nurses are trained to control rather than express their emotions. We hypothesize that there is a link between the strategies racialized nurses use to respond to their emotional pain when they are discriminated against and the strategies they learn and use in their professional capacities as nurses. Barbee observed a decade ago that the nursing profession operates largely on the basis of the colour-blind assumption that 'interpersonal relations are not greatly influenced by group membership' (Barbee 1993, 351). The emphasis on being colour blind while caring for individuals is an obstacle to identifying racism in the profession. Antiracism is paradoxical in that it asks us not to discriminate but insists that we be vigilant about racial discrimination and its effects. We practise equity by constant self-reflection so that we can engage in corrective equilibration practices that countermand the racial elements pervading everyday language in a racially stratified society (Hagey et al. 2005). So-called colour blindness does not facilitate vigilance and equilibration.

Nurses report various ways of dealing with the emotions provoked by racialized conflict. Their varied strategies suggest that there is no one best way to handle emotions triggered by racial discrimination. The transcripts reveal that some nurses maintain a sense of how they respond emotionally to the discrimination they encounter. They interpret their responses and use them in ways that enhance, rather than impede, their efforts to understand the issues in relational conflict with colleagues or supervisors. They feel vulnerable, but sometimes find that articulating their feelings helps them to cope:

> In team meetings ... I have seen situations where discussions may be centred around the dominant culture. I have been very vocal ... in expressing my feelings about it. I think now they do not feel comfortable doing or saying anything that would make me feel uncomfortable. I have been in ... the same environment for quite a while, so they know I wouldn't stand for it.

A racialized nurse in one instance responded with anger and rage:

> There was just a point when I felt that there was a threat of losing my job. I said, 'You can do anything to me, but don't take away something that I have worked at extremely hard.' I drew the line at that ... You just all of [a] sudden get mad and say, '... You have done all of these things to me for many years ... I will not take that when I have educated myself ... I have worked hard for you, and this is how you treat me.'

A nurse who experienced prolonged racial conflict at work said, 'I knew I was being documented. At that time I thought about it in terms of being a hard-boiled egg. You know, you just put it in water and the longer you boil it the harder it becomes' (Turrittin, Hagey, et al. 2002, 663). Her goal was to create change, not in the realm of personal relationships, but in institutional relations between employer, union, and provincial human rights legislation.

Relational Accountability

Racialization can trigger images of victimhood. Walker says she 'felt like a lobster in a boiling pot' when she was not given an opportunity for advancement at work. Images of victimhood are of little use in bringing about change, because they exacerbate 'distortions and hostilities' in relationships, fuel conflict, and engender disconnections. All nurses, racialized and otherwise, have to recognize their differences and reflect upon their position in the workplace hierarchy to realize that change is needed. Walker advocates that instead of adopting images that 'function to support a stance of victimness,' which justifies a lack of relational accountability and forecloses 'opportunities for movement,' we choose relational accountability (2002, 6).

A nurse who experiences racial discrimination and chooses to exercise relational accountability gives offenders an opportunity to learn from their mistakes, change their behaviour, and thus act responsibly by treating others respectfully and fairly. Relational accountability is based on the premise that responsible behaviour will be reciprocated; it encourages everyone to respect 'difference' along with human rights. Acting responsibly as well as making others accountable for how they act is based on the assumption that accountability and responsibility mediate relations and have the potential of promoting racial equality in nursing.

Racism continues to pervade our social institutions, despite the enactment of human rights legislation; thus, relational accountability by itself cannot bring about equitable and safe workplaces. Consequently, we strongly advocate that health-care professionals adopt and use procedures and policies that ensure accountability for eradicating racial inequalities at the workplace. The enthnoracial stratification that exists in hospitals at present does not create a workplace that is free of racism. Implementing racial equality and employment-equity accountability procedures and policies would eventually lead to greater inclusiveness in nursing leadership. However, such changes require the cooperation and support of management and administrative staff in enacting and implementing racially inclusive policies and procedures that address the systemic racism in health-care education and delivery.

In counselling individuals and groups to choose relational accountability, Walker is advocating the possibility of repairing relationships, although she does not stipulate conditions or contingencies. Initiating relational accountability in a racial dispute appears to us to require feeling safe enough to respond to indignities, assessing offenders as having the capacity to learn from their mistakes, and believing that those in authority will act ethically (see Hagey, Lum, et al. 2005). In the scenario reported below, the nurse evidently trusted her manager to do the right thing and felt safe enough disclosing her feelings of hurt, in the belief that the offenders might change:

Even though I am not a member of the Aboriginal community [when a derogatory remark is made about an Aboriginal person], I feel very hurt as a person of colour ... as someone who belongs to a minority power group ... So, I went to my manager. 'You heard what was said ...' I said. 'I didn't like that ... [It] bothers me ... it hurts me,' and she had to do something.

Several of the nurses who were interviewed chose to uphold their dignity and rights and thus acted on the basis of relational accountability. For some of these nurses, relational accountability meant documenting systemic racism or bringing individual racism to the attention of the management. Nurses, particularly racialized nurses, are exhorted by colleagues to 'document, document, document.' Several of the nurses that we interviewed spoke of the importance of such documentation:

Keeping to the nursing practice standards helped me to survive the system ...They wanted me to compromise my nursing principles, and if I had followed what they told me, they could've nailed me with incompetence and all kinds of things ... A particular group of nurses have subsequently ... continuously tried to find fault [with me] ... The only way I can protect myself is by my documentation ... [particularly] legal documentation.

Not only do I challenge them, [but] I feel that I need to role-model when I challenge them. I like to take on a very compassionate kind of [stance] ... I try to [explain] my perspective without really being very judgmental and putting them down. I feel that people behave in certain [ways] not only [as] individuals, but because of the system. And they need to be accountable, but at the same time, I am part of that system and I need to take responsibility [as well] for being accountable.

One black nurse's manager did not give her opportunities to demonstrate the full range of her knowledge and skills on the job:

I was never given the opportunity to be the 'in-charge person.' I'd been monitoring it, so when the situation came up ... I was observant enough to pick up [on it] ... I ... examined all the records ... going back a few years. That was the concrete evidence ... that [I was] consistently placed at the bottom of the pile ... I didn't understand that not being in charge gave the other colleagues power over me. It put me at the bottom of ... the social pecking order. It doesn't matter what you do or how qualified you are. [Others] will view you the way the head person views you.

This same black nurse realized she would be treated with little or no leniency when she failed to sign off a medication. She used documentation to hold her manager accountable:

One time ... I didn't sign off a medication, and [my manager] called me and said I need to fill an incident report ... The patient was alert and awake. According to the College [of Nurses of Ontario], she is right. What's not signed is not given. So I sent for her [the manager] and I said, 'Well, okay, I didn't sign off that medication last night, but you want me to make an incident report? Okay, I will make it. But ... I will make it only when I have done my research.' I researched all the charts ... all the times that medication wasn't signed off. I had all the nurses' names. I said, 'When you have all these nurses fill out an incident report, then I will fill one out.'

In another incident, by creating a paper trail and using bureaucratic procedures to defend herself, this individual again chose relational accountability when her colleagues failed to intervene after a patient discriminated against her:

I was going to do an injection on [a patient] and this was in the scan room and there was a white technologist I was working with – a male – and I went into the patient ... and he did not want me to do his injection. He wanted a white doctor. And I realized this, because I recognize racism as soon as I see it ... So I went to ... tell the doctor that he should come and do this injection ... The technologist went into the room to talk to the patient and when I was going [back] into the room, he [the technologist] slammed the door in my face ... It was 'Get out,' you know ... and I am the one there to do patient care ... So I called my manager to come in and reported to his manager, and then they wanted to set up a meeting on their time and do all that they wanted to do. And I [told] them, 'No, I will set the meeting up. I will write you a letter ... We will do a paper trail and we'll meet. And then [the technologist] apologized. He [said he] was wrong for what he had done and ... he didn't want the grievance to go any further.

Another nurse discovered that adopting 'relational accountability' while advocating for patients enhanced her feelings of self-worth:

I was so strong in my advocacy for the patients. If I had a conflict with a doctor and I knew I was right, I stood up, and usually, because of my strong personality, I got my way ... So, it did create some tension [and] I was threatened with insubordination after a series of things and ... I decided to file a grievance with ONA [the Ontario Nurses' Association, the province's largest union]. The grievance wasn't based on discrimination ... but it was while I was going through the process of the grievance that I realized that I was being discriminated against ... Through ONA's help, I was able to understand, because one of the resources that I got from ONA was Tania Das Gupta's book ... and I came to the conclusion that yes, this is a matter of discrimination ... The outcome was that it was never acknowledged as discrimination ... [It] was a draw ... I stood up for my beliefs and I did get the things I wanted as an outcome ... For me, getting that outcome ... made a total difference for ... my life because ... people were treating me differently ... My life totally turned around.

However, advocating for oneself, especially when one suspects that racism is at issue, is usually complicated (Collins et al. 1998; Hagey, Choudhry, et al. 2001). June Veecock, a union educator who has counselled hundreds of nurses, says:

When we remain silent ... we are contributing to our own oppression. And I know that once you begin to speak, you have to be prepared for what comes. People are accused of making false claims of racism. They are accused of being incompetent and of using racism as an excuse for their incompetence. So that immediately the focus is shifted. The accuser becomes the accused. The victim is then faced with the additional burden of not only having to prove that she is experiencing racism, that this is a racist environment, but also that she is competent. (Calliste 1996, 360–1)

Connecting Despite Barriers to Relationships

In her work as a psychological counsellor, Walker notes that she has frequently advised women to give up behaviour related to the desire for 'victory or power over another being (2002, 6).' Letting go of such behaviour entails willingness to be influenced by others and to give them an opportunity to 'relinquish [their] image of the proper relationship between a white and a black woman [or a person of some other colour], and the opportunity to pay more attention to the actual relationship [one is] living in the moment' (6).

Several of the nurses that we interviewed reported finding strategies that promoted mutuality between themselves and their white colleagues. One nurse's approach was consistent with relational/cultural theory about relating to others in the 'lived moment':

Some ... co-workers... I have developed a close relationship with only because I believe they are more open. If there [are] questions regarding my race, my background, they are open to asking [about them], even if it is stupid questions like 'Why do all black people name their kids Ayesha?' or stuff like that. I don't mind that kind of stuff, but it is the underlying little petty things that I don't like ... When [my co-worker] brought up this Ayesha thing, I just thought it was funny but ... this particular staff [member], any question he has ... he'll come and ask and then he always says, 'Well, I hope you don't mind my asking ... it's just that I haven't really mixed with ... [many] black people,' and I see [him as] more open than most ... With certain staff ... I have developed a close relationship because of that.

Another nurse encouraged mentoring to promote mutuality, and dialogue to maintain connection:

[The registration exams] ... don't prepare you for ... the work life experience, that you are gonna be treated differently ... [New nurses] are absolutely shocked ... They're not prepared. Nobody talks to them about it. It's only when you get into these informal groups ... when you start linking with people and you start looking at people and thinking, okay, so what we do is ... when we see some of the issues [in the unit], we take them out for coffee and say, okay, maybe this is going on ... Let's keep an eye on her and, you know, help her out a little bit.

Before I was more patient, much more willing to give the other the benefit of the doubt. Now I am much clear[er] that there is no doubt in my mind ... I go up to them [new nurses] and tell them, if this [is] happening, talk to me ... making them aware that I know ... They may not know that it is happening. But, hey, there's a reason. If you want to talk, [I tell them], call me ... and we'll talk about it.

Yet another nurse reported setting limits with a white colleague, who then told her what to do to move forward:

On many occasions, you would make a comment or a suggestion, and instead of someone responding to you that, okay, that's another view ... they would say, 'Well, you know, Mary's opinion was better than yours' ... and on one or two occasion[s], I addressed it ... and I said... 'I am not comfortable when you make that statement ... you know, 'Mary said it better' or 'Mary's opinion was better.' And the person told me that she wasn't conscious that she was making this statement, that she would pay attention in the future not to put it that way. She said, 'That's what I mean ... you see, you just speak what you wish and that is not good for you. You have to learn to be diplomatic ... and not express your feelings like this, if you want to move forward...'

Another nurse's comment illustrates that even though she lacked formal authority, non-racialized colleagues were intimidated by her social power:

Her comment to me was, 'I don't think you have been racially disracialized.' I said, 'Well, why not?' She said, 'It's because they're afraid of you.' So I said, 'How so?' She said, 'Well, you're tall, you're black, you're educated, you articulate well, and you are a living threat. So, it's ... not that they're discriminating against you or they're racializing you. It is that you are intimidating to them.'

It is commonplace for racialized nurses to lament being perceived as aggressive and intimidating when they use timeworn strategies to claim equal opportunity or take issue with passive-aggressive approaches to privilege and advantage by in-group members. At a recent national conference sponsored by the Canadian Race Relations Foundation, Zenana Akanda said that 'today's brand of racial discrimination has a friendly face' (Akanda 2003), and her remarks held a special resonance with the audience. Racialized nurses are taken advantage of in socially acceptable ways, and their concerns are smoothed over by pleasantries. In the meantime, they are kept out of the information loop, or worse, set up to fail in times of job competition or cutbacks (Hagey et al. 2005).

One nurse reported, 'I make a point of saying, "Oh, I should know this," or, "You know, that information should be shared."' By insisting that she has the same information needs, this nurse is promoting the kind of relationship envisioned in relational/cultural theory. To get information, she has adopted the tactic of networking:

> They'll talk to you, provided that they can manipulate you ... some of our young coloured nurses ... really are naïve in a way. Some of us ... know what the issues are, and they can't bluff us. But yes, they hold back information. So ... we have to work doubly hard to network to get out of that isolation ... it's a form of power.

Amplifying Difference to Expand Relational Space

The recurring need for racialized nurses to respond effectively when colleagues and patients discriminate has led them, in Walker's terms, to 'amplify difference to expand relational space.' Walker suggests that racialized individuals must listen to their antagonists' narrow views but then question them about broader issues. In this way, racialized individuals will hear themselves giving 'in to fuller voice,' and will be encouraged 'to engage in deeper connection.' They must value their antagonists for their difference ('however awkwardly it might be packaged'). Walker argues that these skills have the potential for shifting 'the usual terms of power' (Walker 2002, 7).

Some nurses reported storytelling as a strategy for sharing differences to come to mutual understanding:

> I could tell a story. I could really tell a story and this is my gift ... When you read my report, I am telling you a story you could visualize. So that is the area that I used to counteract with ... That's my skill, that was my strength, and it still is my strength.

The current transcripts are retrospective, and cannot provide substantive detail on the outcome of these processes for racialized nurses, but we know from informal testimony that supervisors who are seen as fair and just are those who actively listen and sustain connections with racialized nurses through reciprocal favours.

Owning One's Vulnerability

The emotions generated in situations of racial conflict can overpower individuals, particularly if they perceive themselves as victims. Several nurses report having found ways to resist the pain consequent to experiencing discrimination at work (for example, 'I don't need to be loved at work; I get my loving at home'). The demands these nurses make on themselves and the chilly work climate they endure are not unique to their profession. Racialized individuals who encounter racism in other organizations similarly build defence mechanisms rather than address their feelings of vulnerability. Yet Walker suggests that in some situations racialized individuals need to 'soften' themselves for conflict instead of bracing themselves for it, 'since it is in our vulnerability that we find our growing edge' (2002, 7).

This research found that nurses who struggled against racism through their unions and other venues have suffered serious health problems. Consequently, the question of how to engage others in defending an individual's feelings of vulnerability and upholding their rights and privileges is crucial. Our research found that the dispute process is badly in need of reform (Hagey, Lum et al. 2001). Each of the fourteen participants we interviewed reported reprisals for naming racism, despite its being forbidden under the Ontario Human Rights Code. It is true, however, that those complainants who confessed to feeling vulnerable and who gave a senior white male of the organization the right to defend them fared well.

Practising the Power of Naming

As noted earlier, the 1991 Census of Canada showed that racialized nurses in Ontario had only half the chance of becoming managers compared to white nurses (Nestel 2000). (These data have not been assembled for the 2001 census.) What should a racialized nurse who applies for promotion but is not promoted do? While Walker advocates strategies that promote and enhance mutuality and connection at work, she also emphasizes practising 'the power of naming.' In alternative dispute resolution it is commonplace to advocate naming the issue, although such naming increases the risk of temporarily escalating the conflict. Theoretically, naming the issue is crucial in interest-based negotiations. But in identity-based negotiations such as racial disputes, identifying an act as discrimination can be perceived by the victim as violating a moral code of not naming such incidents, since potentially they can involve financial and other liabilities for the employer.

'Naming an injury is a vast act of exposure' (Miller 1986) that can threaten the status quo and induce retaliation and censure by those who operate using the conventional 'power-over-another' paradigm. Walker does not explain how naming should be used in negotiations with employers or colleagues. However, the risks of naming are widely known in the subculture of racialized nurses. For example, according to one nurse:

> If you call the action, [are] willing to be ostracized, to be put down, to be not given ... timely information..., be prepared ... not to get any opportunity. You [have] to fight for everything [and] you gotta put [in] double the work anybody [else does] to get the same position ... It's not equal. It's not fair. But that's the way it is. And, you know, some of the personal prices are very high. The economic price ... you know, you can live with. It's the personal demoralizing, the personal [lack of] satisfaction – those prices are... very high.
>
> Disciplinary action ... is the formal process. Nobody can ... put in a formal process when there is no real hard evidence. But then there is an informal process, where you know ... you are penalized, but not in a way that you can point a finger and say, this is a punishment...
>
> *Interviewer:* Even though it's not formal disciplinary action, there is this informal censoring that goes on?
>
> ... Minority nurses have to be very careful of that, which is a price you pay. And if you're not aware of that price, you always doubt yourself, and I think once you start doubting yourself, they'[ve] won, cause that's what they want.

Another nurse found simple wordplay helped her stand firm in her relationship with clients. Achieving the effect of naming with just her presence and demeanor, she reports thwarting racialized complaints:

> Well, a couple of times [a patient's] family would ask if I am the real nurse and I [would tell] them, RN means 'real nurse' ... When I had a supervi-

sory job, I think I quite shocked a few people ... they wanted to complain
about a nurse of colour and ... said they want[ed] to page the nursing
supervisor ... but the family never continued to complain because they
found that when they saw me, they somehow had nothing to say.

Walker's warning that those who complain must be prepared to 'relinquish any fantasies of happy endings' (2002, 8) because 'the dominant
powers attempt to suppress complaints, by any means necessary, but
most often through humiliation and shaming' (7) is validated by the
experiences of the nurses who filed formal complaints and grievances
documented in our earlier research (Collins et al. 1998).

The double victimization of the complainant, however, may be coming to an end. A number of hospitals in Toronto are experimenting with
new models, such as diversity workplace units, that attempt to deal
with discriminatory practices within the organization. Early results
indicate that preemptive action by such units can promote positive relationships at work. One informant told us that her job requires confronting the offending decision-maker with the shame that will come to the
organization if a formal human-rights complaint is launched. In this
way, the humiliation is not experienced by the complainant, but rather
threatens to overcome those who defend the discrimination or their
perpetrators.

Walker adds to her discussion of naming by describing a practice
called 'defecting in place' (see Fischer 1999) adopted by mothers of the
'disappeared' in Latin America who come together to share their pain
and give one another collective support (2002, 7). These mothers found
a way to 'embrace an alternative model' of power in the most extreme
conditions of domination. While the social context in the nursing profession in Canada is arguably less oppressive than that constraining the
response of the Latino mothers, parallels can nevertheless be identified
in some of the recently emerging anti-racist organizations.

'Defecting in place' may have led to the formation of The Ontario
Association of Black Health Care Providers (OABHCP) in Toronto. In
1995, following a two-day conference to 'End the Silence on Racism in
Nursing' (Calliste 1995), a number of racialized health professionals
found support and a space to meet at Across Boundaries, Canada's first
ethnoracial mental-health centre. Juilette Saunders states:

The Association's founding members ... were motivated to take action as a
result of complaints concerning racist attitudes that nurses at Northwest-

ern General Hospital had been subjected to ... The Association's number-one goal was to promote the development of creative and innovative strat-egies to help its members deal effectively with racism and discriminatory practices in their work environment. The OABHCP's main accomplish-ment was to create a forum for minority nurses to come to and have their issues validated. Many nurses had nowhere to go to speak openly about their issues. There is always strength in numbers, and issues of race and discrimination are often denied by the dominant group. Association mem-bers provided support to nurses whose complaints were heard at arbitra-tion, and informally advised nurses about legal aspects of the grievance/complaint process. (Hagey et al. 2005, 69–70)

When offenders continue to operate from the power-over paradigm despite opportunities to engage in mutuality and connectedness, those who are racially discriminated against can sometimes exercise the option of leaving. As one nurse said, 'I just ask for a transfer to a differ-ent floor.' Others have left nursing altogether, and still others have writ-ten forcefully about nursing as an inhospitable profession to be avoided by women of colour (Hagey, Lum et al. 2001).

Implications for the Political Context of Nursing

Numerous ethnoracially and language-based nurses' associations and social-justice organizations have come together in a broad-based coali-tion to form The Centre for Equity in Health and Society (CEHS). The Centre's mandate includes advocating changes in workplace policies and procedures to ensure more equitable work environments for all nurses. The Centre's recent report to the Canadian Race Relations Foundation (Hagey et al. 2005) calls upon employers and regulatory bodies to reward equity practices and to institute administrative accountability for systemic discrimination. The Canadian Human Rights Act (CHRA) and Employment Equity Act (EEA) were amended in 1996 to preclude the option of hearing cases and hence of imposing penalties that hold employers accountable for systemic discrimination (Beck, Reitz, and Weiner 2002). Consequently, employers, union repre-sentatives, nurses, and colleagues that we have spoken with are com-pelled to either ignore complex escalating conflicts or embark upon expensive grievance arbitrations that neither employers, unions, nor human rights tribunals can afford.

The CEHS report calls for nursing conferences that will help to organize new ways of thinking and speaking, thus precipitating a shift away from the 'discourse of dominance.' We have argued that the essence of racism and the root of the discourse of racial dominance is that one does not necessarily have to be accountable to racialized people. This lack of accountability engenders racial discrimination and is fundamentally conflictual. Racial conflict requires formal and informal administrative tools for restoring accountability within a new cultural paradigm. Shifting to a model for achieving equity through accountability necessitates that nursing and health-care organizations adopt policies and training programs to build ethnoracial competencies and implement accommodation for inequities. The report to the Law Commission of Canada, *Exploring Transformative Justice in the Employment of Nurses: Toward Reconstructing Race Relations and the Dispute Process* (Hagey, Lum, et al. 2001), presents a preliminary accountability tool for evaluating the procedures used to prevent racial discrimination and resolve racial disputes.

Ironically, where there is no accountability and racial discrimination goes unchallenged, those in authority tend to deny that it induces conflict. We argue, however, that this denial has to be transcended if balanced relationships are to flourish. Acknowledging the existence of racism and building accountability programs both go strategically to the source of the problem and avoid discrimination, dominance, hurt, and resentment. Disputes arising from racial discrimination lead to distress and absenteeism among nurses, thus affecting patient care as well as violating human rights (Hagey et al. 2005).

There is a close link between relational accountability and human-rights concerns, although Walker does not discuss this as part of relational accountability and only one of the nurses we interviewed mentioned it. However, it would be unfair to require racialized individuals to rely solely on the offenders' good intentions and willingness to change their behavior. While some offenders may be more or less fair to token individuals, or willing to change their behaviour when made conscious of its harmful effect on others, most nursing departments do not yet have policies or procedures that require accountability for systemic racial discrimination. Relational accountability can be used to lobby for organizational accountability and needs to be done collectively (see *Kawa Whakaruruhau* 1988, a document of Maori nurses demanding cultural safety).

Workplaces are reported as having stressful environments where racial tension is high and systemic racial discrimination is chronic. The CEHS is calling for organizational policies and procedures that will monitor and make key decision-makers accountable for upholding human rights and promoting accountability initiatives. Apologies and reparations go a long way to healing relations, correcting inequities, and preventing repeat offences. The pattern we have documented elsewhere (Hagey et al. 2005) of lashing out against the nurse who has complained about racism is unjust and unacceptable. We are asking our colleagues everywhere to be vigilant about racial discrimination, identify it when it happens, and take a leadership role in intervening against it.

Soares (1997) outlines strategies for contending with resistance to equal access and participation, and describes counter-strategies of resistance that can get around certain situations of harassment. He notes also that accusations of racism are extremely threatening and tend to produce poor outcomes for the complainant. We hope that this study will help nurses to empathize with those disadvantaged by systemic differences and motivate leaders in the profession to break the silence on segregation, stratification, and racial harassment in nursing and the health-care system. Despite these realities, many of the nurses in this study displayed resilience when they experienced racism. The CEHS, along with the Stone Center and the Jean Baker Miller Training Institute, advocates resilience rather than counter-resistance to the widespread denial of equity. Resilience is conceptualized as strengthening relationships, whereas resistance and counter-resistance can run the risk of destroying relationships (see Sparks 1999).

Racialized nursing organizations have been successful at organizing collectively to promote their interests and defend their human rights (Calliste 1995, 1996). Few of the nurses who participated in the research reported here had filed formal grievances or complaints charging their employers with racial discrimination, although they made comments about what nurses should do to improve working conditions (Collins et al. 1998; Hagey, Choudhry et al. 2001). The nurses participating in this study recommended:

- *Speaking up collectively.* 'If we [all] ... say something ... at least we would be heard, but when it's just one of us, it's just like you're silent. Sometimes ... you just get lost in the majority.'
- *Educating nurses at all levels of the profession about diversity and discriminatory practices.* 'For me, one way of combating [the] oppression of

racism is to train and provide professional development for those who are exclusive, but also for us, who learned not to be assertive and claim our rights.'
- *Becoming engaged in the political process and in research for change.* 'I got involved in the union in ... occupational health and safety, and as an occupational health and safety representative for the nurses, I felt I used to get a lot of things done – a lot of actions corrected that normally would have gone to grievance process so ... when the Occupational Health and Safety Act came about in [19]79, I used that as a way to cure a lot of ills, so that was positive.'

It is our hope that by learning about the strategies used by nurses who employ tact to cope with racial discrimination, readers of all ethnoracial provenance may be motivated to learn about racial discrimination and dominance and to find ways to promote equity and diversification of leadership in nursing.

Conclusion

This chapter has discussed the practices advocated by relational/cultural theory, including relational accountability, alongside strategies reported by self-identified racialized nurses who were interviewed for a research project on racism in their profession. The nurses shared their insights about what to do and say when one experiences racial discrimination at work. Many of their strategies reveal resilience, a tactic that is advocated over resistance in relational/cultural theory.

The testimony of some of the nurses demonstrates their desire to give up the mantle of victimhood and adopt individual and coordinated social responsibility. Their strategies echo the cultural ideals of some racialized communities; for example, the belief that racial 'discrimination is [not] an excuse for not being able to achieve personal and professional success' (Andre 2003, 1). The nurses believe it is important to maintain their dignity when responding to those who discriminate against them.

We have offered some preliminary concepts from relational/cultural theory in the hope that the best practices of nurses can be developed further and that our capacities for building consensus can surmount the challenges of white privilege and racial dominance embedded in nursing education (Hagey and MacKay 2000), health and social services (Henry et al. 2000), education, employment, and income (Ornstein 2000). Relational/cultural theory defines power as the capacity to bring about change. A key strategy for change is enabling those who discriminate to save face while at the same time becoming conscious of the inappropriateness of their actions. Clear messages within the relationship can offer offenders the option to choose accountability and nurture the relationship by defending the vulnerability of the racialized nurse.

Relational/cultural theory can offer nurses approaches to developing collegiality at work (Jacobs 2002), in keeping with the philosophy that ethnocultural and racial differences must not prevent professional nurses from finding ways to work inclusively to enhance our mutuality and connection and preserve our collective interests. Perhaps it is natural to feel threatened by colleagues who tell us that they view our language and behaviour as discriminatory. To their credit, the nurses interviewed have often chosen relational accountability and have taken on the task of educating wrongdoers. In the participatory action research component of our study, these nurses advocated for a Canada-wide equity assurance policy: equity assurance of *racial* equality. With them, we believe that relational accountability can support and be supported by organizational structures committed to ensuring all nurses equitable privileges.

Notes

The authors wish to thank Bridget Liriano and Pam Sun for their insights with respect to the discussion of power.

1 Claudine Charley, to whom this paper is dedicated, was a nurse who called upon her colleagues to support her after she was targeted for complaining of racism. A white nurse had unplugged a heart monitor on one of Claudine's patients with the confessed motive of getting Claudine into trouble. In contrast to the reprisals Claudine experienced for filing a grievance, when the white nurse revealed her motive to the arbitration panel, the proceedings were stopped so that she could get legal counsel. This happened during a period when nursing care was under-funded, layoffs were taking place, and nurses feared losing their jobs. More than forty nurses showed up to Claudine's hearings, each laying a daffodil on the podium. Claudine took a cut of $50,000 in her settlement so that she could speak to the media about her story. The media insinuated that Claudine was paid her $250,000 package so

the hospital could get rid of a troublemaker of questionable professional stature. Claudine served on governing bodies such as the Mental Health Reform Committee of the Toronto District Health Council, the Joint Provincial Planning Committee of the Ontario Ministry of Health and the Ontario Hospital Association, which introduced an antiracism policy in 1995. The latter policy has yet to be fully implemented. Claudine died in June 2003 of cancer of the throat.

2 To the best of our knowledge, the participants in this study have not read Walker's research and publications.

References

Akanda, Z. 2003. Racism: Breaking through the denial. Keynote speech at the Canadian Race Relations Foundation award of excellence symposium. Toronto.
Andre, I. 2003. *Share*. 13 February, 1.
Barbee, E. 1993. Racism in U.S. nursing. *Medical Anthropology Quarterly* 7 (4): 346–62.
Beck, J.H., J.G. Reitz, and N. Weiner. 2002. Addressing systemic racial discrimination in employment: The Health Canada case and implications of legislative change. *Canadian Public Policy*, March.
Brock, R.N. 1993. *Journeys by heart: A Christology of erotic power*. New York: Crossroads. Cited in Walker 2002, 3.
Calliste, A. 1995. *End the silence on racism in health care: Build a movement against discrimination, harassment and reprisals.* A conference report for black nurses and other health care workers. Toronto: Ontario Institute for Studies in Education.
– 1996. Antiracism organizing and resistance in nursing: African Canadian women. *Canadian Review of Sociology and Anthropology* 33 (3): 361–69.
Centre for Equity in Health and Society (CEHS). 2005. *Implementing accountability for equity and ending racial backlash in nursing.* Report to the Canadian Race Relations Foundation, Toronto.
Collins, E., A. Calliste, U. Choudhry, J. Fudge, R. Hagey, R. Lee, J. Turrittin, and S. Guruge. 1998. *Making racism seeable: The complaints/grievances filed by women immigrant nurses who are members of designated minorities.* Report to the Centre of Excellence for Research on Immigration and Settlement (CERIS).
Collins, P.H. 1990. *Black feminist thought: Knowledge, consciousness, and the politics of empowerment.* Boston: Unwin Hyman.

Das Gupta, T. 2002. *Racism in nursing*. Report to the Ontario Nurses Association.

Essed, P. 1991. *Understanding everyday racism: An interdisciplinary theory*. Newbury Park, CA: Sage.

Fischer, K. 1999. *Transforming fire: Women using anger creatively*. Mahwah, NJ: Paulist.

Hagey, R., and R. MacKay. 2000. Qualitative research to identify racialist discourse: Towards equity in nursing curricula. *International Journal of Nursing Studies* 37 (1): 45–56.

Hagey, R., U. Choudhry, S. Guruge, J. Turrittin, E. Collins, and R. Lee. 2001. Immigrant nurses experience of racism. *Journal of Nursing Scholarship* 33 (4): 389–94.

Hagey, R., L. Lum, R. MacKay, J. Turrittin, and E. Brody. 2001. *Exploring transformative justice in the employment of nurses: Toward reconstructing race relations and the dispute process*. Report to the Law Commission of Canada.

Hagey, R., L. Lum, J. Turrittin, and R. MacKay. 2005. How the profession of nursing can achieve ethnoracial safety through transformative justice. In *Professionalization of work*, ed. M. Jacobs, 144–64. Toronto: de Sitter.

Henry, F., C. Tator, W. Mattis, and T. Rees. 2000. *The colour of democracy: Racism in Canadian Society*. Toronto: Harcourt Brace.

Jacobs, M. 2002. Creating understanding from research: Staff nurses' views on collegiality. In *Is anyone listening? Women, work, and society*, ed. M. Jacobs, 295–314. Toronto: Women's Press.

Kawa Whakaruruhau (Cultural safety in nursing education in Aotearoa). 1988. Hui Waimanawa, Conference on Maori education, Otautahi (Christchurch), New Zealand.

Marshall. K. 1996. The diversity of managers. *Perspectives*. Statistics Canada. Winter, 24–30.

Miller, J.B. 1986. *Toward a new psychology of women*. 2nd ed. Boston: Beacon. Quoted in Walker 2002, 7.

Miller, J.B., and I. Stiver. 1997. Seeking connection by staying out of connection. In *The healing connection: How women form relationships in therapy and in life*. Boston: Beacon.

Nestel, S. 2000. Obstructed labour: Race and gender in the re-emergence of midwifery in Ontario. PhD thesis, University of Toronto.

Ng, R. 2002. Teaching against the grain: Contradictions and possibilities. In *Is anyone listening: Women, work and society*, ed. Merle Jacobs, 89–116. Toronto: Women's Press.

Ontario Hospital Association and the Ontario Ministry of Health, Joint Policy and Programming Committee. 1995. *Anti-racism organizational change self-assessment tool/anti-racism policy guidelines.*

Ontario Human Rights Code. 1981. Toronto: Government of Ontario.

Ontario Human Rights Commission. 2005. *Policy and guidelines on racism and racial discrimination.* Toronto: Ontario Human Rights Commission.

Ornstein, M. 2000. *Ethno-racial inequality in the city of Toronto: An analysis of the 1996 Census.* Toronto: United Way.

Soares, A. 1997. *Stratégies des résistance et travail des femmes.* Paris: Harmattan.

Sparks, E. 1999. Against all odds: Resistance and resilience in African American welfare mothers. Wellesley, MA: Stone Center/Jean Baker Miller Training Institute, Working Paper 81.

Turrittin, J., R. Hagey, S. Gurige, E. Collins, M. Mitchell. 2002. The experience of professional nurses who have migrated to Canada: Cosmopolitan Citizenship or democratic racism? *International Journal of Nursing Studies* 39 (4): 655–67.

Walker, M. 2002. Power and effectiveness: Envisioning an alternate paradigm. Wellesley, MA: Stone Center/Jean Baker Miller Training Institute, Working Paper 94.

van Dijk, T. 1993. *Elite discourse and racism.* Newbury Park, CA: Sage.

PART THREE

Nation and Identity

Nations comprise 'imagined communities' of traditions or ancestry and seek political expression for them. Nation is not conterminous with state: the state has physical, geographical, and territorial boundaries that do not always coincide with those of the nation. The state may include groups identified by race, ethnic identity, or politics that perceive themselves as a nation and wish to separate from the state, as the Quebecois in Canada sought to in the 1970s. At other times, a racial or ethnic group may be present within the physical borders of the state, as is documented in the chapters in this section, but may yet be excluded from the 'imagined community' of the nation by being absent from national histories, marginalized within institutions, and disparaged in discourses. The meanings attached to physical attributes may mark some as 'outsiders' and 'foreigners' (with labels such as 'Jews,' 'blacks,' 'Muslims,' or 'Arabs') to that which is defined as 'Canadian,' 'American,' or 'German.' Since nation is an arbitrary construct, exclusions and inclusions depend upon the will and pleasure of powerful others. Nations matter more to people as individuals than do states (Appiah 2005, 244).

Political elites construct a nation in their own image by their control of institutions and through public policies. For example, in Canada and the United States, immigrants from European nations have been welcomed, but the arrival of Asians, Africans, and other racialized groups has caused consternation and raised doubts about their ability to assimilate with the nation. Although exclusionary practices, whether legal or social, have been with us throughout the last century, their form and expression change with time, place, and social context. Racism is thus fluid, chameleonlike, and parasitic.

Racialized populations in the United States and Canada had begun to believe that a new, just society was slowly evolving with the legislative, social, and behavioural changes that were widely instituted in myriad forms since the 1960s. However, such hopes were severely compromised after the terrorist attacks in New York City and Washington in September 2001 and the consequent intensification of what has been termed Islamophobia. In 'Racism Masquerading as Nationalism: Wars, Japanese-Americans, and Arab-Americans,' Ezra Yoo-Hyeok Lee contends that the old notion of racial hierarchy – such as who is 'properly American' versus who remains foreign – re-emerges in a new guise in contemporary America. This chapter documents the racism that resulted in the internment of Japanese-Americans and the illusionary choices between Japan and America they were forced to make. Racism that was latent in peacetime was expressed openly in the form of nationalism during World War II, thereby victimizing the Japanese-Americans. Regardless of the choice they made – to demonstrate loyalty to America by going to war or to stay away from the war – Japanese-Americans were marginalized and thought to be outside that which constituted the nation. Racism in the post–September 11 period has changed its form and its target. Now it is expressed as the need to make the world safe from terrorism, which permits the covert articulation of racism against Muslims and Arab-Americans. However, there are similarities between the racism experienced by Japanese-Americans in earlier days and that which is being perpetrated against Arab-Americans at the present time. Now it is cultural racism in the form of Islamophobia that plagues the Arab-Americans and Muslims.

The 'war on terrorism' initiated by the United States has had repercussions on racialized populations in Canada, as it has elsewhere. It could be argued that the new security regulations, anti-terrorism legislation, and border control policies are all necessary to protect Canadian citizens. Charles S. Smith, speaking from an oppositional voice in 'Borders and Exclusions: Racial Profiling in the New World Order,' writes that the new regulations have further intensified the victimization of people of African descent by law enforcement agencies. Racialization of people of African descent has stereotyped them as violent individuals prone to drugs and crime. The media has played a contributory role, criminalizing blacks through reports of illegal and violent activity that portray them as being the perpetrators. The current fear of the Other has made law enforcement based on racial profiling more acceptable to the public, despite its horrendous economic, social, and psychological impact on those so targeted. Smith argues that racial profiling has become an increasingly challenging phenomenon in law enforcement. Whether in urban policing and the deployment of law enforcement in African-Canadian communities or in patrolling the borders of the nation in the aftermath of September 11, there has been a growing racialization of law and law enforcement, with harmful impacts on racialized groups.

Racialized individuals are often citizens in the United States, Canada, and elsewhere. Citizenship entails rights and responsibilities whose specificity is determined by the state; it incorporates beliefs about equality, whether they are of race, gender, or religion. Furthermore, in Canada the Charter of Rights and Freedoms has given individuals the ability to challenge discriminatory policies and practices since the 1980s. Although provisions of the Charter can be used to challenge new regulations and the covert racial profiling engaged in by law enforcement bodies, they are a distressing evidence of racism in contemporary Canadian society.

National and cultural identities change in response to new ideas, political events, people, and evolving beliefs. Cultures are dynamic rather than static; they are transformed in particular social contexts and over time. Individuals seek not only to maintain and preserve their culture, but also to re-imagine and to recreate it. Identity and nationalism are closely connected. The content of the culture is 'incidental'; what is significant is the 'larger task of self definition' (Appiah 2005, 134). What distinguishes 'us' from 'them,' white from racialized populations, is not mere identity but a history that has assigned power to some and made others less powerful (or even powerless). However, who we imagine ourselves to be, how we act, and the stories we choose to tell can construct a nation that accepts the past while struggling and resisting racism.

Nation building is an act of faith. Cecil Foster writes that if we as a society reinvent and re-imagine the beliefs around nation, race, and the state, we can move forward to a time of hope.

Do we continue to follow the strands [nation, race, and state] into what appears to be social dead ends? One strand places us in a nation-state that's an exclusive homeland for a few of humanity's diversity. This would be the case for those who maintain positions of privilege within the nation-state. Another option is that of a nation-state that is radically universal and as diverse as humanity itself, a society that aims to be a reflection of humanity in its entirety, and a country in which all members of humanity are equal and share the same privileges and entitlements of citizenship. (Foster 2005, 156)

One innovative answer that can take us forward is found in Germany's creation of museums that address the anti-Semitism of the past and seek to fill in the voids of history. The Jews were excluded from the German nation and exterminated because of their race. The wrongs of history and the absence of the Jews in German history have been acknowledged, and there are now signs of rapprochement and gestures towards reconciliation. Robin Ostow's chapter, 'From Displaying 'Jewish Art' to (Re)Building German-Jewish History: The Jewish Museum Berlin,' explores the social history and deconstructs the permanent exhibits of two Jewish museums in Berlin in the context of larger debates about the status of Jews in Germany. Berlin's first Jewish museum opened in January 1933 as Germany was about to embark on a catastrophic restructuring of its government, national identity, and way of dealing with minorities. One result was that the Nazis dissolved the Jewish Museum and the Jewish population around it within a few years: the museum was closed in 1938, and the deportation of Berlin's Jews began in 1941. Sixty years later, in September 2001, a new Jewish museum opened in Berlin. A monumental project sponsored largely by the government of reunified Germany, the Jewish Museum Berlin recasts German and Jewish identities and repositions German-Jewish history within and around national history. Both the earlier museum and the modern-day one represent large statements, innovative concepts, and contested positions in contemporary debates regarding the relation of German Jews to the larger society around them and to the German state.

References

Appiah, Kwame. 2005. *The ethics of identity.* Princeton: Princeton University Press.
Foster, Cecil. 2005. *Where race does not matter: The new spirit of modernity.* Toronto: Penguin.

7 Borders and Exclusions: Racial Profiling in the New World Order

CHARLES C. SMITH

The police become omnipresent and spectral in the so called civilized states once they undertake to make the law, instead of simply contenting themselves to applying it and seeing that it is observed. This fact becomes clearer than ever in the age of new teletechnologies ... In such an age police violence is 'faceless' and 'formless,' and is thus beyond all accountability. Nowhere is this violence, as such, to be found; in the civilized world, the spectre of its ghostly apparition extends itself limitlessly.

Jacques Derrida, *On Cosmopolitanism and Forgiveness*

Throughout its history, the Canadian government has developed and implemented laws, policies, and procedures that are now thought to be racist. These have ranged from the sanctioning of slavery and segregation in education and residential accommodations to the racialization of law enforcement, criminal justice, and immigration and refugee determination processes. Canadian laws and social values have oppressed people of Japanese, Chinese, and South Asian origin and people of African descent, among others. Racialized discourses have constructed these same groups of people in negative ways. This has led in contemporary times to racial profiling, a construct related to criminal profiling that has been adopted by law enforcement authorities at Canada's borders and within Canadian cities. Specifically, people of African descent (along with Muslims and those of Arab descent) have been targeted as criminally suspect, and the rule of law is sometimes ignored by law-enforcement authorities in stopping, charging, and apprehending individuals from these communities.

The convergence of domestic tendencies and international influences has made racial profiling a very disturbing phenomenon in the daily lives of people of African descent. As a law-enforcement practice, it is linked to a history of racial oppression for groups who find themselves under its scrutiny in almost every aspect of their public and private life (Adamson and Holman 2002; Hamilton 2003). For members of the dominant group, profiling is a distant matter handled by law-enforcement officials, resulting in an experiential gap that shields them from its rather gritty details and horrendous impact. This protective dynamic, however, has recently been disrupted with reports of racial profiling in domestic law enforcement and local policing (Rankin et al. 2002) as well as at the borders of our nation (Daniels, Macklem, and Roach 2002; Mendes and McAllister 2002; Canadian Bar Association 2001; Law Commission of Canada 2002; Griswold 2002; Canadian Human Rights Commissioner 2001).

Consistent with Canada's history of racialization, racial profiling in law enforcement has established particular borders and exclusions that apply at a number of entryways in our lives. These borders are like the obstacles Kafka's 'K' faces in *The Trial* as he tries to find his accusers, who are everywhere and nowhere. Attempts to identify these boundaries are like K's efforts in *The Castle* to find the meaning of things, while the trail to the person who seems to have the answers appears and then disappears. Often these boundaries are referred to as the geographical borders of a country, but they are also painfully evident in the lives of individuals from racialized groups, particularly those borders within the self, those landmarks by which individuals and communities establish identities, purposefully drawing distinctions between themselves and others. Woven into this is the effect of dominant and subordinate group relations and their racialization within contemporary domestic and global sociopolitical and cultural spheres.

The promise of the 2001 United Nations gathering against racism, xenophobia, and other related intolerances in Durban, South Africa, was totally lost with the attacks of September 11 that same year in New York City. The aftermath of September 11 represents a rather dramatic change from denouncing racism to condoning it domestically and internationally in Canada, the United States, and the United Kingdom. As a result, racial profiling has become even more enmeshed in the fabric of North American and European societies, affecting the way those it impacts see themselves and the world because of how *they* are seen. Dyzenhaus (2002, 21–8) and Gross (2002, 45–7) discuss how anti-terrorism legislation establishes boundaries separating 'us' from 'them' – 'insiders' from 'outsiders' – that are based on stereotypes. Consequently, Macklin argues, 'members of diasporic communities, whatever their immigration status, will experience more than ever how boundaries demarcated by ethnicity, culture, religion, and politicization emerge in sharp relief when viewed through the lens of the state's surveillance camera' (2002, 398).

What is disturbing here is the move to establish what appears to be a permanent policy, through anti-terrorism legislation, in response to an emergency situation. Of equal concern is the failure of the federal and provincial governments in Canada to take decisive action on reports of racial profiling by domestic police forces, including the RCMP. This compels us to consider the normative value of race and racism within communities, and how it continues to be normalized in society's way of thinking and doing things.

Racialization (discussed in detail by Agnew in the introduction to this volume) refers to a process by which those in power construct the social identity of others by attaching meaning to their bodily markers. Such racialization constructs a 'profile' of an individual that law-enforcement agencies use to target and to discriminate. Although the term 'racial profiling' has only recently gained currency, the phenomenon has deep roots in Canadian history. This paper will show that by historically racializing some groups through legislation and by associating criminal activity with people of African descent, Canadian society has facilitated their past and current targeting through law-enforcement policies of racial profiling. I document this by reviewing the history of racialization in immigration and refugee law and policy, in racialized discourses of the media, and in current domestic law enforcement policies and practices. These discussions reveal continuity between earlier periods of racialization and the present time, despite the difference in focus and details. Such profiling shows us that racism constructs national identity and national borders, calling into question how Canada defines itself as a nation.

The Social and Political Context of Racial Profiling

In the last few years, the infamous term 'racial profiling' has mustered its way to the top of the list of common terms employed in public discourse across North America and in the United Kingdom. There have been numerous media articles on this subject (Olson 2000; Radil 2000;

Bain 2000; Cloud 2001; Golab 1999; Arellano and Ashenfelter 2000; Murakami 2002; Barovick 1998; McCain 2000; Goetz 2001). The *Toronto Star*'s series on policing and racial profiling, and particularly the controversy resulting from it, has served to push this issue into the forefront, as has the recent human-rights settlement of Selwyn Pieters in his complaints against Canada Customs (Canadian Human Rights Commission 2002). Furthermore, the Ontario Human Rights Commission recently released the results of its public inquiry examining racial profiling, documenting many stories from individuals claiming that they had been victimized by this practice in a variety of sectors (2003). At the same time, the Ontario Court of Appeal addressed racial profiling in *R. v. Decovan Brown* (Morden 2003), and the Ontario courts dismissed the action initiated by the Toronto Police Association alleging that the *Star*'s series on racial profiling was libelous (Tyler 2003). Shortly afterwards, the Canadian Association of Chiefs of Police addressed this issue at its August 2003 conference and the Nova Scotia Human Rights Commission concluded a tribunal hearing on racial profiling and policing (Powell 2003; Girard 2003).

While these reports and occurrences contextualize racial profiling as a contested terrain, 'September 11 forced a fundamental shift in the racial profiling discourse. The central contention was no longer whether racial profiling was in fact taking place or how to best prevent incidents of racial profiling or even whether the Charter offered adequate remedial measures to address racial profiling. Rather, racial profiling debates in the context of the war against terrorism [now] focus on whether Canadian society can morally, legally or politically condone racial profiling' (Bahdi 2003).

Canadian society has become increasingly security conscious and more willing to allow the state to erect boundaries between 'us' and 'them' than at any time since the end of World War II (Aiken 2001, 1). Consequently, racial profiling supports the sense of comfort and well-being of white Canadians. It has been described as one of the most significant weapons in both the 'war on drugs' and the 'war on terrorism.' Because the concept of war has been directly linked to racial profiling, it is not open for debate, let alone corrective or restorative measures. As a result, it plays havoc with the lives of those it ensnares (Glasser 1999 and 2000). Beare notes that 'since September 2001, terrorism supplements all other lesser threats with a slightly different perspective that focuses more on the nature of the border and the symbolic and/or real reasons for maintaining one's border. The terrorist enemy has become the dangerous foreigner in our midst, with the policing task being to identify, remove, and incapacitate these persons' (2003, 7; see also Macklin 2002, 383–92).

Racial profiling in the new millennium has allowed racism to openly and unapologetically insert itself into policing and security. We see it everywhere around us. For example, Stenning (2003) writes about policing in Canada and the United Kingdom. He examines the impact of policing on racialized groups over the last thirty years and comments on the increasing reliance on private security companies, which operate openly in shopping centres, malls, and public housing complexes. Their presence is a seemingly inescapable sign of comfort against an ever-present threat (from youths, particularly those of African descent) that has been socially constructed as dangerous (Benjamin 2003; Law Commission of Canada 2002, 15–28, 39–41). Since the 1970s, a disproportionate number of African-American students have been at greater risk of receiving school punishments, and more recent evidence suggests that zero tolerance in the schools simply moves the 'problem' from the school to the community, where in many instances, such youths engage in criminal offences (Power 2003, 3–4; Harvard University Civil Rights Project 2000).[1] Similar patterns affecting African-Canadian youths have emerged in places such as Nova Scotia (Power 2003, 4–5; Smith and Lawson 2002, 40–3).[2]

Racial profiling is consistently used in law enforcement in Canada, the United States, and the United Kingdom. For example, in the state of Maryland, African Americans constituted 72 per cent of those stopped by police, even though they only made up 17 per cent of drivers in the state. In the United Kingdom, recent data indicate that people of African descent are stopped anywhere between 7.5 and 27 times more than white drivers. In Ontario, survey results indicate that 43 per cent of African-Canadian respondents have been stopped by police over a two-year period, compared with 25 per cent of white and 19 per cent of Asian respondents. Other data suggest that African-Canadian drivers are 4 times more likely to be stopped more than once and 7 times more likely to indicate that they have been unfairly stopped by police (Smith 2004; Wortley 1997; Tanovich 2002, 151–7).

The hostile interactions between law enforcement and security services and individuals from racialized groups, particularly those of African descent, seem to point to a tacit understanding within the public domain of whom we need to feel 'safe from.' This form of racism has become acceptable in day-to-day existence, and while it can be defined, it is simply not discussed, lending itself to the 'spectral' reality that Derrida speaks of and becoming the illusive source of knowledge that makes the accuser invisible.

Defining Racial Profiling

Since people of African descent are being profiled, we need to examine how this 'border' between them and other people was established historically and at the present time. Perhaps one of the most seminal English-language works contributing to the notion of borders is Matthew Arnold's *Culture and Anarchy*. Writing in the mid-nineteenth century, Arnold argued that culture comprises 'the best that has been thought and said in the world.' On this basis, he articulated a belief that 'the disruptive nature of working-class lived culture... [and] the political dangers that he believe[d] to be inevitably concomitant with the entry of the urban, male working class into formal politics in 1867' would lead to anarchy; thus, 'the social function of culture is to *police* [my emphasis] this disruptive presence'(Arnold 1869/1960, 6). Throughout the twentieth century, Arnold's influence 'has been enormous in that [it] virtually mapped out the way of thinking about popular culture and cultural politics which dominated the field until the late 1950s' (Storey 1993, 27).

Cornel West comments critically that Arnold's references to '"our way," without explicitly acknowledging who constitutes the "we" ... is symptomatic among many bourgeois, male, Eurocentric critics whose universalizing gestures exclude ... or explicitly degrade women and peoples of color. [It also] *links culture to safety* [my emphases] – presumably the safety of the "we" against the barbaric threats of the "them" ... Needless to say, Arnold's negative attitudes towards British working-class people, women and especially Indians and Jamaicans in the Empire clarify why he conceives of culture as, in part, a weapon for bourgeois, male, European "safety"' (1993, 7–8).

Explanations of criminal behaviour that make use of national and racial characteristics have always characterized the modern juridical system. Modern legal institutions evolved with the formation of the nation state in eighteenth- and nineteenth-century Britain. The moral regulation of citizens and their property became one of the primary objectives of state intervention. The identification of law with national interests and of criminality with un-English qualities dates from this process of state formation, and its history remains relevant to the analysis of 'race' and crime today (Gilroy 1991, 77). Ware suggests that concepts of race and belonging are inextricably linked to national histories and identities (2001, 185). In discussing contemporary Canadian experience, Macklin says, 'Boundaries of membership and modes of exclusion can be (and regularly are) redrawn from within the nation. They trace themselves along fault lines that erupt along the surface of our pluralistic, multicultural democratic country when stressed by real or perceived crisis' (2002, 398). Henry and Tator concur by noting that in a racialized society such as Canada, whiteness is an integral part of the dominant culture, while being subtle and even invisible. Whiteness has the power, they argue, to define what is normal with respect to race, class, gender, heterosexuality, and nationality (2003, 8).

Racialization and 'white supremacy' have influenced the body politic in most Western countries and elsewhere (Lipsitz 1998). Racializing is pervasive, broad, and general, while racial profiling is specific; at the same time, however, racialization is part of racial profiling. Knight and Kurnik define a law enforcement 'profile' as 'a set of circumstances, events, or behavior that, when combined with the experience of an officer, may cause heightened suspicion that affects the officer's exercise of discretion in stop and/or arrest decisions ... The term 'racial profiling' appears to broadly connote discriminatory law enforcement practices based on an elective decision by an officer' (2002, 3). In other words, racial profiling implies a degree of mental intent or discriminatory purpose (Verniero and Zoubek 1999, 7).[3]

In Canadian jurisprudence, racial profiling has been defined as 'criminal profiling based on race ... [which] refers to that phenomenon whereby certain criminal activity is attributed to an identified group in society on the basis of race or colour resulting in the targeting of individual members of that group ... [and] is illegitimately used as a proxy for the criminality or general criminal propensity of an entire racial group' (Rosenberg 1999). Bahdi defines racial profiling as a practice that 'involves separating a subsection of the population from the larger whole on the basis of specific criteria that purportedly correlates to risk, and subjecting the subgroup to special scrutiny for the purposes of preventing violence, crime or some other undesirable activity. Racial profiling thus entails the use of race as a proxy for risk either in whole or in part (2003, 3–4).[4]

The war on terrorism has intensified the practice of racial profiling, raising concerns about whether it is valid, credible, or fair to use race as a substitute for real knowledge about an individual's connection to or propensity for terrorist activity. In Canada as in the United States, the question that has garnered the most attention in the debate about the 'war on terrorism' is whether Muslims and those of Arab descent are likely to threaten national security (Bahdi 2003, 3–4). To assess how Canadian society has arrived at this debate on racial profiling and domestic law enforcement, I will next examine the legacy of racism within the history of Canada's immigration and refugee policies.

Racism in Canada's Immigration and Refugee Laws – The Social Context of a Notorious Fact

Racial profiling in Canada has evolved from a history of racialized discourse and through policies of immigration and refugee settlement. The movement of individuals from racialized groups across national boundaries has become suspect – particularly given the racialization of public discourse on immigration and the criminalization of black identities (Economic Council of Canada 1991, 2).[5]

The preference for a white population in Canada's immigration policies is apparent in the acceptance of refugees from the 1950s throughout the 1970s (Aiken 2001, 6). Although Canada received the Nansen medal from the United Nations High Commissioner for Refugees (UNHCR) for its record on accepting refugees from 1976 to 1986, a return to more restrictive measures was evident in 1987 with the arrival of 174 Sikhs in Nova Scotia. This event prompted an emergency recall of Parliament and the introduction of Bills C-55 and C-84 to restructure the in-land refugee determination system and establish the Immigration and Refugee Board.

Smith and Lawson note that while there was an initial phase of tolerance for increased immigration (following the 1970s), public sentiment shifted dramatically in the 1990s towards scrutinizing immigrants and refugees more carefully (2002, 46). In 1992, Bill C-86 was passed into law in an effort to ensure that Canada did not become a safe haven for terrorists and internationally organized crime syndicates. In this bill, terrorism was named as a category of inadmissibility, and refugees could consequently be denied entry to Canada if there were reasonable grounds to believe they would commit terrorist acts or become members of organizations involved in terrorist activities. The bill failed to define terrorism or membership in a terrorist organization. Furthermore, it was thereafter required that convention refugees have an identity document before they could be accepted as permanent residents. A total of 6,000 people were denied entry to Canada in 2000 for not having satisfactory documentation; the majority of these claimants were from countries in Asia, Africa, and Latin America. It is also estimated that since 1993, there have been as many as 5,000 Somalis languishing in uncertainty in Canada as a result of these legislative changes (Aiken 2001, 33).

In 1995, the Canadian government adopted Bill C-44 in response to a murder that was allegedly committed by immigrants of African descent.[6] This bill allowed the Minister of Citizenship and Immigration 'to render an opinion that an immigrant or refugee who was convicted of an offence carrying a maximum sentence of 10 years or more was a danger to the public.' The result of such an opinion was the denial of the right to appeal a deportation order to the Immigration and Refugee Board (Smith and Lawson 2002, 47–52). Data indicate that since 1991, there have been 2,845 individuals deported from Canada, and of these, the overwhelming majority are individuals from racialized groups (Smith and Lawson 2002, 49).

In the same year, the federal government also introduced the Right of Landing Fee, which has been deemed by many as a return of the infamous head tax imposed on people of Chinese ancestry in the late 1800s. The fee is $975 for each successful adult applicant and must be paid prior to landing. This is in addition to the standard application fee, which ranges between $475 and $550 for all permanent-residence applicants and dependants over 22 years of age. It has been estimated that for a family of four with one dependent child over twenty-two years of age, the total cost would be $5,675. These fees, introduced during a time when the primary sources of immigration to Canada were Asia, Africa, Latin America, and the Caribbean, pose a barrier to family reunification (Smith and Lawson 2002, 54).

It has also been alleged that DNA testing to determine family status of individuals seeking to reunite their families has been disproportionately applied by immigration officials to individuals of African descent. The African Canadian Legal Clinic asserts that 85 per cent of African applicants are asked to submit to such testing. The Canadian Council for Refugees has expressed similar concerns regarding specific groups of refugees. Both organizations maintain that this is an unnecessary and intrusive intervention that is applied in many cases before all alternative documentary avenues have been explored. It also imposes a significant cost on the applicant, thereby erecting additional barriers to immigration and family reunification (Taitz 2001, 25, 33; African Canadian Legal Clinic n.d.; Canadian Council for Refugees 1998).

In 1998, Canada stopped a boat carrying 192 Tamil asylum-seekers off the coast of Africa and escorted it back to Sri Lanka; from 1997 to 2002, Canada's interdiction practices have prevented 33,000 people from reaching Canadian borders (Macklin 2002, 385–6). The Canadian Council for Refugees has recently reported on the differential and discriminatory treatment afforded refugee claimants from South Asia and the Middle East. The organization cites nineteen such cases, comparing them to the more favourable treatment received by similar claimants from Kosovo (2003, 8–9). At international airports, people of African descent are stopped more frequently than white people. Wortley notes that seven out of every ten people of African descent included in his study were questioned by Canada Customs officials, compared to only 33 per cent of whites, and that five of every ten people of African descent had their luggage searched, compared to one out of every ten white people. He further points out that of the nine passengers subjected to strip searches, eight were of African descent (1997, 17–20; James 1998). Wortley's report was followed by a Canada Customs study on 'visible minorities' (COMPAS 1999) and a successful human-rights complaint alleging racial profiling by Canada Customs (Canadian Human Rights Commission 2002).

The *Suresh* case, involving an immigrant and alleged member of the Liberation Tigers of Tamil Eelam, is another recent example that illustrates the racialization of Canada's approach to 'terrorism' and immigration (Aiken 2001, 14).[7] Much has also been made in the public media regarding the financing by Tamils in Canada of the allegedly terrorist Tamil Tigers. Henry and Tator have analysed the media's coverage of Tamil immigrants and identify the strong language used to attack the federal government, a number of its cabinet ministers, and what journalists term the Immigration Industry (2002, 113–19). They suggest that in the media, the discussion of immigration follows several rhetorical motifs, including questions about who belongs in Canada, who should be admitted, policies that should be enacted to keep 'them' out and the new actions needed to protect 'our' space as well as national identity, citizenship and culture (2002, 109). While Henry and Tator focus their attention on the *National Post*, other, more recent media reports continue this trend of treating immigrants and refugees suspiciously as either undesirable or as the 'dangerous Other.'[8]

Canada's system of immigration was severely tainted by race and racism even before September 2001. There appear to have been three stages of policy and practice: first, the actual use of race as a tool to determine desirable from undesirable immigrants; second, the attempt to dismantle this approach and to ensure fair access, which, however, still targeted racialized groups for specific labour needs; and third, the resurrection of racial characterization to openly define desirables and undesirables in the name of national security. In all of these stages, race and racism have been operable phenomena both in efforts to restrict and to include. While the openly restrictive covenant of immigration policy was clear in the first stage, it became more inclusive in the second stage in response to the need for labour (Smith and Lawson 2002, 45–6). Although the trends in the third stage are currently a matter of contestation, many suggest that the overt racism of the war on terrorism has led Western nations to draw a sharp line between themselves and others. 'What is perhaps most clear ... is that the overall policy framework ... has not incorporated a strong anti-racist stance. Rather, it has tended to deflect and deny racist influences and outcomes by focusing on nation building and national economic development discourses with imagined futures, such as Canada as a sophisticated niche player' (Simmons 1998, 112). Following September 11, national security might be easily added to this list.

Hunting for Terrorists and the Impact on Immigrants and Refugees

Immigration and refugee policy has targeted specific racialized groups for differential and discriminatory treatment in Canada, paving the way for law-enforcement bodies to engage in racial profiling in the fight against terrorism. The racialization of people of African descent portrays them as threats to national security and sets them up to be racially profiled by law-enforcement agencies. There are some data to support the contention that racial profiling is authorized by and/or collected by the state. Police forces in the states of Maryland and Florida were forced to admit to the official sanctioning of the practice after internal memoranda had been discovered asserting its importance to law and order (Harris n.d., 115). In the United Kingdom, data collection was initiated after the Brixton riots of 1981 through the recommendations of the Scarman report and the introduction of specific legislation (Scarman 1981). In Canada, there is still official denial of the practice, even though several studies document its existence at both the national and local levels. In Ontario, two cities have now adopted strategies to address racial profiling, and Canada Customs has also been ordered to do so.[9]

Historically, 'national security' has served as a useful tool of immigration control, a 'shield for white Canada's fear that foreign Others were corrupting the nation's "racial purity" and political fabric' (Aiken 2001, 5). The spectre of national security has been raised again recently and embedded in law through the adoption of twenty pieces of legislation, including the *Anti-Terrorism Act*, the *Immigration and Refugee Protection Act*, and the *Public Safety Act*; and through amendments to the *Foreign Missions and International Organizations Act*, the Criminal Code, the *Official Secrets Act*, the *Canada Evidence Act*, the *Proceeds of Crime Act*, and the *Aeronautics Act*. Consistent with the International Convention for the Suppression of the Financing of Terrorism,[10] the *Anti-Terrorism Act* also addresses the financing of terrorist organizations.

Given the numerous pieces of legislation adopted or amended to address the threat of terrorism to national security, it is not surprising to find anecdotal evidence of complaints from racialized Canadian residents and those seeking to enter Canada as immigrants, refugees, or visitors. There has been a reported increase in hate activities directed at those of Arab descent and at Muslims, or at those perceived to be Arabs and Muslims, across North America. In Hamilton, a Hindu Samaj was burned shortly after the events of September 11, 2001. During the last months of the same year, Hamilton police recorded a staggering number of reported hate attacks in the same period (Smith 2003, 58–9). Furthermore, the Canadian Muslim Civil Liberties Association has recorded 110 such incidents, and the Canadian Islamic Congress indicates that such acts have increased by 1,600 per cent since September 11 (Bahdi 2003, 21–3). The Ontario Human Rights Commission has received numerous inquiries and complaints. Additionally, several organizations have expressed alarm in discovering that their Muslim colleagues and those of Arab descent have suddenly become subject of workplace discrimination and scrutiny by CSIS (Canadian Arab Federation 2002, 18).

Many of these legislative measures had been normalized in different ways over the past century and have now been elevated to a more extreme level. This is evident in people's experiences of crossing the border to the United States, through such matters as guilt by association, invasion of privacy, inflicting of individual and community turmoil, incursions on personal financial and business development, and restrictions on family reunification and movement within Canada (Beare 2003, 5–26; Aiken 2001, 16–18; Gross 2002, 47; Schneiderman and Cossman 2002, 174–84; Bahdi 2003, 6–16; Davis 2002, 229). As Macklin suggests:

Locating terrorism exclusively in immigration legislation institutionalized in law the figure of the immigrant as the archetypal menace to the cultural, social, and political vitality of the nation. The myriad tropes of the foreign Other – as vector of disease, agent of subversion, corrupter of the moral order and debaser of the national identity – all trade on the exteriorization of threat and the foreigner as the embodiment of its infiltration. Canadian immigration history is replete with examples, ranging from the exclusion of racialized groups on grounds of inferiority and degeneracy, to the deportation of foreign-born labour and social activists in the inter-war years, to the persistent stereotype of immigrants as distinctively crime-prone. In this symbolic order, the border of the state is akin to the pores of the national corpus, and expelling the foreign body serves to restore the health of the nation ... Viewed within a historical and semiotic frame, the equation of terrorism with foreignness follows almost axiomatically. (2002, 392)

Such profiling begins with the powers of law enforcement authorities, including immigration officials, to detain individuals on the basis of reasonable grounds of suspicion that they are involved in terrorist activities or associated with terrorists.[11] This practice of issuing 'security certificates' results in individuals 'being held indefinitely without bail, based on secret evidence which renders them unable to defend themselves and challenge their accusers' (Canadian Arab Federation 2003). The federation cites two cases, one involving a person of Moroccan birth and the other an Egyptian-born father of four children held in solitary confinement for twenty-two months in Toronto. More recently, nineteen men have been held in detention in Ontario under similar circumstances (Sheppard, Small, and Gordon 2003).

There are several examples of Canada's cooperation with the United States in which Canadian citizens and residents have been negatively affected. Within the context of the Smart Border Declaration of June, 2002, these include: the seizing of anti-war videotapes by Canada Customs and Revenue Agency; the 'disappearance, secret detention and deportation' of Maher Arar and six other Canadian citizens of Arab or Islamic origin; and the adoption by the United States of the National Security Entry-Exit Registration System, resulting in the subjection of 14,000 people from 112 countries (10 per cent of whom were Canadians) to special security measures, including lengthy detentions. 'Of the total number of people targeted, 172 had been arrested for various reasons, but only one for reasons "related to terrorism"' (International Civil Liberties Monitoring Group 2003, 8).

The overly broad and vague definition of terrorism and the ways it can be facilitated encourages guilt by association. For example, the definition of terrorism includes participating in charitable organizations, even though such a definition may contradict international agreements concerning membership in terrorist organizations (Aiken 2001, 16–18; Canadian Council for Refugees 2003, 8; Beare 2003, 23; Carter 2002). The new *Charities Registration (Security Information) Act* allows the government to revoke the charitable status of an organization if it is deemed to be involved in terrorist activities (International Civil Liberties Monitoring Group 2003, 11). This legislation can have a profoundly negative impact on the work done by charitable and non-profit associations within Canadian Arab and Muslim communities, affecting a broad range of humanitarian, social-service, and community-development activities.

Furthermore, certain measures within existing legislation can negatively impact on matters of personal privacy, particularly through the sharing of information between policing agencies within Canada as well as between them and law enforcement agencies in the United States. For example, amendments to the Aeronautics Act, and particularly to section 4.83, allow airline carriers to provide passenger information to a government of a foreign state (Bahdi 2003, 10).[12] CSIS and immigration officers are said to be pressuring individuals to cooperate with investigations of others in their communities; if they resist, they may be held in preventative detention, deported, or have their citizenship revoked (International Civil Liberties Monitoring Group 2003, 8; Canadian Council for Refugees 2003, 4).

Legislative and other measures now being considered could further entrench this remarkably hostile treatment. Proposed amendments to the *Citizenship Act*, for example, would allow the government to revoke the citizenship of naturalized citizens. Furthermore, the Justice Department's 'Lawful Access' consultation document suggests that legislation may soon be introduced to allow electronic surveillance and monitoring of all email communications and Internet activity. It may possibly require Internet providers to cooperate in tracking, intercepting, and reporting on suspect communications. Finally, the *Ottawa Citizen* has reported that officials in the Solicitor General's department 'are keen to link justice and police computer-data systems, not only between federal and provincial law-enforcement and justice agencies, but also to explore expansion of the Canada Public Safety Information Network

(CPSIN) to include exchanges of information between Canada and the United States' (International Civil Liberties Monitoring Group 2003, 3, 12).

Racial Profiling in the Media

Racial profiling in the media presents African Canadians as troublesome, criminal and dangerous, thereby deserving the attention conferred on them by the police. After September 11, the media stereotyped Muslims and those of Arab descent as 'terrorists' and 'fanatical, violence loving maniacs' (Bahdi 2003, 12). 'The mass media provide a symbolic platform on which crimes and criminals are paraded before the public and collectively condemned. These media portrayals can be understood as simple morality plays that reaffirm ideas about right and wrong and consolidate the collective conscience' (Benjamin 2003, 33–4). In 'The Black/Jamaican Criminal: The Making of Ideology,' Akua Benjamin explores in detail approximately 266 articles in the *Toronto Sun* on 'Black/Jamaicans' that reported criminal activities, focusing on the connections between stereotypes and the criminalization of African Canadians. Benjamin found that 'in the *Sun*'s news reports on Jamaicans and crime, language and discourse readily recognizable as and conveying a racial profile was used to identify the suspect or perpetrator of the crime' (2003, 250). The effect of these articles, which reproduce stereotypes and racist ideologies about African Canadians and crime, is to aggravate the social exclusion and marginalization of other Jamaicans (1–8).

In a similar vein, Frances Henry and her colleagues, through an examination of articles in the *Toronto Star*, note that African Canadians are stereotyped as criminals and problematized as requiring a disproportionate amount of political attention and public resources. They found that Jamaicans in particular have been stereotyped as criminals (Henry et al. 1995). One of the most important factors in the racializing of crime is the over-reporting of crimes allegedly committed by people of colour – especially black people. The media construct such people as having criminal propensities that do damage to their sense of self and to their perceived social status in the community (Henry and Tator 2002, 164).

In examining 2,840 news articles on crime from the *Toronto Star*, the *Globe and Mail*, and the *Toronto Sun* for two months of each of the years

1994, 1996, and 1997, Henry and Tator found that:

- 39 per cent of the articles in the *Star* and the *Sun* about Jamaicans related to such issues as crime, justice, immigration, and deportation;
- racial identifiers were used twice as often in reports on individuals from racialized groups, particularly African Canadians, than in reports on whites;
- 46 per cent of all crime articles in the *Globe*, 38.5 per cent in the *Star*, and 25.6 per cent in the *Sun* 'used a racial or ethnic descriptor [that] involved Blacks or people of Caribbean origin';
- forty-four of the 102 articles on deportation in the *Star*, *Globe*, and *Sun* focused on African Canadians/Jamaicans, compared to sixteen articles on white people and fifteen on Nazis; and
- approximately 33 per cent of all photos in crime stories depicted individuals from racialized groups, with African Canadians comprising 44 per cent of these images despite representing only 7 per cent of the Toronto-area population. (2002, 167–8)

Henry and Tator use discourse analysis to explore the media's reporting and found that the media developed three discourses on aspects of law and order: gun control; the young offender; and immigration or deportation (2002, 168–80). Following the *Toronto Star*'s series on racial profiling (Rankin et al. 2002), they once again reviewed media reports on the controversy surrounding the series and discovered in them three themes: the impact of authority figures such as the chief of police, the mayor, and others, who denied the veracity of the media reports; the attack on human rights, exemplified in the challenges faced by the Ontario Human Rights Commission when it announced it was conducting an inquiry into racial profiling; and reverse discrimination, which describes the suggestions of the chief of police and others that the *Star* series had victimized them (Henry and Tator 2003, 28–36).

Studies such as these, conducted over a period of years, clearly demonstrate the spectrum of media attention on African Canadians that is a form of racial profiling. Although the *Star*'s research on racial profiling extends the evidence already in the public domain, it is nevertheless significant with respect to the massive amount of data examined and the period of time under scrutiny. The data reviewed included 480,000 incidents in which an individual was charged with a crime or ticketed for a traffic offence over a period of ten years. It supports the premise that African Canadians are 'singled out' by the police for offences related to driving, drugs, and violence. They are held in detention longer than whites. African Canadians are charged more frequently than others. African Canadians are over-represented in reportings of out-of-sight traffic offences in police divisions with low African-Canadian populations as well as in those that do not include a significant number of African Canadian residents. These data support the African Canadian community's anecdotal accounts that they are targeted by the police. More specifically, the *Star* research revealed the following:

- Although representing only 8.1 per cent of Toronto's population, African Canadians comprise 34 per cent of drivers charged with out-of-sight violations, and are over-represented by 4.2 times for out-of-sight driving offences, 3.8 times for cocaine possession and 2.1 times for simple drug possession.
- Despite comprising 63.8 per cent of those charged with simple drug possession (over 10,000 cases), white people were released at the scene 76.5 per cent of the time, compared to a 61.8 per cent release rate for African Canadians. Once they are taken into custody, African Canadians were held for court appearance 15.5 per cent of the time, compared to 7.3 per cent for whites.
- In charges of cocaine possession (over 2,000 cases), 41.5 per cent of African Canadians were released at the scene, compared to 63 per cent of whites people.
- African Canadians comprise 27 per cent of all violent charges, even though they only comprise 8.1 per cent of the population. (Rankin et al. 2002)

The *Star's* evidence supports the contention of African Canadians that racialization forms an alarming backdrop to their lives and enables racial profiling, directly or otherwise.

Domestic Law Enforcement

Frequently, a discussion of domestic law enforcement and racial profiling in Canada draws our attention to recent experience, supporting the belief that the racialization of this discourse is a recent phenomenon parallel to changes in immigration patterns. The historical literature on immigrants and refugees does not extensively explore race and criminal justice, making it difficult to fully understand the experiences of peoples of African descent in Canada and their relationship with law enforcement authorities (Walker 1997; Mosher 1998; Backhouse 1999). Many issues, such as the differential treatment in apprehending, charging, and sentencing members of racialized groups in crimes related to drugs, public order, violence, and so on, have a history that goes back to the early 1900s and continues to the present. In documenting historical media depictions of criminality, Mosher writes: 'While systematic empirical studies concerning the coverage of racial issues by the Canadian press in the early to middle 1900s were apparently not conducted ... [there was] a tendency on the part of Canadian newspapers to make reference to the race of the offenders in their coverage of crime and criminal-justice issues. This focus on the racial characteristics of offenders served to identify Asians and Blacks as alien and influenced, to a certain extent seemingly justified, their differential treatment by the criminal justice system' (1998, 124–6).[13] Sentencing judges regarded 'the testimony of Black offenders as unreliable, which in part explains the greater likelihood of imprisonment' (179).

Mosher's extensive analysis of the racialization of criminal justice focuses on the period between 1892 and 1961. The Commission on Systemic Racism in the Ontario Criminal Justice System documents the ongoing nature of racialization, and the African Canadian Legal Clinic reports the cumulative impact of anti-black racism in Canadian society (Smith and Lawson 2002, 21–34). Reports that use statistics to examine the impact of policing on racialized groups, particularly African Canadians, lay to rest the skepticism about the ability of anecdotes and qualitative studies to reveal the widespread nature of the problem. One of the first such studies, conducted by Phillip Stenning, points to the differential treatment of African-Canadian inmates in three Toronto detention centres in 1994.[14] Stenning makes the following observations:

- African Canadians were significantly over-represented in the major offence category: 58.8 per cent versus 25 per cent for whites and 28.9 per cent for others. This category included robbery (whites, 5 per cent; African Canadians, 29.4 per cent; others, 2.6 per cent) and drug offences (whites, 10 per cent; African Canadians, 19.6 per cent; others 15.8 per cent) (1994, II.9).
- African Canadians were generally treated differently by police, with police behaviour towards them being unfriendly and less polite (1994, II.10–11). Fairly dramatic differences are evident in terms of allegations of police verbal abuse, with African Canadians being sworn at more often by police (58.8 per cent, versus 38.3 per cent for whites and 43.6 per cent for others) and subject to racial epithets

more often, with 31.4 per cent indicating they had been subject to racially derogatory remarks from police officers versus 5 per cent for others (1994, II.14–15).

- In responding to minor offences, police drew their weapons in the act of arresting African Canadians more frequently than with other groups (25 per cent, versus 6.7 per cent for whites and 6.7 per cent for others) (1994, II.23).
- Police use of force both at time of arrest and after arrest was significantly different for African Canadians (33.3 per cent and 31.4 per cent, respectively, versus 25 and 25 per cent for whites and 30.8 and 23.1 per cent for others) (1994, II.24).

These data provide some insight into the unequal relations between police and African Canadians compared to those between police and white or other Canadians. Similar facts were documented for youths in 1993 by the Canadian Civil Liberties Association. The survey, comprising 150 youths, revealed that 71 per cent of individuals from racialized groups who had come in contact with the police, compared to 50 per cent of white individuals, had had negative experiences. Several of these youths alleged that they had been subjected to racial slurs by police officers during questioning (Mosher 1998, 191).

Scot Wortley's research reinforces the widely held perception among African Canadians that they are inordinately and unfairly targeted by the police. He found that 28 per cent of African Canadians believed that they were stopped solely because of their race, and another 13 per cent felt they were stopped for a 'bogus violation.' Consider the following statistics for individuals being stopped by the police for questioning:

- 28.1 per cent of African Canadians report being stopped by police, compared to 18.2 per cent of white Canadians and 14.6 per cent of Chinese Canadians;
- 16.8 per cent of African Canadians report being stopped twice by police, compared to 8.0 per cent of white Canadians and 4.7 per cent of Chinese Canadians;
- 11.7 per cent of African Canadians report being stopped by police 'unfairly' in the past two years, compared to 2.1 per cent of white Canadians and 2.2 per cent of Chinese Canadians;
- 42.7 per cent of African-Canadian males report being stopped by police in the past two years, compared to 22.1 per cent of white and Asian males;
- 28.7 per cent of African-Canadian males report being stopped twice

in the past two years, compared to 9.9 per cent of white and Asian males (Wortley 1997, 2).

In noting these differences, Wortley argues that 'racial differences in the frequency of involuntary police contact are a strong indicator of the extent to which people from different racial backgrounds come under police scrutiny. If it can be documented that certain types of people are more likely to come under police surveillance, it is logical to assume that such people are also more likely to be caught for breaking the law. Thus, racial differences in street surveillance practices may help explain profound racial differences in arrest and incarceration rates (1997, 2). Consequently, and not surprisingly, people of African descent view police negatively (Wortley 1996, 447–50).

Regarding drug-related charges, the Commission on Systemic Racism in the Ontario Criminal Justice System reports the following findings:

- 23 per cent of white Canadians, compared to 30 per cent of African Canadians, are likely to be detained before trial, particularly for drug charges;
- incarceration of African Canadians for drug trafficking increased by 1,164 per cent (from 25 per cent in 1986–87 to 60 per cent in 1992–93). This compares to a 151–per-cent increase in incarceration for whites during the same period;
- for drug charges, accused white Canadians were released more often than African Canadians. African Canadians were also denied bail more frequently, and the conviction rate of African-Canadian men was higher – 69 per cent as opposed to 57 per cent for white men;
- for drug offences, African Canadians were charged 66 per cent and white Canadians 35 per cent of the time, respectively. For simple possession, 49 per cent of African-Canadian men, compared to 18 per cent of white men, were sentenced to prison (1995, 105).

The Commission went on to note that 'no evidence shows that African Canadian people are more likely to use drugs than others or that they are over-represented among those who profit from drug use. Events of the last few years do show, however, that intensive policing of low-income areas in which African Canadian people live produces arrests of large and disproportionate number of African-Canadian male street dealers. Once the police have done this work, the practices and decisions of the crown prosecutors, justices of the peace and judges operate as a conveyor belt to prison' (1995, 83). The Commission reported that between 1987 and 1993, the African-Canadian population in Ontario increased by 36 per cent, while the number of African-Canadian prisoners increased by 204 per cent. In the same period, the number of white prisoners increased by only 23 per cent. The U.S. practice of drug profiling was introduced into Canada in 1994, and the RCMP trained some 10,000 law-enforcement personnel in its use (Tanovich 2002, 152). Despite the Commission's findings, the training continued.

The trail of evidence did not stop there. In another report, African Canadians described examples of 'policing black,' where blacks (young males in particular) were exposed to excessive policing. The study, done in 2000 by the Committee to Stop Targeted Policing, interviewed 167 people, many of whom were African Canadians from low-income populations and users of social agencies. It found that two out of three interviewees reported being assaulted or threatened with assault by police. Actual assaults ranged from being beaten, slapped, punched, and maced. Threats of death were also received (37 per cent). Other intimidation tactics included police harassment (74 per cent), threatening arrest (59 per cent), conducting searches without good cause (54 per cent), arresting individuals on false or improper charges that were eventually thrown out of court (35 per cent), and taking photographs of individuals on the street without their consent (25 per cent).[15] Wortley (with Julian Tanner) reinforced these findings. Their survey of 3,400 Toronto high school students revealed that African-Canadian students were often searched and stopped arbitrarily by the police (2003, 7–9).

'Racial profiling has, thus, created a disproportionately large class of racialized offenders. It has also criminalized many predominantly black neighbourhoods in Toronto, which are commonly referred to by the police as "high crime areas." This criminalization has contributed to the perpetuation of the belief that there is a link between race and crime.' Such beliefs have 'stigmatized the black community, and ha[ve] had a tremendously negative impact on their dignity and self-worth' (Tanovich 2002, 162). Those who were so charged and detained were penalized in other ways as well. Being in prison scarred and traumatized the victims, increased their health risks, and aggravated their difficulties in accessing education and employment.[16]

Conclusion

While racial profiling by law enforcement is critically important in itself, the continued prevalence of this practice must be placed within an overall social and historical context. Racism has marginalized peoples of African descent and their communities in Canada. Racial profiling reinforces this history and magnifies the impact of discrimination faced by African Canadians in every facet of their public and private life. This is very similar to the impact of the anti-terrorism legislation on people of Arab descent (see, for example, the chapter by Lee in this volume) and the place of these laws within a continuous history of Canada's racist immigration laws. These phenomena are also strikingly similar in other countries, particularly in the United States and the United Kingdom.

Given the incredible panoply of legislation adopted, the increased and focused coordination of law enforcement authorities domestically and internationally, the social context of racism in Canadian immigration policies, and the history of anti-black racism, a broad range of debilitating impacts upon racialized communities continues to occur. In the new millennium, race has emerged as an active, probative, and divisive force within Canadian society. Indeed, in looking at the phenomenon of racial profiling in Canada, the United Kingdom, and the United States, particularly following the proscriptions resulting from the recent Iraq war, the war on terrorism, and the war on drugs, it is clear that race is once again a definitive marker within public discourse.

It is difficult not to juxtapose these events with the 2001 United Nations conference against racism, which preceded the September 11 attacks by one month, and to see the global challenge to racism, no matter how qualified, turning into a widespread racist attack. It is as if the will of the world was spun on a coin and the movement towards the goals expressed at Durban reversed overnight. Precedent has been found for continuing and developing new arguments legitimizing racism in state law and policy and in the media through newscasting. However, the blatant and willful promotion of racial profiling is unprecedented, particularly in democratic countries that espouse human-rights laws and constitutional guarantees prohibiting racism.

Whether from a liberal perspective, as articulated by such thinkers as Will Kymlicka (1995 and 1998) and Charles Taylor (1994), or from the more critical perspectives outlined above, Canadian society is addressing issues of race and racism. The percentage of racialized people migrating to or seeking refuge in Canada, the United States, and the United Kingdom has increased substantially in the last fifty years or so through changes in immigration legislation and refugee determination processes. It is therefore imperative that these countries deal not only with racism in law enforcement but more fundamentally, examine the very foundations of the rule of law for its biases. Such work is now being undertaken by critical race theorists who contend that laws and their underlying values reflect the racialized discursive formation within our society (Crenshaw et al. 1995; Delgado and Stefanic 2000).

An increasing number of challenges such as these will provide a basis or starting point from which to confront the problem of racial profiling. To do so will undoubtedly mean questioning the normative value of racism in Canadian society. It will require exhorting governments, the courts, and the media to re-think how racism has an impact on our lives, why it does so, and more importantly, how allowing racism to continue (indeed, aiding and abetting it) causes immeasurable harm to Canada's social fabric. Given the impact of racial profiling on domestic law enforcement and national security, there may be no better time to address this issue than now.

Notes

1 In the United Kingdom, 72 per cent of students who had been expelled from school admitted that they had committed serious offences. In contrast, 72 per cent of students who were in school had committed no offence (Power 2003). Research conducted in the United States by the Harvard University Civil Rights Project indicates that 25 per cent of all African-American students were suspended at least once during a four-year period, and that African-American students make up 42 per cent of the student population but account for 61 per cent of disciplinary actions (2000).

2 Power (2003) draws on information from the Nova Scotia Black Learners Advisory Committee Report on Education, which demonstrates that even though African Canadian youth comprise 8 per cent of the Halifax student population, they account for 16 – 21 per cent of suspensions.

3 Peter Verniero and Paul H. Zoubek, former attorney general and first assistant attorney general, respectively, for New Jersey, write that there are 'more common instances of de facto discrimination by officers who may be influenced by stereotypes and may thus tend to treat minority motorists differently during the course of routine traffic stops, subjecting them more routinely to investigative tactics and techniques that are designed to ferret out illicit drugs or weapons' (1999, 7).

4 In another comment on racial profiling, a Globe and Mail journalist noted

that 'most Canadians will not be terribly inconvenienced ... Instead, the costs will be borne by people who find themselves targets of police suspicion because of their ethnic background, radical political views or association with immigrant communities that have ties with groups deemed to have terrorist fronts' (16 October 2001, qtd in Macklin 2002, 395).

5 For a detailed analysis of the racialization of the discourse on immigration and refugee policies, see contributions by Li and Aiken in this volume.

6 The Bill appeared to be a response to the highly publicized 'Just Desserts' case of the previous year, in which a youth of African descent killed a white woman during a robbery attempt in a downtown Toronto restaurant.

7 Suresh had been recognized as a convention refugee in 1991 and was later served with a security certificate as a result of his involvement in the two Toronto-based agencies that CSIS considered fronts for the Liberation Tigers of Tamil Eelam (LTTE). A federal court upheld the reasonableness of the certificates and decidedly did not engage in consideration as to whether or not the LTTE was a liberation movement. See also Canadian Council for Refugees 1998, 10–23.

8 For example, see 'Canadians Are Expressing Less Tolerance of Foreigners,' *CTV News,* Friday, 10 March 2000, and 'Polls Suggests Intolerance Toward Immigrants on the Rise,' *The London Free Press*, 11 March 2000.

9 The police in Kingston have recently undertaken projects to collect data on individuals stopped by police and their racialized identities. See also Canadian Human Rights Commission 2002.

10 The Convention was adopted by the General Assembly of the United Nations in December 1999 and signed by Canada in February 2003.

11 See the Immigration and Refugee Protection Act, Sections 33 and 34 (1)(f).

12 See also concerns expressed by the Commissioner of Privacy (as he was then) George Radwanski at http://www.privcom.gc.ca/media/nr-c/o2_05_b_021101_e.asp.

13 Mosher later suggests that 'stereotypes and general fears regarding the criminal proclivities of Blacks were prevalent in media reports of the early 1900s. The descriptions of Black criminals emphasized that, like the Chinese, they were prone to involvement in drug and other public order offences such as gambling and prostitution. However, of greater concern to the public was the notion that Blacks were violent and likely to be involved in more serious forms of violence than the Chinese, and thus posed a greater threat (1998, 129).' To support his contention, Mosher cites news reports in several media, including the *Hamilton Spectator, Globe and Mail, London Free Press, London Advertiser, Toronto Daily Star,* and *Windsor Evening Record* (129–34).

14 Stenning's study was conducted with 150 inmates (sixty white, fifty-one black, and thirty-nine other non-white inmates). Although Stenning suggested that the research precludes considerations about police-citizen contacts more generally, when contextualized within the scope of both the historical treatment of African Canadians and contemporary and subsequent studies, the results of this limited research indicate of a pattern of treatment that is pervasive within the criminal justice system.

15 Recent research by Carl James and Robynne Neugebauer provides remarkably similar findings (James 1998; Neugebauer 2000). Based on interviews with fifty African-Canadian youths from six different cities in Ontario, James found that these youths reported that being stopped by police was a common occurrence, primarily attributable to the colour of their skin. Neugebauer conducted interviews with sixty-three African-Canadian and white youths in Toronto and found the same result.

16 Tanovich also writes: 'While there is no evidence that OPCJ (Operation Pipeline/Conway/Jetway) explicitly encourages officers to use race-based pretext vehicle stops as an opportunity to discover contraband, this is a reasonable inference given the American experience.' In the footnote to this point, he adds that 'we may never know the methodology of OPCJ since access to the RCMP training materials will likely be refused on the basis of public interest privilege' (2002, 152).

References

Adamson, L., and B. Holman. 2002. Assessment of security-youth relations in St. James Town (TCHC). In *St. Stephen's Community House Conflict Resolution Service*, 31 October.

African Canadian Legal Clinic. n.d. Fact Sheet no. 2: Immigration. Toronto, ON.

Aiken, S.J. 2001. Of gods and monsters: National security and Canadian refugee policy. *Revue Québécoise de Droit International* 14 (2): 1–51.

Arellano, A., and D. Ashenfelter. 2000. State cops more apt to search black men. *Detroit Free Press*, 21 July.

Arnold, Matthew. 1869/1960. *Culture and anarchy.* Ed. and intro. by J. Dover Wilson. London: Cambridge University Press. Quoted in Storey 1993, 21–2.

Backhouse, C. 1999. *Colour-coded: A legal history of racism in Canada, 1900–1950.* Toronto: University of Toronto Press.

Bahdi, R. 2003. No exit: Racial profiling and Canada's war against terrorism. Unpublished paper.

Bain, B. 2000. Walking while black. *Village Voice*, 26 April–2 May.

Barovick, H. 1998. DWB: Driving while black. *Village Voice*, 15 June.

Beare, M. 2003. Policing with a national security agenda. Paper presented at National Symposium on Policing in a Multicultural Society, Department of Canadian Heritage and Royal Canadian Mounted Police. February.

Benjamin, A. 2003. The Black/Jamaican criminal: The making of ideology. PhD thesis, Ryerson University, Toronto.

Canadian Arab Federation. 2002. *Proudly Canadian and marginalized.* Report on the findings and recommendations of the study Arab Canadians: Charting the future. April.

Canadian Arab Federation. 2003. Security certificate an insult to Canadians. News Release, 30 May.

Canadian Bar Association. 2001. *Backlash: Terrorism and civil liberties.* http://www.cba.org/CBA/National/Cover2001/Dec01asp.

Canadian Council for Refugees. 1998. Notes from roundtable meeting, 14 September.

– 2003. *Refugees and security.* Revised February 2003.

Canadian Human Rights Commissioner. 2001. *Proposed anti-terrorism act casts too wide a net.* http://www.chrc-ccdp.ca/news-comm/2001/NewsComm241001.asp.

Canadian Human Rights Commission. 2002. Minutes of settlement, Mr. Selwyn Pieters and Department of National Revenue (now Canada Customs and Revenue Agency). File no. T650/3801. February.

Carter, T. 2002. Anti-terrorism legislation in Canada and its impact on charities: An overview. *Ontario Bar Association Issues in Charity Law: A Potpourri*, 22 October.

Cloud, J. 2001. What's race got to do with it? *Los Angeles Magazine*, 31 July.

Commission on Systemic Racism in the Ontario Criminal Justice System. 1995. Co-chairs D. Cole and M. Gittens. Toronto: Queen's Printer.

COMPAS. 1999. *Canada Customs visible minority study.* March.

Crenshaw, Kimberlé, N. Gotanda, G. Peller, and K. Thomas. 1995. *Critical race theory: The key writings that formed the movement.* New York: New Press.

Daniels, R.J., P. Macklem, and K. Roach. 2002. *The security of freedom: Essays on Canada's anti-terrorism bill.* Toronto: University of Toronto Press.

Davis, K.E. 2002. Cutting of the flow of funds to terrorists: Whose funds? which funds? who decides? In Daniels, Macklem, and Roach 2002, 200–320.

Delgado, Richard, and J. Stefanic, eds. 2000. *Critical race theory: The cutting edge.* Philadelphia: Temple University Press.

Derrida, J. 2001. *On cosmopolitanism and forgiveness.* London and New York: Routledge. The epigraph to this chapter is found on p. 14.

Dyzenhaus, D. 2002. The permanence of the temporary. In Daniels, Macklem, and Roach 2002, 21–38.

Economic Council of Canada. 1991. New faces in the crowd: Economic and social impact of immigration.

Gilroy, P. 1991. *There ain't no black in the Union Jack: The cultural politics of race and nation.* Chicago: University of Chicago Press.

Girard, Philip. 2003. *Kirk Johnson v. Michael Sandiford and the Halifax Regional Police Service.* Nova Scotia Human Rights Commission Board of Inquiry, 22 December.

Glasser, I. 1999. American drug laws: The new Jim Crow. The Edward C. Sobota Lecture, Albany Law School.

– 2000. Racial profiling and selective enforcement: The new Jim Crow. Unpublished paper, American Bar Association.

Goetz, K. 2001. Racial profiling surveys continue: Thousands questioned in effort to settle suit. *Cincinnati Enquirer,* 8 August.

Golab, J. 1999. Police profiling is vilified as institutionalized racism. *Jet,* August.

Griswold, D. 2002. Don't blame immigrants for terrorism. Cato Institute, 2 February. http://www.cato.org/current/terrorism/oubs/griswold-01 1009. html.

Gross, O. 2002. Cutting down trees. In Daniels, Macklem, and Roach 2002, 45–7.

Hamilton, T. 2003. Everyday life tracked by society's prying eye: Privacy vanishing with surveillance. *Toronto Star,* 10 May.

Harris, D. A. n.d. When success breeds attack: The coming backlash against racial profiling. Unpublished paper.

Harvard University Civil Rights Project. 2000. The devastating consequences of zero tolerance.

Henry, F., and C. Tator. 2001. *Racist discourse in Canada's print media.* Toronto: Canadian Race Relations Foundation.

– 2002. *Discourses of domination: Racial bias in the Canadian English-language press.* Toronto: University of Toronto Press.

– 2003. Racial profiling in Toronto: Discourses of domination, mediation and opposition (final draft). Toronto: Canadian Race Relations Foundation.

Henry, F., C. Tator, W. Mattis, and T. Rees. 1995. *The colour of democracy: Racism in Canadian society.* Toronto: Harcourt.

International Civil Liberties Monitoring Group. 2003. In *The Shadow of the Law,* 14 May.

Immigration and Refugee Protection Act, S.C. 2001. c. 27.

James, C. 1998. 'Up to no good': Black on the streets and encountering police.

In *Racism and social inequality in Canada: Concepts, controversies, and strategies of resistance*, ed. V. Satzewich, 157–76. Toronto: Thompson Educational.

James, R. 1998. Black passengers targeted in Pearson searches? Lawyers plan court fight over 'racial profiling' by customs officials at airport. *Toronto Star, 29* November.

Kafka, Franz. 1925/1998. *The Trial*. Trans. Breon Mitchell. 1998. New York: Schocken.

– 1926/1988. *The Castle*. Trans. Mark Harmon. 1998. New York: Schocken.

Knight, E.A., and W. Kurnik. 2002. The defense perspective on civil rights litigation. American Bar Association.

Kymlicka, W. 1995. *The rights of minority cultures*. Toronto: Oxford University Press.

– 1998. *Finding our way: Rethinking ethnocultural relations in Canada*. Toronto: Oxford University Press.

Law Commission of Canada. 2002. *In search of security: The roles of public police and private agencies*. Ottawa, Ontario.

Lipsitz, George. 1998. *The possessive investment in whiteness: How white people profit from identity politics*. Philadelphia: Temple University Press.

Macklin, A. 2002. Borderline security. In Daniels, Macklem, and Roach 2002, 383–404.

McCain, M. 2000. Racial profiling perceived: Panel hears complaints. *Horizon Magazine,*14 May.

Mendes, E., and D. McAllister, eds. 2002. Between crime and war: Terrorism, democracy and the Constitution. Special issue of the *National Journal of Constitutional Law*. Toronto: Thomson/Carswell.

Morden, JJ.A. 2003. *R. v. Brown, Ontario Court of Appeal*, C37818, April.

Mosher, C.J. 1998. *Discrimination and denial: Systemic racism in Ontario's legal and criminal justice systems, 1892–1961*. Toronto: University of Toronto Press.

Murakami, K. 2002. Thorny racial profiling debate. *Philadelphia Post Gazette,* 12 February.

Neugebauer, R. 2000. Kids, cops, and colour: The social organization of police-minority youth relations. In *Criminal injustice: Racism in the criminal justice system,* ed. Robynne Neugebauer, 83–108. Toronto: Canadian Scholars Press.

Olson, D. 2000. Justice in black and white: The justice gap. *Minnesota Public Radio News*, 13 April. http://www.minnesota.publicradio.org.

Ontario Human Rights Commission. 2003. *Paying the price: The human cost of racial profiling*. December.

Powell, B. 2003. Police chiefs told to help the helpless. *Toronto Star*, 26 August.

Power, A. 2003. Rethinking zero tolerance. Paper presented at the 2nd Annual

Human Rights Symposium: Focus on Racial Discrimination. Toronto, 22–23 May.

Radil, A. 2000. Racial profiling allegations bring calls for statewide data collection. *Minnesota Public Radio News*, 15 June.

Rankin, J., J. Quinn, M. Sheppard, S. Simmie, and J. Duncanson. 2002. Singled out: An investigation into race and crime. *Toronto Star*, 19 October.

Rosenberg, J.A. 1999. *R. v. Richards*. 26 C.R. (5th) 286 Ontario Court of Appeal.

Scarman, Lond. 1981. *Report into the Brixton Disorders*. London: Home Office.

Schneiderman, David, and B. Cossman. 2002. Political Association and the Anti-Terrorism Bill. In Daniels, Macklem, and Roach 2002, 173–94.

Sheppard, M., P. Small, and M. Gordon. 2003. 'Van loads of evidence' in the terror probe. *Toronto Star*, 23 August.

Simmons, Alan. 1998. Racism and social policy. In *Racism and social inequality in Canada: Concepts, controversies, and strategies of resistance*, ed. V. Satzewich, 87–114. Toronto: Thompson Educational.

Smith, C.C. 2003. *Hamilton at the crossroads: Anti-racism and the future of the city*. February. http://www.shci.hamilton.ca/pdf/lessons-learned-final-report.pdf.

– 2004. Racial profiling – then and now. In *Crisis, conflict and accountability*. Toronto: African Canadian Community Coalition on Racial Profiling. March.

Smith, C., and E. Lawson. 2002. *Anti-Black racism in Canada: A report on the Canadian government's compliance with the international convention on the elimination of all forms of racial discrimination*. Toronto: African Canadian Legal Clinic. July.

Stenning, P. 1994. *Police use of force and violence against members of visible minority groups in Canada*. Report prepared for the Solicitor General of Canada. Canadian Centre for Police Race Relations.

– 2003. Policing the cultural kaleidoscope: Recent Canadian experience. In *Police and Society* 7:13–47.

Storey, J. 1993. *An introductory guide to cultural theory and popular culture*. London: Harvester Wheatsheaf.

Taitz, J. 2001. *Exploring the use of DNA testing for family reunification*. International Organization for Migration.

Tanovich, D. 2002. Using the Charter to stop racial profiling: The development of an equality-based conception of arbitrary detention. *Osgoode Hall Law Journal* 40 (2): 145–87.

Taylor, C. 1994. *Multiculturalism: Examining the Politics of Recognition*. Princeton: Princeton University Press.

Tyler, T. 2003. Judge dismisses suit against Star. *Toronto Star*, 25 June.

Verniero, P., and P.H. Zoubek. 1999. *Interim report of the state police review team regarding allegations of racial profiling*. State of New Jersey, 20 April.

Walker, J.W. 1997. *'Race,' rights and the law in the Supreme Court of Canada: Historical case studies*. Waterloo, ON: Osgoode Society for Canadian Legal History and Wilfred Laurier University Press.

Ware, V. 2001. Perfidious Albion: Whiteness and the international imagination. In *The making and unmaking of whiteness*, ed. Birgit Brander Rasmussen et al., 84–213. Durham: Duke University Press.

West, C. 1993. *Keeping faith: Philosophy and race in America*. New York and London: Routledge.

Wortley, S. 1997. The usual suspects: Race, police stops and perceptions of criminal justice. Paper presented at the 48th Annual Conference of the American Society of Criminology. Chicago.

– 2003. Data, denials and confusion: The racial profiling debate in Toronto. Unpublished paper.

– n.d. *Under suspicion: Race and criminal justice surveillance in Canada*. Centre for Criminology, University of Toronto.

8 Racism Masquerading as Nationalism: Wars, Japanese-Americans, and Arab-Americans

EZRA YOO-HYEOK LEE

We might say that racism exists when one ethnic group or historical collectivity dominates, excludes, or seeks to eliminate another on the basis of differences that it believes are hereditary and unalterable.

George M. Fredrickson, *Racism: A Short History*

Imperial racism, or differential racism, integrates others with its order and then orchestrates those differences in a system of control.

Michael Hardt and Antonio Negri, *Empire*

The Return of Repression

Nationalism tinted with racism has been freely articulated in times of war in American history, although such expressions of bias are frowned upon in peacetime. Consider the following two cases: Japanese-Americans in the post–Pearl Harbor period and Arab-Americans (and/or Muslim Americans) in the period following September 11, 2001. After the bombing of Pearl Harbor in 1941, Japanese-Americans were uprooted from their homes, forced into internment camps, and had their property seized, mainly because they were regarded as potential enemies. This internment included both Issei, first-generation Japanese immigrants, and Nisei, second-generation, American-born Japanese-Americans. Two-thirds of the over 120,000 people who became internees were American-born citizens. Since September 11, Arab-Americans (and/or Muslim Americans) have been under a different kind of surveillance as a result of being regarded as potential terrorists in a time of 'war on terrorism.'[1] In this paper, I explore the specific character of these experiences of repression through two kinds of writing that address these racialized moments. In analysing the experience of Japanese-Americans, I offer a critical reading of *No-No Boy*, by John Okada; in the case of Arab-Americans (and/or Muslim Americans), I analyse the journalistic representations of Arab-Americans (and/or Muslim Americans) after September 11. I look at a novel in one case and at journalism in the other because each best describes the disfiguring effects of racism on the psyches of Japanese-Americans in the post–World War II period and Arab-Americans in the post–September 11 era, respectively.[2]

'Arab-American,' an ethnic identity that includes many different groups, is a relatively recent invention, just as 'Asian-American' was in the 1970s.[3] Michael W. Suleiman, in *Arabs in America*, notes that the 1967 Arab-Israeli War and the United States' one-sided pro-Israel policy prompted Arab-Americans to 'organize conferences and publish journals and books in defence of their cause. They wrote fiction, poetry and memoirs declaring pride in and solidarity with Arabs and the Arab community in America' (1999, 10, 13). This historical moment led Arab-Americans to develop an awareness of their homogeneous identity as an ethnic group.[4] Hence, the term Arab-American has served as a useful designation for the political coalition of a variety of Arabic people in the United States, just as the term Asian-American once did for others.

The terms Arab-American and Muslim American tend to be used interchangeably, despite some significant differences. Arab-Americans are 'U.S. citizens and permanent residents who trace their ancestry to or who emigrated from Arabic-speaking places in southwestern Asia and northern Africa, a region known as the Middle East' (*Detroit Free Press* 2001). Thus, the term Arab-American includes a great variety of peoples from different countries collectively called 'the Middle East.' The bond that ties together such different peoples is the Arabic language. However, despite the common misperception that 'Arab traditions are Islamic, or that Islam unifies all Arabs' (*Detroit Free Press* 2001), the majority of Arab-Americans are Christians, some of whom belong to Protestant, Catholic, or Orthodox denominations; only about one quarter are Muslims (Samhan 2006).

'Muslim Americans' are those who have faith in Islam and follow its religious traditions and teachings in the United States. Thus, the umbrella term Muslim American includes many different groups of people, much like the terms African-American, Southeast Asian, European, South-Central Asian, African, and Arab (Council on American-Islamic Relations 2004). Compared with the term Arab-Americans, the term Muslim Americans generally comprises a much more diverse group of people from around the world. I use the term 'Arab-American' in this paper because the terrorists who perpetrated the September 11 attacks have been consistently linked to Islam and to the territory of the Middle East. As a whole ethnic group, Arab-Americans – and those who look like Arabs or as if of Arab descent, regardless of their real identities – have been discriminated against and stereotyped as potential terrorists through racial profiling in the post–September 11 period. Hence, in this paper, the term Arab-Americans includes Muslim Americans unless indicated otherwise. In *Covering Islam: How the Media and the Experts Determine How We See the Rest of the World* (1997), Edward Said notes that the stereotypical image of Islamic or Arabic others has been produced and reproduced through the interaction of power and knowledge. This paper explores the ways in which the old notion of racial hierarchy – such as 'who and what was properly American versus that which remained foreign'(Bussolini 2003, 23) – re-emerges in a new yet not completely different form in twenty-first-century America: the return of repression.

Race, Nation, and Culture

'Racism remains a major international problem at the dawn of the twenty-first century,' despite the struggle against it throughout the last century (Fredrickson 2002, 139). Yet Fredrickson differentiates the racism of the new millennium, which he calls 'cultural racism,' from the racism of the past, as embodied in anti-Semitism in Nazi Germany, white supremacy in the American South in the Jim Crow era, and apartheid in South Africa (4, 13). Culture, Fredrickson notes, serves as the basis of a racial ideology that discriminates against and persecutes others, just as biology did in earlier times. He argues that 'culture can be reified and essentialized to the point where it becomes the functional equivalent of race' (7), and that 'most of the minorities throughout the world that are victimized by discrimination or violence appear to be differentiated from their oppressors more by authentic cultural or religious differences than by race in the genetic sense' (145). As examples, he refers to Irish Catholics in Ulster, Albanian Muslims in the former Yugoslavia, and Buddhists in Chinese-ruled Tibet, to name a few (145). Although some of these groups have been discriminated against and persecuted for a relatively long time, Frederickson suggests that cultural racism has become predominant since the end of the Cold War.[5]

Although culture can become the basis for racisim, Frederickson carefully argues that 'if we think of culture as historically constructed, fluid, variable in time and space, and adaptable to changing circumstances, it is a concept antithetical to that of race' (2002, 7). For this reason, he 'withhold[s] the "R" word' (7), for 'the differences between the ethnic groups involved are [not] permanent and ineradicable' (170); rather, assimilation and socio-economic mobility are open to cultural and ethnic others. He calls this process of assimilation 'culturalism.' Despite Fredrickson's distinction between culturalism and cultural racism, what is still problematic is who has the power and authority to 'allow' for the assimilation and mobility of religiously or culturally different others. This politics of inclusion and exclusion is likely to end in a mere political gesture in the name of multiculturalism.

It is my intention here to explore how ethnic minorities such as Japanese-Americans and Arab-Americans are victimized by the dominant white group in America due to their cultural or religious differences. Hardt and Negri's elaboration of the new racism, or cultural racism, in the American context offers a theoretical framework through which to analyse a complicated and sophisticated racialized system within the American empire (Hardt and Negri 2000, 190–5).[6] They argue that the new racism is not merely confined to the peripheries of empires but is also located at their centres. In particular, Hardt and Negri point to the two opposing sides of the new racism: on the surface, it adopts different forms and strategies by overtly supporting anti-racism and pluralism, but on a deeper level lies a covert racialized system of control (191).

> From the perspective of imperial racist theory ... there are rigid limits to the flexibility and compatibility of cultures. Differences between cultures and traditions are, in the final analysis, insurmountable ... Pluralism accepts all the differences of who we are so long as we agree to act on the basis of these differences of identity, so long as we act our race. Racial differences are thus contingent *in principle*, but quite necessary *in practice* as markers of social separation ... Subordination is enacted in regimes of everyday practices that are more mobile and flexible but that create racial hierarchies that are nonetheless stable and brutal ... Imperial racism, or differential racism, integrates others with its order and then orchestrates those differences in a system of control. (192, 194–5; my emphases)

This racialized system of control is sophisticated in the sense that 'racial exclusion arises generally as a result of differential inclusion' (Hardt and Negri 2000, 194), making possible only a certain degree of assimilation and mobility. If an individual or an ethnic group tries to go beyond certain boundaries, unseen or covert walls are suddenly made visible and serve as a barrier that cannot be surmounted easily. A perfect illustration of this point is the sudden downfall of John Kwang, the rising Korean-American politician in Chang-Rae Lee's novel, *Native Speaker* (1995). Kwang, 'the yellow man,' is victimized by the identity politics of the United States, where until recently the main conflict has been between white and black people. Since racial minority groups such as Asian-Americans and Arab-Americans cannot easily belong to either side of the black/white paradigm, they develop feelings of vulnerability (see Okihiro 1994, 31–63). This shows the gap between the ideal and the reality of American 'multiculturalism,' which has often been represented as a 'melting pot.' Kwang calls this ideal into question:

> But the more racial strife they can report, the more the public questions what good any of this diversity brings. The underlying sense of what's presented these days is that this country has difference that ails rather than strengthens and enriches. You can see what can happen from this, how the public may begin viewing anything outside mainstream experience and culture to be threatening or dangerous. *There is a closing going,*[sic] *Henry, slowly but steadily, a narrowing of who can rightfully live here and be counted.* (Lee 1995, 274; my emphasis)

Multiculturalism, Kwang argues, is a form of racism in disguise, since the dominant group still has the political power of deciding which group among the minorities can be included in or categorized as the so-called mainstream. Hardt and Negri's arguments, along with Kwang's, reinforce Fredrickson's statement that 'culture can be reified and essentialized to the point where it becomes the functional equivalent of race.' As a racialized signifier, culture is used to differentiate and discriminate self from others (Fredrickson 2002, 7).

A fuller understanding of the modus operandi of the new racism, or cultural racism, requires us to go deeper into the relationship between it and nationalism. Étienne Balibar distinguishes between the nationalism of the dominant, which is the nationalism of conquest, and the nationalism of the dominated, which is the nationalism of liberation (Balibar 1991b, 45). Racism in the guise of nationalism is the nationalism of the dominant and of conquest. From this perspective, the distribution of power between the dominant and the dominated groups can be seen as merely unidirectional. Hardt and Negri, however, argue that 'a people is defined not simply in terms of a shared past and common desires or potential, but primarily in dialectical relation to its Other, its outside' (2000, 194). They suggest that in the course of restructuring and rebuilding the empire, the relationship with others should be carefully considered. Nationalism – inventing a people – is not fixed, but flexible, as the empire expands its territories. This invention of a people, however, is flexible only to a certain degree. As the notion of a dialectical relation implies, people can be included or excluded, and recognized or negated. This is often dependent upon the will of the empire, but surely a dialectical relationship recognizes that the other is not powerless or wholly dependent. Rather, power is distributed across relationships, albeit unevenly. This dialectical power relationship between the dominant and the subordinate groups can generate a creative space from which the possibility of resistance and agency in and among minority groups can arise.

In times of war, the space for such a dialectical relationship becomes very narrow, and minority or ethnic minority groups are easily victimized, as documented in many accounts of American history. A system of control, established in the name of homeland security, is quickly reinforced. And nationalism – how the nation is imagined – comes to serve as a discourse of exclusion. This nationalist discourse vis-à-vis racism demands that ethnic groups commit to either side of their hyphenated identities, plunging them into the situation of a forced choice; that is, no choice, in a true sense. On the one hand, both Arab-Americans and Japanese-Americans have been forced to prove their loyalties to America. On the other hand, their belonging to America is or was suspected and suspended, mainly due to their ethnic identities. Their hyphenated identities thus become more pronounced, making them feel divided and marginalized. During wartime, racism masquerading as nationalism exacerbates the physical and psychological alienation and rootlessness that ethnic minority groups – in earlier times, Japanese-Americans and now, Arab-Americans – have already been experiencing.

No-No Boy and Japanese-Americans

Fu-jen Chen sums up the main theme of Okada's *No-No Boy*: 'Ichiro's quest for a sense of self exposes the disfiguring effects of racism and internment, not only on the individual psyche but also on the family and the community. The exposure of a people's sufferings further overshadows the American spirit of equality' (2000, 282). Okada demonstrates how Japanese-Americans in the post–Pearl Harbor bombing period suffer from anti-Japanese racism.[8] On the one hand, there are those who try to belong to American society by consciously giving up their Japanese identities. On the other hand, there are those who try to keep their Japanese identities regardless of the changing or changed political situation after the Pearl Harbor bombing. In addition, there are also those who stand in between: they are represented in the novel by Ichiro and Kenji, even though one seems to choose the Japanese side and the other the American side. Kenji goes to war for America, but Ichiro declines. Like these two characters, Japanese-Americans seemed doomed to lie in between, in spite of the fact that they occupied a broad political spectrum. This was largely due to white America's rejection of their entire ethnic group after the Pearl Harbor bombing, and sometimes because of Japanese-Americans' alienation from their own ethnic group as a result of their explicit political choices. This in-between state of minority ethnic groups brings forth both negative and positive outcomes. In *No-No Boy*, the disruptive effect of racism and internment – the negative consequence of the in-between state – divides Japanese-Americans on personal, familial, and communal levels.

The protagonist, Ichiro, is a 'no-no boy' who refuses to prove his loyalty to America by giving affirmative answers to the two loyalty questions put to all Japanese-American men interned during World War II. The questions were as follows: 'Are you willing to serve in the armed forces of the United States, on combat duty wherever ordered?' and 'Will you swear unqualified allegiance to the United States of America and faithfully defend the United States from any or all attack by foreign or domestic forces, and forswear any form of allegiance of obedience to the Japanese emperor, to any foreign government, power or organization?' (qtd in Ling 1998, 32).

After the Pearl Harbor bombing, Ichiro has to spend two years in an internment camp followed by another two years in prison, due to his disloyalty to America. The novel, which begins after he is released from prison, illustrates his search for an identity.[9] For individuals with hyphenated identities, seeing oneself as 'both/and' rather than 'either/or' or 'neither/nor' is redemptive, since it contributes to the construction of a healthy self-esteem.

So they [Ichiro and Kenji] sat silently through the next drink, one already dead but still alive and contemplating fifty or sixty years more of dead aliveness, and the other, living and dying slowly. They were two extremes, the Japanese who was more American than most Americans because he had crept to the brink of death for America, and the other who was neither Japanese nor American because he had failed to recognize the gift of his birthright when recognition meant everything. (Okada 1979, 73)

The first extreme – the Japanese who was more American than most Americans – refers to Japanese-American 'yes-yes boys' who answered affirmatively to the two loyalty questions and 'voluntarily' went to war to prove their loyalty to America. At the other extreme are the 'no-no boys' who refused to go to war for America and were put in jail. Ironically, however, their disloyalty to America does not enable them to have a sense of belonging to the Japanese side. In the novel, it seems that Ichiro's disloyalty to America proves his loyalty to Japan (his mother thinks so), yet he never feels that he belongs to that country, either. As a result of feeling that he belongs to neither side, Ichiro suffers an identity crisis and in his search to discover his identity, he also witnesses the identity crises of other Japanese-Americans. In the quotation cited above, both the no-no boy and the yes-yes boy are 'dead' – a 'dead aliveness' or a 'living and dying slowly' that anticipates their gloomy destinies. Ichiro's mother represents Japanese immigrants who hold fast to their Japanese identities. After her suicide, he reflects somewhat bitterly:

Did it matter so much that events had ruined the plans which she cherished and turned the once very possible dreams into a madness which was madness only in view of the changed status of the Japanese in America? Was it she who was wrong and crazy not to have found in herself the capacity to accept a country which repeatedly refused to accept her or her sons unquestioningly, or was it the others who were being deluded, the ones, like Kenji, who believed and fought and even gave their lives to protect this country where they could still not rate as first-class citizens because of *the unseen walls*? (Okada 1979, 104; my emphasis)

Ichiro even calls into question the American identity of yes-yes boys such as Kenji because in spite of showing their loyalty to America by sacrificing their lives and limbs during wartime, they were in the end not regarded as 'truly American.' Kenji's loss of a leg in the war and his slow death as a result imply the dark future of yes-yes boys. They cannot be fully accepted into American society, can never be whole, as his incomplete body indicates. Ichiro's rhetorical questions in the quoted passage imply his 'awakenings to the consciousness that the root cause of Ma's madness is the racism of the country to which she had immigrated' (Ling 1998, 43). Ichiro notes: 'Sometimes I think my mother is to blame. Sometimes I think it's bigger than her, more than her refusal to understand that I'm not like her' (Okada 1979, 152). Ichiro's realization of the unseen walls is similar to Hardt and Negri's description of a covert, racialized system of control within the empire. Through another character, Emi, Okada narrates the racism of the country that forces Ichiro, his mother, Kenji, and many other Japanese-Americans into making a choice, or to be exact, into having no choice:[10]

> It's because we're American and because we're Japanese and sometimes the two don't mix. It's all right to be German and American or Italian and American or Russian and American but, as things turned out, it wasn't all right to be Japanese and American. *You had to be one or the other.* (Okada 1979, 91; my emphasis)

Japanese-Americans had to choose one side of their identity: Japanese or American. This 'either/or' choice is problematic in that it was not voluntary but forced, as illustrated in the cases of Ichiro, Kenji, and Ichiro's mother. Whatever their choice, both no-no boys and yes-yes boys would never feel they belonged to America. Ichiro's brother, a would-be yes-yes boy, further illustrates this phenomenon. He has a strong desire to prove his loyalty to America by showing his willingness to go to war, not only to demonstrate his patriotism but also as a self-conscious reaction to Ichiro's disloyalty to the country and his mother's 'insane' loyalty to Japan. His dilemma shows that the forced choice of 'either/or' is in the end no choice at all, because it is likely to lead him to self-destruction rather than self-realization, as yes-yes boy Kenji's gradual death implies.

From a historical perspective, the choice of 'either/or' was largely made for the 120,000 Japanese-Americans who were uprooted from their homes and relocated to internment camps after the bombing of Pearl Harbor, because they were suspected of being potential enemies. German-Americans and Italian-Americans, however, were not made to suffer in this way. 'Whereas "American" is an indication of nationality, not of ethnicity, the term took on extreme racial overtones during the war. Although the U.S. was at war with Germany and Italy, most Americans distinguished between Americans of German and Italian descent and the German enemy and Italian enemy. The same distinction was not afforded Japanese-Americans ... In the world of *No-No Boy*, "American" equals "White"' (Yogi 1996, 64). Japanese-Americans could not belong to the nation as an imagined community – that is, white America – since during the war racism occurred in the form of nationalism. David Goldstein-Shirley deconstructs the racial discourse that successfully invented Japanese-Americans as 'potential enemies' during World War II. He notes that 70,000 of the 120,000 internees were under the age of eighteen and, as American-born Nisei, were citizens. He asks how school-age youths can have been assumed to threaten the United States. Yet nearly two-thirds of the detainees were Nisei (Goldstein-Shirley 2000, 210).

The military leaders never could have carried out this mass internment of American citizens and their families without widespread public support. The context implicitly allowed acting on such biases, for there was a strong anti-Asian sentiment in the United States and especially on the Pacific Coast, where a large number of Japanese-Americans lived. Since 'many white Americans already harbored distrust of Asians, it was remarkably easy to convince them that their neighbors of Japanese descent posed a grave threat to their own security' (Goldstein-Shirley 2000, 211).

Racism and the nationalism of the dominant worked interactively in inventing a discourse of Japanese-Americans as potential enemies before and after the Pearl Harbor bombing. Marita Sturken writes about similar issues, particularly with regard to cinematic representations. In 'Absent Images of Memory,' Sturken discusses how the so-called official American historical discourse of World War II both includes and omits certain images in the course of making the United States 'a triumphant and moral nation.'[11] She notes that absent images include 'the photographs and film footage of Hiroshima immediately after the bomb' and Japanese-American internment camps in America, which she calls 'concentration camps' (2001, 36–7). We witness a similar process of discourse production of the Iraqi people as 'enemies' and the United States as a 'triumphant and moral nation' as America wages war against Iraq. In particular, the media has played a significant role in constructing a particular kind of discourse by showing only selected images, while those that could potentially disrupt the rationale of this war are made invisible or leaked out only intermittently.[12]

Benedict Anderson's widely adopted concept of the nation as an 'imagined community' is problematic from the perspective of the powerless and disadvantaged. '[The nation] is imagined as a community, because, regardless of the actual inequality and exploitation that may prevail in each, the nation is always conceived as a deep, horizontal comradeship. Ultimately it is this fraternity that makes it possible, over the past two centuries, for so many millions of people, not so much to kill, as willingly to die for such *limited* imaginings' (Anderson 1991, 7; my emphasis). Since the dominant discourse includes only white America in the imagined community, as is the case during wartime, there is little space for ethnic minority groups within it. Anderson's statement that the nation is conceived as a deep, horizontal comradeship regardless of inequalities and exploitation is also problematic because it assumes nationalism as a discourse of exclusion, the nationalism of the dominant. And minority groups (and the powerless and disadvantaged) cannot have a sense of belonging to the imagined nation, for a racialized situation forces them to make their choice between 'neither/nor' and 'either/or.' Here 'neither/nor' is the logic of exclusion and 'either/or' the logic of assimilation. Exclusion or assimilation is the gloomy destiny (or forced choice) that ethnic minorities confront within a racialized conflict, as the situation of Japanese-Americans in *No-No Boy* testifies. 'National unity [or nationalism] is always ultimately impossible precisely because it can be represented as such only through a suppression and repression, symbolic or otherwise, of difference' (Stratton and Ang 1998, 135). Thus, nationalism as a discourse on national unity comes into conflict with multiculturalism, which 'can broadly ... be understood as the recognition of co-existence of a plurality of cultures within the nation' (135).

The relationship between nationalism and multiculturalism has been avidly debated by scholars.[13] Integrating multiculturalism as a national ideology should not be impossible, however, because 'the sovereignty that a nation claims to assert as a universal ideal is always reliant on the existence of an 'other,' without whom the nation could not claim its dominant position' (Davidson, Walton, and Andrews 2003, 125). Hence, it could be redemptive and future-directional 'to seize on multiculturalism's more radical potential ... to give up the ideal of national unity itself without doing away with the promise of a flexible, porous, and open-ended national culture' (Stratton and Ang 1998, 160). There is thus the possibility of a different kind of national culture based not upon the nationalism of the dominant, the logic of exclusion, but one that is flexible, porous, and open-ended. Such a national culture can foster multiculturalism as the logic of coexistence of a plurality of cultures within the nation. It is not easy to balance the (in)compatibility of multiculturalism with national unity and imagine another world where its potential can possibly be maximized. But perhaps we can hope to attain that goal. 'Contradictions if well understood and managed can spark off the fires of invention. Orthodoxy whether of the right or the left is the graveyard of creativity' (Achebe 1987, 100).[14]

In *No-No Boy*, Okada seeks such an ideal through Ichiro, whose search for the *telos* of his true identity is characteristically ambivalent, or in between. Such a position allows Ichiro to belong to neither America nor Japan, but nevertheless to have a critical viewpoint of both territories. This can also be a position from which thinking otherwise, or imagining another world, may be made possible. Ichiro, who witnesses how other Japanese-Americans suffer from an identity crisis that stems from feeling that they cannot belong to their 'home,' cannot easily resolve his own identity crisis by making a forced choice rather than a willing and redemptive one. The ending of the novel seems to suggest that Ichiro pursues the logic of 'both/and' in terms of his hyphenated identity:

> A glimmer of hope – was that it? It was there, someplace. He couldn't see it to put it into words, but the feeling was pretty strong ... He walked along, thinking, searching, thinking and probing, and, in the darkness of the alley of the community that was a tiny bit of America, he chased that faint and elusive insinuation of promise as it continued to take shape in mind and in heart. (Okada 1979, 250–1)

The hope growing in Ichiro's heart is a 'glimmer,' 'faint and elusive,' yet he wishes to pursue it. The novel ends with Ichiro beginning another journey to realize his hope for the ideal America that all immigrants and Americans cherish. However, Ichiro's 'resolution [at the end of the novel] ... proves to be no solution at all,' for it implies continuous pursuit (Ling 1998, 48).[15] In retrospect, Okada's ambivalent ending is prophetic of the identity politics of ethnic minority groups in America, because half a century after the publication of *No-No Boy*, the situation is not any better. The America we cherish seems to be still in our hearts. Carlos Bulosan's *America is in the Heart* was written six decades ago, yet it continues to have enduring significance:

> America is not bound by geographical latitudes. America is not merely a land or an institution. America is in hearts of men that died for freedom; it

is also in the eyes of men that are building a new world. America is a prophecy of a new society of men: of a system that knows no sorrow or strife or suffering. America is a warning to those who would try to falsify the ideals of freemen ... All of us, from the first Adams to the last Filipino, native born or alien, educated or illiterate – *We are America*! (1973, 189)

Bulosan's dream of America is similar to Ichiro's and historically antic- ipates Martin Luther King Jr's hopes expressed in his famous 'I have a dream' speech delivered in front of the Lincoln Memorial during the 1963 March on Washington for Jobs and Freedom.

Reading *No-No Boy* in the post–September 11 era offers us an oppor- tunity to slow down and think over the present American situation as articulated metaphorically by Okada: 'It was like being on a pair of water skies, skimming over the top as long as one traveled at a reason- able speed, but, the moment he slowed down or stopped, it was to sink into the nothingness that offered no real support' (1979, 201). Reading *No-No Boy* helps unmask racism in the guise of nationalism, gives us insight into current understandings of multiculturalism in America, and suggests a way of moving forward to realize equality for all Amer- icans. The ideal of America as a community where people of different colours and cultures can harmoniously coexist, Okada argues, can occur if in times of ideological crisis all live up to the so-called Ameri- can ideals of democracy, equality, and liberty. Gary Okihiro, in *Margins and Mainstreams*, asserts that America has managed to maintain its democratic ideals precisely because minorities have challenged the dominant culture and have won victories that validate the rights of all Americans.

> Although situating itself at the core, the mainstream is not the center that embraces and draws the diverse nation together ... And despite its author- ship of the central tenets of democracy, the mainstream has been silent on the publication of its creed. In fact, the margin has held the nation together with its expansive reach; the margin has tested and ensured the guaran- tees of citizenship; and the margin has been the true defender of American democracy, equality, and liberty. From that vantage, we can see the margin as mainstream (Okihiro 1994, 175).

The ending of *No-No Boy* – 'He walked along, thinking, searching, thinking and probing, and, in the darkness of the alley of the commu- nity that was a tiny bit of America, he chased that faint and elusive insinuation of promise as it continued to take shape in mind and in heart' (Okada 1979, 251) – illustrates how ethnic minorities (and other minority groups) have struggled in the course of upholding the so-called American democratic ideals. Okihiro's claim is, as it should be, more widely supported in the post–September 11 period, in which dissenting voices have precipitously been suppressed.[16]

September 11 and Arab-Americans

Many recent studies draw a parallel between Japanese-Americans in World War II and Arab-Americans in the post–September context, identifying a connection between war and racism in American history.[17] In particular, O'Brien (2001) raises some important yet difficult questions: 'Do all Americans now have fewer rights? Or only some Americans, people identified as "suspected terrorists" or "Arab-looking" or "Muslim"? If we agree that because of September 11, the rights of some or all should be restricted, another vexing question arises: to what degree and for how long?' (419) After surveying several cases to consider the restrictions on constitutional and human rights during wartime in American history, O'Brien concludes that 'racial and ethnic profiling will be tolerated in practice (even if profiling is not considered right in principle) in measures aimed at ensuring the safety of travelers and in initiatives to investigate terrorism' (421).[18] Herein lies another contradiction between theory (or principle) and practice. Keeping a perfect balance between the two is not easy; however, this is not a sufficient reason to suspend the constitutional and human rights of certain citizens. It is abhorrent to think that non-citizens such as immigrants and visitors should live under surveillance, or that Americans should impose other forms of control on them during national emergencies such as a war.[19] Non-citizens, too, need to have their human rights protected. Yet the post–September 11 situation in the United States shows that the constitutional and human rights of Arab-Americans are being seriously violated in the name of 'homeland security.'[20] In such circumstances, the 'home' imagined by those in the mainstream cannot be the same as that imagined by those in the margins. Furthermore, the post–September 11 U.S. situation also shows the conflict between national unity (or imposed nationalism) and multiculturalism. Racial groups with obvious racial signifiers, such as names, physical features, and appearances, can be easily discriminated against. Religious and cultural differences powerfully influence the stereotype of Arabic or

Islamic others as terrorists or potential terrorists. Such a stereotype, according to O'Brien, is an invention largely based upon inaccurate and misguided information: 'All terrorists, even the majority of terrorists, are not Arabs, Middle Eastern, or Muslim. In fact, of the 87 terrorist incidents in the United States between 1984 and 1998, only two were linked to an Arab group. Just as very few Christians are extremists and perform violent acts, such as bombing abortion clinics, only a tiny proportion of Arabs are extremists, and only a minute number of extremists are terrorists' (O'Brien 2001, 421–2).

The stereotyping of Muslims or Arabs as terrorists is a discourse that is guided and produced ideologically. Such biased and misinformed knowledge of others has been constructed by those in power and privilege without or regardless of its truthfulness. In Foucauldian terms, this damaging stereotype of others serves as a discourse that occupies the imaginative geography in the minds of Western people (Said 1979, 49–73). The media and so-called experts have played a tremendously powerful role in depicting Arabs or Arab-Americans as potential terrorists and inscribing such a negative image on the minds of American people.[21] Such knowledge production of others has been strengthened in the post–September 11 period in spite of vigorous and systematic resistance by scholars such as Said, who have attempted to discredit it by deconstructing the Western discourse about Islam and Arabs.[22] 'I am not saying that Muslims have not attacked and injured Israelis and Westerners in the name of Islam. But I am saying that much of what one reads and sees in the media about Islam represents the aggression as coming from Islam because that is what "Islam" is. Local and concrete circumstances are thus obliterated. In other words, covering Islam is a one-sided activity that obscures what "we" *do*, and highlights instead what Muslims and Arabs by their very flawed nature *are*' (Said 1997, xxii). What 'we' read and see through the media in the West is just what is *re*-presented. The images and news about Muslim or Arabic others, who are located far away from 'us,' are merely what is delivered to us, not part of our own experience. Such images and news are often a partial and fabricated view of others. This, according to Said, is how the racialized discourse about Islam and about Arabs is made and remade. Such a racialized discourse about Arabs – one that had already been constructed before September 11 – emerges in a time of war in complicity with nationalism and is used to differentiate others and discriminate against them. Thus, the notions of how other Americans treat Arab-Americans and how Arab-Americans feel about themselves are completely different before and after September 11. The testimony of one New Yorker – who is a U.S. citizen, ethnically Bangladeshi, and with Muslim connections – reveals this:

> I became a United States citizen four years ago because of my long love affair with New York ... I am a Bangladeshi woman and my last name is Rahman, a Muslim name ... Before last week, I had thought of myself as a lawyer, a feminist, a wife, a sister, a friend, a woman on the street. Now I begin to see myself as a brown woman who bears a vague resemblance to the images of terrorists we see on television and in the newspapers. I can only imagine how much more difficult it is for men who look like Mohamed Atta or Osama bin Laden. As I become identified as someone outside the New York community, I feel myself losing the power to define myself. (Rahman 2001)

The bombing of Pearl Harbor drastically changed the life of Japanese-Americans, as did September 11 for Arab-Americans. This woman's experience rivals that of Ichiro, who could belong to neither side of his hyphenated Japanese-American identity.[23] Yet her case is somewhat different in the sense that she does not list 'Arab' as one of her identities. This suggests that she is like the yes-yes boys, who pursued assimilation into American society by intentionally giving up their ethnic identities; she seems to have been successful in her quest to be included in American society before September 11. However, the events of September 11 have drastically changed her situation, for since that time 'cultural difference' has served as a racialized signifier that excludes her and makes inconsequential her strong desire to belong to the New York community. Just as skin colour can never be erased, so too cultural difference seems to be permanent. In such a racialized atmosphere, she can easily be recognized and categorized as an Arab-American rather than simply as an American, despite her personal choice. Her words – 'As I become identified as someone outside the New York community, I feel myself losing the power to define myself' – seem to suggest that the changed political situation suddenly plunges her into the logic of 'neither/nor' and 'either/or,' options also faced by other ethnic minorities in a racialized context. However, those are no choices at all, for regardless of her decision, with her identity dependent upon recognition or misrecognition by the dominant group, she cannot fully belong to American society. Consequently, this woman's definition of herself is easily negated.

The drastically changed situation of Arab-Americans, and particularly of Muslim Americans, is described by Shahid Athar:

> The average middle-class, mosque-going Muslims who run grocery stores, are office workers or students, are totally confused at what they should do or say. Should they side with the terrorists overseas or with the superpower that is bombing the innocent civilians in hospitals and houses there in order to free the whole world of these terrorists? How can we present Islam to those who stereotype, profile and even call us their enemy? On record are close to 1,000 cases of such hate crimes since September 11. Is the FBI our friend or our foe? Will our children get admission to schools of flight training, biochemical research and nuclear physics or will we ever feel comfortable flying as a passenger in an airplane? Will our women in hijab be able to go shopping without any fear? The joy of being a Muslim in America is gone, at least for now. (Athar 2003, 10)[24]

An American Muslim's testimony shows how September 11 and its aftermath – particularly 'the war against terrorism' – plunges Arab-Americans into an oppositional deadlock of being either friends or enemies.[25] They are forced to choose one side (American) and give up the other side (Arab) to prove their loyalty to America. If they refuse to do so, they are automatically considered as belonging to the enemy (as implied in George W. Bush's statement, 'Either you are with us or you're with the terrorists'). But even if they somehow show their loyalty as Americans, they are still branded as 'bad Arabs' by some, since their names and external images – racialized signifiers that mark their cultural difference – betray their Arabness. In fact, many Arab-Americans have been attacked (both verbally and physically), interrogated, and detained for no specific reason. Many cases since September 11 attest to how hard it is for Arab-Americans to escape the web of racial stereotyping – the logic of 'neither/nor' and 'either/or' – in the post–September 11 period.[26] Like the fictional Ichiro and real-life Japanese-Americans in wartime, Arab-Americans have also been suffering from racism in the guise of nationalism, which is a discourse of exclusion.

The dynamics of inclusion and exclusion construct the racial stratification that prevails in the United States. Racial formation is still largely predicated upon the dichotomy of black and white and thus completely 'ignor[es] the gradations and complexities of the full spectrum between the racial poles [of black and white]' by making minorities such as 'Asians, American Indians, and Latinos invisible' (Okihiro 1994, 62). In

Whitewashing Race, Michael Brown and others similarly deconstruct the conservative consensus that racism in America has been defeated since the civil rights movement in the 1960s, focusing on the dynamics of black and white in racism in America. 'It is because the black/white binary persists in America as a feature of everyday life and is crucial to the commonsense understanding of racism. It persists, in large part, because "whiteness" has always been important in defining who is and who is not an American ... To further complicate matters, whiteness in the United States has never been simply a matter of skin color. Being white is also a measure, as Lani Guinier and Gerald Torres put it, "of one's social distance from blackness." In other words, whiteness in America has been ideologically constructed mostly to mean "not black"' (Brown et al. 2003, x). The ideological construction of whiteness has remained constant, despite the increasing numbers of Asians and Latinos in the United States and the development of a black middle class. Racism in the United States at the present time 'continues to be defined by a dichotomy not between black and white, but between black and non-black ... The relationship of African Americans to whites therefore remains fundamental to any analysis of racial inequality' (xi).

The race classification of Arab-Americans illustrates the workings of the black/white binary, in which 'whiteness' has always been the final measure in defining who is and who is not truly American. Arab-Americans are considered to be more like Asian Americans and Hispanic Americans instead of being included as whites (Samhan 2006), even though 'Arabic-speaking peoples [were] viewed as part of the "white race" during the earlier period of Arab immigration' (Suleiman 1999, 12). In addition, according to the U.S. census, Arabs are officially classified as white, along with the European majority (Samhan 2006). 'Phenotypically, Arabs range from black to blond and blue eyed. However ... Arabs are represented in the media as not quite white and not quite colored ... the popular representation of Arabs "taints" but does not color them enough to be considered a racial minority. The tainting of Arabs ... is accomplished through a racialization of Islam' (Joseph 1999, 259).

The sense of belonging has started to fluctuate among Arab-Americans, just as it did for Asian-Americans, due to the changed political situation in America. It is difficult to determine 'where Arabs fit on the ever-changing prism of race in America' (Samhan 1999). The dominant white society sometimes conveniently categorizes Asian-Americans as being more like white people so as 'to "discipline" African Americans (and other minorities according to the model minority stereotype),' so that the whiteness of Arab-Americans completely depends upon the political need of the dominant majority (Okihiro 1994, 62). These two ethnic minority groups can easily be considered to be more like black people, if the political situation so dictates. Here again, the logic of 'both/and' is redemptive, because it allows Arab-Americans to form their identities in a healthy way, without being forced to choose sides. The race classification of both Japanese-Americans (or Asian-Americans) and Arab-Americans as 'not quite white' should not be regarded as insulting or incomplete, but rather as marking difference and moreover, as 'envisioning possibilities beyond the hyphen' in identity formation (Ty and Goellnicht 2004, 10). From this perspective, Arab-Americans can explore ways to overcome the marginality of being ethnically identified as 'not quite white' and of being negatively stereotyped as potential terrorists.

Conclusion: Beyond the Hyphen[27]

Double consciousness, or the 'sense of always looking at one's self through the eyes of [the dominant] others' (Du Bois 1903) that ethnic minority groups experience seems to be inescapable if 'our identity is partly shaped by recognition or its absence, often by the *mis*recognition of others' (Taylor 1995, 225). Their forced choice of 'neither/nor' or 'either/or' results from misrecognition or non-recognition by the dominant group. Nationalism as a discourse of exclusion is another form of non-recognition or misrecognition of others. In this regard, the logic of 'both/and' is what minority groups must seek, with 'dogged strength,' so as to '[keep] ... [their hyphenated identities] from being torn asunder,' (Du Bois 1903). Henry Louis Gates' reinterpretation of double consciousness as an ironic stance – a double voice that is capable of critiquing the dominant culture – offers room for resistance and agency in and among minority groups. He writes: 'Voice presupposed a face, but also seems to have been thought to determine the very contours of the black face' (Gates 1986, 11). From this perspective, the character Ichiro's ambivalence – his double consciousness – can be reinterpreted as his double voice, from which resistance and agency are generated. Arab-American writer Lisa Suhair Majaj's suggestion for Arab-Americans – although written before September 11 – is still quite appropriate: 'At century's end, our split vision may be our most important legacy, forcing us to direct our gaze not only backwards, to the past, but forward, to an as-yet-unwritten future' (Majaj 1999, 77). The wholesome acceptance of their double identities as double voices will help ethnic minority groups to form affirmative identities.

To do so, however, requires great struggle on the part of ethnic minorities. This struggle has always contributed constructively to upholding the so-called democratic ideals that most Americans believe to be their own. In other words, the margin as mainstream is where thinking otherwise, or imagining another world, can be made possible. 'The change [of envisioning possibilities beyond the hyphen] has come about because at times, historical circumstances have pressed Asian North Americans to create *alternative spaces* from which to speak and to imagine in order to survive. Asian North Americans have developed *new ways* of perceiving and thinking about themselves, and along with new representations, new social psyches have emerged' (Ty and Goellnicht 2004, 10; my emphases). The narrowing or exclusive vision of America and Americans, often supported by the so-called mainstream, will be overcome by the inclusive vision, imagined and cherished by those on the margins. It is that inclusive vision that will foster a flexible, porous, and open-ended national culture in which the potential and ideal of multiculturalism – the logic of coexistence – can be truly maximized.

Notes

I would like to thank Dr Imre Szeman and Dr Donald Goellnicht in English and Cultural Studies at McMaster University and the editor of this volume, Dr Vijay Agnew, for helping me make this essay a much better one.

1 For the concept of the other and the enemy in Western history, see Harle 2000 and Anidjar 2003.
2 There are many journalistic representations but no substantial fictional representations of Arab Americans in the post–September 11 era.
3 The discovery in 1970 of *No-No Boy*, originally published in 1957 and republished in 1976, is the outcome of the emergence of ethnic studies such as Asian-American studies (Inada 1976, iii–vi; see also Chin 1976).
4 See Suleiman 1999 for a short informative history.
5 The rise of cultural racisim is also closely related to the recent proliferation of the studies of nations and nationalism. After the demise of the Soviet bloc, many welcomed and supported the idea that globalization would create a world without borders and an end to the nation-state. But over the last decade, as globalization intensifies, we see instead the rise of nationalism.

The nation-state continues to play a significant role in the era of globalization, albeit in a quite different manner.

6 On the new racism, or cultural racism, in France and Great Britain, see Balibar 1991a; Todorov 1993, 156–57; and Gilroy 1990.

7 For a discussion of the complicated and dynamic relationship between racism and nationalism, see Balibar 1991b and Mosse 1995.

8 In this chapter I discuss only Japanese-Americans after the Pearl Harbor bombing, although Japanese-Canadians had similar experiences. For the autobiographical representations of Japanese-Canadians' internment experience, see Takashima 1971; Nakano 1980; and Kogawa 1981, 1986. For the discussion of both cases, see Holsinger 1991 and Amoko 2000.

9 John Okada does not directly describe the everyday life of Japanese-Americans during internment. Instead, he describes the psychological effects of racism and of their internment in post–World War II America. For the internment-camp life of Japanese-Americans, see Harth 2001, a collection of memoirs. The last chapter of the book includes Japanese-Americans' critical responses to the internment camps. See also the documentary film *Something Strong Within*, a collection of home movies on Japanese-American life in internment camps which is included in the documentary film *9066 to 9/11*.

10 Emi is one of the Japanese-Americans in the novel who hopes to become more American than most Americans, just like Kenji, the yes-yes boy.

11 The recent Hollywood movie *Pearl Harbor* (2001), made to commemorate the sixtieth anniversary of the Pearl Harbor bombing by the Japanese army on 7 December 1941, shows how the inclusion and omission of certain images work in inventing Japanese-Americans as 'enemies,' thereby illustrating Sturken's argument.

12 In her article 'Regarding the Torture of Others,' Susan Sontag discusses the politics of visual images in the Internet and digital era. After arguing about the political role of the Abu Ghraib prison photos, which were accidentally leaked and made public, she concludes: 'The pictures will not go away. That is the nature of the digital world in which we live ... In our digital hall of mirrors, the pictures aren't going to go away. Yes, it seems that one picture is worth a thousand words. And even if our leaders choose not to look at them, there will be thousands more snapshots and videos. Unstoppable' (Sontag 2004). Susan Buck-Morss elaborates the political impact of visual images in the era of globalization by noting that visual images, which are locally produced yet widely distributed, can contribute significantly to the formation of global imagination and resistance; see Buck-Morss 2004.

13 For a detailed discussion of this issue, see Bennett 1998, which includes theoretical and empirical on nationalism and multiculturalism.

14 This is reminiscent of 'the role of the imagination in social life' (Appadurai 2000, 6) and the 'social imaginary' (Taylor 2004, 24–30). Both argue the ways in which social imagination shared by collectivities can contribute to transforming reality.

15 Ichiro's position is very close to that of intellectuals in the dark moments of America after September 11. 'The intellectual's provisional home is the domain of an exigent, resistant, intransigent art into which, alas, one can neither retreat nor search for solutions. But only in that precarious exilic realm can one first truly grasp the difficulty of what cannot be grasped and then go forth to try anyway' (Said 2004, 144).

16 For a discussion of censorship in post–September 11 America, see Butler 2004. Butler mourns the fact that America called for war and isolated itself from the global community by heightening nationalist discourse and extending surveillance mechanisms, reminding us of the simple truth that we and others can be injured. Butler suggests that the powers of mourning and violence can lead us not to retaliation but to the awareness that our life is fundamentally dependent upon anonymous others, and that the recognition of such inevitable interdependency of our lives can form the basis for global political community where no one controls others.

17 See Bussolini 2003; Leong and Nakanishi 2002, 54–104; Marable 2003; and O'Brien 2001. For a documentary film, see *9066 to 9/11* (2004). Leong and Nakanishi offer a variety of responses from Asian Americans to the events of September 11, 2001.

18 Agamben identifies how some emergency measures adopted by Western countries in times of war become governing norms afterwards: 'One of the essential characteristics of the state of exception – the provisional abolition of the distinction among legislative, executive, and judicial powers – here shows its tendency to become a lasting practice of government' (2005, 7). Moreover, he relates 'the state of exception as a paradigm of government' to the political situation in America after September 11 as shaped by the Bush administration. For a detailed discussion, see Agamben 2005, 1–31; see also Giroux 2004 and Butler 2004.

19 Maher Arar (a Syrian-Canadian) was arrested in New York's Kennedy Airport on 26 September 2002 as he was traveling to Montreal from Tunisia and was later deported to Syria, where he underwent unbearable torture. This is a good case that shows how the Bush government has treated visitors to the United States after September 11. There are numerous other cases.

20 The human rights of Iraqi soldiers in Abu Ghraib prison and of prisoners at Guantanamo Bay have been seriously violated (Giroux 2004, 26; see also Butler 2004, 50–100).

21 For a comprehensive and groundbreaking study of the misrepresentation of Arabs in Hollywood films, see Shaheen 2001.
22 Since September 11, books and articles have been published in an attempt to eradicate stereotypes of Islam and Muslims (see for example Buck-Morss 2003, 2), although it is doubtful how significant such anti-hegemonic discourses could be in instituting a significant change.
23 Here 'Arab-American' is used as an umbrella term that includes both Christian and Muslim Arabs in order to emphasize that identity formation – 'defining oneself' – is pretty much dependent upon the recognition or misrecognition of others.
24 Herein lies the problematic concept of 'the different value of different lives' behind America's war against Iraq (Pilger 2003, 9). On September 11, innocent civilians were killed; Americans mourned for them and supported the war. However, few Americans have mourned in public for the many more innocent civilians in Iraq, including children, who were killed during the two Gulf wars. Allocating different human value to certain people, according to Giroux, is a characteristic of neoliberal culture, 'a politics in which radical exclusion is the order of the day, and in which the primary questions no longer concern equality, justice, or freedom but are now about the survival of the slickest in a culture marked by fear, surveillance, and economic deprivation ... The question that currently seems to define neoliberal "democracy" is "Who has a right to live or does not?"' (2004, xxii).
25 In *Healing the Wounds of September 11, 2001 (Reflections of an American Muslim)* Athar unmasks the hypocrisy of America's war against Iraq, noting that 'all 19 of the alleged hijackers of Sept. 11 were Saudis. Iraq had never attacked the US. Therefore, in the opinion of millions of protesters all over the world, invasion of Iraq was not justified. If the theory of presence of weapons of mass destruction is valid, then all nations have the right to attack other nations, including us, on the basis of that theory, as we have more weapons of mass destruction than anyone else' (2003, 37–8).
26 For the ill treatment of Arabs or Arab-Americans or Arab-looking people after September 11, see Cusac 2002. Many other accounts can also be found on the Internet.
27 The heading 'Beyond the Hyphen' is borrowed from Ty and Goellnicht 2004.

References

Achebe, Chinua. 1987. *Anthills of the savannah*. London: Heinemann.
Agamben, Giorgio. 2005. *State of exception*. Trans. Kevin Attell. Chicago: University of Chicago Press.

Amoko, Apollo O. 2000. Resilient ImagiNations: *No-no boy, Obasan*, and the limits of minority discourse. *Mosaic* 33 (3): 35–55.

Anderson, Benedict. 1991. *Imagined communities*. Rev. ed. London and New York: Verso.

Anidjar, Gil. 2003. *The Jew, the Arab: A history of the enemy*. Stanford: Stanford University Press.

Appadurai, Arjun. 2000. Grassroots globalization and the research imagination. *Public Culture* 12 (1): 1–19.

Athar, Shahid. 2003. *Healing the wounds of September 11, 2001 (Reflections of an American Muslim)*. Bloomington, IN: 1st Books.

Balibar, Étienne. 1991a. Is there a 'neo-racism'? In *Race, nation, class: Ambiguous identities*, ed. Étienne Balibar and Immanuel Wallerstein, 17–28. London and New York: Verso.

– 1991b. Racism and nationalism. In *Race, nation, class: Ambiguous identities*, ed. Étienne Balibar and Immanuel Wallerstein, 37–68. London and New York: Verso.

Bell, Bernard W. 1987. *The Afro-American novel and its tradition*. Amherst, MA: University of Massachusetts Press.

Bennett, David, ed. 1998. *Multicultural states: Rethinking difference and identity*. London and New York: Routledge.

Brown, Michael K., Martin Carnoy, Elliott Currie, Troy Duster, David B. Oppenheimer, Marjorie M. Schultz, and David Wellman. 2003. *Whitewashing race: The myth of a color-blind society*. Berkeley and Los Angeles: University of California Press.

Buck-Morss, Susan. 2003. *Thinking past terror: Islamism and critical theory on the left*. London and New York: Verso.

– 2004. Visual studies and global imagination. *Papers of Surrealism* 2 (Summer). http://www.surrealismcentre.ac.uk/publications/papers/journal2/index.htm.

Bulosan, Carlos. 1973. *America is in the heart: A personal history*. Intro. by Carey McWilliams. Seattle and London: University of Washington Press. First published in 1943, New York: Harcourt, Brace.

Bussolini, Jeffrey. 2003. The Wen Ho Lee affair: War on terrorism or war on liberty? In *Implicating empire: Globalization and resistance in the 21st century world order*, ed. Stanley Aronowitz and Heather Gautney, 15–30. New York: Basic.

Butler, Judith. 2004. *Precarious life: The powers of mourning and violence*. London and New York: Verso.

Chen, Fu-jen. 2000. John Okada (1923–1971). In *Asian American novelists: A bio-bibliographical critical sourcebook*, ed. Emmanuel S. Nelson, 281–8. Westport, CT: Greenwood.

Chin, Frank. 1976. Afterword: In search of John Okada. In *No-no boy*, by John
  Okada, 253–60. Seattle: University of Washington Press.
Council on American-Islamic Relations (CAIR). 2004. Ethnicity of Muslims
  pie chart. 11 August. http://www.ispi-usa.org/Intro_muslims/
  ethnicitymuslims.gif.
Cusac, Anne-Marie. 2002. Ill-treatment on our shores. *The Progressive*. March.
  http://www.progressive.org/mag_cusacmarch02.
Davidson, Arnold E., Priscilla L. Walton, and Jennifer Andrews. 2003. *Border
  crossings: Thomas King's cultural inversions*. Toronto: University of Toronto
  Press.
Detroit Free Press. 2001. 100 questions and answers about Arab Americans: A
  journalist's guide. Available online at http://www.freep.com/legacy/
  jobspage/arabs.htm.
Du Bois, W.E.B. 1903. Of our spiritual strivings. In *The souls of black folk*, ed.
  with intro. by David W. Blight and Robert Gooding-Williams, 37–44. Boston:
  Bedford Books, 1997. Quoted in Bell 1987, 12.
Fredrickson, George M. 2002. *Racism: A short history*. Princeton: Princeton University Press. The epigraph to this chapter is found on p. 170.
Gates Jr, Henry Louis. 1986. Introduction: Writing 'race' and the difference it
  makes. In *'Race,' writing, and difference*, ed. Henry Louis Gates Jr, 1–20. Chicago: University of Chicago Press.
Gilroy, Paul. 1990. One nation under a groove: The politics of 'race' and racism
  in Britain. In *Anatomy of racism*, ed. David Theo Goldberg, 263–82. Minneap-
  olis: University of Minnesota Press.
Giroux, Henry A. 2004. *The terror of neoliberalism: Authoritarianism and the eclipse
  of democracy*. Boulder, CO: Paradigm.
Goldstein-Shirley, David. 2000. Enemies in their own land: The internment of
  Japanese Americans during World War II. In *Asian American studies: Identity,
  images, issues past and present*, ed. Esther Mikyung Ghymn, 207–16. New
  York: Peter Lang.
Guinier, Lani, and Gerald Torres. 2002. *The miner's canary*. Cambridge, MA.:
  Harvard University Press, 224. Quoted in Brown et al. 2003, x.
Hardt, Michael, and Antonio Negri. 2000. *Empire*. Cambridge, MA: Harvard
  University Press. The epigraph to this chapter is found on p. 195.
Harle, Vilho. 2000. *The enemy with a thousand faces: The tradition of the Other in
  Western political thought and history*. Westport, CT: Praeger.
Harth, Erica, ed. 2001. *Last witnesses: Reflections on the wartime internment of Jap-
  anese Americans*. New York: Palgrave.
Holsinger, M. Paul. 1991. Told without bitterness: Autobiographical accounts
  of the relocation of Japanese-Americans and Canadians during World War II.

In *Visions of war: World War II in popular literature and culture*, ed. M. Paul Holsinger and Mary Anne Schofield, 149–59. Bowling Green, OH: Bowling Green State University Popular Press.

Inada, Lawson Fusao. 1976. Introduction to *No-no boy*, by John Okada, iii–vi. Seattle: University of Washington Press.

Joseph, Suad. 1999. Against the grain of the nation – the Arab. In *Arabs in America: Building a new future*, ed. Michael W. Suleiman, 257–71. Philadelphia: Temple University Press.

Kogawa, Joy. 1981. *Obasan*. Toronto: Penguin.

– 1986. *Naomi's road*. Toronto: Oxford University Press.

Lee, Chang-rae. 1995. *Native speaker*. New York: Riverhead.

Leong, Russell C., and Don T. Nakanishi, eds. 2002. *Asian Americans on war and peace*. Los Angeles: UCLA Asian American Studies Center Press.

Ling, Jinqi. 1998. Writing the novel, narrating discontents: Race and cultural politics in John Okada's *No-no boy*. In *Narrating nationalism: Ideology and form in Asian American literature*, 31–52. New York and Oxford: Oxford University Press.

Majaj, Lisa Suhair. 1999. New directions: Arab American writing at century's end. In *Post-Gibran: Anthology of new Arab American writing*, ed. Munir Akash and Khaled Mattawa, 67–77. Maryland: Kitab.

Marable, Manning. 2003. 9/11: Racism in a time of terror. In *Implicating empire: Globalization and resistance in the 21st century world order*, ed. Stanley Aronowitz and Heather Gautney, 3–14. New York: Basic.

Mosse, George L. 1995. Racism and nationalism. *Nations and Nationalism* 1 (2): 163–73.

Nakano, Takeo Ujo, with Leatrice Nakano. 1980. *Within the barbed wire fence: A Japanese man's account of his internment in Canada*. Toronto: University of Toronto Press.

9066 to 9/11: America's concentration camps, then ... and now? 2004. Akira Boch, director. Japanese American National Museum.

O'Brien, Ed. 2001. In war, is law silent? Security and freedom after September 11. *Social Education* 65 (7): 419–25. http://www.downloads.ncss.org/lessons/650704.pdf.

Okada, John. 1979. *No-no boy*. Seattle: University of Washington Press. First published in 1957, Rutherford, VT: Charles E. Tuttle.

Okihiro, Gary Y. 1994. *Margins and mainstreams: Asians in American history and culture*. Seattle and London: University of Washington Press.

Pearl Harbor. 2001. Michael Bay, director. Buena Vista Home Entertainment, Inc.

Pilger, John. 2003. *Rulers of the world*. London and New York: Verso.

Rahman, Anika. 2001. Fear in the open city. *New York Times*, 19 September.

Said, Edward. *Orientalism*. 1979. New York: Vintage.

– 1997. *Covering Islam: How the media and the experts determine how we see the rest of the world*. Rev. ed. New York: Vintage.

– 2004. The public role of writers and intellectuals. In *Humanism and democratic criticism*, 119–44. New York: Columbia University Press.

Samhan, Helen. 1999. Not quite white: Race classification and the Arab American experience. In *Arabs in America: Building a new future*, ed. Michael W. Suleiman, 209–26. Philadelphia: Temple University Press. http://www.aaiusa.org/foundation/355/not_quite_white.

– 2006. Arab Americans. http://www.aaiusa.org/foundation/358/arab_americans.

Shaheen, Jack G. 2001. *Reel bad Arabs: How Hollywood vilifies a people*. New York and Northampton: Olive Branch.

Something Strong Within. 1995. Robert A. Nakamura, director. Japanese American National Museum.

Sontag, Susan. 2004. Regarding the torture of others. *The New York Times*, May 23. http://donswaim.com/nytimes.sontag.html.

Stratton, Jon, and Ien Ang. 1998. Multicultural imagined communities: Cultural difference and national identity in the USA and Australia. In *Multicultural states: Rethinking difference and identity*, ed. David Bennett, 136–62. London and New York: Routledge.

Sturken, Marita. 2001. Absent images of memory: Remembering and reenacting the Japanese internment. In *Perilous memories: The Asia-Pacific War(s)*, ed. T. Fujitani, Geoffrey M. White, and Lisa Yoneyama, 33–49. Durham: Duke University Press.

Suleiman, Michael W. 1999. Introduction: The Arab immigrant experience. In *Arabs in America: Building a new future*, ed. Michael W. Suleiman, 1–21. Philadelphia: Temple University Press.

Takashima, Shizuye. 1971. *A child in prison camp*. Montreal: Tundra.

Taylor, Charles. 1995. The politics of recognition. In *Philosophical arguments*, 225–56. Cambridge, MA: Harvard University Press.

– 2004. *Modern social imaginaries*. Durham and London: Duke University Press.

Todorov, Tzvetan. 1993. *On human diversity: Nationalism, racism, and exoticism in French thought*. Trans. Catherine Porter. Cambridge, MA: Harvard University Press.

Ty, Eleanor, and Donald C. Goellnicht, eds. 2004. *Asian North American identities: Beyond the hyphen*. Bloomington and Indianapolis: Indiana University Press.

Yogi, Stan. 1996. You had to be one or the other: Oppositions and reconciliation in John Okada's *No-no boy*. *Melus* 21 (2) (summer): 63–77.

9 From Displaying 'Jewish Art' to (Re)Building German-Jewish History: The Jewish Museum Berlin

ROBIN OSTOW

In her introduction to this volume, the editor (quoting Fredrickson 2002) notes that although the concept of racism dates back to ancient times, the term became widely used with the persecution of Jews in Europe in the 1930s. The first museum to be discussed in this chapter opened in Berlin in early 1933, just a few days before Hitler came to power, and struggled to survive and to boost the morale of the city's Jewish community until it was closed by the Nazis in 1938.

Theorizing the relation of anti-Semitism to racism is complicated partly because the practices of these forms of oppression and our understandings of them are historical: they have changed in the past, and they continue to change. A further complication, as Karen Mock argues, is that in the case of Jews, religious and racial boundaries coincide (1996, 12–132). But this addresses the situation today, which is contested. In pre-modern Europe, Jews were identified largely as a religious group. They could escape discrimination and persecution by converting to Christianity, as many Jews did in Spain in the last years of the fifteenth century.

Sander Gilman's essay 'Are Jews White?' documents how starting in the late seventeenth century, much of Europe's scholarly literature described Jews as 'black,' or at least 'swarthy.' 'For the eighteenth- and nineteenth-century scientist the 'blackness' of the Jew was not only a mark of racial inferiority, but also an indicator of the diseased nature of the Jew' (2000, 231). Gilman notes that by the end of the nineteenth century, 'Western European Jews had become indistinguishable from other Western Europeans in matters of language, dress, occupation, location of their dwellings and the cut of their hair,' but they were still seen by scientists as a 'distinct racial category' (233).

In North America, Everett Hughes was one of the first social scientists to write about Nazism. His 1955 essay 'The *Gleichschaltung* of the German Statistical Yearbook' documents parts of the process of racialization discussed in Agnew's introduction to this volume by highlighting the changes in categorization in Germany's statistical yearbook from 1932 through 1952. Hughes found that 'race in the pre-Nazi Yearbooks was a characteristic of stallions ... Men ... had religion. They were Christians of Protestant or Roman-Catholic confession, or they were Israelites' (1971, 519). After the enactment of the Nuremberg Laws in 1935, the category 'Israelites' was replaced in German statistics by 'Jews' and 'Jewish mixtures' of the first and second degree. Jews had become a race.

Some of the subtleties and complexities of the intersections of Jewishness and blackness in the twentieth century and today are articulated in Vijay Agnew's interview with Frances Henry in this volume, in which Agnew quotes Henry's 1994 statement: 'I am no stranger to *racism* [my italics]. I have felt it personally as a Jewish refugee from Hitler's Germany.' Yet two decades earlier, Henry described her study of Jews and their non-Jewish neighbours in the Nazi Germany she fled as an 'ethnohistory' (1971, 6). This discrepancy in terminology points to changes in the social sciences in North America over thirty-five years.

This chapter examines the social histories of two Jewish museums in Germany's capital city and deconstructs their exhibits, not in the general context of anti- Semitism, but with respect to Nazism, a regime whose policies and ideology centred on race. Berlin's first Jewish museum opened in January 1933 just as Germany, under a new Nazi government, was about to embark on catastrophic changes in its government, its national identity, and its way of dealing with minorities, especially racial minorities. One result of this restructuring was that the Jewish Museum and the Jewish population around it were dissolved by the Nazis within a few years.[1] The museum was closed in 1938, and the deportation of Berlin's Jews began in 1941. Sixty years later, in September 2001, a new Jewish museum opened in Berlin. A monumental project, sponsored largely by the government of reunified Germany – in local parlance, the 'Berlin Republic' – the Jewish Museum Berlin announces a recasting of German and Jewish identities and a repositioning of German-Jewish history within and around national history. Although there is no institutional continuity linking the two museums, both represent large statements, innovative concepts, and contested positions in contemporary debates regarding the relation of German Jews to the larger society around them and to the German state. The first museum serves as an example of attempted cultural resistance in the face of racist oppression. The establishment of the second museum in 2001 points to the difficulties of overcoming the legacy of Nazism even sixty years after Hitler's defeat.

The Jewish Museum 1933–38

This was the largest Jewish museum in Europe. It was based on the most modern approach to Jewish culture,[2] and it was the last one to open before the Nazis began to close and plunder Jewish museums as part of their program of extermination of European Jewry.[3] Like its counterparts in Danzig, Warsaw, and other cities, Berlin's museum originally housed a collection that consisted mostly of coins, medallions, and portraits that had been donated to the Jewish community.[4] As in Warsaw, the establishment of the museum in Berlin was delayed by institutional inertia and lack of interest. Albert Wolf, the Dresden jeweller who willed his collection to Berlin's Jewish Community, died in 1907, but no one in Berlin even bothered to unpack the crates until ten years later. From 1917 to 1930, Wolf's collection, along with new acquisitions, was displayed in three rooms of the Jewish Community's administrative building (Oranienburger Straße 31) as the 'Art Collection of the Jewish Community.'

The museum project became more dynamic when curator Karl Schwarz (1885–1962) and collector Salli Kirschstein (1870–1935) became involved in the late 1920s. Rather than displaying 'leftovers from the past,' Kirschstein wanted to produce a 'lively display and a source for observation and knowledge. A Jewish museum ... can be of inestimable value for holding our people together. But, at the same time, it must be able to influence the attitude of non-Jews towards Jews and Judaism, as the lack of knowledge about Jewish life was, and still is, one of the strongest factors in anti-Jewish views' (Jacobson 1928, 88). (Unless otherwise noted, all translations from German are my own.) Its goal, then, was to attract both Jewish and non-Jewish visitors to instill pride in the former and to provide knowledge to combat anti-Semitism in the latter.[5] Schwarz's idea was to use the museum to encourage modern Jewish art by commissioning and displaying works of contemporary Jewish artists, rather than merely hanging up items from the past that had been acquired or donated.

The opening of the Jewish Museum on 24 January 1933 (just a few days before Hitler came to power) was reported in the Jewish and non-

Jewish (including the foreign) press. Fifty years later, James Yaakov Rosenthal (1903–97), the correspondent for the Jewish Telegraphic Agency, remembered the event as 'the last significant, still relatively unclouded though twilight-tinted, major Jewish cultural event in what was then the capital of the (Third) Reich. Everyone who had anything to do with Jewish life and faith was among those assembled, as well as everyone with any standing in Jewish or in general cultural and intellectual life' (Rosenthal 1980, 1982). At a time when most Jewish museums were displaying medieval gravestones, old artifacts, and portraits of local notables, the new museum in Berlin foregrounded twentieth-century art based on epic Jewish themes reaching back to the Bible. On the walls of the front gallery hung three large oil paintings: Lesser Ury's *Jeremiah* (1911) and *Moses* (n.d.), and Jakob Steinhardt's *Prophet* (1913/14). Against the walls were busts of two major German-Jewish intellectuals: Moses Mendelssohn (1729–86), the father figure of bourgeois Berlin Jewry,[6] and Abraham Geiger (1810–74), a rabbi and leading intellectual figure in Reform Jewry and in the *Wissenschaft des Judentums* (Science of Judaism).[7] On a pedestal in the middle of the gallery, the object that commanded the immediate gaze of the visitor was Arnold Zadikow's statue of *David* (1921).[8] Photos of the statue show David standing naked, proud, and handsome. His body radiates physical and spiritual strength. Slingshot in hand, he greets the public and guards the exhibit.

As (male) Jewish heroes, the Biblical David and eighteenth-century Berlin's Moses Mendelssohn represent physical and historical antitheses. Where Mendelssohn had an ugly and deformed body that harboured a powerful and open mind, Zadikow's *David* was a muscular warrior whose classical proportions met twentieth-century German criteria of beauty.[9] Mendelssohn was a local hero, associated with an era when German Jews had no power but earned the respect of the larger society through their intellectual achievements. David, by contrast, was associated with Jewish military and political power, and pre-dated both Christianity and Germany. Zadikow (1950) commented on his statue: 'Das ist meine Antwort an Hitler und die Nazis' (This is my answer to Hitler and the Nazis). Abraham Geiger, the most recent figure in the front gallery, represented the modern historical approach to Judaism, which led to the establishment of Jewish museums in many of Europe's major cities. With this front gallery, the Jewish Museum announced a distinguished German-Jewish tradition of art and philosophy, strength and beauty, and a proud history dating back to the Old Testament.

The halls that followed continued the display of modern Jewish art, including paintings by Camille Pissarro (1830–1903), Max Liebermann (1847–1935), who donated a self-portrait to the museum, and Max Oppenheim (1885–1954). A prominent feature of the modern art exhibit was the large oil painting *Sie Wandern* (*Exile*, 1904) by Samuel Hirszenberg (1865–1908), which attracted considerable attention among the European Jewish public. It depicted a group of Jews huddled together, walking through the snow across a barren landscape, presumably fleeing a pogrom in the East. Zionists in particular saw the painting as a major statement of the tragedy of Jewish life in the Diaspora (Cohen 1998, 230–4). In the face of increasing Nazi persecution, Berlin Jews came to identify with it (Simon 2000, 138–9).

Beyond this gallery, two rooms displayed ceremonial objects dating back to the sixteenth century; a third room contained religious artifacts by modern silversmiths; and a fourth room featured archeological displays from Palestine and medallions. The next room was devoted to modern Jewish graphics, the history of Berlin's Jewish community, and displays of Jewish holidays. Local history, including portraits of community leaders and sections devoted to holidays, were standard features of pre-war Jewish museums. The permanent exhibit ended with two synagogue installations.

Schwarz's display expanded the purview of Jewish museums from portraits, old ceremonial objects, and local history to include modern art and ritual crafts, and archeological finds from Palestine. The archeological exhibits extended Jewish history to pre-date Christian and European history and gestured to Zionism, which located the centre of Jewish history in the Middle East. Schwarz himself was a Zionist. Six months after opening Berlin's Jewish Museum, he left Germany to become the founding director of the Tel Aviv Museum. In 1930s Berlin, showcasing the longer course of Jewish history and expanding the geographical panorama eastwards may have provided comfort and perhaps a false assurance of continuity under the increasing pressure of German anti-Semitism.

Beyond these innovations, the permanent exhibit of Berlin's Jewish Museum voiced a strong, affirmative position in the debates of the pre-war years regarding the existence of 'Jewish art.' The first books announcing and promoting Jewish art appeared in Germany in the late 1920s (Schwarz 2001; Cohn-Wiener 1929). But many intellectuals believed that 'Jewish' art did not exist, and some commentators perceptively predicted that the concept of Jewish art could become a weapon to be used against Jews (Simon 2000, 69). Curt Glaser argued that all the efforts to bring various kinds of modern Jewish products together in the 'Jewish Museum' did not demonstrate the existence of 'Jewish art.' The permanent exhibit did not convince him that a painting by Rembrandt on an Old Testament theme should not hang in a Jewish museum, while a still life or landscape by someone like Max Liebermann should.

Simon (2000) and Schwarz (2001) describe the museum's career under the Nazi government. Subject to increasing harassment, some of its key staff members emigrated: the director, Karl Schwarz, in spring 1933; his successor, Erna Stein, in 1935; and the curator, Rahel Wischnitzer-Bernstein, in 1936.[10] At the same time, as Jewish artists were excluded from German museums and galleries, they turned to the Jewish Museum, the only one that could exhibit their work. And as Berlin's Jews were forbidden to participate in German public life, many began to turn inward and came to the Jewish Museum to learn more about their Jewishness and to draw pride and strength from their history and cultural achievements. Simon argues that the museum's intense program of special exhibits – eighteen in five years – supported the morale of Berlin's Jews by highlighting heroic figures in European Jewish history, Jewish crafts, and the holiday of Chanukah, which is associated with a miracle and with light. As Berlin's wealthier Jews began to emigrate and Germany's smaller Jewish communities were dissolved, the curators appealed for donations to the museum. Thus, as Germany's Jewish population disappeared, the museum's inventory grew.

Simon (2000) interprets the Jewish Museum's short history as an example of *Aufbau im Untergang* (building in the midst of destruction). Others see it as one more example of the naiveté of German Jews regarding their acceptance and integration into Germany (Bendt 1987, 200–9). James Young comments: 'It is almost as if the museum had hoped to establish the institutional fact of an inextricably linked German-Jewish culture, each a permutation of the other, as a kind of challenge to the Nazis' assumption of an essential hostility between German and Jewish cultures' (2000, 156).

The Jewish Museum was effectively closed by the Nazis right after *Kristallnacht* (the night of broken glass) in November 1938 and its inventory was confiscated.[11] Surprisingly, a large part of the collection survived the war in Berlin, in the cellar of the former Ministry of Culture on the Schlüterstraße. After the war, these objects, mostly paintings, were sent in different directions. Some are now displayed at the

Hebrew Union College in Cincinnati; some at the Skirball Museum in Los Angeles; a few are hanging in the Centrum Judaicum, the museum of the history of Berlin's Jewish Community; and others are in the Israel National Museum in Jerusalem. Many, including Zadikow's *David* and Hirszenberg's *Sie Wandern*, have been lost.

Post-war Concepts for a Jewish Museum in Berlin: 1969–2000

In the early post-war years, there was no idea of reviving Jewish communal life in Germany. And non-Jewish Germans, busy rebuilding their own lives, had no interest in reopening a Jewish museum they had liquidated. The impulse to re-establish a Jewish museum in Berlin dates from the late 1960s, when Heinz Galinski (1912–92), then president of West Berlin's Jewish Community, went public with his claim that the city had an obligation to replace the Jewish museum which the Nazis had dismembered. Reiner Güntzer, who was then in charge of Berlin's municipal museums, negotiated with Galinski, who told him, 'I don't want a repetition of the ghetto at the higher level of a cultural institution.' He 'wanted the history of Jewish people to be exhibited in the Berlin Museum.'[12]

In 1971, the (West) Berlin Museum mounted a major exhibit entitled 'Achievement and Fate. 300 Years of the Jewish Community in Berlin: 1671–1971.' This exhibit focused on *berühmte Leute*, Berlin Jews who were famous in the 1920s. It nostalgically evoked pre-Nazi Germany as a *heile Welt* (a world in a state of grace) and generated public discussion around the need for a Jewish museum in West Berlin, as part of the Berlin Museum. The committee formed to carry the project was a grass-roots initiative of Berlin Jews and non-Jews.[13] In 1975, the (West) Berlin Senate approved the establishment of a Jewish department in the Berlin Museum. And in 1979, Vera Bendt was hired as department head.

In the seventies and eighties, debates around the proposed museum focused on the institutional arrangements, particularly the location. But they were framed by larger understandings of the position of Jews in post-war (West) German society. Vera Bendt carried the initiative for fifteen years (1979–94), expanding the Judaica collection and pressing for a building (Bendt 1995, 1992, and 1987). She saw the museum as a site of *Begegnung* (encounter), 'a place where two groups that have problems with each other come together and become intimate with each other and each learns to understand the problems of the other).'[14]

Bendt's boss, Reiner Güntzer, envisioned a museum where Jewish history would be exhibited from a German point of view, because 'this is a German museum ... the Berlin Municipal Museum exhibits Jewish history from the point of view of the non-Jewish majority'.[15] Güntzer admired Heinz Galinski as a 'German patriot, a man who integrated himself into the non-Jewish society, *despite* everything that happened ... Galinski gave us the chance to belong to "the decent people."' Integrating a Jewish museum into the city museum would likewise offer non-Jewish Berliners a chance to belong to the 'decent people.' Güntzer planned to mount an exhibit about the recently deceased Jewish leader. But Galinski's widow, horrified by the idea of this exhibit, refused to cooperate.

The debates and conflicts around Berlin's Jewish museum project unfolded against the backdrop of two decades of discussions and confrontations in Germany regarding memories of the Holocaust, German guilt, and the place of Jews in German history and in contemporary Germany. The eighties and nineties saw unprecedented numbers of publications, media reports, conferences, and artistic productions on Jewish-related issues, including Holocaust commemoration rituals and monuments (Bodemann 1996). Offe (2000) describes the establishment in those years of up to 100 mostly very small Jewish museums, in towns with no Jewish inhabitants. These museums all arose out of years of heated controversy, informed by a broad spectrum of guilt and defenses against guilt on the part of the local residents. The museums tended to be housed in former synagogues, which had been used as warehouses, cinemas, and even firehouses after the war.[16] The restoration of these buildings and their rededication as Jewish sites was seen by many Germans as a chance to reconnect with the pre-1933 era and through this, to attain a new, positive identification with local history. Reiner Güntzer's vision of a museum that would allow Germans to belong to the 'decent people' suggests that the debates and politics around the Jewish museum in Berlin were informed by similar dynamics. Offe argues further that by allowing Germans to recreate or rescue the remnants of local Jewish culture and to identify with it, Jewish museums provide a bridge to a healing process through which Germans can overcome the trauma they suffered as a result of their own history.

In 1988, the (West) Berlin Senate approved the financing for a Jewish museum that was to be administratively part of the Berlin Museum, but would have a name and quarters of its own. A year later, the architectural design of Daniel Libeskind was selected for the building. The son of Holocaust survivors, Libeskind was born in Łodz, Poland in 1946.

He emigrated to Israel where he trained as a musician. He then studied history in the United States and later earned a degree in architecture in the United Kingdom. His design for the museum has a zigzag shape. In Germany, it is often described as a lightning bolt and as a deconstructed Star of David. British historian John Breuilly sees it also as a deconstructed swastika.[17] It has no public doors to the outside: visitors enter only through the basement of the adjacent Berlin Museum. And it features 'voids' – empty towers that represent the voids left in Berlin history and Jewish history by the Holocaust. The building is constructed around intersecting axes: one leads to annihilation; one to the garden of exile; and the third to continuity.

With an area of 10,000 square metres, Libeskind's building dwarfs the Berlin Museum next to it, the yellow *Kollegienhaus*, a historic baroque structure that was originally a Prussian courthouse. Libeskind's cutting contours, small windows, and the harshness of the facade make no concessions to the surrounding Kreuzberg cityscape. This structure presumes hard boundaries separating Germans and Jews. Most important, its design reduces German-Jewish history to the Holocaust. In fact, in 1998, historian Julius Schoeps suggested using the Libeskind building as a national Holocaust memorial and housing the Jewish museum elsewhere. Young points to the uncanny quality of the structure, particularly its irregular surfaces that cause visitors to feel off balance and estranged from their environment. Whereas the earlier concepts for a Jewish museum within Berlin's municipal museum centred on integration, Libeskind's design is about the 'interpenetration' of Jewish and German history (Young 2000, 174). The lightning-bolt building and the adjacent *Kollegienhaus* meet only underground. The 'voids' serve as a physical interference with chronological display. 'This is ... an aggressively antiredemptory design built literally around an absence of meaning in history, an absence of the people who would have given meaning to their history' (179). Thomas Lackmann, a German, sees the building as an architectural penetration of Berlin's cityscape, a mark of Jewish revenge and German humiliation and loss of control of their capital city (2000, 73). Libeskind's concept caused a sensation, and enthusiasm for the museum grew.

The fall of the Berlin Wall in November 1989 brought a reorganization of plans for the Jewish museum. With the political unification of Berlin, municipal finances began to tighten, and in 1991, the city tried to stop the project. At the same time, Berlin's (unsuccessful) bid for the 2000 Olympics and a wave of skinhead terror against Germany's minorities swayed public opinion in favour of the Jewish museum. As the discussions and politics around the Jewish museum merged with the debates and events surrounding German unification, the Jewish museum became a national project. Anderson (1983) and Bennett (1995) point to the role of museums in nation building, which in the Berlin Republic was informed by the frightening memory of the Third Reich, an example of a nation out of control that was responsible for war, genocide, and defeat. As late as 1999, in an interview in the news weekly *Die Woche*, Michael Naumann, who was then minister for culture, referred to Germany as 'a country which, after the war, established itself, not as a nation, but as a society which communicates with itself in a moral-ethical confrontation with its own history' (Naumann 1999). Building a Jewish museum in Libeskind's zinc lightning bolt became part of the process of crafting a positive national identity out of this confrontation with Nazism and the Holocaust.

The decision to go ahead with the *Libeskindbau* (Libeskind building) was followed by years of conflict regarding what would be housed in the new structure and the relationship between the Jewish and the Berlin museums. Reiner Güntzer made plans to put the Jewish museum in the basement of the Libeskind building and use the space above ground to display Berlin history, with Jewish life artifacts 'integrated into it.'[18] In 1994, art curator Amnon Barzel replaced Vera Bendt as director. He demanded use of the entire building as a museum that would focus on Jewish history as a prism for viewing global problems such as war, displacement, and divided cities (Barzel 1996, 1995). As an Israeli who spoke little German and had no previous work experience in Germany, Barzel proved unable to negotiate the routes through Berlin politics. In 1997 he was dismissed, and an American, Michael Blumenthal, was brought in as director.

Blumenthal was born in 1926 and raised in Berlin as an assimilated Jew. In 1938, he emigrated with his family to Shanghai, and then to the United States. There, he served as CEO of Bendix Corporation in the fifties and sixties. From 1977 to 1979, he was secretary of the treasury in the Carter administration, which translates elegantly into German as '*Finanzminister*.'[19] Blumenthal is a member of the board of Daimler-Benz, and speaks flawless German. He secured the exclusive use of the Libeskind building (which was completed in 1996) as well as the *Kollegienhaus* for the Jewish museum. He also put together the financing for what had become an enormous museum project to be carried by the federal government, the city, and private donations.

It was Blumenthal who decided that the Jewish museum would be a history museum, and he delegated the day-to-day operations of the project to Tom Freudenheim, another emigrated German Jew, who had made his career largely at the Smithsonian Institution in Washington, D.C. Jeshajahu (Shaike) Weinberg was brought in to organize the permanent exhibit. Weinberg, who was born in Poland and spent part of his adolescence in Berlin before emigrating to Palestine, had been the founding director of Israel's Diaspora Museum and later of the U.S. Holocaust Memorial Museum in Washington, D.C. It was his idea to build a high-tech exhibit around a chronological story line that would narrate Jewish history as a part of German history, including 'elements of integration and elements of tension.'[20] In the late 1990s, then, after years of being mired in fractious politics, the plans for the Jewish museum began to coalesce under the leadership and protection of three Jewish men who had some biographical connection to Germany, but had most recently been working in the United States. And this was part of the increased American cultural presence in Berlin after the withdrawal of the U.S. military in 1994.[21]

The course set by this triumvirate aimed at defusing Libeskind's lightning-bolt structure by reintroducing the theme of integration and using a continuous chronology to create what Blumenthal called a 'safe environment' for the visitor (Lackmann 2000, 243). When Weinberg died in early 2000, a German design firm, Würth & Winderoll, was awarded the contract for the permanent exhibit. This firm designed the *Haus der Geschichte der Bundesrepublik Deutschland* (House of the History of the Federal Republic of Germany), Germany's federal museum of the post-war period, which also uses high-tech, interactive exhibits and a chronological narrative to articulate Germany's national identity.

A few months later, Freudenheim was replaced as project director by Ken Gorbey, the director of exhibition and research development at the Te Papa Tongarewa Museum in Wellington, New Zealand. Gorbey is neither German nor Jewish. He doesn't speak German and has no expertise in German or Jewish history, but his super-sized museum, also based on a high-tech, interactive permanent exhibit, is a popular success.[22] Te Papa displays New Zealand as a dynamic nation where descendants of European colonizers coexist successfully with descendants of the all-but-exterminated indigenous people in a harmonious relation with the natural environment.

The dimensions of Gorbey's interactive Te Papa exhibit, which covers an area the size of three rugby fields, and the museum's animated website announcing: 'Dinosaurs Roar into Life at Te Papa' fueled the anxieties of some Germans regarding the displays to be installed in Libeskind's lightning bolt. In his book, *Jewrassic Park* (2000), Lackmann references Steven Spielberg's popular film about dinosaurs that come back to life to threaten humans. He fantasizes the Berlin museum as the incorporation of the reanimated ghosts of Jewish victims who take revenge by scarring the centre of the capital city and devouring German history.

If Libeskind's building engaged the German public's charged feelings and images around Jews and Germans, and what Young refers to as 'the constant, free-floating anxiety that seems to accompany every act of Jewish memorialization in Germany' (2000, 154), Berlin's Jewish community, by contrast, reacted to the museum project with a decided lack of interest. Historian Cilly Kugelmann (1996) points out that as Polish-Jewish Holocaust survivors, the members of West Germany's post-war Jewish communities had no interest in German-Jewish history and maintained a largely hostile relation to the state. Offe (2000) notes that this situation began to change in 1997. When Reiner Güntzer fired Amnon Barzel, Berlin's Jewish community protested and demanded representation on the board of directors. Since then, local Jewish communities have taken a more active interest in Jewish museums in other cities as well; for example, in Fürth in the late 1990s.

The Jewish Museum Berlin 2001: Two Millennia of German-Jewish History in 3,000 Square Metres

The new Jewish Museum Berlin is one of the Berlin Republic's three federal museums. The others are the *Deutsches Historisches Museum* (German Historical Museum) in Berlin and the *Haus der Geschichte der Bundesrepublik Deutschland* in Bonn. Together, they articulate a tripartite national history: the Roman era to 1944 is narrated in the *Deutsches Historisches Museum* in what had been East Berlin; West, East, and reunified Germany after 1945 are displayed in Bonn; and two millennia of German-Jewish history are housed in the Libeskind building in the former West Berlin.

The Jewish Museum's opening in September 2001, officially designated as an 'act of state,' and referred to in the German press as a 'world event,' was attended by 850 personages and dignitaries, including Chancellor Gerhard Schröder, President Johannes Rau, and former U.S. secretary of state Henry Kissinger. Broder (2001) points out that perhaps the most important message of this museum is visible already in the foyer, where a 1.5-by-2-metre transparent plaque lists the names of the museum's non-government sponsors and donors: banks; industrial, commercial, and media enterprises; and private individuals. The German businesses that employed slave labour during the Third Reich and the descendants of the Jews who were forced to work in the concentration camps participated in this museum project together. The gala opening marked the return of the dead Jews, not only as ghosts in a museum, but more importantly, as *Paten* (godparents) in a new, centralized republic (Broder 2001, 264, 266). In this role, they no longer threaten Germany. Rather, they bless and protect it.

To enter the exhibit, the visitor descends a flight of stairs to the subterranean display area. Underground are three corridors with white walls in which recessed vitrines showcase documents and personal belongings of Jews who fled the Nazis and of those who were murdered. Two corridors, or axes, lead respectively to the eerie garden of exile, which consists of forty-nine tilted concrete pillars containing willow trees, and to death, a dark, empty chamber. These axes and the installations they lead to do not tell the story of the Holocaust. The Libeskind basement is rather what van Alphen has termed a 'Holocaust Effect' or 'an unmediated confrontation with Nazism or with the Holocaust by means of a re-enactment' within the realm of art (1997, 11).

Holocaust installations are found in all of Europe's post-war Jewish museums. Although these museums deliberately distinguish themselves from Holocaust memorials and consciously aim to display Jewish life rather than death, each features a major Holocaust installation which functions as a kind of internal memorial. In Prague's Jewish museum, it is the Pinkas synagogue with the names of the 77,297 Czech and Slovak Holocaust victims painted on the walls. In the Jewish museum in Paris, it is Boltanski's installation about the deported inhabitants of the building that now houses the museum. And in Vienna's Jewish museum the *Schaudepot* (viewable storage area) on the top floor showcases ceremonial objects and personal belongings – the inanimate remains of pre-war Vienna's Jewish population.

In most Jewish museums, the Holocaust installation is placed towards the end of the permanent exhibit, at its chronological place in Jewish history. But in Berlin, appearing at the very beginning, Libeskind's Holocaust installation frames the historical narrative that follows. In the Libeskind basement, Jews are shown as victimized, but not as passive objects of Nazi genocide. Rather, they are presented as subjects who make choices and take action. In particular, the letters and objects in the vitrines reveal the persecuted Jews as individuals who thought about what was happening around them and made plans. This focus on Jewish subjectivity and activity is maintained throughout the permanent exhibit.

Libeskind's third path, the axis of continuity, leads to a staircase which takes the visitor up three stories to the beginning of German-Jewish history. The entrance is marked by a neon sign suspended from the ceiling displaying the date in real time in Hebrew and the friendly greeting: 'Welcome to two millennia of German-Jewish history.' Mustroph (2001) and Broder (2001) point out that since most European states trace their national history to the Middle Ages, in this museum, German-Jewish history is longer, in fact, almost twice as long as the history of Germany's neighbours. Is this slick misrepresentation? Or poetic licence – Lackmann's feeling that after the Holocaust, German-Jewish history seems over-dimensional?

Although the exhibit text states that the Jews first came to the Rhineland with the Roman legions, the first German Jew displayed is a replica of a painted medieval male face on a cube of plexiglass mounted on a red pillar. The text underneath identifies Issak, a Jew who brought Charlemagne an elephant from Baghdad in 801.[23] The image of Issak positions Jews as merchants who enriched Germany's rulers by bringing them gifts. The exhibit then takes the visitor through the Middle Ages, followed by sections on Rural and Court Jews. A major focus of the permanent exhibit is Moses Mendelssohn and the Enlightenment. As in the pre-war Jewish Museum, Mendelssohn is displayed as the enlightened Jew who turned outward towards Christians, won their respect, and contributed to both Jewish and German philosophy. But the new Jewish Museum adds another dimension of Mendelssohn's life that is often minimized, if not forgotten: Mendelssohn, the observant Jew whose children converted to Christianity.[24] The Jewish Museum Berlin highlights the interface between Jewish and non-Jewish society. Rather than ignoring converts, or dismissing them as traitors, it explores the complexities of their existence.[25]

Most of the installations focus on what Broder (2001) called 'Good Jews,' the upper middle classes, and especially those who contributed to German culture and industry. And their history is narrated, in places, in the ironic mode. For example, one of the most popular sections of the permanent exhibit, 'In the Bosom of the Family 1850–1933,' highlights the interplay of family, religious observance, and business. It features portraits of some of Germany's leading Jewish bankers and industrialists and their families, home movies from the 1930s, blow-ups of newspaper advertisements for husbands and wives (including a private detective's report on one prospective husband), a children's play area, and a parlour complete with a piano, a vitrine with six menorahs and children's books about Chanukah. A two-metre Christmas tree in this parlour represents another interface between Jewish and Christian culture and changes in observance.

Parlour installations were commonly found in pre-war Jewish and non-Jewish museums. Purin traces the history of living rooms as museum exhibits to 1870 when the *Germanisches Nationalmuseum* (German National Museum) installed displays of old-style German interiors as part of an attempt to make museums more popular. He also points out that in the years around the turn of the twentieth century, ethnographic museums used room installations to emphasize the importance of space in national identity (Purin 1995, 137–9). Hödl points out that with secularization, many Jews began to cultivate family life as a substitute for religion. Maintaining a bourgeois family was also seen as evidence that Jewish life was European and compatible with Christian culture (Hödl 2002, 56–7). Whereas most living room installations are sentimental, in the Jewish Museum Berlin the detective's report and the Christmas tree point to the tensions of pre-war Jewish life in Germany and interrupt any evocation of nostalgia.

The section 'Persecution, Resistance, Extermination 1933–45' tells the story of the Holocaust in Germany, but it centres on Jewish reactions to persecution. These included communal fundraising for Jews who became impoverished, the Jewish organization of artists and performers expelled from German cultural institutions, and the preparations and schooling for emigration and going underground – hiding or living with false identity papers. Though the title of this area includes the word 'resistance,' what's displayed is cultural resistance. The few instances of Jewish political resistance appear in a small corner at the end of the section.

The presentation of the most recent era of German-Jewish history, 'The Present: 1945 until Today,' focuses on the Jewish Holocaust survivors who rebuilt Jewish communities in both post-war Germanies, on their children, and on the relationship of the two generations with the larger society around them. The most dramatic displays are videotapes showing the displaced persons camps, Hannah Arendt discussing the Eichmann trial, and Jews in Frankfurt/Main mounting the stage to stop the opening performance of Fassbinder's play *Garbage, the City and*

Death in 1985. The protagonist of this play, a Jewish real estate specula-
tor who is ruining the centre of the city, is a thinly disguised reference to
Ignaz Bubis, then president of Frankfurt's Jewish Community.[26]

The history ends with another ironic exhibit called '*So einfach war das:
Jüdische Kindheit und Jugend in Deutschland seit 1945*' ('It Was So Simple:
Jewish Childhood and Youth in Germany since 1945'). This collection of
stories about growing up Jewish in the post-war Germanies illustrates
that in fact, it was anything but simple. German-Jewish history, then,
proves to be about survival, and about learning to live with tension.

This grand sweep of 'two millennia of German-Jewish history' is
exhibited in 3,000 objects (about half of them authentic), supplemented
by sounds and activities: wheels to turn, purple drawers (containing
additional information) to pull out, questions to answer, and notes to
write. The clutter has all but hidden Libeskind's voids. The exhibit has
met with criticism from many sides, starting at the opening ceremonies.
Broder's review in *Der Spiegel* noted that it ignores Rosa Luxemburg
and even more importantly, Karl Marx, whose writings changed half
the world and who was a Jewish anti-Semite. 'This kind of figure could
serve to illustrate the entire tragedy of emancipated Jewry ' (Broder
2001, 264, 266). Although Marx was brought into the exhibit in 2005, the
post-war section makes no mention of the philosopher Gershom
Scholem, who in the 1960s wrote about what he called the 'myth of German-Jewish dialogue.' Most of the museum's visitors, though, are not
Jewish and are not familiar with Jewish history. They arrive in record
numbers – 660,000 in 2003 – and return positive comments to the visitor
research department.

Conclusion

The inaugurations of Berlin's two major Jewish museums mark the
beginning and end of the long curve of German and German-Jewish
history, which began with the onset of Nazism and ended with the
post–Cold War emergence of the Berlin Republic. Both museums were
large by the standards of their times and introduced new concepts into
their displays of Jewish history and culture in Germany. The pre-war
museum was the first Jewish museum to foreground modern Jewish
art. The statue of the Biblical warrior guarding the exhibit and the Pal-
estine-oriented displays mark a shift in the sensibilities of the German-
Jewish middle classes, which until the 1930s had identified unambiv-
alently with Germany.

The Jewish Museum Berlin exhibits German-Jewish history in a lightning-bolt building designed by a child of Holocaust survivors. The building and its message have been modified, but this is nonetheless a significant departure from the more common practice in Europe of housing Jewish museums in restored synagogues or in villas of the pre-war wealthy. The museum's explorations of the lives of Jewish converts to Christianity and its ironic displays represent contested positions today. The emphasis on the re-establishment of Jewish life in Germany after 1945 represents a recommitment to Germany.

These two museums didn't merely refract the metamorphoses of the larger society and the Jewish community around them. They became part of those changes. In the 1930s, as Berlin's Jewish artistic and middle classes came under the increasing pressure of Nazism, the Jewish Museum, as an arm of the Jewish Community, provided cultural sustenance. It displayed positive Jewish images and histories as a response to the anti-Semitic culture that occupied public space in Germany. Its later exhibits in particular featured historical examples of strength and perseverance in adversity.[27] Ultimately, Berlin's Jewish Museum shared the fate of the community around it.

Berlin's new Jewish museum began as a grass-roots initiative of local Jews and non-Jews. It then became a section of the municipal museum, and after 1989, a part of the reorganization of Berlin as the national capital of reunified Germany. The museum's concept and institutional arrangements evolved within the debates at the heart of post-war (West) Germany's confrontation with its Nazi past. Within this confrontation, the Jewish museum became associated with national redemption, but also with fantasies of annihilation, represented by the images of lightning bolts and dinosaurs. For two decades, the discussions and conflicts around the museum project seemed like an endless purgatory. Young (2000, 191) saw the German debates around public memorialization of pre-war European Jewry as a positive process. But they produced no consensus regarding the museum's concept or content. The architectural design and plan for the permanent exhibit were provided by Daniel Libeskind, Michael Blumenthal, and Shaike Weinberg, three Jewish men who had some European background but were working in the United States, and by Ken Gorbey, a New Zealander with no ties to Jewishness or to Germany. On the basis of this cultural development aid from overseas, the Jewish museum took shape. Its realization became a part of nation building in the early years of the Berlin Republic. And today the Jewish Museum in Berlin is one of Germany's three federal museums.

In this museum, size is an important part of the message. The dimensions of the Libeskind building, the number of installations and display objects, the two-millennia expanse of German-Jewish history, and the three-day, 850-guest gala opening all point to the size of the problem the Germans were faced with. (Exhibiting the legacy of Nazism is not for the faint of heart.) Like the Berlin Republic around it, the Jewish Museum Berlin is not unproblematic, but it is large and solid. The lightning-bolt effect of Libeskind's zinc building has been softened on the outside by landscaping and in the courtyard by picnic tables (and jazz concerts in the summer). Inside, Libeskind's angular walls are covered in many places by large red, yellow, and orange panels, which lend warmth to displays of Jews struggling against German anti-Semitism. Libeskind's voids all but disappear behind the colour and clutter. In the gift shop, the zigzag logo decorates t-shirts, baseball caps, writing pads, and shopping bags.

The Jewish Museum Berlin is about exorcising the ghost of the Holocaust and removing the shadow it cast over German history. This is accomplished through clothing a violent history and a tense present in warm colors, and by providing a visitor-friendly environment. The ultramodern building by a world-class Jewish architect is perhaps the greatest attraction. In 2006, Berlin is less than a totally happy European capital. Economic stagnation and restructuring continue to cause high unemployment and to lower the standard of living of many who are still working. The European Union evolving around Germany is bringing frustration, anxieties, and fewer positive results. In 2005, the salaries of many of the museum's employees were slashed. But thousands of schoolchildren, local museum goers, and foreign tourists walk through the German-Jewish history that is now part of the national history of the Berlin Republic, seven days a week. And, more often than not, they leave wearing a T-shirt with a zigzag on the front. Jews in Germany are no longer a problem.

Notes

1 The term 'restructuring' in this chapter refers to a basic change in social structure that resulted from deliberate social engineering on the part of an elite. I feel the term is appropriate in speaking about Nazi Germany, and if it also raises questions about social change today, all the better. .

2 By using the phrase 'the modern approach to Jewish culture' I mean that

instead of merely displaying antiques, Berlin's Jewish Museum focused on modern Jewish art, commissioning and displaying works of contemporary Jewish artists. This was unique in the world of Jewish museums, and is discussed later in this chapter.

3 Europe's first Jewish museum was established in Vienna in 1895. Jewish museums appeared in Danzig in 1904, Prague in 1906, Warsaw in 1910, Amsterdam in 1932, and in other cities as well. The only Jewish museum the Nazis did not dissolve was the one in Prague, which was expanded to become a 'central Jewish museum' intended to display the inanimate remains of an extinct race (Ostow 2003).

4 The history of this museum has been pieced together by Simon (2000). The discussion that follows relies heavily on his work.

5 These goals were shared by the Jewish museums in Vienna and Prague as well (Ostow 2003 and 2006).

6 The philosopher Moses Mendelssohn was the major figure of the Jewish enlightenment in eighteenth-century Germany. An observant Jew, he was nonetheless a leader in Germany's movement for religious tolerance, and a spokesperson for opening Jewish society to the larger culture around it. During the Cold War, a bust of Moses Mendelssohn was on display in the buildings of the Jewish Communities of both East and West Berlin. As a figure associated with one of the most positive eras of local history, Mendelssohn approached the status of patron saint, or even, in anthropological terms, a totem. And since he fathered a large family, of which several members converted, many Jewish and non-Jewish Berliners are literally his descendants.

7 The *Wissenschaft des Judentums* was a nineteenth- and early-twentieth-century movement, based in Germany, to apply modern practices of scholarship to the study of Jewish religion and culture.

8 Arnold Zadikow (1884–1943) was a Jewish sculptor in Munich. For his biography, see Simon 2000, 46–8 and 148–50; and Schwarz 2001, 297. The statue of David, his most important work, was lost during World War II.

9 For a discussion of images of Jewish and non-Jewish bodies, see Gilman 1991.

10 All three went to Palestine.

11 This was the first nation-wide pogrom of the Nazi regime against the Jews of Germany. The museum was officially dissolved in December 1939.

12 Güntzer was referring to the Berlin Museum on the Lindenstrasse in Kreuzberg. These and all subsequent quotations from Güntzer are from an interview with him on 18 July 1996.

13 For a discussion of the role of these kinds of groups in cultural politics, see

Bodemann 1994, 57–8. He refers to groups composed of Jews, people with Jewish ancestry, people who define themselves as Jews but don't meet Orthodox Jewish religious requirements, wannabe Jews, and non-Jews who concern themselves with Jewish culture and, particularly with Holocaust related matters, as 'Judaizing terrain.'

14 Vera Bendt, personal communication, July 1996. German sociologist Erhard Stölting located Bendt's idea in the post-war (West) German concept of the 'Begegnungsort' (place of encounter). It is a site for a 'Begegnung' (encounter) – a kind of love-in, but a love-in with deep intellectual and spiritual dimensions. The idea is that people who hate each other should come together to work through their problems with each other, and ultimately come to love each other. Personal communication with Stölting, July 1996.

15 Güntzer added that Jews have the right to exhibit their history from their point of view and to have it paid for by the public, but that should be done in the Centrum Judaicum, the museum of the Berlin Jewish Community.

16 Offe (2000) points to the firehouse as a disguised reference to *Kristallnacht* (The Night of Broken Glass), when throughout Germany, synagogues were set on fire by Nazis and other Germans.

17 Personal communication with John Breuilly, 8 April 1999.

18 Funding had originally been designated for building a Jewish museum, but once construction began, the Berlin Museum started to think of housing other collections there as well. Part of the unification of Berlin was the unification of its two municipal museums - the Märkische Museum in the East and the Berlin Museum in the West. Space became tight, and the city claimed that Heinz Galinski had agreed to a 'Mischnutzung' (mixed use) of the building in exchange for funding for a Jewish high school (gymnasium). This claim was contested by both the Society of Friends of the Jewish Museum (Gesellschaft für ein Jüdische Museum in Berlin e.V.) and Berlin's Jewish Community.

19 The identity of *Finanzminister*, ironically, assigns Blumenthal the traditional role of Jews in pre-modern Germany as financial advisors, money lenders, and money minters to royalty and aristocracy.

20 Interview with Jeshajahu Weinberg 27 August 1998, Berlin.

21 This was particularly evident in the opening of the American Academy in Berlin in 1998.

22 Located in a city of 3.7 million inhabitants, Te Papa hosts approximately 4 million visitors a year (Reiche 2001).

23 But the small print on the plexiglass dates the face at 1170, some 350 years later.

24 The text points out that four of Mendelssohn's six children converted.

25 The museum has maintained that this is an important part of German-Jewish history in the face of criticism, particularly from Jews who view exogamy and conversion as forms of treason. See Mark 2001.

26 Fassbinder's *Garbage, the City and Death* also sparked debates among Jewish and non-Jewish civil libertarians about the relative importance of prohibiting anti-Semitic incitement and protecting freedom of speech.

27 In 1937, the museum mounted an exhibit on Don Jizchak Abrabanel who led the Jewish community into exile at the time of its expulsion from Spain. A second exhibit featured Akiba Eger, an orthodox scholar and rabbi in Germany.

References

Anderson, Benedict. 1983. *Imagined communities: Reflections on the origins and spread of nationalism.* London: Verso.

Barzel, Amnon. 1995. *Ein Jüdisches Museum für Berlin: Konzeption und räumliche Plannung.* Berlin: Stiftung Stadtmuseum Jüdisches Museum.

– 1996. *Zum Jüdischen Museum Berlin.* Unpublished document.

Bendt, Vera. 1987. Das Jüdische Museum. In *Wegweiser durch das jüdische Berlin: Geschichte und Gegenwart*, ed. Vera Bendt, Stefi Jersch-Wenzel, Thomas Wenzel, and Nicola Galliner, 200–9. Berlin: Nicolai.

– 1992. Das Integrationsmodell. *Museumsjournal* 11 (April): 28–31.

– 1995. *Daniel Libeskind in seinem Verhältnis zur Museumskonzeption.* Unpublished manuscript.

Bennett, Tony. 1995. *The birth of the museum: History, theory, politics.* New York: Routledge.

Bodemann, Michal. 1994. A reemergence of German Jewry? In *Reemerging Jewish culture in Germany: Life and literature since 1989*, ed. Sander Gilman and Karen Remmler, 46–61. New York: New York University Press.

– 1996. *Gedächtnistheater. Die jüdische Gemeinschaft und ihre deutsche Erfindung.* Mit einem Beitrag von Jael Geis. Berlin: Rotbuch.

Broder, Henryk. 2001. Es ist vergeblich. *Der Spiegel* 39, 24 September.

Cohen, Richard. 1998. *Jewish icons: Art and society in modern Europe.* Berkeley: University of California Press.

Cohn-Wiener, Ernst. 1929. *Die jüdische Kunst - Ihre Geschichte von den Anfangen bis zur Gegenwart.* Berlin: Martin Wasservogel Verlag.

Fredrickson, George. 2002. *Racism: A short history.* Princeton: Princeton University Press.

Gilman, Sander. 1991. *The Jew's body.* New York: Routledge.

– 2000. Are Jews white? Or, the history of the nose job. In *Theories of race and racism: A reader*, ed. Les Back and John Solomos, 229–37. London: Routledge.

Henry, Frances. 1971. *Victims and neighbors: A small town in Nazi Germany remembered*. South Hadley, MA: Bergin and Garvey.

Hödl, Klaus. 2002. Jüdische Identität und Museum. Das Wiener Jüdische Museum im 19. Jahrhundert. *Transvaal* 1 (2002): 47–67.

Hughes, Everett. 1971. The *Gleichschaltung* of the German Statistical Yearbook. In *The sociological eye: Selected papers on work, self and the study of society*, 516–23. Chicago: Aldine Atherton.

Jacobson, Jacob. 1928. *Jüdisches Jahrbuch für Groß-Berlin*, 2nd ed., pp. 88ff. Quoted in Simon 2000, 27 and 163, n. 48.

Kugelmann, Cilly. 1996. Das Jüdische als Exponat der Zeitgeschichte. *Wiener Jahrbuch für Jüdische Geschichte, Kultur und Museumswesen* 2:43–56.

Lackmann, Thomas. 2000. *Jewrassic Park: Wie baut man (k)ein Jüdisches Museum in Berlin*. Berlin: Philo.

Mark, Jonathan. 2001. Exhibition of Apology. *New York Jewish Week*, 14 September.

Mock, Karen. 1996. Anti-semitism in Canada: Realities, remedies, and implications for anti-racism. In *Perspectives on racism and the human services sector: A case for change*, ed. Carl James, 120–33. Toronto: University of Toronto Press.

Mustroph, Tom. 2001. Das Leben geht in den Mittelpunkt. *Neues Deutschland*, 11 September.

Naumann, Michael. 1999. Interview in *Die Woche*, 22 January.

Offe, Sabine. 2000. *Ausstellungen, Einstellungen, Entstellungen: Jüdische Museen in Deutschland und Österreich*. Berlin: Philo.

Ostow, Robin. 2003. Religion as treasure: Exhibits of rituals and ritual objects in Prague's Jewish Museum. In *Der Kanon und die Sinne. Religionsästhetik als academische Disziplin*, ed. Susanne Lanwerd, 152–68. Luxembourg: Études Luxembourgeoises d'Histoire & de Sciences.

– 2006. Longing and belonging – home and exile. The Jewish Museum in Vienna: An anti-Heimat Museum? or a Heimat Museum with an accent? In *Der 'Virtuelle Jude' – Konstruktionen des Jüdischen*, ed. Klaus Hödl, 71–82. Innsbruck: Studien Verlag.

Purin, Bernhard. 1995. Isidore Kaufmann's little world: The 'Sabbath Room' in the Jewish Museum of Vienna. In *Rabbiner, Bocher, Talmudschuler: Bilder des Wiener Malers Isidore Kaufmann 1853–1921*, ed. Tobias Natter, 128–45. Wien: Jüdisches Museum der Stadt Wien.

Reiche, Jürgen. 2001. Te Papa Tongarewa oder Welche Vorbilder eigentlich hat das Jüdische Museum Berlin? *Museumsjournal* 3 (15): 4–6.

Rosenthal, James Jaacov. 1980. Letter to Hermann Simon, 9 June.

– 1982. 'Letzte Post' – Museumweihe 1933. *Nachrichtenblatt des Verbandes der Jüdischen Gemeinden der DDR*. Dresden, December. Quoted in Simon 2000, 39, 165, n. 75.

Schwarz, Karl. 2001. *Jüdische Kunst - Jüdische Künstler: Erinnerungen des ersten Direktors des Berliner Jüdischen Museums*, ed. with introduction by Chana Schütz and Hermann Simon. Berlin: Hentrich & Hentrich.

Simon, Hermann. 2000. *Das Berliner Jüdische Museum in der Oranienburger Straße*. Berlin: Hentrich & Hentrich.

van Alphen, Ernst. 1997. *Caught by history: Holocaust effects in contemporary art, literature, and history*. Stanford, CA: Stanford University Press.

Young, James E. 2000. *At memory's edge: After-images of the holocaust in contemporary art and architecture*. New Haven: Yale University Press.

Zadikow, Arnold. 1950. In *Mitteilungen der Congregation Beth Hillel*, no. 78. Quoted in Simon 2000, 48 and n. 166.

PART FOUR

Nation, Citizenship, and Belonging

Historically, Canadian national identity has been defined as white, despite the presence of racialized people. At Confederation in 1867, the national project was to meld Canada's different regional identities into a nation with a distinct culture and identity, but this attempt to homogenize and unify was riddled with tensions because it was both elitist and racist. The nineteenth-century Canada First movement believed in the superiority of the English-speaking, Celtic, Teutonic, and Scandinavian people over those who were French-speaking, Métis, and French Canadian. Such a definition excluded some groups from the 'cultural nation' (Hoerder 1999, 11). Similarly, farming families were made more welcome than craftsmen and immigrant labourers, although all paid taxes and contributed to the national economy.

Gatekeepers like Clifford Sifton, minister of the interior in Prime Minister Laurier's government, 'never included all inhabitants of their state into the nation, rather, they propounded a special role for their culture and class' (Hoerder 1999, 12). European citizens adopted this exclusionary construction of nation as they recorded their everyday routines in life writings. In these narratives, black people are described as 'curiosities' and only occasionally as neighbours or co-workers (Hoerder 1999, 285). Asians – Chinese, Japanese, and Indians – were absent from these accounts because they were compelled to work in job ghettos with members of their own communities, were excluded from almost all social interactions, and lived isolated lives away from the dominant white society. Aboriginal people were sometimes mentioned in these accounts, but only in passing.

Canada was constructed as a white nation through the nineteenth century, but from the mid-twentieth century the identity of Canada as a nation and people came to be redefined by the presence, participation, and disputations of racialized citizens. Political changes in the 1960s consequent to the Royal Commission on Bilingualism and Biculturalism recognized the presence of white ethnic populations that were neither English nor French. The formal enunciation by political leaders of a Canada that was multicultural within a bilingual framework gave recognition, however limited, to the presence of white and racialized groups in Canada. The documentation by racialized groups of their absence from histories, their silent omission from national stories, and their marginal presence in various discourses whether in the media or elsewhere have created a new and different realization of who 'we' are as a people and as Canadians. 'Modern political communities are bound together through representation in which the community is itself an actor; and what binds each of us to the community – and thus to each other – is our participation, through our national identity, in that action' (Appiah 2005, 245).

Citizenship is a legal status nations confer on their populations that gives them rights but also imposes obligations and responsibilities. In Canada, immigrants can become citizens within a few years of their arrival. Potentially they are equal to all others and can enjoy the benefits that citizenship confers, despite their different race. Yet legal citizenship rights, such as the ability to vote, are to be distinguished from the substantive exercise of rights and responsibilities of citizenship. In this section, the authors contend that citizenship is inflected by race, class, and gender, making some more equal than others and circumscribing the rights to equality of racialized populations. Citizenship, academics argue, is also experienced subjectively through a sense of belonging to a group, community, movement, and the nation. However, for racialized women the sense of belonging to the Canadian nation is negated in everyday life by the social, economic, and political exclusions and marginalization they encounter. These routine expressions and reminders of continuing inequalities, racism, and discrimination are played out within social movements, despite their members' greater consciousness of issues of inequality. Consequently, participation in progressive movements, such as the women's movement in Canada, is problematic for racialized people and limits their ability to be 'good citizens.'

The contemporary usage of terms such as 'borders' and 'boundaries,' 'exclusions' and 'inclusions' directs our attention to the fault lines that divide people whose cultures and identities seem different from that which is defined as 'Canadian.' In 'The Conundrum of Inclusion: Racialized Women in Public Policy Reports,' I show the difficulties of inclusion by examining the development of feminist theories with particular reference to Canada. Feminist theories have struggled with the need to reconcile the many differences of identity among women and to formulate some understanding of their varied oppressions. In the 1970s, the exclusion of race from feminist theories alienated racialized women, who challenged the focus on gender. Their critiques eventually led to a better understanding of the intersection of oppressions and to the specific forms in which they are manifested in groups of women. Over time, however, feminist theories have become complex and very abstract.

In this chapter, I juxtapose feminist theories with their application in governmental reports and in commissioned research by the public policy research committee of the Status of Women Canada. I start by documenting the exclusion of racialized women and their concerns from the 1970 Royal Commission on the Status of Women. Subsequent attempts to include the diverse identities of women have proven to be conflictual and highly politicized (for example, on the Canadian Panel on Violence Against Women 1991). Status of Women Canada has attempted to reconcile theories of intersectionality and the range of identities that it generates by selectively choosing to document the concerns of the most disadvantaged women. They have commissioned reports on specific groups of women (such as Aboriginal women and immigrant women). These reports reveal that oppressions continue to bedevil women and that some Canadians have yet to realize their dream of equality.

In 'From Africa to Canada: Bordered Spaces, Border Crossings, and Imagined Communities,' Gillian Creese explores ways in which racialized women who have recently migrated to Vancouver negotiate the complex and contradictory processes of belonging. The discourses of Canadian nation building imagine community through narratives of a multicultural immigrant society, yet 'Canadian' remains a bordered space that only partially admits racialized immigrants. Immigrants are thus compelled to negotiate a series of ongoing and seemingly unending border crossings within Canadian society. The educational credentials, work experiences, accents, and cultural practices of immigrants exclude them from the 'imagined' Canadian nation; consequently, they experience (re)settlement as an uneven and contradictory process and 'belonging' in Canada as an uncertain and ambiguous notion.

Racialized individuals have interrogated the ideology and practice of race and have shown that whiteness is a race, albeit a privileged one.

Theories of identity, subjectivity, and voice do not always address the difficulties of transgressing the colour line. At the same time, academic discourses from many disciplines make the point that struggling against racism is not only the responsibility of victims or of racialized populations in general, but of all of us who believe in a socially just society. Whereas racialized individuals have documented the race line that excludes them economically, politically, and socially, we know less about the experiences of white people who attempt to make common cause with racialized groups. In 'Being White and Thinking Black: An Interview with Frances Henry,' I examine the difficulties encountered by white scholars who research and write on racism. I review theories of social construction, subjectivity, and hybridity to portray the dilemma of racial identity and scholarship. Through an interview with Henry, a distinguished academic who has studied racism in Canadian society, the chapter questions current beliefs about perspective, voice, and race. Frances Henry is a white Jewish woman who experienced the Nazis' treatment of Jews as a child, married a black man, and has mixed-race children. Henry's colour and her research on racism locate her in a contradictory and difficult situation, and I ask if her childhood experience of being a victim of the Nazis gave her a particular affinity for studying racism against blacks. The interview traces the slowness to include race in university curricula, the evolution of theories on 'the insider' versus 'the outsider,' cynicism among the public about research on race, the skeptical attitude of the Canadian judicial system towards accepting expert testimony on racism, white/black personal and professional relations, and the dilemma of being a white woman raising mixed-race children.

References

Hoerder, Dirk. 1999. *Creating societies: Immigrant lives in Canada*. Montreal: McGill-Queen's University Press.

10 The Conundrum of Inclusion: Racialized Women in Public Policy Reports

VIJAY AGNEW

Equality is an ideal, but inequality is often the experience of many racialized women. Scholars have interrogated inequalities based on race, class, and gender, along with their innumerable intersections, and have documented the theoretical and empirical difficulties of overcoming exclusions and becoming inclusive, as the chapters in this collection indicate. Historically, the rise of nation-states has sometimes led to identifying segments of population as the Other, thereby rationalizing their exclusion from the exercise of the rights of citizenship. In contemporary Canadian society, such invidious distinctions have been eliminated from formal citizenship rights; constitutionally, all citizens are equal, without distinctions of race, class or gender. However, there is disagreement among scholars about how to define citizenship so as to include not only its formal expression, but also the individual's ability to exercise substantially the political, social, economical and psychological rights and responsibilities it confers.

In the past, citizenship often assumed as its norm the masculine, white, heterosexual, and able-bodied (among other things) individual, thereby implicitly excluding and marginalizing others. For example, exclusions in the early part of the twentieth century took the form of discriminatory immigration legislation, labour practices, and the right to vote. In contemporary times, scholars avidly debate the definition and meaning of citizenship in the context of the Charter of Rights and Freedoms, which recognizes equality of all citizens and prohibits discrimination based on identities (Tastsoglou and Dobrowolsky 2006). Will Kymlicka, in his seminal work *Multicultural Citizenship*, notes that citizenship is 'an inherently group-differentiated notion' (1995, 124). Citizenship is multilayered, multifaceted and 'inflected by identity, social positioning, cultural assumptions, institutional practices and a sense of belonging' (Yuval-Davis and Werbner 1999, 4). Furthermore, it is fluid and dynamic, changing with time and social context.

'A contemporary "politics of citizenship" must take into account the role which the social movements have played in expanding the claims to rights and entitlements to new areas' (Rosaldo 1999, 255). The politics of citizenship addresses issues of class and inequality, as well as questions about membership posed by feminist and anti-racist movements. For example, the feminist struggle led to the recognition of women's rights to formal citizenship in Canada; however, making it a substantive right by working to eliminate marginalization and exclusion has been an ongoing exercise that has peaked and waned over time. '[Citizenship] opens up spaces and arenas of freedom – of conflict, unpredictability, intimacy, the right to be different – while restricting and structuring these spaces by procedural hedges about limits. It orders conflict, channels and tames it; it labels and classifies collective difference; it determines how, where and when difference may be legitimately 'represented,' and who counts as 'different' in the political arena, itself a social construct' (Werbner and Yuval-Davis 1999, 2).

This chapter begins with a historical overview of the dilemmas raised in working towards substantive equality for racialized women within a feminist context. I argue that the recognition of formal rights based on sex exposes other dilemmas, such as the theoretical understanding of who is a woman and the empirical application of this understanding in public policy discussions and formulations. Diversity in feminist conceptualizations (and theories) of gender, identity, location, epistemology, and discourse has opened up the debate about diversity in interpretation and application. The feminist and anti-racist movements have moulded the subjectivity of their members, encouraging them to assert their rights and protest marginalization and exclusion. 'Citizenship as a subjectivity is deeply dialogical, encapsulating specific historically inflected cultural and social assumptions about similarity and difference' (Werbner and Yuval-Davis 1999, 3). In the post–World War II period the feminist movement in Canada demanded a more equitable distribution of resources, a greater accountability of public policies to the specific needs of women, and a recognition of and responsiveness to women's identities through non-discrimination. Inequality and social position are thus critical in the study of citizenship.

This chapter also demonstrates the nature of inequalities within the feminist movement and the difficulties of representing all women in public policy debates. However, despite numerous problems, the solution does not lie in abandoning the debate about rights and responsibilities; rather, such problems indicate the need to reformulate the debate in ways that serve the most disadvantaged women and make it possible for them to exercise formal and substantive citizenship. Following a brief survey of the feminist movement in Canada since the 1970s, I analyse two key Royal Commission reports – one on the status of women and the other on violence against women – to show how our understanding has evolved regarding gender and the complexity of integrating diverse individuals with varying identities to a common cause. Reports from 2000 onwards indicate that for some women, achieving gender equality remains a distant dream.

The Sex and Gender Divide of the 1970s

The questions 'Who is a woman?' and 'What are her rights?' would have been easy to answer three decades ago but are now a matter of intense discussion among feminists and others. Feminist theories have evolved with our understanding of women's experiences. The word 'gender' was popularized by the second wave of feminism when it sought to distinguish sex, or the physical attributes that defined people as males and females, from the socio-cultural meanings assigned to the body, such as masculinity and femininity. The distinction that was made between sex and gender was empowering for women because it disputed the notion that 'biology is destiny' and suggested instead that societal norms had constrained their freedom to develop their human potential. Women's lack of participation in politics, for instance, had less to do with their sex than with the norms imposed by society on their bodies. Feminists went on to argue that the public and private spheres are not discrete and isolated but are interconnected, and that women's lack of power in one area leads to their subordination in the other. Society has assigned differential values to the work (paid and unpaid) that women perform and this has had consequences for their subordinate status in society. It was invigorating for women to discover that what had been previously viewed by society as women's lack of achievements was in reality a matter of lack of opportunities. In this initial phase, feminists tended to minimize differences of sex and instead privileged gender.

In the 1980s, it became part of the common wisdom to assert that gender was a socially constructed category. Postmodern and post-structuralist feminists went on to argue that gender is not a stable category but temporary, fluid, and shifting. The meanings attached to gender are not universal; rather, they are specific and derive from particular social contexts, in relationship to other subjects. Every society and culture understands, configures, and represents gender identities in particular ways. For example, the identity of a Chinese woman is different in China than it is in a Chinatown in a North American city or in a suburb of Toronto. Similarly, a woman's power or its lack thereof is contextually defined rather than being constant and fixed.

The sex/gender distinction that had initially helped women to answer so many questions about themselves, individually and collectively, came to be viewed with scepticism as feminists' knowledge and understanding about women's lives evolved. Sex and gender were perceived as binary categories and therefore problematic, since one category was usually privileged over the other. Feminist deconstructionists argued against the binary distinction between sex and gender and asserted that the body and its functioning are formed not in isolation or outside culture, but in interaction with society and culture (Andermahr, Lovell, and Wolkowitz 2000, 103). They added that sex is only one of the many distinctions that constructs gender, but rejected the notion that it functions 'along with' or 'alongside' race, class, nationality, ethnicity, or any other category; rather, they stated that gender is constructed through and by these distinctions.

The sex/gender distinction also came to be discussed as the difference between essentialist and anti-essentialist perspectives. Essentialist arguments claim that there are innate differences between men and women and reject the notion that gender is socially constructed. Feminists like Mary Daly have argued for a unique female identity, while some French feminists have supported the concept of a uniquely female mode of discourse. In North America, such thinking came to be known as 'women's ways of knowing,' 'women's knowledge,' and 'women's experiences.'

Anti-essentialists, however, assert that patriarchy positions women as 'other,' which signifies difference. Judith Butler, one of the foremost theorists of deconstructive feminism, argues that 'gender distinctions only have meaning within a phallocentric order built on a system of binary differences' (1990). Gender identity is maintained through the fixed opposition of male and female, with each category defined by its difference from the other. Butler suggests that far from being innate, 'gender constitutes a set of gestures which are performed upon the surface of the body' (Gamble 2001, 200). Allison Weir explains that Butler's fundamental claim is 'that any identity is always and only the product of a system or logic of power/language which generates identities as functions of binary oppositions, and seeks to conceal its own workings by making those identities appear natural' (Weir 2000, 44). Hélène Cixous and Luce Irigaray note that 'female bodies are highly metaphorical and ironic, and do not necessarily denote belief in the existence of a fundamental female identity' (Gamble 2001, 225). Such interpretations suggest that there is no integral overlap between sex and gender and that, for example, a person with a woman's body can adopt masculinity (as a gendered norm) through transsexual, transgendered identities.

Butler favours dismantling the sex/gender divide, but other feminists like Evelyn Fox Keller and Anne Phillips are for retaining the distinction. Fox argues that given the exigencies of the human reproductive system, every society needs some way of distinguishing the body and has built a superstructure of cultural meaning around this socially necessary function. Similarly, Phillips supports maintaining the distinction between sex and gender, for 'we will continue to need some way of disentangling the differences that are inevitable from those that are chosen, and from those that are simply imposed (qtd in Andermahr, Lovell, and Wolkowitz 2000, 104). However, despite such theoretical debates, the social understanding within a particular culture or society of the characteristics that constitutes a female body and its associated norms is intuitively grasped and followed in practice by its members.

Historicizing Gender and Race

In the 1970s, feminist theory was criticized for ignoring racism and treating gender as a universal and ahistorical category that encompassed the experiences of all women. Racialized women had adopted 1970s feminist slogans that identified all men as 'the enemy' and all women as suffering 'common oppression.' But after the initial enthusiasm for articulating the common experiences of gender, some feminists began to critically examine these slogans and their assumption that gender represents the primary source of women's oppression. This reexamination spawned a vigorous and far-ranging critique of feminist theories in Britain, the United States, and Canada. Racialized women used historical data to demonstrate that class and race were as powerful as gender in oppressing and exploiting women (Agnew 1996; Bannerji 1997; Calliste and Dei 2000).

Race, like gender, is socially constructed in the sense that the dominant group in a society, characterized by unequal social relations with others, selects certain physical traits and attributes significance to them. These traits, such as skin colour, shape of eyes, and hair texture, are then associated with moral, psychological, or social norms and values. Over time, the association of physical characteristics with a set of values comes to be seen as natural, normal, and inevitable. The correlation between people's physical traits and their encoded attributes does not have to be scientifically established, and indeed proof is irrelevant. The association between physical traits and norms and values derives its strength from the widely accepted belief in race. The content of these socially constructed concepts changes and shifts over time (Agnew 1996; Fleras and Kunz 2001). (The term 'race' is extensively explored in my introduction to this volume and by Aiken in Chapter 2). The word 'racialized' came to be commonly used by women to refer to their identity, stigmatization, and ostracism as a discrete racial category characterized by traits or attributes that were thought to be typical (Ontario Human Rights Commission 2005, 9).

Racialized women were concerned about theorizing the relationship between race and gender. Angela Davis and bell hooks were among the first black women in the United States to question how race, along with gender, oppressed women. Hooks's *Feminist Theory from Margin to Center* (1984) and *Talking Back: Thinking Feminist, Thinking Black* (1988) were highly influential in starting a debate among racialized women on their own experiences in North American and European societies in the period following World War II. Hooks argued that racial identity and racism distinguish the experience of black and, by implication, other racialized women and are as significant as gender in oppressing them. Black women, she maintained, look to the comfort of home and family relations as a safe harbour from the racism of the larger society. Gender oppresses them, no doubt, but only in tandem with race and class. In Canada, this debate was taken up by feminists such as Himani Bannerji, Linda Carty, Dionne Brand, Agnes Calliste, Roxanna Ng, and Akua Benjamin.

Writings of racialized women in the United States, Britain, and Canada ignited a vigorous debate on the relationship between race, gender, and class. New insights into other structures of oppression put white women on the defensive, and they were stricken with guilt about having been ethnocentric in viewing the family and society from their own specific location as white, university-educated women (Segal 1987).

Reflecting on the debates of the 1980s, Akua Benjamin notes that 'as women came to question their feminism,' they entered 'a real battleground,' for there was 'a lot of conflict and a lot of turmoil' (interview in Rebick 2005, 139). It was only over time, and with much discussion, that the relationship between the different structures of oppression could be understood. For example, the question arose as to whether there was a hierarchy of oppression, in the sense that some structures of oppression might be more significant than others. If that was not so, then could women add up the many structures of oppression that intersected in their identities? Elizabeth Spelman strongly opposed such an additive method, arguing instead that women's identities and their oppression are integrated and inseparable. She noted that 'one's gender identity is not related to one's racial and class identity as the parts of pop-bead necklaces are related, separable and insertable in other "strands" with different racial and class "parts"' (Spelman 1988, 15).

Some forms of oppression seem to be experienced by all women, while others are not. The critical issue was to seriously account for the differences. Audre Lorde has observed that it is the social significance attached to these differences, rather than the differences themselves, that forms the basis of exclusion and separation; it is historically created social differences that divide women and distort the relations between them (Rothenberg 1990, 42–54). By accounting for differences among women, however, we broadened the categories and structures of oppression to include other aspects such as sexuality, age, and disability. Furthermore, these types of oppression were seen to intersect in different permutations in people's identities, adding to the complexity of the debate. By the 1980s, it was widely acknowledged that there are many axes of women's oppression and that these are both integrated and interrelated. Thereafter, it became the norm to use the term 'intersectionality' to refer to the cross-cutting nature of oppression in different identities.

Diversity in Knowledge Construction

Feminist epistemologists have deconstructed knowledge to show how power relations are embedded in language and to identify a method for posing insightful questions about women and by women that document the 'truths' of their socio-political oppression and marginalization. Lorraine Code provides the following critique of androcentric knowledge: 'Theories and methodologies in the social sciences "objectify" the human subjects they study. Experiments are designed to predict human behavior and to analyze it quantitatively, for only behavior amenable to statistical analysis is judged worthy of scientific study. The methodology produces explanations of personality and of social structures that take into account neither the consciousness of the subjects studied nor the meanings and interpretations of their experiences for these subjects' (Code 1991, 34). Instead of seeking universal truths, feminist epistemologists prefer to document contextualized, partial truths about specific groups of women. In doing this they hope to accord women authority as knowers and producers of knowledge and thus empower them (Code 2000, 170).

The individual's identity, location, and positioning determine her perspective and therefore her discovery of truth. Sandra Harding, a highly respected philosopher, has argued that a woman's experiences provide her with a unique starting point, or as she later called it, 'a feminist standpoint' for discovering certain biases in science (Harding, 1987). Dorothy Smith's seminal work questions the seemingly normal, the routine events and relationships of our daily lives and the power relations that structure them. Feminists, she recommends, should ask questions that are generated by women's lives and address their concerns; in other words, feminists need to view themselves and society from a woman's perspective. In explaining how the standpoint of women in the everyday world might be explored, she writes that 'so far as their everyday worlds are concerned, we rely entirely on what women tell us, what people tell us, about what they do and what happens. But we cannot rely upon them for an understanding of the relations that shape and determine the everyday. Here then lies our work as social scientists, for the investigation of these relations and the exploration of the ways they are present in the everyday are and must be a specialized enterprise, a work, the work of a social scientist' (Smith 1987, 110). Some questions that arise from such an approach are: 'Is the feminist standpoint an essentialist understanding of gender?' 'Does such thinking polarize male/female identities and make them binary categories?' 'Is cognitive authority associated only with gender, or does it also include race, class, sexuality, culture, and age, among many other differences?'

Patricia Collins, a black sociologist, disputes the idea that gender provides insight into women's everyday lives; rather, she argues strenuously in favour of acknowledging the differences in women's lives. She rejects gender as a unified category of women, noting instead the need for research on black women to include questions derived from their identities and experiences (1991). Harding observes that different cultures organize the production of knowledge in different ways and may be better able to address questions that relate closely to their experiences (1998). Ristock and Pennel support a feminist standpoint, since it is 'grounded in awareness of women's subordination [and] ... makes for a more comprehensive and ethical understanding than is possible for their masculinist counterparts, even those who hold emancipatory goals' (Ristock and Pennel 1996, 5). But Gamble points out that 'none of the research into the "difference and dominance" tradition begins to address how language, personal identity and social context interact or how that interaction sustains unequal gender relations' (Gamble 2001, 146).

Feminist standpoint theory is problematic in another way: if there is no generic woman and few experiences common to all women, there can be no location from which to speak for all women, even within a specific group. Gayatri Spivak, the distinguished deconstructionist, questions the assumption that a woman's identity means that she speaks for women from a position of 'knowledge.' She prefers instead to highlight the cultural and discursive construction of female subjectivity and cautions against the urge to claim to know or speak on behalf of other women on the basis of shared or common identities (Spivak 1990).

Politics of Discourse: Names and Naming

The emphasis on the social construction of identity – and thus on language and discourse – has drawn some feminists to Michel Foucault's theories of how power relations construct knowledge. Henry and Tator explain that 'discourse is most closely associated with language and with the written or oral text ... Discourse is the way in which language is used socially to convey broad historical meanings. It is language identified by the social conditions of its use, by who is using it and under what conditions' (Henry and Tator 2002, 25). Language is the site for the cultural production of identity but it can never be neutral, objective, or detached, because it is never free from the socio-cultural and economic influences that produced it.

As racialized women engaged in discourse analysis, they discovered that they were largely absent from discourses on feminism and ethnicity in Canada up to the early 1980s (Agnew 1996). When they were discussed, they were located as marginalized 'others' and were represented in a stereotypical and racist manner. More often than not, they were perceived as homogeneous groups rather than as individuals with diverse identities and experiences. Asian and black women energetically took on the task of documenting their history. But the first stumbling block was the issue of 'naming' themselves. They too encountered the difficulty of not appropriating the experience of other more disadvantaged women and speaking for the entire group. Instead, they had to admit to speaking partial truths that were limited in their applications.

The discourse by racialized women on naming themselves is an example of the politics of disempowered women speaking for themselves and resisting the oppression of white, middle-class feminists and the rest of society. There was disagreement not only between racialized women and society at large, but also among racialized women themselves as to the most appropriate term that would incorporate both their race and their immigrant status.

Historically, the terms that have been used in the post–World War II period have been 'visible minority women,' 'non-white women,' 'immigrant women,' 'Third World women,' and more recently, 'women of colour,' 'black women,' and 'racialized women.' In deconstructing these terms, we found norms and assumptions underlying them that suggested that these women were outsiders, foreigners, inferior, and different. The term 'visible minority women' was criticized because it attributed significance to skin colour and implied that the women it referred to were not only different but also inferior. Referring to women as 'non-white' was problematic because it carried the assumption that white women are the norm. The term 'immigrant women' was supposed to be neutral, objective, and polite, but it encoded racist and class distinctions between these women and the rest of society. The label 'Third World women' was used to refer to women who came from poor countries, spoke English hesitatingly, and were employed in manual jobs.

Racialized women asserted that power relations are embedded in a terminology that reflects social and political realities, influences perceptions, and determines the material and social reality of individuals and groups. Thus although at one level the debate was about racialized women finding a name, claiming the right to speak for themselves, and defining their subject position in their history and politics, its subtext was about dislodging relations of power. Racialized women claimed the right to describe (and thus to name) themselves and their oppression on their own terms and to redefine the differences between them and 'Canadian' women.

Discourse analysis was a valuable tool, for it revealed the biases hidden in many categories and definitions, but its emphasis on language was criticized. Some feminists argued that the significance of language does not mean that the social perceptions of identities evaporate and lose all meaning in everyday practice. 'Identities and social relations imply at least some degree of continuity, and individual identities, however open-ended, provisional and "in process" cannot readily be expunged. They may be etched into the very fabric of the body, into gestures, lineaments and markers of who we are ... These lineaments disclose what we have been. While they may not determine, they surely have some consequences for what we may become' (Andermahr et al. 2000, 124).

Politics and Positionality

Gender, race, class, sexuality, ability, and age are some of the axes of oppression that affect women. These axes determine individuals' experiences and construct their sense of self and identity. The centrality of identity in feminist politics led to the proliferation of new political groups and progressive social movements such as the gay and lesbian rights movements, the disabled women's network, and immigrant women's organizations. The politics of these movements focused on issues that stemmed from their subjective positions or identities and were thus different from conventional broad-based politics such as those found in the peace movement.

The focus on identity validated the differences between individuals and enabled them to mobilize other women with similar identities, but it had the disadvantage of tying individuals to their identity and thereby constraining them. Black and South Asian feminists expressed frustration at always being perceived through the prism of race and thus implicitly excluded from other discussions. Marxists argued that the emphasis on the personal had replaced 'What is to be done?' with 'Who am I?' Andermahr points out that 'unreflective identity politics represent a form of essentialism in which experience can be transparently transposed into discourse to "speak for itself" and a subjectivism in which "only I speak for me."' (Andermahr et al. 2000, 126). But others like De Lauritis maintain that some form of strategic essentialism was necessary for feminist politics.

Theorization about identity and subjectivity made for endless differences and led to fragmentation and dissension among feminist scholars. Sunera Thobani, reflecting on her tenure as president of the National Action Committee on the Status of Women, notes that the inability of many white women to accept women of colour as leaders or as capable human beings makes 'battles' between women inevitable (Rebick 2005, 240). Grewal suggests that solidarity between women can be expressed, not through 'totalitarian effacement of difference' nor by 'delirious celebration of a limitless and ever-proliferating "indifference,"' but through practical relations 'constructed through forms of dialogue and struggle that presuppose a common commitment to ending all forms of oppression and exploitation, however organized through the intertwining of race, class, gender sexual orientation, or cultural difference, and that work out, and work through, the differences from there' (Grewal and Kaplan 1994, 225–6).

Over time, the emphasis on discourse, language, and identity shifted to academic feminism and to its practice in women's studies. Many readers protested that the language of some feminist writing had become extremely convoluted and nearly inaccessible. Catherine MacKinnon complained that some feminist debates are purely intellectual, utterly divorced from the realities of working-class women (1991). Naomi Wolf criticized feminism for adopting 'an exclusive and elaborate professional jargon which amounts to no more than pig-Latin' (1994, xxvi) and Camille Paglia attacked it for having become rigid and doctrinaire – a 'bourgeois prison' (1994, ix).

The consciousnesses of the 'self' or 'identity' led to the disintegration of the politics of 'sisterhood.' Although women attempted to work with the ideal of coalitions and alliances between women's organizations, in everyday practice it was difficult to operate within these alliances, which led to conflicts and tensions. Nancy Hartsock questioned the direction of feminism, asking sceptically: 'Why is it that just at the moment when so many of us who have been silenced begin to demand the right to name ourselves, to act as subjects rather than objects of history, that just then the concept of subjecthood becomes problematic?' (Hartsock 1990, 163).

Others like Roiphe, Wolf, and Sommers – sometimes referred to as post-feminists – found much that was problematic in feminist theorizations and politics. Katie Roiphie felt that feminists were intolerant of dissent; she wished to 'invent ways to talk about politics and sex and responsibility that allow for independence of thought' (1994, xxiii).

Christina Sommers argued against what she calls the 'gender feminists' who describe society as a patriarchy and a 'male hegemony' that keeps women 'cowering and submissive.' She believes that this type of feminism is divisive and has little support in the American population at large. Instead, she supports 'equity feminists' – 'women who want for women what they want for everyone: fair treatment without discrimination' (1994, 22).

Gender and Diversity in Royal Commission Reports: An Overview

Feminist theory has encouraged women to identify, question, and resist oppression by the practices and discourses of dominant groups. Debates within women's organizations, academia, and public institutions require that feminists continually re-evaluate their concepts and reformulate their theories. This process has moved feminism from a narrow focus on combating gender bias to more dynamic programs with broader goals and objectives. Carol Bacchi notes that every issue affects women and therefore recommends that we ask 'What's the problem?' when we seek to analyse policy. If we do so, we can approach policy critically to 'reflect upon representations offered both by those who describe something as a problem and by those who deny the issue problem status.' She argues that we have to view targets of public policy in the context of how they are represented and talked about in political debate and policy proposals. Policies that seek to present 'solutions' to 'problems' are only one of a range of possible choices available to us. The choice of what we do and how we do it depends on the preconceptions (assumptions and norms) embedded in our representation and analysis of the 'problems,' the language used to discuss them, and their effect or material consequences on us (Bacchi 1999, 2).

Report of the Royal Commission on the Status of Women

The Royal Commission on the Status of Women was the formative event in the development of government policy on women. The commission was appointed in 1967 at the behest of the Committee for Equality of Women in Canada (a group representing many women's organizations) and the Fédération des femmes du Québec (FFQ), who both pressured the government to investigate the condition of Canadian women (Dobrowolsky 2000, 19). The commissioners were to 'inquire into and report upon the status of women in Canada, and to recommend what steps might be taken by the Federal Government to ensure for women equal opportunities with men.' The commission set out three goals that it specifically wished to investigate: 'equal opportunity with men,' 'an adequate standard of living,' and 'freedom to choose a career.'

Women's organizations in Canada had been somewhat influenced in their demands by the civil rights movement in the United States and the demands of the Québecois for recognition of their social, political, and economic contributions to Canadian society. The public hearings that accompanied the work of the Royal Commission on Bilingualism and Biculturalism (established in 1963) created a consciousness of rights among the population. The other European-origin populations that were excluded from the deliberations of the commission felt aggrieved and made representations to politicians about their desire to be included. The final report of the Bilingualism and Biculturalism Commission noted that the French and the English were the country's two 'founding nations' or 'charter groups,' and that Canada would be a multicultural nation within a bilingual framework. Although complete equality remained a goal for the other European ethnic groups, the commission's work was significant in that it officially recognized the cultural diversity of the Canadian population.

Although cultural diversity gained a foothold in Canadian public policy, it did not inform the work of the Royal Commission on the Status of Women as such. The commission did not have an explicit conceptual framework or a shared philosophy other than its commitment to the 'equal rights' approach, which coexisted with general notions of the value of a specifically 'female culture' (Bégin 1992, 29). At the time there was little feminist literature available. Nevertheless, the report starkly reveals the feminist bias of the times, claiming that women are discriminated against on the basis of their gender alone. Although sex (the term gender had yet to become common) was thought to be the main culprit in women's inequality, the commissioners recognized the class and regional differences among women and divided them up into separate categories. There was no recognition that race might also be a barrier to attaining the three goals the commission set out to investigate.

The Royal Commission on the Status of Women provided a comprehensive report on the situation of women and made 163 recommendations in nine areas: women in the Canadian economy, education, women and the family, taxation and child care allowances, poverty, participation of women in public life, immigration and citizenship, criminal law, and women offenders (Crow and Gotell 2000, 70–87). Its plan for action was as follows:

> We recommend that a federal Status of Women Council, directly responsi-
> ble to Parliament, be established to (a) advise on matters pertaining to
> women and report annually to Parliament on the progress being made in
> improving the status of women in Canada, (b) undertake research on mat-
> ters relevant to the status of women and suggest research topics that can
> be carried out by governments, private business, universities, and volun-
> tary associations, (c) establish programmes to correct attitudes and preju-
> dices adversely affecting the status of women, (d) propose legislation,
> policies and practices to improve the status of women, and (e) systemati-
> cally consult with the women's bureau or similar provincial organizations,
> and with voluntary associations particularly concerned with the problems
> of women. (Royal Commission on the Status of Women 1970)

The report discussed women as one category, although it paid some attention to those who live in poverty or in remote communities. In discussing poverty, it focused on three groups: 'sole support mothers,' 'elderly women,' and 'Indian, Metis, and Eskimo women.' The report addressed what it called 'immigrant women' over four pages, arguing that 'gender' was the only source of oppression and locating their problems in the culture of their ethnic and racial groups. In discussing women who do not speak English or French, the report noted that 'the social customs of some immigrant communities may not permit the housewife to leave home in the evening to attend the language classes and other courses that she badly needs' (1970, 361). But it conspicuously failed to question issues such as the scheduling of these classes, who was eligible to attend them, where they were held, or their curricula. There was no exploration of responsibilities relating to child care or to the material survival of the family that might make it impossible for women to attend language classes.

The language of the report is condescending and patronizing. Immigrant women are treated as objects, as passive rather than active participants in defining themselves or identifying their problems. Race and class differences are presented as add-on characteristics of some women rather than as integral components of race, class, and gender oppression. The notion of gender oppression remains primary; there is no mention at all of oppression based on sexual orientation or disability.

The Royal Commission on the Status of Women report informed public policy for the next two decades. It supported the lobbying efforts of women's groups to eliminate the discriminatory aspects of legislation and to introduce new and creative programs for ensuring women's equality. The report was, however, silent on violence against women. In the years since its publication, a consciousness had developed about the pervasiveness of violence and its implications for women's equality.

Canadian Panel on Violence Against Women, 1991

Status of Women Canada prepared the first federal plan for action, entitled *Towards Equality for Women* (1979), in which they identified violence against women as a public policy issue. The report recommended that the government undertake a major study on the problem of violence against women, establish a national clearinghouse on information on the subject, and review amendments to the Criminal Code on the offence of rape (Levan 1996, 322).

Women's organizations were divided on whether women could depend on the government to reduce the impact of violence against them. Some wanted the government to establish a royal commission to investigate violence against women, while others thought that women's organizations should do this themselves. But the 1989 Montreal massacre that killed fourteen women outraged Canadians and lent a sense of urgency to the issue. Thirty women's organizations, with the support of many units of provincial and municipal governments, formally petitioned the federal government to establish a royal commission on violence against women. The Canadian Panel on Violence Against Women was appointed in 1991 and submitted its report *Changing the Landscape: Ending Violence – Achieving Equality* in 1993.

Whereas the Royal Commission on the Status of Women had made little effort to include racialized women in its work, the Canadian Panel on Violence Against Women included one native woman, one immigrant woman, and one man. In addition, a four-member 'Aboriginal Circle' was set up to act as an advisory committee with a focus on those aspects of the problem that most closely affected aboriginal women. Despite this attempt to increase the panel's ethnic diversity, a dispute immediately broke out about whether it was sufficiently representative of racial minority women and women with disabilities. Furthermore, although the panel had obtained the cautious support of Judy Rebick, then president of the National Action Committee on the Status of

Women (NAC), there was intense dispute about whether the panel was accountable to the women's organizations that had lobbied for it or to the federal government that had appointed it.

The relationship of the Aboriginal Circle to the panel was not well defined; to resolve its indeterminate character, its members were eventually incorporated into the panel. Even more difficult to resolve, however, was the dispute about the panel's representation of women from cultural and racial minorities and women with disabilities. The panel offered to set up an advisory committee that more accurately 'reflected the diversity of Canadian women.' Despite a lack of enthusiasm for this initiative, it was nonetheless carried out. The advisory committee drew half of its membership from women with links to feminist organizations, while the other half hailed from 'various environments' such as 'police, judicial, academic, and elderly women' (Canadian Panel on Violence Against Women 1993, B4). But the appointment of the advisory body raised additional questions, and the panel was asked by Canadian women's organizations to define its relationship with the committee. For example, it was asked: 'What were the "real powers" of the advisory committee?' 'Did it have access to information that was collected by the panel?' 'Did they have the power to accept or reject the panel's decisions?' (B4).

The panel's concessions over membership did not satisfy some women's organizations; consequently, the Congress of Black Women and the National Organization of Immigrant and Visible Minority Women, along with the National Action Committee, refused to participate in its proceedings or to support its work (Levan 1996). The panel, however, saw the difficulties it confronted as being endemic to all government agencies. It noted that 'the under-representation of minority women and women experiencing multiple forms of oppression is a problem for all decision-making structures in Canada and will be an abiding concern in the future. The Panel could not resolve this complex issue alone.' It went on to acknowledge that 'our failure to resolve [this issue] has clearly resulted in disarray and a sense of powerlessness within both the Panel and the feminist community' (Canadian Panel on Violence Against Women 1993, B4).

The panel's report made 494 recommendations on a wide range of issues but did not prioritize any of them. It identified problems concerning sponsorship, immigration status, and the exploitation of women who come into Canada as domestic workers. The report strongly reflected the perspective of activist racialized women who had been voicing the concerns of women from their groups (Agnew 1998) and stated unequivocally that 'efforts to overcome violence against women can no longer be dissociated from the struggle against sexism, racism, intolerance and inequality (Canadian Panel on Violence Against Women 1993, B4). It noted that some people think that violence is part of others' cultures but argued that this belief betrays a racist attitude: 'Racism, cloaked in the more respectable mantle of "cultural considerations," results in the stereotypes about violence being part of the "culture" of the people. This can be an excuse for non-intervention within the legal system and other services based on the misinformed fear of interfering with the practices of another culture. However no cultural practices or norms can be used to justify violence' (1993, 80).

The report found that there were 'three major impediments' faced by women who experienced violence and sought help from social services: 'racism from those involved in service delivery; a lack of services specifically focused on their needs, even when the demographics of the community would demand such availability; and the peripheral role that women of colour play in the structuring and delivery of mainstream services ... A lack of specialized services leaves women of colour isolated and more likely to return to the violent situations from which they were seeking escape' (Canadian Panel on Violence Against Women 1993, 82).

The minister for Status of Women, Mary Collins, responded to the panel's report by noting that the government would adopt a 'zero tolerance' policy towards violence against women, but she declined to allocate any resources to the problem and was consequently severely criticized by women's organizations.

The panel's report lends substance to some feminist theoretical orientations. For example, it demonstrates that identity is important but that including people of diverse identities is problematic in practice and raises theoretical difficulties. Theoretically speaking, the panel had adopted an essentialist perspective on identity by equating physical attributes (one man and one Native woman) with diversity (it also included what it called one immigrant woman). Yet although much was debated, no one questioned such an equation. No one asked whether white women could represent issues of racialized women, or why it was necessary to include racialized women at all. Could all the members of the panel have been black or South Asian or disabled, or could the panel have relied on one white woman to represent her entire ethnic group? The failure to ask such questions reveals the gap between feminist politics and practice and its theories.

Theoretically, it is possible to provide an answer to the difficulties of incorporating diverse individuals and perspectives without equating their physicality with their ideology. Razack reconciles the differences between essentialism and non-essentialism by suggesting that we should be focusing on the relationships between women of varying identities and accounting for the differential and changing power relations between them.

> It begins with anti-essentialism and the recognition that there is no one stable core we can call woman's experiences. Equally important, it is a politics guided by a search for the ways in which we are complicitous in the subordination of others. If we take as our point of departure that systems of domination interlock and sustain each other, we can begin to identify those moments when we are dominant and those when we are subordinate. Our implication in various systems of domination means that there are several ways in which we can perform ourselves as dominant at the same time that we understand ourselves to be engaging in liberatory politics. (1998, 159)

Feminists of all persuasions may at times be engaged in liberatory politics, yet unknowingly become dominant and complicit in the subordination of others (Agnew 1998, 159).

The 'problem' to be discussed by the panel was violence against women, but it could be argued that such a representation constructs women as victims. Roberta Clarke suggests that 'feminists reframe the issue moving from women as victims (violence against women) to men as aggressors (violence by men), *while* holding states responsible for the many ways in which they support the production of violent men' (qtd in Bacchi 1999, 179). The goal in such reframing would be to change social structures that are complicit in producing violent men and to pressure governments to not condone the excesses of such men; rather, governments should initiate measures that would punish them severely and thus deter others from similar acts (179).

Reports by Status of Women Canada

In the 1990s, Canadian women of varying identities challenged certain practices, institutional arrangements, and social interactions that were embedded in public policy documents. They argued that the goal of a more inclusive definition of citizenship would be to recognize the many layers of differences between people and to remove fixed and immutable boundaries of otherness.

Public policy debates in the 1990s focused on gender and diversity by identifying themes such as poverty or homelessness and then examining how they impact different groups of women, or by examining the situation of specific groups such as First Nations Women, Aboriginal Women, and women at risk. Similarly, existing policies such as those relating to pension, disability, employment equity, and immigration have been analysed for their impact on groups of women; for example, the Employment Equity Policy in Canada (Bakan and Kobayashi 2000), Gendering Immigration/Integration (Status of Women Canada 1998), and Income for Women with Disabilities (Doe and Kimpson 1999). Such an interpretation of diversity enables us to be inclusive of a wide range of groups of women and respond to their needs by adopting the gender lens and identifying gaps in public policies that detract from their citizenship status.

The feminization of poverty has been an ongoing concern of women's groups and of public policy since the 1970s. Women's poverty crosses many axes of oppression, such as religion, ethnicity, race, disability, age, and marital status. Poor women are found in almost all ethnic and racial groups, but some women are particularly vulnerable to poverty because of limited education and marketable skills, childcare responsibilities, and systemic biases in the labour market. These problems have been extensively discussed in the literature; however, there are differences in perspective of what constitutes both the 'problems' and their 'solutions.' Some argue that the problem lies in the dependence of women on social programs and that the answer is to inculcate greater self-sufficiency through restrictive social policies. However, women's groups demand their rights as citizens to an equitable share of the nation's resources and emphasize the need to recognize the contributions they make to the well-being of their children and thus of society.

Davies and others, in *Social Policy, Gender Inequality, and Poverty* (2001), discuss the situation of women who rely on social security programs, explaining why they are poor. Using quantitative and qualitative methodologies, they provide a gender analysis of social assistance and Employment Insurance policies. Women's poverty – and therefore their need for social security programs – is a multifaceted problem that stems from the gender ideologies of the family that guide the choices women make from childhood onwards about education, employment, marriage, and motherhood.

Gender role expectations mean that women sometimes make choices that have grave economic consequences in later life; one example is early pregnancies that lead to dropping out of school. Women's responsibilities within the family make it difficult for them to seek and keep employment. Childcare responsibilities further skew the employment pattern of married women and keep them trapped in low-paying jobs. Women become 'dependent' on social programs, but the programs may not be particularly responsive to their life circumstances. Furthermore, the lack of availability of supportive programs like daycare keeps them trapped in poverty and unable to become economically independent.

The *Canada Health and Social Transfer Act* of 1995 led to 'sweeping changes' to the administration and funding of programs, eroding some of the gains women had made in previous decades. These changes 'jeopardized income security by providing provinces with greater autonomy over spending decisions (thereby reducing national standards for social assistance) and by limiting the availability of funds' (Davies et al. 2001, 73). The consequences of these changes were different for women than they were for men, since women's responsibilities for childcare and the lack of available daycare made it harder for them to meet the new qualifying regulations (based on number of hours worked and supplementary work).

Since poverty is related to a lack of employment, fewer women rely on Employment Insurance (as opposed to social assistance) for survival. Employed women need greater flexibility to quit their jobs (which becomes necessary at times to meet children's needs) and require more benefits when they are out of work. Supportive social policies will enable women to fulfill their gender role obligations and become economically independent and self-sufficient.

Davies and others (2001) argue that the problem of poverty is amenable to resolution if public policies prioritize women's needs and requirements throughout their life. They make far-ranging recommendations for policies and programs that would ensure proper education in childhood and enable young women to avoid teenage pregnancies, or if pregnant, to stay in school. Similarly, they recommend that public policies be designed taking into account the family context in which women make their decisions. They suggest a need to increase the rate of social assistance so women have a better standard of living, are able to improve their health and well-being, reduce their stress, and enhance their ability to parent their children. The authors reiterate the recommendations made by several other studies to make daycare more easily accessible and available to poor women, thereby enabling them to explore work and educational opportunities.

Aboriginal women are the poorest of the poor. Carolyn Kenny notes that despite much research, the poverty of Aboriginal women remains endemic (2002). In examining their situation several questions arise. Are Aboriginal women poor because of the intersection of race, class, and gender that particularly disadvantages them? Or does the 'problem' lie in public policies that exclude and marginalize the women? Alternatively, is it the particular historical and social circumstances that continues to oppress Aboriginal women? Why are their citizenship rights not being honoured? What are the perceptions of Aboriginal women about their ongoing poverty and limited education and work opportunities?

A plethora of other studies on Aboriginal women by members of the larger society have led to scepticism about the value of such research. Aboriginal women argue that the research done on them has seldom represented their points of view faithfully, and that few productive and meaningful outcomes have emerged. Consequently, in an effort to win over the subjects of her research, Kenny (2002) scrupulously adopted the methodology recommended by the Report of the Royal Commission on Aboriginal People. The Commission suggested that researchers respect the culture, languages, knowledge, and values of the Aboriginal people and adopt their standards for 'legitimating knowledge.' These methods – conducting research in a collaborative way and minimizing power relations between the researcher and the researched – parallel those used by feminists. It is important, feminists suggest, to identify the perspective of the people involved and to give priority to the voice or viewpoints of those being studied. Kenny identifies four primary questions:

1. What have you experienced in attempting to advance your education and find meaningful work?
2. Have you experienced conflict between realizing your work goals and living a 'cultural' life? What have they been?
3. What do you recommend in terms of policy changes that would diminish these conflicts?
4. What do you need in a general sense to support coherence between your cultural life and your work life?

In responding to these questions, Aboriginal women noted emphatically that they did not want to be 'fighting the same fight' generation after generation. Their primary recommendation was that public policies be more sensitive and responsive to their life circumstances by allocating resources to facilitators who are thoroughly familiar with the everyday lives and the organizations that the Aboriginal women have developed for themselves. Facilitators would help the women design and develop policies (as opposed to imposing them from above). However, the Aboriginal women who participated in this study wanted guarantees that policies they identify as critical for their well-being will be implemented before they participate in any further research. There are seventeen other recommendations of varying nature, ranging from better childcare policies to a more appropriate educational curriculum, but a common thread of empowering and enabling Aboriginal women to take charge of their lives runs through them all. Considerable attention was given to the inequities of the Indian Act and the need to reform it, so that women can be equal participants in the governance of their communities.

Conclusion

Citizenship involves social and political participation as well as individual and community rights. It is about rights, but also about duties and obligations. Asserting rights requires participation in civil society, and the exercise of the right to participate reveals the barriers and obstacles that need to be confronted and disputed, whether they lie in the construction of knowledge or in formulations of public policy. Citizenship is not a given; rather, it is a process that takes shape through the exercise of rights and responsibilities, and thus is about both status and practice. It is contested and negotiated in situations of unequal power and authority (Dobrowolsky and Jenson 2004).

This chapter has documented how racialized women recognize the many structural constraints that operate to limit them and deny them full membership within a movement. But they are not mere victims; rather, they are active participants in civil society and exercise their human agency to contest their marginalization and exclusion. Yuval-Davis notes that the notion of citizenship should be differentiated from that of belonging. 'If citizenship signifies the participatory dimension of belonging, identification relates to the more emotive dimension of association. Feeling that one is part of a collectivity, a community, a social category or yearning to be so is not the same as actually taking part in a political community' (qtd in Ralston 2006, 173).

The nation is an 'imagined community,' an arbitrary social construction dependent on the will and pleasure of its proponents. The politics of identity have discursively produced a subjectivity among racialized activists, who contend that Canada has historically defined itself as a white nation. They have challenged such characterization by documenting not only the beliefs that 'we' value, but also the disjuncture between ideals and practice. The struggle lies not only in documenting the 'truth' as they perceive and understand it, but also in finding innovative ways to reconcile these truths with a history of marginalization and exclusion. The conundrum lies in how to include, for such inclusions continue, at times, to have the sediment of bias within them.

Women of all identities are an integral part of the Canadian nation. Racialized women have made considerable strides since 1970 in gaining equality, both formally and substantively, with white Canadian women. But some women, such as those who live in poverty or are Aboriginals or disabled, continue to lag behind others who have enjoyed greater equality and experienced more fully the rights and obligations of citizenship. Bureaucrats and politicians, along with many segments of the broader society, have enthusiastically adopted the concept of diversity, yet problems of religious, ethnic, and racial discrimination continue. There is a lack of studies that ask questions about the experience of racialized, lesbian, and disabled women with the complaints process of the Human Rights Commission. What changes are needed to better address the needs of racialized, lesbian, and disabled women? Women's representation in decision-making bodies is critical. Women need to collectively reflect on how a fair process of selecting women can be put into place. They need to recognize how important it is to evaluate current ad hoc strategies and change them in order to better represent the diversity of women in all federal, provincial, and municipal decision-making bodies. Since citizenship is a process, it is through various forms of political struggle that individuals define themselves and find a place in the nation. Participation in civil society gives concreteness and substance to their membership in the nation.

References

Agnew, Vijay. 1996. *Resisting discrimination: Women from Asia, Africa, and the Caribbean and the women's movement in Canada.* Toronto: University of Toronto Press.
– 1998. *In search of a safe place: Abused women and culturally sensitive services.* Toronto: University of Toronto Press.

Andermahr, Sonya, Terry Lovell, and Carol Wolkowitz., eds. 2000. *A glossary of feminist theory.* London: Arnold.

Bacchi, Carol. 1999. *Women, policy and politics: The construction of policy problems.* London: Sage.

Bakan, Abigail, and Audry Kobayashi. 2000. *Employment equity policy in Canada: An inter-provincial comparison.* Ottawa: Status of Women Canada.

Bannerji, Himani. 1997. Geography lessons: On being an insider/outsider to the Canadian nation. In *Dangerous territories: Struggles for difference and equality in education,* ed. Leslie Roman and Linda Eyre, 23–42. New York: Routledge.

Bégin, Monique. 1992. The Royal Commission on the Status of Women in Canada: Twenty years later. In *Changing times: The women's movement in Canada and the United States,* ed. Constance Backhouse and David Flaherty, 21–38. Montreal: McGill-Queens University Press.

Butler, Judith. 1990. *Gender trouble: Feminism and the subversion of identity.* New York: Routledge.

Calliste, Agnes, and George Dei, eds. 2000. *Anti-racist feminism: Critical race and gender studies.* Halifax: Fernwood.

Canadian Panel on Violence Against Women. 1993. *Changing the landscape: Ending violence – achieving equality.* Ottawa: Panel on Violence Against Women.

Code, Lorraine. 1991. *What can she know? Feminist theory and the construction of knowledge.* Ithaca, NY: Cornell University Press.

– ed. 2000. *Encyclopedia of feminist theories.* London: Routledge.

Collins, Patricia. 1991. *Black feminist thought: Knowledge, consciousness, and the politics of empowerment.* New York: Routledge.

Crow, Barbara, and Lise Gottell. 2000. *Open boundaries: A Canadian women's studies reader.* Toronto: Prentice-Hall.

Davies, Lorraine, Julie Ann McMullin, William R. Avison, and Gale L. Cassidy. 2001. *Social policy, gender inequality, and poverty.* Ottawa: Status of Women Canada.

Dobrowolsky, Alexandra. 2000. *The politics of pragmatism: Women, representation, and constitutionalism in Canada.* Don Mills, ON: Oxford University Press.

Dobrowolsky, Alexandra, and Jane Jenson. 2004. Shifting representation of citizenship: Canadian politics of 'women' and 'children.' *Social Politics* 11 (2): 154–80.

Doe, Tanis, and Sally Kimpson. 1999. *Enabling income: C.P.P. disability benefits and women with disabilities.* Ottawa: Status of Women Canada.

Fleras, Augie, and Jean Kunz. 2001. *Media and minorities: Representing diversity in a multicultural Canada.* Toronto: Thompson Educational.

Gamble, Sarah, ed. 2001. *The Routledge companion to feminism and postfeminism.* London: Routledge.

Grewal, Inderpal, and Caren Kaplan, eds. 1994. *Scattered hegemonies: Postmodernity and transnational feminist practices*. Minneapolis: University of Minnesota Press.

Harding, Sandra. 1987. *The science question in feminism*. Ithaca, NY: Cornell University Press.

– 1998. *Is science multicultural? Postcolonialism, feminisms, and epistomologies*. Bloomington: Indiana University Press.

Hartsock, Nancy. 1990. Foucault on power: A theory for women? In *Feminism/postmodernism*, ed. Linda Nicholson 157–75. New York: Routledge.

Henry, Frances, and Carol Tator. 2002. *Discourse of domination: Racial bias in the Canadian English-language press*. Toronto: University of Toronto Press.

hooks, bell. 1984. *Feminist theory: From margin to center*. Cambridge, MA: South End.

– 1988. *Talking back: Thinking feminist, thinking black*. Toronto: Between the Lines.

Kenny, Carolyn. 2002. *North American Indian, Métis and Inuit Women speak out about culture, education and work*. Ottawa: Status of Women Canada.

Kymlicka, Will. 1995. *Multicultural citizenship: A liberal theory of minority rights*. Oxford: Clarendon.

Levan, Andrea. 1996. Violence against women. In *Women and Canadian public policy*, ed. Janine Brodie, 319–54. Toronto: Harcourt Brace.

MacKinnon. Catherine. 1991. From practice to theory, or What is a white woman anyway? *Yale Journal of Law and Feminism* 4:413–22.

Ontario Human Rights Commission. 2005. *Policy and guidelines regarding racism and racial discrimination*. Toronto: Ontario Human Rights Commission.

Paglia, Camille. 1994. *Vamps and tramps*. New York: Vintage.

Ralston, Helen. 2006. 'Citizenship, identity, agency and resistance among Canadian and Australian women of South Asian origin.' In Tastsoglou and Dobrowolsky 2006, 172–188.

Razack, Sherene. 1998. *Looking white people in the eye*. Toronto: University of Toronto Press.

Rebick, Judy. 2005. *Ten thousand roses: The making of a feminist revolution*. Toronto: Penguin.

Ristock, Janice, and Joan Pennell. 1996. *Community research as empowering: Feminist links, postmodern interruption*. Don Mills, ON: Oxford University Press.

Roiphie, Katie. 1994. *The morning after: Sex, fear, and feminism*. Boston: Little, Brown.

Rosaldo, Renato. 1999. Cultural citizenship, inequality and multiculturalism. In *Race, identity and citizenship: A reader*, ed. Rodolfo Torres, Louis Miron, and Jonathan Inda, 253–61. Oxford: Blackwell.

Rothenberg, Paula. 1990. The construction, deconstruction, and reconstruction of difference. *Hypatia* 5 (1): 42–57.

Royal Commission on the Status of Women in Canada. 1970. *Report of the Royal Commission on the Status of Women in Canada*. Ottawa: Information Canada.

Segal, Lynne. 1987. *Is the future female? Troubled thoughts on contemporary feminism*. London: Virago.

Smith, Dorothy. 1987. *The everyday world as problematic: A feminist sociology*. Toronto: University of Toronto Press.

Sommers, Christina. 1994. *Who stole feminism? How women have betrayed women*. New York: Simon and Schuster.

Spelman, Elizabeth. 1988. *Inessential women: Problems of exclusion in feminist thought*. Boston: Beacon.

Spivak, Gayatri. 1990. *The post-colonial critic: Interviews, strategies, dialogues*, ed. Sarah Harasym. London: Routledge.

Status of Women Canada. 1979. *Towards equality for women*. Ottawa: Status of Women Canada.

– 1998. Gendering immigration/integration: Policy research workshop proceedings and a selective review of policy research literature 1987–1996. Ottawa: Status of Women Canada.

Tastsoglou, Evangelia and Alexandra Dobrowolsky. 2006. *Women, migration and citizenship: Making local, national and transnational connections*. Aldershot, UK: Ashgate.

Weir, Allison. 2000. From the subversion of identity to the subversion of solidarity? Judith Butler and the critique of women's identity. In *Open boundaries: A Canadian women's studies reader*, ed. Barbara Crow and Lise Gotell, 43–50. Toronto: Prentice-Hall.

Wolf, Naomi. 1994. *Fire with fire: The new female power and how to use it*. New York: Fawcett Columbine.

Yuval-Davis, Nira, and Pnina Werbner, eds. 1999. *Women, citizenship and difference*. London: Routledge.

11 From Africa to Canada: Bordered Spaces, Border Crossings, and Imagined Communities

GILLIAN CREESE

To belong to Canada is to be treated equally, I think that's when I would think I belong here. Right now, they look at me and right away they think that I don't belong here, you know. So belonging is to be seen as if I equally belong here, not you know as somebody who is passing through.

(Lwanzo, Interview 10)[1]

Migration to Canada is an unsettling experience, one of leaving familiar worlds behind to create new homes in a strange, sometimes perplexing, and not infrequently unfriendly environment. Migration is a gendered and racialized process that is shaped by class, sexuality, immigration status, country of origin, language, age, presence of close family, and size of ethnic community in local Canadian contexts (Abu-Laban 1998; Agnew 1996, 2003; Boyd 1997, 1999, 2001; Creese and Dowling 2001; Dhruvarajan and Vickers 2002; Dossa 2002, 2004; Dyck and McLaren 2002; Giles and Preston 1996; Lee 1999a, 1999b; Lo et al. 2001; McLaren and Dyck 2004; Ng 1990, 1998; Pratt 2002, 2004; Preston and Giles 1997; Thobani 2000; Walters and Teo 2003). Migration may also be voluntary or involuntary, embedded in social processes of neo-colonialism, globalization, growing inequalities, and, not infrequently, political conflict. For some, adjustments in Canada may be minimal and a sense of belonging may develop quickly; for others, migration is a massive dislocation that involves life-long processes of negotiating bordered spaces within Canada, creating conditions in which belonging is always contingent and partial.

My own experience as an immigrant in a British family is of the former variety. Arriving in Canada as a young child, my main sense of an immigrant experience was the absence of extended family nearby. As far as I (and they) can remember, my parents' London accents and white skins proved no barrier to anything, from jobs to housing to new networks of friendship that quickly developed in Canada. Though the absence of extended family was no doubt felt strongly, particularly in the early years, there was little dislocation otherwise. Institutional structures and culturally accepted practices were, in most respects, very familiar. The combination of Anglo dominance and white privilege provided a context in which feelings of belonging in this new space – both our own sense of inclusion and that conveyed by others – were unproblematic. Being British somehow encapsulated being Canadian: there appeared to be no contradiction between the two; there were few psychic, social, or cultural borders in need of traversing; and over time the latter identity came to predominate without any apparent sense of loss or ambiguity.

As contemporary trends in immigration make clear, this is not the reality experienced by most newcomers to Canada today. Most recent immigrants enjoy neither white-skinned privilege nor the ease of Anglo dominance that, for all the emphasis on multiculturalism, continues to shape the basic institutional arrangements in Canada. Today, migration reflects global diversity. Among immigrants who arrived between 1990 and 2000, for example, 58 per cent came from Asia, 20 per cent from Europe, 11 per cent from the Caribbean, Central and South America, 8 per cent from Africa, and 3 per cent from the United States; 73 per cent of recent immigrants are people of colour (Statistics Canada 2003a, 6 and 10).[2] There has been a three-fold increase in the number of Canadians of colour since 1981, from 1.1 million to 4 million; people of colour now constitute 13.4 per cent of the total population (Statistics Canada 2003a, 10). Most immigrants settle in the major urban centres, especially Toronto, Vancouver, and Montreal. In 2001, for example, immigrants made up 44 per cent of the population of Metropolitan Toronto and 37.5 per cent of Greater Vancouver; 37 per cent of the population of both cities identified as people of colour (Statistics Canada 2003a, 28–9, 35).[3]

Whiteness and Anglo dominance do not seamlessly coincide. Immigrants from Britain come from many different ethnic origins. In addition, those from former British colonies, including India and many parts of Africa, were raised in contexts in which British institutional structures predominated and English was the primary language of education – albeit in a context that inscribed British superiority over local cultures, traditions, institutions, and languages. Still, in travelling from one former British colonial context to another, it is questionable to what degree migrants of colour are able to capitalize on their fluency in English and their familiarity with British institutional arrangements. Settlement experiences in Canada are shaped not only by language fluency and cultural familiarity, but perhaps more importantly, by processes of racialization. Processes of racialization are such that a privileged British or Commonwealth heritage can readily be erased when not attached to white skins. This paper addresses one group in Canada who experience this erasure of their English fluency and historical Commonwealth ties – black women who migrated from African countries once colonized by Britain.[4] For these women, (re)settlement in Vancouver involves negotiating a seemingly endless series of bordered spaces – in the labour market, in neighbourhoods, and in cultural imaginations – that emphasize their 'difference' from 'Canadians,' denying their Commonwealth experiences and making belonging uncertain at best.

Multiculturalism and Belonging

Nation-states are multiply bordered spaces. As Brah writes, borders are 'arbitrary dividing lines that are simultaneously social, cultural and psychic; territories to be patrolled against those whom they construct as outsiders, aliens, the Others; forms of demarcation where the very act of prohibition inscribes transgression; zones where fear of the Other is the fear of the self; places where claims to ownership – claims to "mine," "yours," and "theirs" – are staked out, contested, defended, and fought over' (1996, 198).

Nation-building projects define political, geographical, social, and psychic borders that rely on 'imagined communities' of belonging.[5] 'Imagined communities' operate through discourses of citizenship that tend to homogenize and erase differences internal to the nation, and separate citizens from (both internally and externally located) 'Others.' Canada's colonial history exemplifies such nation-building projects, embedded in British and French exploitation of resources, and in attempts to construct a white British and French Canada in which British economic, political and social structures, cultural values, and immigrants would predominate (Abu-Laban 1998; Arat-Koc 1997; Li 2003; Perry 2001; Stasiulis and Jhappan 1995).

The 'imagined nation' of Canada was (and is) embedded in images of whiteness,[6] in spite of the continued vitality of First Nations communities and the fact that early migration included people from Africa and

Asia (Gonick 2000; Li 2003). Imagining a white British and French nation simultaneously helped to subordinate 'others' and erase their presence from early Canadian history. According to John Porter (1965), a 'vertical mosaic' of ethnic and racialized (and gendered) power and privilege crossed all major social institutions by the 1960s.[7]

More recently, nation-building processes have became more complex and contradictory, unsettling these historical imaginings of community (Satzewich and Wong 2003). The introduction of the points system in 1967 shifted immigration away from Europe and towards other parts of the world, particularly Asia; multiculturalism replaced Anglo-conformity as official policy in the 1970s; the recruitment of immigrant investors, entrepreneurs, and professionals altered the class dynamics of immigration processes; and the growth of the women's and civil rights movements created a climate in which issues of gender and racial equality were placed on the public agenda. New discourses of nationhood emerged, with a pluralist multicultural Canada at the centre (Mackey 2002). By the late twentieth century, ethnic differences among European groups had ceased to be a central fault line in Canadian society, while leaving in place 'a strong "coloured mosaic" of racial differences' (Lian and Matthews 1998, 476; see also Henry and Tator 2002; Henry, Tator, Mattis, and Rees 1995; Lautard and Guppy 1990; and Li 1998).

New discourses of nationhood focus on multiculturalism. As Eva Mackey (2002) argues, multiculturalism and difference are deeply embedded within national images of Canada. Indeed, multicultural discourses mediate Canada's complex colonial history: simultaneously displacing First Nations peoples, maintaining Anglo dominance vis-à-vis Quebec, placing immigration flows in hierarchical relations that privilege 'traditional' (i.e., European) immigrant groups, emphasizing cultural pluralism over substantive equality, and distinguishing Canada from the United States as an ostensibly more tolerant and pluralist society (Mackey 2002, 16).[8] Therefore, as Mackey demonstrates, discourses of multiculturalism both contain and regulate difference.

Moreover, although images of multicultural Canadians have a central place in the public imagination, they are abstracted from concerns with substantive equality and embedded in notions of 'tolerance' and cultural maintenance (Abu-Laban and Gabriel 2002; Bannerji 2000; Das Gupta 1999). Multicultural images also remain racialized in complex ways, with common-sense discourses constructing people of colour as immigrants, and immigrants as people of colour (Abu-Laban and Gabriel 2002; Bannerji 2000; Gonick 2000; Ng 1990; Razack 1998; Thobani 2000).[9] Such processes erase the 'Canadian birthright' of many people of colour (Pratt 2004) and erase the immigrant status of many who migrated from Europe or her former 'white settler-colonies.' The implication is that white ethnic communities have a longer lineage that somehow makes them 'more Canadian' than others. So while many Canadians may claim an immigrant heritage, it seems clear that some people are *defined* by that status while others are not, and some are never able to escape an immigrant designation no matter how deep their Canadian roots.

There is, therefore, a disjuncture between nationalist discourses that paint Canada as a pluralist immigrant society and the realities of 'othering' faced by immigrants (and other Canadians) of colour. Tropes of multicultural inclusion notwithstanding, immigrants of colour negotiate shifting boundaries of 'Canadianness' in which it is often made clear they are not fully accepted. Formal Canadian citizenship – a status that 84 per cent of immigrants possess[10] – does not mean that one belongs to the imagined community of 'Canadians' (Creese 2005; Gonick 2000). Instead, belonging is negotiated in specific material sites – in neighbourhoods, workplaces, schools, shops, and street corners. These sites are gendered, classed, racialized, and sexualized spaces through which we all define and redefine identities (Anthias 2002a; Brah 1996; Dyck and McLaren 2002; Fortier 2000). Brah refers to these as 'diaspora spaces': 'the point at which boundaries of inclusion and exclusion, of belonging and otherness, of "us" and "them" are contested' (1996, 208–9).

Immigrants must navigate these social, cultural, and psychic borders to traverse the gulf between 'other' and 'us,' or 'immigrant' and 'citizen' (Brah 1996). Most often, immigrants of colour are consigned to what Anzaldúa refers to as 'the borderlands' or the ambiguous 'spaces in between' (Anzaldúa 1987; 2000).[11] Successful border crossing implies a sense of belonging that, as Anthias argues, must include a home 'in the imagining of a collectivity' (Anthias 2002b, 277). In this sense, imagined meanings of 'Canadian' constitute a 'diaspora space' in which immigrants of colour struggle to gain entry. For black women who migrated from Commonwealth African countries, negotiating belonging involves navigating a complex series of bordered spaces – in the labour market, in neighbourhoods, and in cultural imaginations – mediated by multicultural discourses of nation-building superimposed on an imagined white community. These daily (and partial) border crossings are exemplified in the erasure of shared Commonwealth leg-acies, including pre-existing English language fluency; a process that challenges claims to 'Canadian' identity and belonging.

African Immigrants in Vancouver

This chapter explores some of the ways bordered spaces are negotiated by black women who have migrated from diverse countries in sub-Saharan Africa previously colonized by Britain.[12] It draws on two focus groups and twenty-four interviews with women who migrated from Ghana, Kenya, Malawi, South Africa, Sudan, Swaziland, Uganda, Zam-bia, and Zimbabwe.[13] Participants came through a variety of immigra-tion streams (refugee, independent immigrant, and family class),[14] and all but one were either landed immigrants or Canadian citizens at the time of the interviews.[15] All spoke English before arriving in Vancouver and were educated within education systems modelled on British ones. Many had advanced university degrees, some of which were obtained locally after settling in Canada.

In spite of the diversity of countries of origin, language, religion, and culture, similarities in the women's experiences in Vancouver and shared ambiguities about the possibility of belonging in the local com-munity have given rise to a new pan-African identity in the local con-text. This enunciation of an 'African community' coexists with diverse national identities rather than overriding them, but it is increasingly an identity through which the women talk about their community in Van-couver. The social geography of Vancouver – as distinct from places with different histories and much larger black populations, such as Tor-onto, Montreal or Halifax[16] – shapes experiences and identities in sig-nificant ways. For those who participated in this study at least, their African origins and immigrant experiences seem to suggest less in com-mon with Canadian-born black people or those who migrated from the Caribbean, the United States, or other parts of the world than with each other. Similarly, their racialized black bodies suggest few similarities with non-black migrants from Africa. It is a *black African immigrant* experience that shapes their emerging notions of community and strug-gles over belonging.

Vancouver is Canada's third largest city, and after Toronto, its second most diverse.[17] A recent United Nations report ranked Vancouver fourth in the world in terms of its percentage of foreign-born popula-tion.[18] According to the 2001 Census, 37.5 per cent of the population of the greater metropolitan area are immigrants,[19] and 37 per cent identify as people of colour (Statistics Canada 2003a, 35 and 58).[20] Within the City of Vancouver proper, 46 per cent of the population are immigrants and 49 per cent of the population identity as people of colour, the largest group of whom define themselves as Chinese in origin (30 per cent of the city's population).[21] In this context of embodied diversity within Vancouver,[22] African immigrants who are black form a very small minority. According to the 2001 Census, only 1 per cent of the population of Greater Vancouver identify themselves as black.[23] Slightly fewer identify their ethnic origins as 'African,' with a much smaller number of those (less than half of 1 per cent) also identifying as 'black' or 'African (black).'[24] Among immigrants, the 2001 Census records 3 per cent of all immigrants in Greater Vancouver are from Africa, spread unevenly over its various municipalities (British Columbia Ministry of Community, Aboriginal and Women's Services 2004).[25] As the dispersal across municipalities suggests, there is no neighbourhood or district that can be identified as the centre of an African community, or any sub-group thereof. Thus by any measure, black African immigrants have the distinction of being both hyper-visible (in relation to the majority populations of European and Asian origins) and a tiny minority (in terms of sheer numbers) in the Vancouver area. It is within the social geography of visibility and of minority locations that African immigrants negotiate the local landscape and act to create an emerging African community in Vancouver.

Racializing Language, Placing Immigrants

The expansion of English across much of the globe was an integral part of centuries of British imperialism. As Willinsky reminds us, language 'was used to regulate and police access to authority and knowledge among colonized peoples' (1998, 191). The legacy of this 'intellectual project of imperialism' is a world in which English lays claim to status as a world language, and yet 'native speakers' in predominantly white English-speaking nations remain its privileged purveyors. Willinsky cautions that the 'frame of mind' in which one listens to those speaking English 'may still bear traces of the history of imperial conquest and dominance' (194).

As Norton argues, language is learned, communicated, and understood in the context of broader power relations (2000). The ability to be recognized as linguistically competent involves both the 'right to speak' and the 'power to impose reception,' or the right to be heard (9). In an immigrant context, neither the right to speak nor the right to be heard can be taken for granted. As Pierre Bourdieu notes, 'speech always owes a major part of its value to the value of the person who utters it' (Bourdieu 1977, 652). Different English accents provide cues to where a person was raised as a child, what their first language might be, and even their gender, class background, and racialized bodies, not all of which are equally valued by dominant members of the society. In the context of Vancouver, where nearly 40 per cent of residents are immigrants from somewhere else, many English accents can be readily identified as 'non-local'. Non-local accents do not enjoy equal ability to speak and be heard. Some, like British and Australian English accents, most often attached to white skins, seem to be accepted in the local environment without difficulty. Others are defined as 'foreign' accents, a socially constructed notion in a diverse cosmopolitan city. Moreover, accents defined as foreign are markers that both reinforce a speaker's 'non-Canadianness' and serve to discount social competencies in other areas (Creese and Kambere 2003; Henry 1999; Norton 2000; Scassa 1994).

Black African women in Vancouver live the legacy of British imperialism on many fronts, but nowhere more clearly than in their struggle to be recognized as competent speakers of English. Denigration of 'African English' accents is recounted as a daily occurrence, cited in the failure to get access to jobs, promotions, rental houses, adequate services, proper medical attention, and experienced through the daily correcting of pronunciation that friends, co-workers, and strangers alike seem to feel entitled to. In an erasure of their Commonwealth heritage, English-as-second-language (ESL) status is often assumed. As Kavuo recounts, she got used to people asking, 'Where did you learn your English, did you learn it on the plane over here?' (Kavuo, Interview 23). Indeed, some women recalled being pressured to take English-as-second-language classes in Canada, even though they have spoken English since childhood.

The erasure of prior English-language competency merges with the devaluation of 'African English' in the local Vancouver context:

It seems that somehow they put you in a spot where you become defensive. You have to defend how you talk. When they correct me I just say well this is the way you pronounce it, but this is the way I pronounce it. (Mapendo, Focus Group 1)

I don't know even if I live for how many years here, I don't think that will end. I don't think I can actually have the, the very accent they want me to have, and I will still have, always have those problems here, different ways like I pronounce things. (Vatisi, Interview 8)

It seems clear that these struggles over language competency are not so much issues of miscommunication – where the meaning is really not understood – as negotiations over power and social location. Indeed, misrecognition often seems intentional. As Abasi notes: 'I think people who do it on purpose, just to make you, let you know that you are speaking with a different accent' (Abasi, Interview 18). The construction of accent difference is a reaffirmation of immigrant status that serves to differentiate African women from other Canadians in daily encounters. In this way, the imagined nation is 'discursively patrolled through accents' (Creese and Kambere 2003, 566).

The everyday denigration of 'African English' is part of the symbolic reproduction of difference and otherness, a form of symbolic violence that has clear material consequences. Accents are markers for constructing general competencies (or incompetencies) as employees, neighbours, mothers, citizens, and the like. As Bizima observes, 'Since we can't talk like them, it's really hard to convince them that you can talk sense' (Bizima, Interview 5). The ways in which the content of one's speech is disregarded, trivialized, or simply not heard serves to silence and marginalize African women. As Sangara suggests, an African accent seems to render her speech unintelligible because the listener is preoccupied with locating her 'foreign' body:

Because that accent first of all, turns them off. I mean it just turns them right off, you know, that accent turns them right off. I mean when you get, I mean the thing is like when you speak, people are not prepared to listen to you. They hear the accent, that's all they hear. It takes some kind of person to listen to what you have, forget about the accent business. Yes, and that's what I call it. Once you open your mouth, the first day, they won't even understand what you say, what's going on in their minds 'where is she from, where is she from, where is she from?' (Sangara, Interview 9)

Moreover, as Kabugho explains, the act of locating one's 'foreign accent' is bound up with disentitlement to material resources: 'If you speak English in your accent, people will know that you are from Africa and by the accent they cannot give you a job, or a house.' (Kabugho, Focus Group 1). For example, several women recounted how their employment qualifications were deemed impressive on paper, but in interviews an employer's body language, comments, or curtness (one interview scheduled to take half an hour lasted no more than a few minutes) made it clear their accents were a barrier to employment.

Thus language creates a double disjuncture in African women's lived experiences in Vancouver: first, as women who hail from Commonwealth nations, English is understood as one of their own languages, and taking their own fluency for granted, the erasure of English competency is troubling and surprising; and second, the dominant discourse of Canada as a pluralist multicultural society makes perplexing the everyday denigration of the 'foreign' (be it accents, educational credentials, or people). Muhindo's comments get to the heart of this puzzle by locating her experiences in the processes of racialization:

> When you come here, you come from a continent or a country that was originally colonized by the British. You had your education, you were taught by the British. You speak your good English, but somehow they ask you 'What colour is your English?' (Muhindo)[26]

'African English' is, after all, embodied by black African speakers. How can denigration of one's 'African accent' be separated from response to one's African body? Thus for most of the women in this study, disparaging 'African English' was understood quite clearly as racism. As Mabunda argued, 'Language is a tool that has been used against us ... a systemic barrier that was put within the system to put us down' (Mabunda, Focus Group 1). For Mabunda, disparaging 'African English' accents is nothing less than an excuse for racial discrimination.

Some women despaired of their inability to localize their accents the way their children can and thereby be better accepted in the local community. More commonly, however, women refused to counsel such an abrogation of their identities and instead sought to reaffirm their African English heritage. As Vatisi commented, 'I tell them I was taught by the British, the original people of the English language, so how come you do not understand me?' (Vatisi, Interview 8). Similarly, Vira argued:

> What's wrong with my accent? As far as I am concerned, oh my God, that's a blessing from God, that's so beautiful, I like my accent. Come on Africans, stick to our customs, to our accents. One day, we will have our

offices and we will be, and the white people will come, also asking for job, and I will ask, 'How can you improve your accent?' (Vira, Interview 20)

Vira's comments clearly place the construction of 'local'/acceptable and 'foreign'/unacceptable accents back in the realm of larger power relations within Vancouver, and point to language competency as a 'diaspora space' where belonging and otherness is contested. Indeed, she envisions that these power relations could change in the future. Equally important, her comments reflect the growth of a pan-African identity in Vancouver as one way in which belonging can be reconstituted in the African community's own terms.

Labour Market Borders

The labour market constitutes another 'diaspora space' where otherness is constructed and contested. Although immigration policies focus on recruiting skilled workers, professionals and entrepreneurs, the Canadian labour market devalues all things – be it experience, educational credentials, or workers – construed as 'foreign.' African immigrant women must negotiate multiple borders to attain work and like many other immigrants, they commonly experience deskilling and under-employment.

Immigrant women encounter a gendered and racialized labour market that relegates most of them to low paying jobs. Like most labour markets, the Canadian labour market remains fundamentally gendered, with women concentrated in 'traditional' women's jobs, particularly in the clerical and sales and service sectors, and earning substantially lower pay than men across all occupational groups and educational levels (Statistics Canada 2000).[27] Aboriginal women, women of colour, and recent immigrants fare much worse in the labour market than their white, native-born, and non-Aboriginal counterparts. The former have lower rates of employment, higher rates of unemployment, lower wages, and are concentrated in less desirable and more 'non-standard' jobs (Fudge and Vosko 2003; Statistics Canada 2000, 2003b). A significant body of research documents a large and growing wage gap between immigrant and non-immigrant Canadians that particularly disadvantages recent immigrants (Aydemir and Skuterud 2004; Badets and Howatson-Leo 1999; Chui and Zietsma 2003; Frenette and Morissette 2003; Hiebert and Pendakur 2003; Li 2000, 2003; Picot and Hou 2003) and a wage gap between Canadian-born people of colour and whites that disadvantages people of colour, even when controlling for differences in education, occupation, and other human capital (Pendakur and Pendakur 1998, 2004; Tran 2004). Thus the ways in which immigrant women of colour are integrated into the Canadian labour market provides an example of what Anthias has referred to as 'disempowering' inclusion (2002b, 285).

Immigrants' central focus on employment is critical in an era of neo-liberal restructuring, where individual self-sufficiency has become paramount (McLaren and Dyck 2004). The 'ideal immigrant' is defined as an economically productive one who contributes skills, capital, and other resources to the Canadian economy. In this context, immigrant women use 'paid work as a primary entry point for negotiating their positions as mothers, immigrants and citizens' (44). Discourses of 'good' immigrant women centre on interconnections between mothering work and paid work, while local employment practices present obstacles to achieving this ideal state.

Most immigrants quickly discover that the local labour market is a 'bordered space' designed to restrict entry. The first border is the demand for Canadian work experience. In most cases, years of work experience attained elsewhere are summarily dismissed as meaningless. As Bizima commented, 'They look at what you have attained here in Canada, and not what you already had from back home. That does not count' (Bizima, Interview 5). In fact, recent research on declining incomes of immigrants shows that 'roughly one-third of the deterioration appears to be due to a persistent decline in the returns to foreign labour market experience which has occurred almost exclusively among immigrants originating from non-traditional [non-European] source countries' (Aydemir and Skuterud 2004, 3). The incongruity of multicultural discourses honouring difference and labour market practices that privilege the local – especially in a city where nearly 40 per cent of people originate from somewhere else – is not lost on the women in this research. Where, Kizito and Lwanzo ask, would you like us to attain our Canadian experience if no one will give us a job?

Whenever you apply, they ask you for Canadian experience. And if you have never worked here, where will you get experience? (Kizito, Interview 11)

People will tell you, people told me, if you get Canadian education that will be much easier. So I said, oh right then, but that was not the whole story, it's not just Canadian education. You need much more than that. Now they are telling me, you need Canadian experience. So I said, give me a break, where do I get Canadian experience? It's right here! If I get employed, I will get it right here, you know. (Lwanzo, Interview 10)

Negotiating initial entry to the labour market is often frustrating, time consuming, and particularly disheartening for independent immigrants who were recruited for their skills and education. As Media explained, high hopes can be quickly dashed:

I came with high hopes because, before I came I even searched on the internet, and I found at that time Canada was advertising 250,000 jobs. And I found, I tried to find out whether I was in the categories of the people they would want. Yes, this is me. This is me, only to come here and I got the surprise, the jobs are not there. (Media, Interview 4)

The most common routes to eventually finding employment are volunteer work to get some 'Canadian experience' on one's résumé,[28] enrolling in local courses and training programs to gain Canadian educational credentials, or seeking employment in one of the few areas that do not require Canadian experience – but from which it is also difficult to move on – such as temporary labour agencies, unskilled labour, or home work (Creese 2005).

Demands for Canadian educational credentials constitute another border in the local labour market. Although independent immigrants are admitted on the basis of their educational and occupational qualifications, most quickly find that they cannot practise their professions within Canada because their educational qualifications are not recognized by Canadian employers or professional associations (Basran and Zong 1998; Bauder and Cameron 2002; Geddie 2002; Henin and Bennett 2002; Li 2003; Reitz 2003). As Ndalula and Sangara explained:

The qualifications that I had back home, I came here so I looked into the system, I see that if you have any qualifications they are not accepting it. But there is a lot of, let me say discrimination, because you are not a Canadian, you are from Africa. So that made me to realize myself, I said let me go back to school. I have Canadian experience, and then I will bring out what I have. (Ndalula, Interview 14)

I consider myself an educated person, if I have two bachelors degrees, and a masters degree, what else do you get? Then, when you apply for job, it's just, I mean certain things are not considered relevant. They don't give you a chance to try and see what you can give them. Very relevant, somebody calls you for sales, for example, customer service, he just hears your accent. (Sangara, Interview 9)

Of course some 'foreign' degrees (attained in Britain, the United States, and sometimes western Europe) are more likely to be accepted at face value than others (attained in Africa, Asia, Latin America, or the Caribbean), resulting in a racialized 'discounting' of immigrants' educational credentials and skills that has increased over the last two decades (Reitz 2003). Coming from Commonwealth countries, some women had educational credentials that were clearly recognized as equivalent to those attained in the United Kingdom. Even for these women, their African educational credentials were not accepted in Canada:

My credentials were issued by UK, they told me they would accept UK qualifications, and yet when I presented them, they had all these reasons, you know. And then I checked in their manual, in their regulations. They would say, they would say, credentials accepted by UK. And then when I asked them, I said, this is what your regulations say, how come you are not honouring mine? And they didn't even reply to me. (Lwanzo, Interview 10)

This racialized evaluation of educational credentials is further illuminated in Li's research (2003). He shows that the undervaluation of university degrees (relative to white native-born Canadian degree holders) is greatest for immigrant women of colour with foreign degrees, but a significant wage gap also exists for immigrants of colour who earned their degrees within Canada. Thus those who pursue higher education within Canada still find it difficult to get jobs and salaries commensurate with their skills and education. As Konate and Kavuo commented, a Canadian degree does not make their African bodies disappear:

It is a lot of frustrations. You go to school, you finish, and you can hardly find a job. You go to school, you are just going for yourself, it's not like the community need you. The only time they hire the black person is when they are desperate. No, watch it, look around you, and the moment they get somebody better than that, they give the white person a position, a better position in the workplace. And you, the black person, you can be working in that place for fifty years, you can be staying there, no room for advancement, nothing. (Konate, Interview 2)

You find people who came here and have engineering degrees and still can't find work in engineering. Yes, I know they have to take their refresher courses and all that, but it's so difficult for them to find work because at the end of it, the qualifications are not the only thing that are going to give you the job. It's your accent, it's how you look, you know. (Kavuo, Interview 23)

The result of degree 'discounting' by employers and professional associations is deskilling and downward social mobility for highly skilled immigrants. Trained doctors, nurses, engineers, computer specialists, teachers, social workers, accountants, mechanics, and other skilled workers are all required to retrain in Canada before they will be considered for jobs in their fields. For many immigrants, retraining involves years in university, a cost which is often prohibitive, and they are still unlikely to reap the same rewards as their white native-born counterparts. The erasure of educational credentials and the professional expertise associated with them denies more than a person's human capital, it denies a person's value as a citizen and helps to reproduce immigrants of colour as cheap labour (McLaren and Dyck 2004). Thus the labour market constitutes one more 'diaspora space' where African women are constructed as others, differentiated from and inferior to those with local Canadian experience, education, and accents, and where there is an ongoing struggle for recognition of one's abilities and contributions. These struggles shape African women's experiences of what it means to belong in Vancouver. As Nzanzu and Ndungo reflect, we should not underestimate the ways that treatment in the labour market undermines one's sense of belonging in the local community:

The question of settling here is not, when you come in here, they give your pots and pans and then show you welfare. Do you understand what I am saying, it's not settling. What I mean by settling, some of them that come here, they already have a profession, you know, you have to tailor their needs towards that and show the easiest and the shortest way to be able to get to that. I will give you an example: if somebody is a doctor, and the person comes here, and the person is trying to get a license to practice. OK, so the person should be able to say, 'While you are doing that, this is another alternative you can do, to be able to get to your goal.' You have to have, what we call short-term goals and you have to have your long-term goals, so you use the short-term goals to get the long-term. OK, because

there's nothing [else] that can give you self-esteem, that will give you settlement to be able to be yourself, do you understand. What is happening
is that when they come here, they lose themselves. Because when you
already a doctor, you come here to sell pizza and you come here to drive a
taxi, and you do that, you are going to have problems with your marriage,
and you are going to have problems with your children, you are going to
have problems with the society. (Nzanzu, Interview 13)

First of all, I think my accent, and the education being foreign, has really
affected my settlement here. Because if they didn't treat my education as
foreign, as they do, I would have settled the first day I got here. Same to my
husband, you know, it would have been all easy for us, like a continuation
of life, you know. The problem is when you go for those interviews when
you apply for independent, you know immigrant status. That you know,
what you have is what you will continue to be and that did not happen for
us. So that really affects [us] and when you go sit in an interview, you
would almost, it's almost obvious, that someone will not employ you
because you are talking with an accent, not because you cannot talk
English and not because you are not learned, you know. (Ndungo, Interview 26)

As Nzanzu and Ndungo suggest, it is hard to imagine feeling one
belongs in the local community when experiences in the labour market
persistently reinforce the inadequacy and 'foreignness' of one's education, training, skills, experience, and accent, and thus reinforce a perceived lack of worth as workers and as citizens.

Negotiating Spaces of Belonging

The African women who participated in this study experienced a profound disjuncture between formal citizenship and the difficulties
involved in negotiating the diaspora space of 'Canadian.' As Bara commented:

Isn't that amazing that I have the documents, that I am declared, declared
Canadian citizen. Yet there are places where I know that I would have to
take the back seat because, because my being Canadian is not classified as
maybe, should I say, first grade Canadian? (Bara, Interview 30)

Similarly, Konate observed:

I am counted as a Canadian citizen, but my privileges here is limited. So that citizenship is an illusion. (Konate, Interview 2)

What might it feel like to be a 'first grade Canadian,' to make Canadian citizenship 'real' rather than illusory? Comments from Ndungo, Kavuo, Lwanzo, Abasi, and Bara about what it means to belong somewhere, with the full implication that they do not feel they really belong in Canada, provide some clues about how 'Canadian' is constructed in everyday interactions:

I feel I belong in Kenya. Because that is where I was accepted. Nobody ever doubted you, who you are, or whatever you are doing, or who, you know, nothing, there was nothing totally that made you feel like an outcast. But here, now and then, you get that feeling of like you are an outcast, you know. (Ndungo, Interview 26)

You belong the day you feel you don't have to defend yourself ... Or until the day they are not racist, I don't know. Belonging is, for me, I already feel I belong because I am here. I have a right to be here. I am already here, you know. I feel I belong, and I am going to do everything I can just anybody else would, raise the children just like anybody else would who has lived here all their life, born here, and raised here. But of course belonging is, you would feel also good if you don't get some of the questions you get. Not, you know, you don't get asked all the 'where did you do this, how did you do that, did you live in a house like this.' I guess maybe more just accepting of people, acceptance of the way you are, the way you talk. (Kavuo, Interview 23)

To belong to Canada is to be treated equally, I think that's when I would think I belong here. Right now, they look at me and right away they think that I don't belong here, you know. So belonging is to be seen as if I equally belong here, not you know as somebody who is passing through. (Lwanzo, Interview 10)

When you belong, I think it means that you are one, and you get access like everyone else. You are not treated differently, you are accepted and you are not different. [Interviewer: Do you feel you belong in Canada?] Not completely ... not 100 per cent because I don't get equal opportunities like everyone else. I may get equal opportunities, writing down on paper like you know, I am a Canadian citizen, I am able to do what other Canadians can do as the government stipulates I can get, like child tax benefit,

I can get medical, B.C. Pharmacare, I can get like tax return like most people. But there are some things that the government can't keep an eye on, like when you are going to look for a house, you are looking for, they are not there to watch you, when you are looking for a job especially. (Abasi, Interview 18)

When I first came here, it took maybe minimum of three years for me to first just feel like I belong, because every move, everything, I would compare with back in South Africa. So, that was a very big sense of not belonging to where I was. I would compare it with South Africa, compare it – at home, we don't do this, at home, we don't do this – until of course you have to confront yourself, and you say, 'Where is home now?' Then home is this Canada, but now the question is 'Am I taken as a Canadian? Am I considered Canadian?' So, those are the poles that an immigrant will always experience: yes to feel 'I belong here,' yet I don't belong here because I am not accepted. Because belonging also has to do with being accepted for who you are and feeling at home and comfortable. (Bara, Interview 30)

To feel one belongs in Canada is to feel accepted no matter what you do, how you sound, or what you look like; to be treated the same as other 'Canadians'; and to be perceived to belong to this place just as much as anyone else. As Bara notes, one's perceptions of belonging change over time as familiarity increases, roots grow and deepen, and 'home' shifts to where one is located in the here and now. However, notwithstanding changes with the passage of time, the multiple ways that categories of immigrant/foreign/deficient are reproduced in daily encounters – through responses to accents, bodies, and perceived abilities – mitigate a greater sense of belonging. African women, as Ntombi notes, find themselves located 'in-between,' seeking in others some recognition of their 'Canadianness': waiting 'for people to recognize, oh, he or she is a Canadian citizen' (Ntombi, Interview 3).

One way that participants in our research negotiate spaces of belonging is through the creation of a pan-African community. The small size of the African community in Vancouver makes this particularly challenging. As Kakoto observes, 'Here we are so few it's hard to find each other' (Kakoto, Interview 12). In contrast to much larger communities, particularly the Chinese and South Asian communities, where dense networks of shops, restaurants and other businesses, ethno-specific organizations, and residential patterns create vibrant and visible spaces within the city, Africans feel largely invisible as a cultural, social, or political presence in the local landscape. As Ndalula comments:

> If we are many here, we can establish a place like the Indians, or the Chinese people. They have the place they establish and you know that area as Indian zone. If you go there it's almost India, little India. If we are many as Africans, we will have a place to establish ourselves, this is African area. They have Chinese, India. So if we are many, we will do so. (Ndalula, Interview 14)

The importance of numbers means more than a space within the city to call one's own. It is also connected to the development of networks of support and opportunity, including networks for employment and business patronage. With a larger African community 'it will be easy for you to get a job. It will be easy for you to do your business' (Ougila, Interview 28). In fact some participants clearly identified the development of African-owned businesses as a central strategy for the creation of broader support networks in a developing African community. As Ndalula and Vira commented:

> What advice I would give the Africans? If we can love each other and if we can establish a business like other people do, we will not find it so difficult. Because like, for example, what I see like the Chinese people, they have stores all over, they have restaurants all over, and they employ their own people – only their own people. You can't go there, you are from Africa or you are Japanese, you are [not] working in a Chinese restaurant or any store of Chinese. The Indian people, the same. So Africans we should help each other and when ever we have something we have to get our brothers' share from what we have. (Ndalula, Interview 14)

> Since we are just minority group, that's our problem. I don't, I don't know, maybe they are there, some ideas of what should be done, honestly. Because you go to agencies, they are only white Canadians, or they are government-owned agencies, and you have to go through them. There is no way, unless we Africans, we start our own businesses, and our own stuff, that's the only way we can, you know, we can accommodate our black fellow. (Vira, Interview 20)

As Ougila, Ndalula, and Vira remind us, the small size and spatial dispersal of the African community shapes the nature of settlement in the local context.[29] African women recount feeling both highly visible in an environment where so few people are racialized as black, and invisible in terms of support services, community infrastructure, or political clout. Laziati eloquently captures this contradiction which results in a pressing need for specific services, and yet limited ability to pressure for change:

> I wish we had more people to, to be a political force and to have a voice because it seems like right now, we are the forgotten minority. Because we are so small in number we don't have any political clout, we cannot organize ourselves and sign up lots of people for nomination for parliament of whatever. So, yeah, we really don't seem to have a voice, yet we are taxpayers as well. We also are property owners. We have children here. We contribute to the economy and to the, to the society but we don't seem to have any say politically or otherwise ... I think what we need to do, is to really organize ourselves and make ourselves known. Start making ourselves known. You know, get out there, talk to the MP, talk to the mayors, talk to whoever, you know, that is in a position of power, about us because no one is going to do it for us except us. No one is going to say 'Oh my goodness, I think we have just forgotten those poor African people'. You know no one cares except for us. We are the ones that have to say, 'We are here and we are Canadians and we are taxpayers as well and we need to know what is happening to our community. What services are being delivered for our community? How is our community benefiting from our taxes?' (Laziati, Interview 6)

Embedded in discourses of citizenship rights, Laziati's comments chart a strategy to make claims as 'Canadians' drawing on discourses as parents, property owners, workers and tax payers, all the while recognizing that liberal democracy responds to numbers which the African community in British Columbia cannot muster.

That the African community should organize under a pan-African banner was a view held by most research participants. Unity among Africans and the creation of a strong African organization oriented towards fostering change in British Columbia, rather than along national lines oriented towards events in Africa, emerged as a central strategy for negotiating belonging. This movement towards pan-African organizing is based on shifting identities in the local context. Several women were vehement in their assertions that in their experience in Canada, national African identities were secondary:

> I don't feel like I have to associate with only Ugandans. I don't feel like I should maybe, Ugandans especially. As long as we are Africans, we are

one, we are, you know, we are recognized as African community, so not Ugandan community necessarily. So I feel like I belong to the African community. (Fulani, Interview 21)

I identify myself as an African. [Interviewer: OK, tell me, why not your country of origin?] Well, because when you come here, it doesn't matter where you come from, you know, they just lump you in one thing. And of course, I am not going about what people dictate to me. But for me, as an African, I have always felt more of a bond than other Africans, fellow Africans. So for me, I am an African first before my own country. (Laziati, Interview 6)

You see an African lady. You don't see Nigerian. That's when you see me, you see an African ... [Interviewer: OK, what does this identity mean to you, being an African?] It means that I am African. What it means to me, that I am African, you know. What identity means to me, as an African, nothing can change that in me. Nothing can shake that. That's who I am and I thank God. (Sangara, Interview 9)

Differences among national cultures, languages, religions, and other elements of identity remain but were considered less important than the commonalities experienced as Africans and the support and understanding based on shared experiences.

The African community? It's like you understand each other. You have common understanding of what life is all about so you don't have to explain yourself when you say, when you have got, you like to share with people, which is part of our culture. (Lwanzo, Interview 10)

I always say as an African, you better understand who I am as an African and where I come from, and what my values are. And what life has been, for us. And then of course, coming here, and being viewed as a minority, and as people of colour, you, you begin to feel that you have to identify with some people of your own, you know colour and background. (Laziati, Interview 6)

Not surprisingly, the expression of a distinct African identity and community in Vancouver leads to increasing pressure for the development of a unified African organization able to advance the community's needs and desires in the local political arena. Community organizing is a strategy to provide greater support within the community (by creating, for example, an African immigrant services organization) and to enhance the political weight of small numbers (to lobby various levels of government on issues of concern to the community). Organizing as a community is, in turn, another way of negotiating belonging. Not only will organizing help provide greater unity among the African community itself, but it will also lead to greater recognition of that community's presence within the local landscape:

> But maybe if the Africans united together as just Africans, then you feel, as a big group of just Africans, you would be more powerful. Maybe you would open your own businesses, employ your people and, because you find that the Asians. They have big companies run by Asians and they hire just their people. That way, you tend to be more out there, people know about you. (Kavuo, Interview 23)

> We have to get together, do something for people to recognize us and say, and then 'Oh yes they belong here.' Like for people, when they recognize you, they know that you are there. But when they don't recognize you, they just say, they can't say you belong. You have to get together, get together, Africans. Get together and then do something, do something. Bring some ideas, do something for people to know us. (Ntombi, Interview 3)

> Like if we have Africa community, so like if we really have Africa community, meeting once in a month, so with that, we see ourselves, seeing ourselves, that will help us to know what we can do for we change our life here in Canada. Because whereby everybody is staying on their own, how can we make a move, how can we make a change? Everybody is staying on their own, like we don't have community, we don't have meeting. So it's really hard for us to do something. But whereby we have a strong community as an African, not Nigerian community, just the Africa community, at least we meet once in a month, then we'll know what to do. And then maybe they will see that maybe Africans are many here, oh, you see. Maybe then, we can be bringing our market, then see what we can do for this community to know us, you know. (Ougila, Interview 28)

Shifting identities and community formation among African women reflect the construction of new imagined communities – as African – in a local context that excludes them from the broader imagined community of 'Canadians.' Organizing as an African community may, in turn, be one step towards greater recognition of an African presence and contribution to the broader community.

Conclusions

Black women who migrate from former British colonies in sub-Saharan Africa to Vancouver encounter a seemingly endless series of bordered 'diaspora spaces' in which inclusion and exclusion, belonging and otherness are contested. These spaces are mediated by multicultural discourses of a pluralist immigrant society embedded in a historically imagined white community. African women experience the erasure of their Commonwealth heritage – connections they expect to share with others in Canada – as their pre-existing facility with English and their British-modelled educational credentials are challenged and dismissed as inadequate. The result is that African women are constructed only through 'difference.' Accents, bodies, credentials, experience, and capabilities are denigrated as foreign/immigrant/deficient in a form of symbolic violence that racializes African women and places them in subordinate locations in workplaces, neighbourhoods, and discourses of nation-building.

What distinguishes the experience of African women in Vancouver from many other immigrant groups in Canada is the juxtaposition of hyper-visibility (in a context where only 1 per cent of the population are racialized as black) and real minority status (where only 3 per cent of all immigrants come from Africa). In the face of these demographic realities and exclusion from the imagined community of 'Canadians,' belonging is negotiated through the formation of a new pan-African identity and the struggle to organize within the African community. Thus organizing the African community is a central strategy not only to improve life's chances for community members and their children, but also to make the community's presence felt within the larger society and thereby gain a space from which to make claims as Canadians of African origin.

Notes

I would like to thank my friends and collaborators Edith Ngene Kambere and Mambo Masinda for their invaluable work as research assistants, for their ongoing advice and counsel, and for their unfailing encouragement that we should undertake this project. Although neither is able to devote the time to help in writing up these results, this paper owes much to their influence and advice. Whatever errors remain are of course my responsibility. I am grateful to all the women and men who agreed to participate in this project, and who trusted that telling their stories might, in the long run, help create change. I would also like to thank Anisha Datta and Brandy Wiebe for their conscientious work as research assistants, and Leslie Roman and Nikki Strong-Boag for their helpful comments on an earlier draft. In addition, I am grateful to the Vancouver Centre of Excellence for Research on Immigration and Integration in the Metropolis (RIIM) for funding the pilot project, and the Social Sciences and Humanities Research Council of Canada for funding the main study.

1 All research participants are referred to using pseudonyms.
2 'Visible minority' is the Canadian government terminology for people 'other than Aboriginal peoples, who are non-Caucasian or non-white in colour' (Statistics Canada 2003a, 10). The term 'people of colour' is more commonly used by those racialized as non-white.
3 At the same time, it should be remembered that three out of every ten people of colour are born in Canada, and many can trace their Canadian heritage back several generations (Statistics Canada 2003a, 10).
4 Although I do not hold essentialist views that one must limit research fields to those bearing on one's own social location, I recognize the validity of feminist postcolonial and post-structuralist critiques of white northern feminists appropriating marginalized voices and reproducing relations of power and privilege while 'othering' and exoticizing research subjects. As a privileged white academic, it was with much hesitation that I decided to undertake this project to explicate the experiences of black women and men who recently migrated from Africa. I would not, and indeed could not, have done this work without the participation, ongoing conversations, support, and whole-hearted enthusiasm for the project expressed by Edith Ngene Kambere and Mambo Masinda, and the trust of all those women and men who agreed to be interviewed. I have tried to negotiate these multifaceted power relations in an effort to speak 'with' or 'beside' rather than 'for' those who participated in this study (Dossa 2004, 22; Strong-Boag and Gerson 2000, 5–6). The text reflects this effort with the use of extensive quotations from interviews. It will be up to others, particularly those within the African community, to assess how well I have succeeded in this task.
5 I use Anderson's (1991) notion of 'imagined communities' as the commonsense construction of who belongs (and who does not) within nation-states.
6 As many North American scholars have pointed out, whiteness is an unsta-

ble, historically contingent, and contested category (see for example Frankenberg 1993; Jacobson 1998; and Rasmussen et al. 2001). In the Canadian context, more and more European ethnic communities were redefined as 'white' over time.

7 See Roberta Hamilton (1996) for a gendered reading of the vertical mosaic.

8 It is hard to argue that colonization and nation-building in Canada is less assimilationist and racist than in the United States, though it has been configured somewhat differently given different histories (especially the predominance of slavery in the United States and the presence of Quebec in Canada). In spite of a long assimilationist history in Canada, popular ideologies often contrast Canadian pluralism with American assimilation. See, for example, Daiva Stasiulis and Nira Yuval-Davis, *Unsettling Settler Societies* (1995).

9 As Wenona Giles has demonstrated in her study of Portuguese women in Toronto, some non English-speaking migrants from some parts of Europe are racialized in ways similar to migrants of colour (Giles 2002). See also Franca Iacovetta, *Such Hardworking People* (1992), for similar historical arguments about Italian immigrants.

10 After three years in Canada immigrants may apply for Canadian citizenship. In 2001, 84 per cent of those eligible to apply were Canadian citizens (Tran, Krustec, and Chui 2005).

11 As Gloria Anzaldúa argues, those who inhabit the 'borderlands' or 'the spaces in between' shift back and forth across borders, never fully belonging in any space (1987; 2000).

12 The participants in this research are referred to as black or African, rather than African-Canadian, because that is how they identify themselves.

13 The pilot project of two focus groups, conducted in 2002, involved twelve women and was funded by the Vancouver Centre for Research on Immigration and Integration in the Metropolis (RIIM). The larger project, funded by the Social Science and Humanities Research Council of Canada, involves interviews with thirty-one women and thirty men from diverse countries in sub-Saharan Africa. These interviews were conducted in 2004. This paper draws on twenty-four of these interviews with women who migrated from countries that were once British colonies. Interviews with men have not been analysed yet so it is not possible at this time to assess the degree to which women's and men's experiences are different. However, gender differences will constitute a major theme of the overall project.

14 Independent immigrants are assessed through a points system that focuses on education, occupation, and knowledge of the two official languages, English and French (a sub-set of business immigrants are assessed largely in terms of investment capital); family class immigrants are immediate

dependants of Canadians or landed immigrants and are not assessed through the points system; refugees are either selected abroad from among those designated as refugees by the UNHCR or from those who travel to Canada to make an inland refugee claim (which may or may not ultimately be successful).

15 At the time of the interviews one woman was a refugee claimant, twelve were landed immigrants, and eleven were Canadian citizens.

16 Toronto, Montreal, and Halifax all have significant black populations with long-established histories in each city. For an overview of diversity of black communities across the country see Mensah 2002. For research on black women specifically, see Agnew 1996; Brand 1993; Bristow 1994; Calliste 2000; Daenzer 1997; Elabor-Idemudia 2000; Thornhill 1989; and Wane, Lawson, and Deliovsky 2002. For research on African immigrants, see Adjibolosoo and Mensah 1998; Danso and Grant 2000; Elabor-Idemudia 2000; Mensah 2002; and Mensah and Abjibolosoo 1998.

17 For a good overview of issues of immigration and diversity in Toronto, see Siemiatycki et al., Integrating Community Diversity: On Whose Terms? (2001).

18 Toronto ranked second only to Miami, followed by Los Angeles and Vancouver (Conway-Smith 2004).

19 Here, the term immigrant refers to all those who are not Canadian-born. As indicated in note 10, the vast majority of landed immigrants (the legal term for those granted permanent resident status in Canada) are also Canadian citizens.

20 To put trends in Vancouver in a national context, 18.4 per cent of the total population of Canada are of immigrant background and 13.4 per cent are people of colour (Statistics Canada 2003a, 5–10).

21 Figures for the City of Vancouver, also based on the 2001 Census, are drawn from Multicultural Profiles for B.C. Communities, in British Columbia Ministry of Community, Aboriginal and Women's Services; http://www. mcaws.gov.bc.ca/amip/rpts/profiles.htm (accessed 9 July 2004).

22 For more on the changing diversity of Vancouver, see Hiebert 1999a and 1999b.

23 In the census metropolitan area of Vancouver, 18,410 people identified as black out of a population of 1,967,480 (Statistics Canada, 2001 Census) www12.statcan.ca/English/census01 (accessed 17 July 2004).

24 Altogether, 17,465 people identified as 'African,' though this includes many Africans who are white or Asian in ethnic origins; for example, 20 per cent of all those with African descent in the Vancouver area came from South Africa, and the majority of these people are likely to be white. There were 6,320 people who identified as 'African (Black)' and 1,680 identified as

'Black,' in all 46 per cent of all those who claimed African descent. In addition, it is likely that some Africans who are Black identified themselves by their country of descent (Statistics Canada, 2001 Census) www12.stat-can.ca/English/census01 (downloaded October 20, 2003).

25 According to the 2001 Census, immigrants from Africa constitute 2 per cent of immigrants in the City of Vancouver and Surrey, 3 per cent in Richmond, 4 per cent in Coquitlam, 5 per cent in Burnaby, New Westminster, and the City of North Vancouver, 6 per cent in Port Coquitlam and West Vancouver, 7 per cent in Port Moody, and 9 per cent in the District of North Vancouver (British Columbia Ministry of Community, Aboriginal & Women's Services, 2004). On one level, these figures can be a bit deceiving. The municipalities with the highest percentages of immigrants from Africa, such as West Vancouver, North Vancouver, Port Coquitlam, and Port Moody, actually have the lowest proportions of immigrants overall and lower percentages of people of colour than more diverse areas such as Vancouver, Burnaby, Richmond and Surrey. In addition, it is very likely that many of the African immigrants living in the more affluent suburbs of North and West Vancouver are white South Africans.

26 This quote comes from a participant in a multi-ethnic focus group with immigrant women conducted in 1997 as part of a larger longitudinal study of settlement issues in East Vancouver. Muhindo is originally from Uganda.

27 For full-time workers across all occupations, women average 72.5 per cent of men's earnings; women with university degrees earn 73.6 per cent of their male counterpart's earnings (Statistics Canada 2000, 156).

28 Women, more than men, seemed to be pressured to perform volunteer work to gain some 'Canadian experience' for their résumés (Lee 1999b). It is particularly difficult for mothers to perform unpaid work and pay for childcare. In addition, for many, volunteer work is a concept that is considered demeaning (Creese 2005).

29 We did not ask why people choose to live in the neighbourhoods they do. However, the high price of real estate in Vancouver (which for some years has been the most expensive in the country) is clearly implicated in a more general pattern among recent immigrants of dispersal across the outer, less expensive suburbs.

References

Abu-Laban, Y. 1998. Keeping 'em out: gender, race, and class biases in Canadian immigration policy. In *Painting the maple: Essays on race, gender, and the construction of Canada*, ed. V. Strong-Boag, S. Grace, A. Eisenberg, and J. Anderson, 60–82. Vancouver: UBC Press.

Abu-Laban, Y., and C. Gabriel. 2002. *Selling diversity: Immigration, multiculturalism, employment equity, and globalization*. Peterborough, ON: Broadview.

Adjibolosoo, S., and J. Mensah. 1998. *The provision of settlement services to African immigrants in the Lower Mainland of B.C.* Part 2. Victoria: Ministry Responsible for Multiculturalism and Immigration, Community Liaison Division.

Agnew, V. 1996. *Resisting discrimination: Women from Asia, Africa, and the Caribbean and the Women's movement in Canada*. Toronto: University of Toronto Press.

– 2003. *Where I come from*. Waterloo: Wilfred Laurier University Press.

Anderson, B. 1991. *Imagined communities*. London: Verso.

Anthias, F. 2002a. Diasporic hybridity and transcending racisms: Problems and potentials. In *Rethinking anti-racism: From theory to practice*, ed. F. Anthias and C. Lloyd, 22–43. London: Routledge.

– 2002b. Beyond feminism and multiculturalism: Locating difference and the politics of location. *Women's Studies International Forum* 25 (3): 275–86.

Anzaldúa, G. 1987. *Borderlands: the new mestiza/La frontera*. San Francisco: Aunt Lute Books.

– 2000. *Interviews/Entrevistas*, ed. A. Keating. New York: Routledge.

Arat-Koc, S. 1997. From 'Mothers of the Nation' to migrant workers. In *Not one of the family: Foreign domestic workers in Canada*, ed. A. Bakan and D. Statisiulis, 53–79. Toronto: University of Toronto Press.

Aydemir, A., and M. Skuterud. 2004. Explaining the deteriorating entry earnings of Canada's immigrant cohorts: 1966–2000. Statistics Canada, Analytical Studies Branch Research Paper Series.

Badets, J., and L. Howatson-Leo. 1999. Recent immigrants in the workforce. *Canadian Social Trends* 52 (Spring): 16–22.

Bannerji, H. 2000. *The dark side of the nation: Essays on multiculturalism, nationalism and gender*. Toronto: Canadian Scholars' Press.

Basran, G., and L. Zong. 1998. Devaluation of foreign credentials as perceived by visible minority professional immigrants. *Canadian Ethnic Studies* 30 (3): 6–23.

Bauder, H., and E. Cameron. 2002. Cultural barriers to labour market integration: Immigrants from South Asia and the former Yugoslavia. Working Paper Series No. 02-03, Vancouver Centre of Excellence Research on Immigration and Integration in the Metropolis.

Bourdieu, Pierre. 1977. The economics of linguistic exchanges. *Social Science Information* 16 (6): 652. Cited in Norton 2000, 8.

Boyd, M. 1997. Migration policy, female dependency, and family membership:

Canada and Germany. In *Women and the Welfare State*, ed. P. Evans and G. Wekerle, 142–69. Toronto: University of Toronto Press.

– 1999. Integrating gender, language, and race. In *Immigrant Canada: Demographic, economic, and social challenges*, ed. S. Halli and L. Driedger, 282–306. Toronto: University of Toronto Press.

– 2001. Gender, refugee status, and permanent settlement. In *Immigrant women*, ed. R.J. Simon, 103–23. London: Transaction.

Brah, A. 1996. *Cartographies of diaspora: Contesting home*. London: Routledge.

Brand, D. 1993. A working paper on Black women in Toronto: Gender, race and class. In *Returning the gaze: Essays on racism, feminism and politics*, ed. H. Bannerji, 220–42. Toronto: Sister Vision.

Bristow, P., ed. 1994. *'We're rooted here and they can't pull us up': Essays in African Canadian women's history*. Toronto: University of Toronto Press.

British Columbia, Ministry of Community, Aboriginal and Women's Services. 2004. *Multicultural Profiles for B.C. Communities, 2001*. http://www.mcaws.gov.bc.ca.

Calliste, A. 2000. Nurses and porters: Racism, sexism and resistance in segmented labour markets. In *Anti-Racist feminism*, ed. A. Calliste and G.S. Dei, 143–64. Halifax: Fernwood.

Chui, T., and D. Zietsma. 2003. Earnings of immigrants in the 1990s. *Canadian Social Trends* 70 (Autumn): 24–8.

Conway-Smith, E. 2004. Toronto second in proportion of foreign-born. *Globe and Mail*, 16 July.

Creese, G. 2005. Negotiating belonging: Bordered spaces and imagined communities in Vancouver, Canada. Working Paper Series No. 05-06, Vancouver Centre of Excellence Research on Immigration and Integration in the Metropolis.

Creese, G., and R. Dowling. 2001. Gendering immigration: The experience of women. *Progress in Planning* 55 (3): 153–62.

Creese, G., and E. N. Kambere. 2003. What colour is your English? *Canadian Review of Sociology and Anthropology* 50 (5): 565–73.

Daenzer, P. 1997. Challenging diversity: Black women and social welfare. In *Women and the welfare state*, ed. P. Evans and G. Wekerle, 269–90. Toronto: University of Toronto Press.

Danso, R., and M. Grant. 2000. Access to housing as an adaptive strategy for immigrant groups: Africans in Calgary. *Canadian Ethnic Studies* 32 (3): 19–43.

Das Gupta, T. 1999. The politics of multiculturalism: 'Immigrant women' and the Canadian state. In *Scratching the surface: Canadian anti-racist feminist thought*, ed. E. Dua and A. Robertson, 187–205. Toronto: Women's Press.

Dhruvarajan, V., and J. Vickers. 2002. *Gender, race, and nation: A global perspective*. Toronto: University of Toronto Press.

Dossa, P. 2002. Modernization and global restructuring of women's work: Border-crossing stories of Iranian women. Working Paper Series No. 02-09, Vancouver Centre of Excellence Research on Immigration and Integration in the Metropolis.

– 2004. *Politics and poetics of migration: Narratives of Iranian women from the diaspora*. Toronto: Canadian Scholar's Press.

Dyck, I., and A.T. McLaren. 2002. 'I don't feel quite competent here': Immigrant mothers' involvement with schooling. Working Paper Series No. 02-12, Vancouver Centre of Excellence Research on Immigration and Integration in the Metropolis.

Elabor-Idemudia, P. 2000. 'Challenges confronting African immigrant women in the Canadian workforce'. In *Anti-Racist feminism*, ed. A. Calliste and G.S. Dei, 91–110. Halifax: Fernwood.

Fortier, A.M. 2000. *Migrant belongings: Memory, space, identity*. Oxford: Berg.

Frankenberg, R. 1993. *The social construction of whiteness: White women, race matters*. Minneapolis: University of Minnesota Press.

Frenette, M., and R. Morissette. 2003. Will they ever converge? Earnings of immigrant and Canadian-born workers over the last two decades. Statistics Canada, Analytical Studies Branch Research Paper Series.

Fudge, J., and L. Vosko. 2003. Gender paradoxes and the rise of contingent work: Towards a transformative political economy of the labour market. In *Changing Canada: Political economy as transformation*, ed. Wallace Clement and Leah Vosko, 183–209. Montreal: McGill-Queen's University Press.

Geddie, K. 2002. Licence to labour: Obstacles facing Vancouver's foreign-trained engineers. Working Paper Series No. 02-21, Vancouver Centre of Excellence Research on Immigration and Integration in the Metropolis.

Giles, W. 2002. *Portuguese women in Toronto: Gender, immigration, and nationalism*. Toronto: University of Toronto Press.

Giles, W., and V. Preston. 1996. The domestication of women's work: a comparison of Chinese and Portuguese immigrant women homeworkers. *Studies in Political Economy* 51:147–81.

Gonick, M. 2000. Canadian = blonde, English, white: Theorizing race, language and nation. *Atlantis* 24 (2): 93–104.

Hamilton, R. 1996. *Gendering the vertical mosaic: Feminist perspectives on Canadian society*. Toronto: Copp Clark.

Henin, B., and M. Bennett. 2002. Immigration to Canada's mid-sized cities: A study of Latin Americans and Africans in Victoria, B.C. Working Paper

Series No. 02-22, Vancouver Centre of Excellence Research on Immigration and Integration in the Metropolis.

Henry, F, 1999. Two studies of racial discrimination in employment. In *Social inequality in Canada*, 3rd ed., ed. J. Curtis, E. Grab, and N. Guppy, 226–35. Scarborough, ON: Prentice-Hall Allyn and Bacon Canada.

Henry, F., and C. Tator. 2002. *Discourses of domination: Racial bias in the Canadian English-language press.* Toronto: University of Toronto Press.

Henry, F., C. Tator, W. Matttis, and T. Rees. 1995. *The colour of democracy: Racism in Canadian society.* Toronto: Harcourt, Brace.

Hiebert, D. 1999a. Local geographies of labour market segmentation: Montreal, Toronto and Vancouver, 1991. *Economic Geography* 75 (3): 339–69.

– 1999b. Immigration and the changing social geography of greater Vancouver. *BC Studies* 121:35–82.

Hiebert, D., and R. Pendakur. 2003. Who's cooking? The changing ethnic diversity of labour in Canada, 1971–1996. Working Paper Series No.03-09, Vancouver Centre of Excellence Research on Immigration and Integration in the Metropolis.

Iacovetta, F. 1992. *Such hardworking people: Italian immigrants in postwar Toronto.* Montreal: McGill-Queen's University Press.

Jacobson, M.F. 1998. *Whiteness of a different colour: European immigrants and the alchemy of race.* Cambridge, MA: Harvard University Press.

Lautard, H., and N. Guppy. 1990. The vertical mosaic revisited: Occupational differentials among Canadian ethnic groups. In *Race and ethnic relations in Canada*, ed. P. Li, 189–208. Toronto: Oxford University Press.

Lee, J.A. 1999a. *Immigrant settlement and multiculturalism programs for immigrant, refugee and visible minority women: A study of outcomes, best practices and issues.* Report submitted to the British Columbia Ministry Responsible for Multiculturalism and Immigration.

– 1999b. Immigrant women workers in the immigrant settlement sector. *Canadian Woman Studies* 19 (3): 97–103.

Li, P. 1998. The market value and social value of race. In *Racism and social inequality in Canada*, ed. V. Satzewich, 115–30. Toronto: Thompson Educational.

– 2000. Earning disparities between immigrants and native-born Canadians. *Canadian Review of Sociology and Anthropology* 37 (3): 289–311.

– 2003. *Destination Canada: Immigration debates and issues.* Don Mills, ON: Oxford University Press.

Lian, J., and D.R. Matthews. 1998. Does the vertical mosaic still exist? Ethnicity and income in Canada. *Canadian Review of Sociology and Anthropology* 35 (4): 461–81.

Lo, L., V. Preston, S. Wang, K. Reil, E. Harvey, and B. Siu. 2001. Immigrants' economic status in Toronto: Rethinking settlement and integration strategies. Working paper no. 15, Joint Centre for Excellence on Research on Immigration and Settlement. http://www.ceris.metropolis.net.

Mackey, E. 2002. *The house of difference: Cultural politics and national identity in Canada*. Toronto: University of Toronto Press.

McLaren, A.T., and I. Dyck. 2004. Mothering, human capital, and the 'ideal immigrant.' *Women's Studies International Forum* 27:41–53.

Mensah, J. 2002. *Black Canadians: History, experiences, social conditions*. Halifax: Fernwood.

Mensah, J., and S. Adjibolosoo. 1998. *The demographic profile of African immigrants in the Lower Mainland of B.C.*, Part 1. Victoria: Ministry Responsible for Multiculturalism and Immigration, Community Liaison Division.

Ng, R. 1990. Immigrant women: The construction of a labour market category. *Canadian Journal of Women and the Law* 4 (1): 96–112.

– 1998. Work restructuring and recolonizing Third World women: An example from the garment industry in Toronto. *Canadian Woman Studies* 19 (1): 21–5.

Norton, B. 2000. *Identity and language learning: Gender, ethnicity and educational change*. Harlow, UK: Pearson Education.

Pendakur, K., and R. Pendakur. 1998. The colour of money: earnings differentials among ethnic groups in Canada. *Canadian Journal of Economics* 31 (3): 518–48.

– 2004. Colour my world: Has the majority-minority earnings gap changed over time? Working Paper Series No. 04-11, Vancouver Centre of Excellence Research on Immigration and Integration in the Metropolis.

Perry, A. 2001. *On the edge of empire: Gender, race and the making of British Columbia, 1849–1871*. Toronto: University of Toronto Press.

Picot, G., and F. Hou. 2003. The rise in low-income rates among immigrants in Canada. Statistics Canada, Analytical Studies Branch Research Paper Series.

Porter, J. 1965. *The vertical mosaic: An analysis of social class and power in Canada*. Toronto: University of Toronto Press.

Pratt, G. 2002. Between homes: Displacement and belonging for second generation Filipino-Canadian youth. Working Paper Series No. 02-13, Vancouver Centre of Excellence Research on Immigration and Integration in the Metropolis.

– 2004. *Working feminism*. Philadelphia: Temple University Press.

Preston, V., and W. Giles. 1997. Ethnicity, gender and labour markets in Canada: A case study of immigrant women in Toronto. *Canadian Journal of Urban Research* 6 (2): 135–59.

Rasmussen, B., E. Klinenberg, I. Nexica, and M. Wray, eds. 2001. *The making and unmaking of whiteness*. Durham, NC: Duke University Press.

Razack, S. 1998. *Looking white people in the eye*. Toronto: University of Toronto Press.

Reitz, J. 2003. Occupational dimensions of immigrant credential assessment: Trends in professional, managerial, and other occupations, 1970–1996. Paper presented at the conference on Canadian Immigration Policy for the 21st Century. http://www.utoronto.ca/ethnicstudies/research.htm.

Satzewich, V., and L. Wong. 2003. Immigration, ethnicity and race: the transformation of transnationalism, localism, and identities. In *Changing Canada: Political economy as transformation*, ed. W. Clement and L. Vosko, 363–90. Montreal: McGill-Queen's University Press.

Scassa, T. 1994. Language, standards, ethnicity and discrimination. *Canadian Ethnic Studies* 26 (3): 105–21.

Siemiatycki, M., T. Rees, R. Ng, and K. Rahi. 2001. Integrating community diversity in Toronto: On whose terms? Working paper no. 14, Joint Centre for Excellence on Research on Immigration and Settlement. http://www.ceris.metropolis.net.

Stasiuilis, D., and R. Jhappan, 1995. The fractious politics of a settler society: Canada. In *Unsettling settler societies: Articulations of gender, race, ethnicity and class*, ed. D. Stasiulis and N. Yuval-Davis, 95–131. London: Sage.

Stasiulis, D., and N. Yuval-Davis. 1995. *Unsettling settler societies: Articulations of gender, race, ethnicity and class*. London: Sage.

Statistics Canada, 2000. *Women in Canada 2000: A Gender-based statistical report*. Ottawa: Ministry of Industry, Catalogue no. 89-503-XPE.

– 2001. *Census of Canada*. http:// www.statcan.ca.

– 2003a. *Canada's ethnocultural portrait: The changing mosaic*. 2001 Census Analysis Series, 21 January. Catalogue no. 96F0030XIE2001008.

– 2003b. *The changing profile of Canada's labour force*. 2001 Census Analysis Series, 11 February. Catalogue no. 96F0030XIE2001009.

Strong-Boag, V., and C. Gerson. 2000. *Paddling her own canoe: The times and texts of E. Pauline Johnson Tekahionwake*. Toronto: University of Toronto Press.

Thobani, S. 2000. Nationalizing Canadians: Bordering immigrant women in the late twentieth century. *Canadian Journal of Women and the Law* 12 (2): 279–312.

Thornhill, E. 1989. Focus on black women. *Socialist Studies* 5:26–36.

Tran, K. 2004. Visible minorities in the labour force: 20 years of change. *Canadian Social Trends* 73 (Summer): 7–11

Tran, K, S. Kustec, and T. Chui. 2005. Becoming Canadian: Intent, process and outcome. *Canadian Social Trends* (Spring): 8–13.

Wane, N., E. Lawson, and K. Deliovsky, eds. 2002. *Back to the drawing board: African-Canadian feminisms*. Toronto: Sumach.

Walters, J., and S.Y. Teo. 2003. Social and cultural impacts of immigration: An examination of the concept of 'social cohesion' with implications for British Columbia. Working Paper Series No. 03-03, Vancouver Centre of Excellence Research on Immigration and Integration in the Metropolis.

Willinsky, J. 1998. *Learning to divide the world: Education at empire's end*. Minneapolis: University of Minnesota Press.

12 Being White and Thinking Black: An Interview with Frances Henry

VIJAY AGNEW

Introduction

In her 1991 book, *No Burden to Carry*, Dionne Brand expressed the sentiments of many racialized academics when she wrote that 'Canadian scholarship overall has been preoccupied with English and French concerns, to the exclusion of Canadian people of non-European origin. This, at best, is xenophobic; it is also racist' (11). Racism lies in the absence or marginalization of racialized populations in accounts of Canadian history and society, the use of white Canadians as the norm to which others are explicitly or otherwise compared, the denigration of the 'homes' and heritages of racialized people, and their individual or collective exclusion through inhospitable attitudes. Historically, the imagined Canada has been constructed as a white nation (Hoerder 1999).

In the last decade, a body of literature has emerged that analyses the experiences of racialized groups such as Aboriginals, Chinese, South Asians, and blacks from diverse disciplinary perspectives. Racism as a subject has also been accorded status and respect in most disciplines, and there are many studies that either discuss its meaning, history, and significance, or use the lens of race to analyse public policies such as immigration, national and border security, and refugees (Li 2004; Aiken 2001; Macklin 2001). Similarly, the history and politics of racialized women have been documented and a substantial body of literature now exists. This literature has grown enormously, although Canadian scholarship on racism is not yet of the calibre of the writings of Stuart Hall (in Britain) or of American scholars such as Paul Gilroy or Patricia Williams. However, in the hands of the next generation of scholars perhaps it will continue to develop and become more dynamic.

White scholarship on colonized subjects has been criticized for its biases and for constructing those cultures and societies as the 'Other' (Said 1978). Such scholarship, it is alleged, has treated the colonized, subordinate, or disempowered culture, group, or society as an object of study and not as a participating and engaged subject. The 'truth' about the Other documented in such writings is now considered to be biased, ethnocentric, or plain racist. Critics of these accounts have questioned the privileged position of the author vis-à-vis the subject and have made explicit the power relations embedded in such scholarship. Questions have been raised about the right of the dominant group to speak on behalf of the disempowered, as when males write about females, whites about blacks, and heterosexuals about gay and lesbian rights. Disputing the authority of the powerful, the disempowered and the subordinate have struggled to give voice to their understanding and thus play a role in constructing knowledge.

The scholarly discourse on race and racism in Canada is multidisciplinary and has been written by authors of diverse identities. Throughout the 1980s and 1990s, identity became a significant concept in epistemology and a site of contestation. Initially, identity was viewed as comprising socially significant criteria such as race, gender, class, and sexuality, and their intersections in particular groups and individuals. Identity is not fixed but is historically determined, and since it is constantly negotiated within societies and cultures, it is fluid and changing. Subjectivity 'encompasses conscious and unconscious dimensions of the self, such as one's sense of who one is in relation to other people' (Henry 2002, 250). I discuss this in greater detail in the introduction to this volume and note that subjectivity is discursively produced; in other words, it is created through a process. It is the affect of conscious and unconscious forces, embodied; it is also an expression (or an affect) of power (Code 2000, 398).

Postmodern analyses, such as those of Judith Butler, cast doubt on the significance of physicality or the body, particularly in discussions of gender and race. Butler's writings have spawned a debate on how to reconcile, intellectually and theoretically, the tension between the socially constructed body (meanings imposed upon the body) and essentialism (a set of innate physical differences) (Butler 1990; Weir 2000). The conventional understanding of identity politics proposed solidarity based on commonalities (for example, sexual identity among feminists in the 1970s and race among the proponents of civil rights), but its unintended affect was to exclude and silence different perspectives that emerged from racialized women. Identity politics minimized the different social and political contexts in which people lived.

The debate on identity has become further complicated by globalization and migration, processes that have disrupted the 'relatively settled character of traditional cultures and collectivities structured around ideas of nationality, race, class and gender' (Proctor 2004, 109). Identity is now constructed through participation in global economies that compel individuals to mobilize themselves in their search for economic opportunities, which may take them to different countries sequentially. Transnational migrants participate in different cultures, manifesting their ethnic (group) culture in different locations; consequently, their sense of self is fluid as it emerges from such movements. Furthermore, contemporary transnational migrants are not simply acted upon by the dominant society, but may participate in conscious and deliberate ways to manage perceptions of who they are as well as the meanings attached to their race and culture (Ong 1999).

If identity is not fixed or pure but rather is contingent, the simple binaries of white/black or male/female are disrupted. Furthermore, this contingency raises the question once again about voice and authority. Who has the right to speak and for whom? If the physical body is not significant in and of itself, then associating voice and authority with an 'insider' by virtue of her or his skin colour or sex is an open and controversial issue. Scholars such as bell hooks and Patricia Collins have struggled theoretically to give primacy to the 'insider' as the knower while at the same time disputing the significance of the physical body (hooks 2003; Collins 2000). For Hall, as discussed in the introduction of this volume, significance lies not in fixed or conventional criteria like race or sex but in self-reflexivity, recognizing the multiple positionings that are incorporated in an identity, as well as its contingency on social, political, and cultural contexts (Proctor 2004, 119).

In recent studies of the global diaspora, hybridity and hybrid identities have been used to define identity and perspective. A hybrid perspective is neither indigenous nor exogenous (Code 2000, 260). Homi Bhabha views hybridity favourably because it provides a space in which individuals can continually negotiate with the culture in which they find themselves and thereby gain a better understanding of self and society (Bhabha 2000). But others, like Inderpal Grewal and Caren Kaplan, are more critical of hybridity because not all facets of such an identity are equal and symmetrical; rather, they are uneven because they stem from histories that transcend individual intentionality (1997).

The interview with Frances Henry that follows illustrates how subjectivities are constructed and negotiated within and adopted to historical and social circumstance.

Frances Henry's transgression of boundaries challenges our understanding of the simple white-versus-black binary. Although she is white, she is married to a black man, has adult mixed-race children, and has spent her academic career studying racism against black people. She has a distinguished record of research and publication on racism. Henry received her early training as an anthropologist and has maintained an interest in Trinidadian religions, recently publishing *Reclaiming African Religions in Trinidad* (2003). Since her retirement from York University, she lives in Trinidad for part of the year. She is a hybrid, but not in the way it is generally understood in the literature as having been born in one country or within one culture while also participating in another dominant, usually white, culture. Rather, Henry is a white woman who is immersed, both personally and professionally, in black culture. In whose voice does she speak? In the following interview, I try to have her answer that question.

Crossing over boundaries can sometimes marginalize individuals from the communities of their birth or origins as well as from their chosen one. For example, immigrants often feel distanced from the societies that they have left behind but also feel insignificant and inconsequential with respect to the dominant white communities in Canada. Nevertheless, Bhabha argues that marginality is not necessarily disempowering but that it can be a site from which a unique perspective and a different understanding of self and society emerge (2000). Frances Henry has participated in the black cultures of Canada and Trinidad as a wife, mother, scholar, and activist. Her choices have located her at the margins of both Jewish and black communities, and at one time, at the edge of the social anthropology community. How should we locate the individual vis-à-vis her scholarship? Is she an insider or outsider with respect to racism? What is the significance of whiteness for her, and how has it affected her scholarship? These are some of the questions addressed in the interview.

Frances Henry is Jewish. Until the age of eight, she lived in a small town in Germany where she and her family were victims of the Nazis. She has experienced anti-Semitism, but does that give her a particular empathy and insight into racism against blacks? Anti-Semitism, writes Karen Mock, the current director of the Canadian Race Relations Foundation, is 'simply hostility directed against the Jews solely because they are Jews' (1996, 120). But Mock answers yes and no to the question of whether anti-Semitism is racism. She explains:

> Attacks against Jews come from two distinct sources, religious *and* racial. Therefore, the word 'racism' is not wholly applicable; but neither is the term 'religious intolerance' sufficient ... People of colour are more often subjected to racist attacks and systemic discrimination than are Jews (regardless of their colour or visibility by virtue of dress). It is also true that because of its religious dimension, the hatred directed against Jews differs from that directed against visible minorities. But racism is racism, and ... [it] is a clear component of anti-Semitism ... That it is a consequence of hate mongering is not in question. (1996, 132)

In her acknowledgments to *The Caribbean Diaspora in Toronto: Learning to Live with Racism*, Henry gives us an insight into her feelings. She writes, 'I am no stranger to racism. I have felt it personally as a Jewish refugee from Hitler's Germany where much of my family was wiped out. I have since experienced it as the mother of two Black children growing up and going to school in Canada ... Over the years, I have witnessed my husband's struggles to maintain dignity and decency in the face of sometimes outrageous provocation' (1994, xi).

Do her own experiences make Henry sensitive to what it means for blacks to survive, produce, labour, and create their own imaginative world within a culture and society that is sometime hostile to their presence?

I have known Frances Henry professionally for several years. When I was a junior academic at York University in the 1980s, Frances was an established and well-respected scholar. Over the years we have had occasion to meet at conferences on immigration, race, and ethnicity. In 2004, while attending the Ninth Metropolis Conference on Immigration in Geneva, I asked Frances casually over lunch how she had survived a lifetime of thinking, researching, and writing about race and racism. 'Was it difficult?' I enquired. She laughed enigmatically in response. Sensing that perhaps there might be a story worth listening to, I persuaded her to discuss her work formally in an interview. A month later, we met twice in Toronto at my house and recorded two interviews that were taped and transcribed. I asked her open-ended questions, some of which were blunt, others curious and probing. Frances's answers record her experiences of being a white, Jewish woman doing research on racism.

Interview

VIJAY: Frances, you are Jewish and your parents and grandparents were victimized during the Nazi regime in Germany. Did that give you a particular affinity for working on racism?

FRANCES: That's a good place to begin because if you go back into an individual's history far enough, invariably you find some incidences or experiences that predispose them to work in certain areas. That is very dramatically true for me. I started life as a very severe victim [of racism]. My parents and I got out of Germany at the last possible moment, in March, and the war was officially declared in September 1939. The rest of the family didn't [escape]. I published my memories of this time in *Victims and Neighbors: A Small Town in Nazi Germany Remembered* (1984), which describes both the kindness of neighbours and the incremental and horrific prosecution of Jews. The experience of being a victim naturally predisposed me for the rest of my life to be [empathetic] towards people who feel they have been victimized by other people's power, even if it may not be so in reality. My personal experiences were fundamental to the kind of research that I eventually did.

My sense of being different, which started in Nazi Germany, continued in the United States. When I arrived there I was eight years old. I was put into school, not knowing a word of English. To the other seven- or eight-year-old kids I was German – that meant I was a Nazi, because they had no understanding of the difference between Nazis and non-Nazis. So to little kids, if you're German you're a Nazi, and I was continually mocked for being a German Nazi, plagued [by such taunts], until I was twelve or thirteen. This experience of being 'Othered,' as we would put it today, had a very strong impact on me. I guess that enters in very, very closely to [the kind of research] that I became involved with in later life.

Growing up in the United States, particularly in Brooklyn, New York, I was surrounded by African Americans [and what the media referred to as] the 'black situation' and the 'black problem.' I had personal experiences with black people when I was fairly young; the one that had the most influence on me subconsciously was when I was about nine or ten. My parents had to redo their professional credentials after coming to the United States and had very little money. Sending me to a summer camp was out of the question, so for the holidays they would send me to my uncle's chicken farm in New Jersey.

A little ways down the road from my uncle's farmhouse was a black family; they didn't own the farm, I think they were leasing or renting. It was a large family with one or two children of my age. They were the only kids in that area, so I would go over there to play with them. One of the kids in the family was a girl roughly about my age, and one afternoon we went to the outhouse because they didn't even have a toilet, and stripped down naked. Both of us examined each other and she saw what I had, I saw what she had, and lo and behold it was the same thing. That made an incredible impression on me and [created the] understanding that although she was quite dark skinned and I was white, we had the same physical and sexual apparatus. That was a huge psychological moment in my early life, which gave me the realization of what equality is all about.

Growing up in New York, it is very easy to become a lefty – sort of left of centre or socialist. When I was in my teens, Henry Wallace was running for president on a socialist ticket, which happened, I think, for the first time in the United States and I don't think [has] happened ever since. At the age of thirteen or fourteen, I became an active campaigner for Henry Wallace and his progressive, socialist ideas.

VIJAY: Can you describe your intellectual, social, or psychological struggles to decolonize your mind? I mean, sometimes we internalize biases and values of the larger society without realizing it. What has been your experience?

FRANCES: I didn't really have to do that. I went to Brooklyn College, which in my time was the centre of leftist political ideology and of ethnic but not racial diversity. Poor Italian and central European kids went there. Like all women of my age and generation, I had a lot of anti-female experiences in my student days. But they didn't make me feel inferior; in fact, they gave me an impetus to go on. The one that I remember most strikingly was at Brooklyn College when I was in my fourth year as an undergraduate. I was already married to my first husband and I was majoring in European History and it suddenly occurred to me that if I continued as a historian, I would be working with documentation, and I wanted to work with people. Quite by chance, I came across Ruth Benedict's *Patterns of Culture.* I read that and thought, oh my God, this is what I want to do.

So I went to speak to the chair of the anthropology department at Brooklyn College, who was an archeologist, and told him that I would like to do graduate work in anthropology. He didn't listen to what I was saying. I was sporting a ring. He had observed that and said, 'You are already married, you're going to be having children soon, so what is the point of going on for further education in this or any other field?' He was rude in a very nasty kind of way. Obviously, that was the end of the conversation. I was furious. I emerged from that incident with a 'to hell with you' attitude. I was absolutely determined to go to graduate school in anthropology, and I did. I was never really colonized, in that sense, and when explicit comments were made such as this one, I just came out fighting even harder and being stronger.

VIJAY: What about decolonizing your mind about race? You lived amongst blacks, you were familiar with them, but still the larger society has biases.

FRANCES: Yes. Well, as you know – and it might exist in some quarters today – white women who consort with blacks are seen as prostitutes, whores, or tarts. Some of that [abuse] was thrown directly towards me. [On the other hand,] I have been an academic all my life. The university is a world in and of its own, and you can live within it both professionally and socially without being exposed to the slings and arrows of the outside world. So I was shielded by the university. You know [the abuse] when you see it walking down the street and people stare or make rude comments. I mean, come on, who gives a damn? I really couldn't care less.

There are people who believe that I got into anti-racist research and writing because I was married to a black person. That's not true. My personal ideology was already in place by the time I met my husband, Jeff. The romantic involvement with a black person was not the catalyst; rather, it was almost the last thing in a series of events.

VIJAY: Did you become involved with the feminist movement in Canada?

FRANCES: No. I've always felt, from a theoretical point of view, that certain variables are more primary than others at creating social situations, and for racialized people – maybe not all but a great many of them – race is the dominant variable in the diasporic situation. Therefore I decided not to split my research interests and to focus on race and racism and to keep immigration and integration as the dominant variables. I haven't really discounted gender; one of the first articles I did in the 1960s was on women domestics in Canada. I have always tried in my research and writing to be as inclusive of gender and class as possible. However, as the racial problems emerged out of the feminist movement, [the time] wasn't exactly conducive to becoming a part of [the movement]. At that time I would have been seen as one more dominant white woman who was trying to appropriate the black voice.

VIJAY: In the 1980s, the feminist movement was questioned for its racial biases and there were discussions about appropriation, voice, and the privileged position of the insider based on culture. How did you react to that?

FRANCES: That's a very difficult scenario. I've always had problems with the idea of the insider as the only one who really knows, and still do. Anthropological fieldwork is based on the notion that an outsider goes somewhere, learns enough about a society or group or culture with the help of local respondents, and is able to make some sense of it. Anthropology got tainted by the criticism that no outsider can really understand [a group, culture, or society]. The insiders got more powerful and began asserting themselves; I also agree with that [development].

[Many] of our traditions in the social sciences are based upon expropriated, outside, erroneous, biased, and prejudicial knowledge. So we have to contend with the history of our disciplines, which pretended, in one way or another, to be able to know and to analyse – [and this became] a privilege of famous white scholars. It's chilling. We're guilty of having expropriated people and everything they stand for, but that doesn't mean we're *all* guilty. It doesn't mean that we can't isolate the good from the bad stuff; nor does it mean that all of us should be excluded on the basis of the sins of the pioneers in these disciplines. But it's hard to make that argument in the face of people who expose their pain and say that you can't possibly understand. They're dealing with the situation emotionally, not analytically. There is a certain degree of distancing you must do or else you can't research, write, or think.

I think both perspectives, that of the insider and the outsider, are valuable and complementary; it is not an either/or situation. An insider may have the pain attached to humiliating experiences which the outsider can only glimpse at, but the skills to analyse where that pain comes from and what it means and how it destabilizes a person, group, and society can only come from somebody who is trained in a social science discipline. I have very strong views on the notion of being an insider, and the whole question of appropriation has to be recognized and explored fully, but that does not exclude analysis by outsiders.

VIJAY: In the 1970s, did your research on racism marginalize you in the academy?

FRANCES: I have to answer yes and no to that question. I didn't really start working on racism until I had done a substantial amount of research and writing in Caribbean anthropology. By the time I got working on racism I was an established Caribbean specialist in social anthropology and had obtained tenure and promotion. I couldn't really be touched [i.e., threatened with dismissal or loss of job]. I was untouchable.

Now that's on the official level, but informally there were all kinds of problems. I started my research on racism when I got to York University in 1971, and there I was asked to teach a course called 'Ethnicity, Stratification, and Pluralism.' The person who used to teach it decided she didn't want to do it any more. I said no, I want to teach a course on race and racism. There was real negativism, I would say, even hostility towards teaching a course like that. The department was afraid of a course that had race and racism in its title; they said it would be too difficult to get it past the university's administrative machinery and have it approved. Then there were people in the department who didn't want a course on race and racism, and they argued that the study of racism was sociology, not social anthropology. In a more traditional anthropology department, like that at the University of Toronto, you might have had a course on the genetics of race.

At first I thought, the main thing is to get the course taught, let's worry about the labelling later. So I taught it as 'Ethnicity, Stratification, and Pluralism' for two or three years. I would say to my students, look folks, this is a course on race and racism and here is the outline of the readings; if you don't want this, leave. A few people did leave but not a whole lot. Eventually I thought, let's fight the battle and [try to have it approved as a course on racism]. It created a fairly tense series of circumstances. The course was very successful in terms of enrolment, so the department couldn't get rid of it. I was the only one in the whole bloody university at that time who was teaching racism. Gradually we added a few more courses throughout the university.

I think the issue at York was that racism was a very alien field. They had something like six or seven non-white professors in the whole faculty. There were about four people of African descent, a couple of South Asian descent, and that's about it. So really, it wasn't an issue [in the 1970s]. I was at Wilfred Laurier the other night giving a lecture, and people said to me, 'Oh, York is the centre for the study of anti-racism.' Right – it's the centre today but when I started it was a desert. So the university, at least, has come a long way.

That was the beginning, and one had to work slowly to get race and racism legitimized as a subject area. We then moved to the second stage of this process. [The university hired people with the same ethnicities as their subject matter.] The racialized people who have been hired at the university currently suffer from the same exclusivity and chilly environments that existed in the past. So their presence has not really altered the underlying dynamic, which is still, I think, one of aversion for many people. So, right – the university has open hiring and they go all out of their way to hire and create a diverse environment, and then what happens to the people once they're in there? They still feel excluded. People from disadvantaged communities are at lower levels; there are not many in decision-making capacities at most institutions, yet. They are just not part of the dominant authority structure. We still have a long way to go for that to happen.

The older white people who started the research and teaching on racism or the Caribbean got pushed out. That certainly happened to me. I was informally excluded. For example, Black Studies, when it was first proposed at York University, didn't include me because I'm not black. My work is on blacks; it didn't matter. So these kinds of exclusionary features were certainly evident at York while I was still there and they're still very evident right now, as we speak.

I see [such exclusions] as an inevitable stage in the evolution of social history; I'm not personally affronted by it because I understand it. But it does give you a feeling that no matter what you do you're marginalized: you're marginalized from the white authority structure at the beginning [because of your research], and then you're marginalized by the racialized authority structure later on [because of skin colour]. So it's been a no-win situation. But when you reach a certain point in your career it doesn't really matter; you just do what you have to or want to do.

VIJAY: Did the Urban Alliance on Race Relations that sponsored some of
your earlier work in the 1970s and 1980s believe that you should
have a black writing or research partner?

FRANCES: The Urban Alliance on Race Relations was started in 1975 by
a group of concerned citizens, including the late Wilson Head [a
black academic at York University who pioneered research on racism
in Canada]. At that time, the Urban Alliance was structured in com-
mittees on education, justice, and so on. When the decision was made
to do research, a committee was struck, and it reflected the membership of the Urban Alliance. On that committee, there was Dharma
Lingam, a South Asian, and Susan Ing, a Chinese, but the research
specialists were people like me and Jeffrey Reitz [a white male sociologist at the University of Toronto]. I brought in Effie Ginsburg, a
white female graduate student at York, who had statistical and analytic skills that I didn't have.

VIJAY: In the 1970s and 1980s when you wrote your earlier reports on
racism, there was no sense that only blacks had a special prerogative
for writing on racism. How did the mainstream and the black community regard some of your earlier reports?

FRANCES: The first study I did was an attitude survey called the *Dynamics of Racism in Toronto* (1978), and it was received very poorly by
mainstream society. This was the first indication that there was racism in Canada, and the response of mainstream society to the reports
was to deny, even in the face of research evidence. They said that
[such allegations] were absurd, it was absolutely not true. I was even
accused of making up the data and finagling the numbers. It was just
ridiculous. I was absolutely furious. I was really very angry and very
hurt that people, or the journalists, would even think that I would be
capable of falsifying data to make an ideological point. That was very
distasteful. Such denials still happen today. In *Discourses of Domination*, Carol Tator and I wrote that the principle assumption [behind]
denials of racism is that it does not exist in a democratic society.[1]

But the black community, small as it was at that time, much smaller
than today, reacted very favourably. They said what people still say
today: you're not telling us anything new, we know this, we've experienced it, but it takes white validation and serious research that
hopefully will get people to pay attention to it. Validate the victim's
experience.

The one circumstance that hit us badly, I think, Jeff more than me, was when the study *Dynamics of Racism in Toronto* came out. When that research was reported in the newspapers, we were living in the Bathurst and Eglinton area in a very large beautiful house. We had a lovely dining room that had a large window facing our back garden, and there was a laneway behind that. One day we were all sitting there when a gun or a rifle shot hit our dining room window – it didn't shatter the glass, it was clearly some kind of BB gun. This incident happened directly after that report got attention in the newspapers. We're almost positive that it was some racist or white supremacist or both out there in the laneway shooting at us.

I also received a lot of hate telephone calls and a lot of hate mail. That led to changing the telephone number and de-listing it and subsequent to that, I never give out my home telephone number. Sometimes, at the university, I would have my telephone calls screened. I think the hate mail, which was always anonymous, came from the neo-Nazi white supremacist racist network, the very people that we are now charging at the Human Rights Commission.

In 1985, Effie Ginzberg and I published *Who Gets the Work? A Test of Racial Discrimination in Employment*, which provided documentary evidence of the allegations made by racialized people of the racism of employers. [The methodology of] *Who Gets the Work?* [which used actors to pose as job applicants] was seriously challenged. [It was argued] that potential employers were lied to, since the individuals were not real job applicants. So it was entrapment, and therefore, quite unethical. Another line of attack was that if [racism in employment] was really true, then the discriminating employers must be identified and charged at the Human Rights Commission. So we had to counteract by saying no, this is research, it's not entrapment, we're not out to get these employers because they discriminated or to charge them with human rights violations. Both arguments come down to denial and an effort to undermine the results of our research. The denial of racism is still happening today in certain public quarters; for example, [in] the denial of racial profiling. [The public response is] that it can't happen, it doesn't happen. Carol and I have recently documented this in *Racial Profiling in Toronto: Discourses of Domination, Mediation, and Opposition* (2005).

VIJAY: Did you personally encounter racism in the 1970s?
FRANCES: Worse than that, as an interracial couple Jeff and I were refused accommodation in a rental property in Burlington and in

Montreal. In Montreal, I had seen an apartment and wanted to rent it, but the landlord didn't have the lease papers with him and he said: 'No problem, I'll drop over later this evening.' Good. He dropped over and he saw my son Terry, who was then two years old, playing on the floor, and suddenly he said, 'Oh, no, no. You can't rent this apartment, that's totally out of the question,' and walked out. There was no mechanism in Montreal that I could find [for] charging this man. I don't think there was a Quebec Human Rights Commission. It was not a criminal situation so there was nothing I could do about what happened. But these things have a way of working out for the best because we realized we could not keep on renting, and we managed to get a down payment together to buy a house.

VIJAY: So it's experiences like these that made you interested in studying racism?

FRANCES: Oh yes, absolutely. I was always interested, but being subjected to racial discrimination directly in Canada, 'the race-free society,' [heightened my interest]. For example, we were in London, England, last month, and I noticed there were an extraordinary number of interracial couples. Yet I began to notice that people were looking at us a lot and then I began to speculate why. It's because of our age. Nobody raises an eyebrow seeing young people but [it seemed that people were curious] at seeing this elderly couple on buses and subways. Looking [out of] curiosity is fairly harmless, whereas as you know, [experiencing] actual discrimination is much harder.

VIJAY: In researching and thinking about the Other, what have you learned about yourself, particularly about being white?

FRANCES: Studies of whiteness are incredibly important for the theoretical understanding of race. The whiteness perspective has made a very, very important contribution to our understanding the interracial dynamic and the power relations that flow from it. It has led me to think of how I've perceived myself, but I haven't made much progress on that because I'm still searching. I've only ever seen myself as white in relation to others who are not white. I have never really sat down and thought [about] what being white means to me personally, other than it probably doesn't mean a hell of a lot or else I would not have lived my life the way I have. At some level it probably must have, but I'm really not sure. I'm really not sure.

I have never felt conflicted about being white. I always felt that although I'm not a person of colour, still, having had the Jewish experience, I know not only intellectually and professionally but also emotionally what victimization by race really means. I don't think I've ever had any real difficulties or suffered any guilt for being white, probably again because of my German background.

VIJAY: Did your research on racism and your interracial family make you marginal to the Jewish and the black community?

FRANCES: I have very little to do with the Jewish community, in fact, nothing at all. I'm not an observant Jew; I don't go to synagogue. I don't really like much about the traditional religion though I identify with it culturally and historically. I have no contact with any Jewish community group. The only exception is the League for Human Rights of B'nai Brith, because they're involved in anti-racism and its past director, Karen Mock, is a professional and personal friend. But there's no real tie or attachment.

The only constraint is my being American. It's not a difficulty, but if tensions ever arise, they have nothing to do with being Jewish – it's mainly with being American. In my family, we are all basically anti-American, including me. Nevertheless, the United States is the country that afforded me refuge and without that I'd have been dead. So I have a very strong emotional attachment to the United States and to being American, because that's the nation that rescued me. But I have deep distaste for its politics, its domestic and foreign policy, and its choice of leaders. There's very little I like about the United States, but I have that emotional commitment to it nevertheless. Nobody else in my family or [among] the people that I am friendly with share that, so that sets me apart more than anything else.

The black community is made up of many different cultures and groups and the people have come from various parts of the world; for example, Africa, the Caribbean, the United States, and Britain. The older members of the Caribbean community that I know were always supportive of my research. The younger members ... who don't know me probably have no feelings one way or the other. The black intellectuals in this community have largely negative feelings about my research, based upon race ownership.

VIJAY: What do you mean by race ownership?

FRANCES: Well, they feel that regardless of my past and regardless of my affiliations, I have no business writing about their stuff.

VIJAY: Perhaps there is a fear of appropriation?

FRANCES: Yeah, that's been very evident. There are exceptions, but generally speaking that's pretty much the feeling. So in that sense, I've been marginal to the black intellectual community.

VIJAY: As a Jewish woman growing up in New York you experienced discrimination. Does that make you feel an insider to the black experience?

FRANCES: Sure. I've profited from [that experience] because I understand that the effects of discrimination, no matter who you are, are basically the same. So from that sense, I've always been attuned to racism, as I am towards anybody who's a victim of discrimination.

VIJAY: But blacks don't consider that important?

FRANCES: No, not really. There's considerable antipathy among black intellectuals toward Jews and Judaism that has a long history in the United States. In contemporary times, it is expressed in the Israel and Palestine situation, so the relationship that used to exist in the United States between progressive Jews and progressive blacks in the Civil Rights movement is long gone. [Many] black intellectuals are very anti-Semitic at this point for all kinds of historical reasons. Black intellectuals identify me as a Jew as well as a white woman, which probably makes it worse at this point in time rather than better.

VIJAY: So in essence, despite the fact that you have experienced racism, it comes down to the colour of your skin.

FRANCES: Oh, pretty well. Sure. My research doesn't matter to the way I am perceived by certain groups.

VIJAY: Does the social construction theory hold up for you, or do you think it is essentialism?

FRANCES: The social construction theory does hold up, if you look at it from the point of view of who's doing the constructing. If the communities of colour, or the blacks, are doing the constructing of white people based upon the whiteness of their skin, it's still about theory; you just have to turn it around. It is still whiteness, yes, but it's their construction of whiteness, in this instance. And their construction of whiteness does not allow for individual differences or individual variations. So in that way it's essentialism.

VIJAY: It's essentialism because as a white person you are assumed to have certain characteristics, even if you have a lifetime of work to prove otherwise.

FRANCES: Right, exactly. A contemporary parallel is the Englishwoman Margaret Hassan in Iraq. She was born an Englishwoman, married to an Iraqi, and had been working on Iraqi causes for what, thirty-five years in Iraq? She was nevertheless murdered by insurgents in 2004.

VIJAY: For being white and British?

FRANCES: Yes. It's a bind, isn't it? Well, it's the same thing that racism is based on – you are never perceived as an individual in your own right; rather, you are representing something larger – the white race or the white community or white privilege. When racialized people are not seen as individuals [we refer to it as racism]. It's the same for white intellectuals who are trying to help or at least have an understanding of the issues and problems. Nevertheless, they are tarred with the same brush, the way [whites] have always tarred people of colour.

Such stereotyping has never mattered to me personally because I understand the dynamics, what's behind it, what it means. It's part of the whole victimization process. So I guess I'm not too upset.

VIJAY: There seems to be a permanent colour line, and perhaps your work and personal life should have given a different message to people.

FRANCES: But it didn't and it doesn't, in fact. Well, that's one of the things we have to suffer. But there is another side of this coin. One of the major hallmarks of [being] an academic is that you train and teach future generations. I have received enormous recognition from students, not only in terms of having taught the right kind of approach, but [in] their eventual placement in universities. Now that's a tremendous reward. It's enormously gratifying to know that you touched somebody at age twenty-five who is now fifty and a senior professor, or a senior lawyer, or a judge somewhere. It's a continuing contribution to have helped to frame and shape minds. You feel you have made a difference.

VIJAY: Describe an incident when you felt that black activists in Canada accepted you as an ally.

FRANCES: I don't think that there has been any such incident.

VIJAY: Really! Never?

FRANCES: No, that has never happened.

VIJAY: What about the Canadian Race Relations Foundation?

FRANCES: No, I have never been nominated to its board. Carol Tator and I went to some of their early meetings. I am one of their founding members, but we were never asked to be part of [the] management. We have received small grants from them; for example, they funded the racial profiling study. Similarly, a politician would not get any brownie points for nominating me to a board of an association such as the Canadian Race Relations Foundation. They have got to nominate a black person. In the early 1990s when the New Democratic Party formed the government in Ontario, Carol and I never got any recognition in terms of appointments. No recognition whatsoever, despite the fact that anti-racism was very, very strong on their agenda. The government needed to get the electoral support of the racialized communities so all their appointments were members of those communities. If you're a politician [and] you want policy advisors and people who are in the know, then you appoint people from that community, not people who are attached to it or because they study white racism against it. That doesn't earn you any political advantage.

VIJAY: Can you describe an incident in which you were accused of appropriating the black experience for your professional advancement?

FRANCES: I can't think of a single incident as such, but I'm sure it's happened. I'm almost positive it's happened, but I can't pinpoint any particular incident.

VIJAY: Can you pinpoint your feelings at a time when you felt that accusation explicitly or implicitly?

FRANCES: I don't think I can even do that, not really. I guess it's because a long time ago I developed an 'I don't give a shit' attitude. I do what I want.

VIJAY: Sometimes racialized people are accused of using the 'race card' to promote their careers. What are your views about that?

FRANCES: In a way, we have all done that because we all use whatever it is we study to promote our careers. We use everything that [helps] us to raise our profile or give us mobility. So what is the difference between using your status as a person of colour in a basically white society or as a specialist in some area of study? What is wrong in using your personal position to advance yourself when that also happens to be your area of scholarship? I know people who use the race card are looked down upon for taking advantage of political correctness and so on. But basically, why not, when it is not only who you are, but it is also your field of study?

VIJAY: The other side of the coin is that white people have always used the race card.

FRANCES: Of course, but they've used it so unconsciously that they're not even aware of it. The white establishment that has run all these [institutions] has always done it. It's just that they haven't been recognized for what it is – white power and white privilege.

VIJAY: You have extensive experience at being an expert witness. How does being white and having academic expertise on racism play out in the courtroom?

FRANCES: I have been an expert witness [many times] in the justice system and in the human rights arena, but not always successfully. In the past, there have been judges who would not allow me to testify on racism because they thought that such testimony would not be helpful to the courts and it was irrelevant to the case at hand. That has happened a number of times. The same thing has happened in the human rights area, where the decisions of the tribunal were that the work I do is prejudiced and [that] I come in with a biased perspective. In other words, if the issue in question is race, I say yes, racism exists, and therefore my testimony and writings are [viewed as] biased.

That happened in August of this year [2004]. A tribunal for the Canadian Human Rights Commission [dealing] with a case of employment discrimination wrote, explaining their decision. They said that first of all they disallowed my report and therefore disallowed my appearance as an expert witness on the grounds that I essentially begin with the bias that racism exists and therefore, it exists in this case. The second reason [for disallowing my testimony] was that I do not provide the normal evidentiary baseline – that is, statistics and numbers – and I deal with issues that cannot be proven or tested, such as a chilly environment or an atmosphere where whiteness prevails. They argued that my report [would not have been] useful to them. But [the frustration is that] racism is not subject to statistics and to testing.

[Such incidences] have happened many times. The decisions regarding my work [or that of others] as biased or prejudiced stem from the lack of understanding that social science cannot be objective; it is not the same as manipulating chemicals in a chemistry lab. If social scientists do not produce numbers, then [some assume it comes down to] personal opinion, and they argue: who says your opinion is any more useful than that of anybody else? Anybody who says racism is pervasive in Canadian society is automatically assumed to be a biased individual. Such attitudes are still very prevalent in both [the justice and human rights] systems. This is not a matter of disrespect for my expertise but has much to do with the denial of racism. Such views are not directed against me personally but against the theoretical and ideological doctrine of racism.

However, many times I have been accepted as an expert witness. A lot of judges have been accepting and have listened carefully and attentively, asked questions, used my appearance for educating themselves, and have shown empathy and sympathy for the aggrieved victims of racism. There have been many positive examples in the human rights tribunals. The point I'm making is that even within those systems, there are people in high positions who subscribe to the denial of the racism mechanism and [that attitude] affects how they deal with someone like me.

VIJAY: Do you find judges more accepting now than they were ten years ago?
FRANCES: Absolutely, there is no question about that. It has changed because of the sensibility of some members of the system to the changing social reality around them. However, not everyone is sensitive to change, so the old attitude and behaviour prevail as well. There are judges who still maintain that race, ethnicity, and culture are not relevant. Some lawyers and judges believe that all blacks are criminally prone. They think, just put them into the right situation, tempt them, and you know they'll be criminals because it's within them. In the *Colour of Democracy* (2000), Carol Tator and I document the case of Antonio Lamar of the Supreme Court of Canada, and his

public expression of racist views for which he subsequently apologized. But then people in the justice system see the bottom of the barrel. A judge [may not] have the opportunity to meet black people as neighbours, at the local church, or at the golf club. The only ones he or she sees are those who have been charged with criminal activity, rightly or wrongly. Judges, like police officers, see the underbelly all the time.

VIJAY: Do you feel guilty for being white and enjoying the privilege of skin colour? How do you reconcile with this, given that your spouse is black and your children are mixed race? You have some privileges that your family is inherently denied.

FRANCES: This affects us, but it doesn't affect us in Canada, not in any overt way. It affects us a lot in Trinidad, where we've been for many years and now live part-time every year. Trinidad has a colonial history, and there is a fair-sized white elite made of old-time families and expatriates. The main determinant of class in the Caribbean is skin colour and related racial features; there is a gradation from white to near-white, to brown, and finally to the black-skinned lower class. Like any colonized society, there is enormous white privilege. For example, when you go through bureaucratic procedures like buying a house, a car, getting a driver's licence, or purchasing a ticket on the ferry, whatever relates you to authority, all white people [have an] advantage. They are privileged in the most obvious ways, like queue-jumping. I can go right to the head of the line, get the tickets and leave; now, how does that make me feel and how does it make Jeff feel? Over the years, we have come to agree that if it prevents Jeff from being humiliated and abused by some two-bit functionary, why not? I think it's a cold-hearted practicality of dealing with the logistics of living in a tough world and particularly of trying to make things easier as you get older and less able to manage. Besides, I feel we have paid our dues to society.

In terms of my own inner feelings about it, I'm not even sure that being Jewish has made that difference. I feel very bad for my daughter, Miriam, and my son, Terry, because they experience racism. Physically [i.e., in terms of skin colour], Miriam and Terry are exactly in the middle of their mother and father. Of course, it also depends on who is doing the looking; my children are perceived as light-skinned blacks and they both emphasize it. Terry, for twelve or more years, has worn dreadlocks down to his rear, so he announces his identity very, very powerfully. Miriam does that to a lesser extent, but she too plays up her curly hair.

Miriam has not had too many instances of racism, although she's had some. Terry has had a lot. We know about it, we talk about it, and we deal with it. It saddens me that he has had to go through these experiences. Both of our children are very strong individuals; we deliberately trained them that way, knowing that they would have to go through these experiences. So they're not damaged by the racism they have encountered; they've been strengthened by some of these struggles and they understand them for what they are, and so neither one of them has been made to feel inferior. But now and again I feel sad that they have had to go through these humiliating experiences, as every person of colour has had to. But I really don't feel guilty; I don't know if I should but I really don't.

It is interesting how the family network has turned out. My granddaughter is thirteen. She is Terry's daughter; her mother is white and my granddaughter is one of these genetic happenings – she's phenotypically white. You would never suspect that she has any black in her unless you knew the family history. She's very fair, she has much lighter skin than I have, but there is a slight pigmentation that you see in summertime. But you have to look closely. She has brown, auburnish, straight but wavy hair.

My granddaughter has completely identified with her black father because her mother is not in the picture and he is the primary caregiver. So the bond is totally with the black father, Jeff, and me. She feels that she is too white, she hates herself for being too white, and she wants to have a brown complexion like her father. She sits out in the sun to get darker. She is trying rather desperately to identify with the black parent. For years we've tried to tell her that what's inside is what's important. She's conflicted: a black father, a black grandfather, and a white grandmother – where does she fit into this?

VIJAY: What are the particular dilemmas of a white woman raising children of mixed race?

FRANCES: The main problem is that I had to explain the circumstances of life to very young children in trying to prepare them as they moved forward in life. It is hard; you can only do it incrementally as they grow older. I'm not sure I was always successful at it and neither was my husband, I think because it is really difficult to get across to children that they are as good as everybody else and that race makes no difference. Miriam was much more sensitive to racism than Terry. It was difficult to prepare them for the fact that they were going to be humiliated for no reason, for not having done anything. In grade eight Miriam had a major racist incident, and we had to put her in a private school. Trying to explain the dynamics of racism to her, which we did and which she accepted, was deeply, deeply hurtful. To see your child in pain because she'd been called a black bitch is really quite awful. It was difficult to deal with her pain. Dealing with that kind of hurt was hurtful to us.

VIJAY: Do you advocate or support black and white intimate relations in Canada?

FRANCES: I have often been criticized for my views on interracial marriages. At York University, I used to teach courses on Caribbean anthropology and the Caribbean diaspora. These classes were almost always, I'd say, 75 per cent filled with white women. Why were they in that class? It was almost invariably because they had black Caribbean boyfriends. As the term would progress, they would come to me and spill out their guts; what were they going to do? Should they marry or partner with this man? The advice I always gave was: have a ball, have a great time, enjoy, but do not marry and do not get into a permanent relationship. 'But why not?' they would ask – 'You did it.'

I would try to go through and tell them that it is not the racial but the cultural difference that makes such relationships difficult. As [young white Canadian women], they didn't know anything about Caribbean male/female relations and cultural norms. But the boyfriend does and the chances are that unless [these women] have enormous sensitivity or know a great deal about his background more than taking a course in Caribbean anthropology, they're not going to like it. So they'd walk out of my office very dejected, because they'd come to see me with the expectation that well, I'm the role model who has done it so why shouldn't they, and I'd given them just the opposite advice. I really believe the problem is intercultural. If you're interracially related, after a while, in terms of a good relationship, that's totally meaningless. But the cultural upbringings of two people who come from different areas of the world never go away, and that's where the problems emerge. But try to tell that to young people in love.

In the Caribbean, gender relations are still very problematic; men are very patriarchal, for the most part. Despite the professionalism among women in recent times, women are still basically seen in very traditional roles. They're not expected to be assertive in any way. Then there is a deep-seated belief in, for want of a better word, male promiscuity. Men can have several relations but women are not allowed to; they do, but normatively they're not allowed to. It's not only true in the Caribbean but elsewhere as well, but it is very predominant and powerful there. That's not to say that men don't [act promiscuously] here – of course they do, but in the Caribbean it's almost an expectation. You're not a man unless you're doing it everywhere. So I think that can be problematic, unless the white woman knows her partner extremely well. There are always individual circumstances [when an intercultural relationship works], but as a general pattern I think it is very difficult.

VIJAY: So even if society makes it easier to rent an apartment or they don't get stared at quite as much, you still do not support intercultural marriages?

FRANCES: I think so. Marriage is a difficult relationship and then you add differences of upbringing, socialization, and cultural norms. You're adding to the tensions that are already there, almost by definition. The rate of failure in intercultural relationships or formal marriages is relatively high. It's more than just societal perceptions. Jeff and I have had to work out all kinds of cultural differences that have nothing to do with race or religion but simply with cultural outlook.

VIJAY: How have you survived? It must be very emotionally tense.

FRANCES: No it wasn't, it really isn't. It is tough to work in the human rights field. Academics and activists who are involved in this field, in general, have an unshakeable faith in the equality of all human beings. There are very few universals, but that is certainly one of them. Such a belief is not a doctrine. It's more than that; it becomes your essence. Frontline workers who put their lives on the line in the pursuit of equality certainly have it. I have it to a certain extent. I think that's a characteristic you must have to work on anti-racism. You have to be able to withstand the challenge to your belief in equality from kooks, racists, ignorant, and ill-informed people, and say to yourself that their views don't count. You must have the strength to write off some people.

You have to build personal strength and confidence if you are in an academic area in which you are likely to be the subject of criticism. It is particularly true in the sensitive interpersonal, interracial, and intercultural matters.

The only way this work on anti-racism has been in the slightest bit painful is the fact that I have never got a single award from any racialized community that I have advocated for – particularly the black community. I've been invited many times to give talks and I've been treated very well, but in terms of [being given] an award – a certificate or a trophy – not once. Not even by the Urban Alliance on Race Relations, of which I was a founding member and under whose support I did some of my major research. An award is public recognition that disadvantaged people always use as a symbol of an individual's contribution or work. If you read the black community papers, they are constantly giving awards for this, that, and the other thing. The fact that I've never been a recipient of any awards – you know, I notice its absence. The black community cannot take that public step of identifying a white pioneer in the struggle. I am never going to be identified for an award, no matter what my allegiance to the black community and my interracial family. But then I know not to expect it, so it's all right.

VIJAY: Has there been change in Canadian society?

FRANCES: Change has taken place over the course of my professional life. There has been improvement at certain levels ... If you look carefully at certain institutions and some societal dynamics there has been a change; for example, in the justice system. In the last ten years some important decisions have been made that favour the racial equality cause. More of such decisions are coming out all the time. They don't make many waves, but they are instrumental because they help to build up case law on these issues and it moves us to creating a more equitable justice system in Canada.

Similarly, there has been some significant movement in the human rights field, although it is also heavily bureaucratized. There are many minor human rights cases that have succeeded. In the race field there is the class action [suit] led by the National Capital Alliance on Racism (NCAR), an Ottawa group, which found that Health Canada was discriminatory towards South Asian scientists in their employ. That is really a landmark decision because it's not a small private employer; rather, it's the government of Canada. There are many similar decisions at the provincial level. Those are signs of some change, but there are also institutions, like the police, that

steadfastly maintain they're not racist. It's just, you know, the few
rotten apples.

Generally there is a much greater awareness and acceptance that
racism exists. Things are changing, albeit slowly. The struggle is endless.

Note

1 'The assumption is that because Canada is a society that upholds the ideals
of a liberal democracy, it cannot possibly be racist. The denial of racism is so
habitual in the media that to even make the allegation of bias and discrimination and raise the possibility of its influence on social outcomes becomes a
serious social infraction, incurring the wrath and ridicule of many journalists and editors' (Henry and Tator 2002, 229).

References

Aiken, Sharryn. 2001. Manufacturing 'terrorists': Refugees, national security
and Canadian law, Part 2. *Refuge* 19 (4): 116–33.
Bhabha, Homi. 2000. The vernacular cosmopolitan. In *Voices of the crossing*, ed.
Ferdinand Dennis and Naseem Khan, 133–42. London: Arts Council of
England.
Brand, Dionne. 1991. *No burden to carry: Narratives of black working women in
Ontario 1920 to 1950*. Toronto: Women's Press.
Butler, Judith. 1990. *Gender trouble: Feminism and the subversion of identity*. New
York: Routledge.
Code, Lorraine. 2000. *Encyclopedia of feminist theories*. New York: Routledge.
Collins, Patricia. 2000. *Black feminist thought: Knowledge, consciousness, and the
politics of empowerment*. New York: Routledge.
Grewal, Inderpal, and Caren Kaplan, eds. 1997. *Scattered hegemonies: Postmoder-
nity and transnational feminist practices*. Minneapolis: University of Minnesota
Press.
Henry, Frances. 1978. *The dynamics of racism in Toronto: A research report*. Tor-
onto: York University.
– 1984. *Victims and neighbors: A small town in Nazi Germany remembered*. South
Hadley, MA: Bergin and Garvey.
– 1994. *The Caribbean diaspora in Toronto: Learning to live with racism*. Toronto:
University of Toronto Press.

– 2003. *Reclaiming African religions in Trinidad: The socio-political legitimation of the Orisha and spiritual Baptist faiths.* Jamaica: University of West Indies Press.

Henry, Frances, and Effie Ginzberg. 1985. *Who gets the work? A test of racial discrimination in employment.* Toronto: Urban Alliance on Race Relations and The Social Planning Council of Metropolitan Toronto.

Henry, Frances, and Carol Tator. 2002. *Discourses of domination: Racial bias in the Canadian English-language press.* Toronto: University of Toronto Press.

– 2005. *Racial profiling in Toronto: Discourses of domination, mediation, and opposition.* Toronto: Canadian Race Relations Foundation.

Henry, Frances, Carol Tator, Winston Mattis, and Tim Rees. 2000. *The colour of democracy: Racism in Canadian society.* Toronto: Harcourt Brace.

Hoerder, Dirk. 1999. *Creating societies: Immigrant lives in Canada.* Montreal: McGill-Queens University Press.

hooks, bell. 2003. *Teaching community: A pedagogy of hope.* New York: Routledge.

Li, Peter. 2004. *Destination Canada.* Toronto: Oxford University Press.

Macklin, Audry. 2001. Borderline security. In *The security of freedom*, ed. Ronald Daniels, Patrick Macklem, and Kent Roach, 383–405. Toronto: Toronto University Press.

Mock, Karen. 1996. Anti-semitism in Canada: Realities, remedies, and implications for anti-racism. In *Perspectives on racism and the human services sector: A case for change*, ed. Carl James, 120–33. Toronto: University of Toronto Press.

Ong, Aihwa. 1999. *Flexible citizenship: The cultural logics of transnationality.* Durham, NC: Duke University Press.

Proctor, James. 2004. *Stuart Hall.* London and New York: Routledge.

Said, Edward. 1978. *Orientalism.* New York: Vintage.

Weir, Allison. 2000. From the subversion of identity to the subversion of solidarity? Judith Butler and the critique of women's identity. In *Open boundaries: A Canadian women's studies reader*, ed. Barbara Crow and Lise Gotell, 43–50. Toronto: Prentice-Hall.

Contributors

Vijay Agnew is a professor of Social Science and the former director of the Centre for Feminist Research at York University. Her book *Resisting Discrimination: Women from Asia, Africa, and the Caribbean and the Women's Movement in Canada* (University of Toronto Press, 1996) won the Gustav Myers award as an 'outstanding book on the subject of human rights in North America.' Her other books are *Diaspora, Memory, and Identity: A Search for Home*, ed. (University of Toronto Press, 2005); *Where I Come From* (Wilfrid Laurier University Press, 2003); *In Search of a Safe Place: Abused Women and Culturally Sensitive Services* (University of Toronto Press, 1998); and *Elite Women in Indian Politics* (Vikas, 1979). In 1998, the minister of multiculturalism, Hedy Fry, appointed Agnew to the External Research Advisory Committee of the Status of Women.

Sharryn J. Aiken is an assistant professor in the Faculty of Law at Queen's University, where she teaches immigration and refugee law, international human rights, and administrative law. Prior to moving to Kingston, Sharryn practised immigration and refugee law as a staff lawyer with legal aid clinics in Toronto and in private practice. During that time, she appeared before the Supreme Court of Canada in a number of precedent-setting refugee cases, including *Suresh v. Minister of Citizenship and Immigration*. A past president of the Canadian Council for Refugees, Sharryn has been actively engaged in public advocacy on immigration and refugee issues for the past decade. She is editor-in-chief of *Refuge*, an interdisciplinary journal on forced migration, and co-chair of the Equality Rights Panel of the Court Challenges Programme.

Gillian Creese is a professor in the Department of Anthropology and Sociology at the University of British Columbia, and leader of the Social

Domain at the Vancouver Centre of Excellence for Research on Immigration and Integration in the Metropolis (RIIM). She has written widely on issues of immigration and racialization in Canada, and on trade unions as sites of struggle for women and racialized minorities. Her most recent book is *Contracting Masculinity: Gender, Class, and Race in a White-Collar Union, 1944–1994* (Oxford University Press, 1999). Other recent publications include (with Edith Ngene Kambere) 'What Colour is your English?', *Canadian Review of Sociology and Anthropology* (2003); (with Veronica Strong-Boag) 'Women's Issues in Canada,' in *Women's Issues in North America and the Caribbean* (ed. Cheryl Kalny, 2003); and (with Robyn Dowling) 'Gendering Immigration: The Experience of Women,' *Progress in Planning* (2001).

Tania Das Gupta is an associate professor in the School of Social Sciences in Atkinson Faculty of Liberal and Professional Studies, York University. Her research interests are in anti-racist critiques of state policies, anti-racism and the labour movement, and immigrant women.

Rebecca Hagey is an associate professor at the Faculty of Nursing, University of Toronto, and teaches in the Community Nursing Program. She is a founding member of Anishnawbe Health Toronto, Canada's first urban Aboriginal Community Health Centre, and is also a founding member of the First Nation House at the University of Toronto. Her research interests include indigenous knowledge pertaining to diabetes in Aboriginal populations and consensus-building strategies for promoting accountability of systemic racism in nursing and in health care.

Ezra Yoo-Hyeok Lee is a PhD candidate in the Department of English and Cultural Studies at McMaster University in Hamilton, Ontario. His doctoral research is on postcolonial literature and cultural studies, with a particular focus on globalization and comparative literary and cultural studies, and Asian North American literatures.

Peter S. Li is a professor of Sociology at the University of Saskatchewan and chair of the Economic Domain, Prairie Centre of Excellence for Research on Immigration and Integration. His research areas are race and ethnicity, immigration, and multiculturalism. His latest book is *Destination Canada: Immigration Debates and Issues* (Oxford University Press, 2003). His other books include *Race and Ethnic Relations in Canada* (Oxford University Press, 1999), *The Chinese in Canada* (Oxford University Press, 1988, 1998), and *The Making of Post-War Canada* (Oxford University Press, 1996). He has served as a consultant and advisor to several Canadian federal departments on immigration, multiculturalism, race relations, and social statistics policies. In 2002, he received the Outstanding Contribution Award from the Canadian Sociology and Anthropology Association. He has been elected President (2004–05) of the Canadian Sociology and Anthropology Association.

Lucia Lo is an associate professor of Geography at York University. She was leader of the Economic Domain of the Centre of Excellence for Research on Immigration and Settlement (CERIS), and leader of the Transportation and Commerce Research Thrust of Geomatics for Informed Decision Making (2003–5). She has written extensively on Chinese immigrants in Toronto, particularly their residential patterns, labour market performance, businesses and entrepreneurship, and consumer behaviour. Her paper with Shuguang Wang on 'Settlement Patterns of Toronto's Chinese Immigrants: Convergence or Divergence' in the *Canadian Journal of Regional Science* (1997) is considered pioneering research on Chinese sub-ethnicity. Her current projects include 'Infrastructure in the York Region: A GIS Analysis of Human Services' (funded by Infrastructure Canada); and 'Economic Adjustment of Adult Immigrants: Role of Educational Institutions' (funded by the Canadian Council of Learning).

Jean McDonald is a doctoral candidate in Social Anthropology at York University. Her anthropological and political project aims to challenge processes of illegalization in the context of citizenship, racism, and nationalism. In particular, she examines the everyday practices that make and unmake illegality in Toronto. Jean is a founding member of No One Is Illegal in Toronto.

Robin Ostow is a Fellow at the Centre for Russian and Eurasian Studies, University of Toronto, and assistant professor in the Department of Sociology, St Francis Xavier University. She has written extensively on Jews and Jewish culture in both Cold War Germanies and in reunified Germany. Her publications include: 'Imagined Families and "Rassenschande": Germans and Russians, Nation and Gender at the Ravensbruck Memorial,' *Journal of European Area Studies* (2001); *Die Ostdeutsche Juden und die deutsche Wiedervereinigung* (Wichern Verlag, 1996); and *Jews in Contemporary East Germany: The Children of Moses in the Land of*

Marx (Macmillan, 1988). She recently guest-edited a special thematic issue of the *Journal of East European Jewish Affairs* on Post-Soviet Jewish Immigration to Germany (Winter 2003). Her edited volume *(Re)Visualizing National History: Museums and National Identities in Europe in the New Millennium* (University of Toronto Press) will appear in July 2007.

Krishna Pendakur is an associate professor in the Department of Economics at Simon Fraser University and researches economic inequality, poverty and discrimination. He is the associate editor for *Journal of Business and Economic Statistics* and co-organizer of the Applied Welfare Economics Study Group in Verona, Italy.

Ravi Pendakur has a PhD in Sociology from Carleton University. He has been a researcher with the Canadian government since 1988 and is currently the assistant director of Social Research at Social Development Canada.

Charles C. Smith currently lectures on Cultural Pluralism in the Arts at the University of Toronto Scarborough and is the equity advisor to the Canadian Bar Association. In the past, he has served as equity advisor to the Law Society of Upper Canada and as manager of the Access and Equity Centre in the former Municipality of Metropolitan Toronto.

Jane Sawyer Turrittin is a social anthropologist who has carried out research on women and work in West Africa and in Toronto, Ontario. Since 1995, Jane has been involved in action research on equity issues in nursing in conjunction with a team that is now associated with the Centre for Equity in Health and Society, Toronto.

Shuguang Wang is professor and Chair of the Department of Geography at Ryerson University in Toronto, Canada. His research and writing focus on ethnic economy and the internationalization of retailing. Some of his recent publications include 'Penetrating the Great Wall and Conquering the Middle Kingdom: Wal-Mart in China,' in S. Brunn, ed., *Wal-Mart World: The World's Biggest Corporation in the Global Economy* (2006); (with Y. Zhang and Y. Wang), 'Opportunities and Challenges of Shopping Centre Development in China: A Case Study of Shanghai,' in *Journal of Shopping Center Research* (2006); (with L. Lo), 'The New Chinese Business Sector in Toronto: A Spatial and Structural Anatomy of Medium & Large-Sized Firms,' in E. Fong and C. Luk, eds., *Chinese*

Ethnic Business: Global and Local Perspectives (2006); and (with M. True-love) 'Evaluation of Settlement Services Programs for Newcomers in Ontario: A Geographical Perspective,' in *Journal of International Migration and Integration* (2003).